STUDIES IN IMPERIALISM

general editor: Andrew S. Thompson
founding editor: John M. MacKenzie

When the 'Studies in Imperialism' series was founded more than thirty years ago, emphasis was laid upon the conviction that 'imperialism as a cultural phenomenon had as significant an effect on the dominant as on the subordinate societies'. With well over a hundred titles now published, this remains the prime concern of the series. Cross-disciplinary work has indeed appeared covering the full spectrum of cultural phenomena, as well as examining aspects of gender and sex, frontiers and law, science and the environment, language and literature, migration and patriotic societies, and much else. Moreover, the series has always wished to present comparative work on European and American imperialism, and particularly welcomes the submission of books in these areas. The fascination with imperialism, in all its aspects, shows no sign of abating, and this series will continue to lead the way in encouraging the widest possible range of studies in the field. 'Studies in Imperialism' is fully organic in its development, always seeking to be at the cutting edge, responding to the latest interests of scholars and the needs of this ever-expanding area of scholarship.

Sites of imperial memory

Manchester University Press

Sites of imperial memory

Commemorating colonial rule in the
nineteenth and twentieth centuries

Edited by Dominik Geppert and Frank Lorenz Müller

MANCHESTER
UNIVERSITY PRESS

Published by MANCHESTER UNIVERSITY PRESS
ALTRINCHAM STREET, MANCHESTER M1 7JA
www.manchesteruniversitypress.co.uk

British Library Cataloguing-in-Publication Data
A catalogue record for this book is available from the British Library

Library of Congress Cataloging-in-Publication Data applied for

ISBN   978 0 7190 9081 3   hardback

First published 2015

Typeset in 10/12pt Trump Mediaeval
by Graphicraft Limited, Hong Kong
Printed in Great Britain
by TJ International Ltd, Padstow

CONTENTS

[v]

CONTENTS

ILLUSTRATIONS

ILLUSTRATIONS

CONTRIBUTORS

Stefan Creuzberger is Professor of Contemporary History and Director of the Research and Documentation Centre of the Dictatorships in Germany at the University of Rostock (Germany). His research focuses on German and Soviet History. He has published and edited various books, e.g. *'Geistige Gefahr' und 'Immunisierung' der Gesellschaft. Antikommunismus und politische Kultur in der frühen Bundesrepublik* (München: Oldenbourg 2014), *Die Berliner Republik. Beiträge zur deutschen Zeitgeschichte seit 1990* (Berlin: be.bra Verlag, 2013), *Westintegration und Neue Ostpolitik. Die Außenpolitik der Bonner Republik* (Berlin: be.bra Verlag, 2009), *Stalin. Machtpolitiker und Ideologe* (Stuttgart: Kohlhammer, 2009), *Die sowjetische Besatzungsmacht und das politische System der SBZ* (Weimar; Köln; Wien: Böhlau, 1996) and *Gleichschaltung unter Stalin? Die Entwicklung der Parteien im östlichen Europa 1944–1949* (Paderborn; München; Wien; Zürich: Ferdinand Schöningh Verlag, 2013).

Victor Enthoven teaches global history at the *Vrije Universiteit* Amsterdam. His research focuses on the early modern period, with a particular interest in the Atlantic World. He has published *Riches from Atlantic Commerce: Dutch Transatlantic Trade and Shipping, 1585–1817* (Leiden: Brill Academic Publishers, 2003), *The Navigator: The Log of John Anderson, VOC Pilot-Major, 1640–1643* (Leiden: Brill Academic Publishers, 2010), and *Geweld in de West. Een militaire geschiedenis van de Nederlandse Atlantische wereld, 1600–1800* (Leiden: Brill, 2013). He is currently working on a book on the Dutch in the Atlantic World.

Dominik Geppert is Professor of Modern History at Bonn University. He was a Research Fellow at the German Historical Institute from 2000 to 2005 and Heisenberg Fellow of the Deutsche Forschungsgemeinschaft in 2006/2007. His main fields of research are international history and intellectual history of the nineteenth and twentieth centuries as well as British and German contemporary history. His most recent studies include *Die Ära Adenauer* (Darmstadt: Wissenschaftliche Buchgesellschaft, 3rd edition, 2012) and *Pressekriege. Öffentlichkeit und Diplomatie in den deutsch-britischen Beziehungen, 1896–1912* (Munich: Oldenbourg, 2007). His most recent book puts the current European crisis in historical perspective: *Ein Europa, das es nicht gibt. Die fatale Sprengkraft des Euro* (Munich: Europa Verlag Gmbh, 2013).

Richard Goebelt serves as the Vice-Director Brussels Office of a German association in Belgium. He holds a Master's degree in modern history and international law from the *Freie Universität* Berlin and is currently starting doctoral research on the transnational confluence of Indian and British memory cultures. A former freelancer at the Military History Research Institute he has published several academic articles.

Xavier Guégan is Senior Lecturer in Colonial and Post-colonial History in the Department of History at the University of Winchester, UK. He specialises in the history of British and French imperial and post-colonial history, and in particular the cultural implications in South Asia, the Maghreb and the Ottoman Empire. His most recent publications include *The Imperial Aesthetic: Photography, Samuel Bourne and the Indian Peoples in the Post-Mutiny Era* (forthcoming), and two volumes co-edited with Martin Farr, *The British Abroad since the Eighteenth Century*, vol. 1: *Travellers and Tourists* (Basingstoke: Palgrave Macmillan, 2013) and vol. 2: *Experiencing Imperialism* (Basingstoke: Palgrave Macmillan, 2013).

Katja Kaiser studied history, linguistics and English literature at Berlin's *Freie Universität*. She was a research fellow at the Museum of Cultural History in Magdeburg and trainee as well as curator at the German Historical Museum Berlin. She specialises in German colonial history, gender studies, museology and history of collections and has published a book and essays on these subjects. For her PhD thesis her focus has shifted to German colonial botany.

James Koranyi teaches Modern European History at Durham University. His research focuses on nineteenth- and twentieth-century east-central European history, especially on Romania, Hungary, Germany and the Habsburg Empire. His work encompasses the areas of memory, minorities and space. He has published on German people from Romania and is currently completing a monograph on Romanian German memory cultures in the twentieth century.

Shraddha Kumbhojkar teaches Practice of History at the University of Pune, India. Her research interests include Ancient and Modern India, popular culture and modernity in western India and the Neo-Buddhist culture today. She has authored *Nationalism, Literature and Creation of Memory* (Pune: Sugawa Prakashan, 2008) and edited the collection *19th Century Maharashtra: A Reassessment* (Newcastle upon Tyne: Cambridge Scholars Publishing, 2009). Her current research projects include *Inclusive Growth, Caste and Software Professionals: A Survey*, *Modernity and Popular Theater in late 19th Century India* and *Orientalism, Modernity and Religious Thinking*. She has presented her research at various conferences in Europe, Russia and Asia. She also does volunteer work to provide education and support to destitute children.

Barak Kushner teaches at the University of Cambridge and researches Japanese and Chinese modern history. His first book was *The Thought War – Japanese Imperial Propaganda* (Honolulu: University of Hawai'i Press, 2006). The second, *Slurp! A Culinary and Social History of Ramen – Japan's Favorite Noodle Soup* (Leiden: Brill, 2012), was awarded the 2013 Sophie Coe Prize. *Men to Devils, Devils to Men: Japanese War Crimes and Chinese Justice* is forthcoming from Harvard University Press. Since 2013 Barak has led an ERC funded project, 'The Dissolution of the Japanese Empire and the Struggle for Legitimacy in Postwar East Asia, 1945–1965.'

Maria Misra teaches, writes and researches on the history of India and the British Empire at the University of Oxford where she is a Fellow at Keble College. Her books include: *Business, Race and Politics in British India* (Oxford: Oxford University Press, 1998); *Vishnu's Crowded Temple: India since the Great Rebellion* (London: Penguin Books, 2007). She is currently working on a cultural history of Indian cities. Dr Misra has also written and presented a three-part TV series on Channel 4: *An Indian Affair*, exploring issues of race and culture in India in the eighteenth and early nineteenth centuries. She is on the Editorial Board of the *Journal of Global History*.

Frank Lorenz Müller teaches Modern European History at the University of St Andrews. His research focuses on nineteenth-century Europe with a particular interest in the history of politics and its culture, especially within a monarchical context. He has published *Britain and the German Question. Perceptions of Nationalism and Political Reform 1830–1863* (Basingstoke: Palgrave, 2002), *Die Revolution von 1848/49* (Darmstadt: Wissenschaftliche Buchgesellschaft, 2002) and *Our Fritz. Emperor Frederick III and the Political Culture of Imperial Germany* (Cambridge, Mass; London.: Harvard University Press, 2011). Since 2012 he has led the AHRC-funded research project 'Heirs to the Throne in the Constitutional Monarchies of 19th-Century Europe' (http://heirstothethrone-project.net/).

Berny Sèbe is a Lecturer in Colonial and Postcolonial Studies at the University of Birmingham. His research examines the relations between metropolitan and colonial history in Britain and in France since the nineteenth century, as well as the modern history of the Sahara. He is the author of *Heroic Imperialists in Africa: The Promotion of British and French Colonial Heroes, 1870–1939* (Manchester: Manchester

University Press, 2013) and he has co-edited *Echoes of Empires: Identity, Memory and Colonial Legacies* (London: I. B. Tauris, 2014). Since 2012, he has led the AHRC-funded project 'Outposts of Conquest: The History and Legacy of the Fortresses of the Steppe and the Sahara in Comparative Perspective (1840s to the present day)' (www.birmingham. ac.uk/forts).

Winfried Speitkamp teaches Modern and Contemporary History at the University of Kassel. His main fields of research range from cultures of memory and politics of memory to colonial and African history. He has published *Deutsche Kolonialgeschichte* (third edition, Ditzingen: Reclam Publishers, 2014), *Kleine Geschichte Afrikas* (second edition, Stuttgart: Reclam, 2009), *Erinnerungsräume und Wissenstransfer. Beiträge zur afrikanischen Geschichte* (editor, Göttingen: V & R Unipress, 2008), and other books on constitutional history, the protection of monuments and European cultural heritage. Forthcoming is *Afrikanische Tierräume. Historische Verortungen* (editor together with Stephanie Zehnle, Köln: Rüdiger Köppe Verlag, 2014).

John Stuart is Associate Professor of History at Kingston University, London. He teaches British, British imperial and world history, and researches and writes on the history of Protestant overseas missions from Britain in the nineteenth and twentieth centuries. His work focuses on the interaction between mission, non-Western nationalism and imperialism and on the activities of mission, church and ecumenical organisations in the aftermath of Western imperial and colonial rule. Among his published works are *British Missionaries and the End of Empire: East, Central, and Southern Africa, 1939–64* (Wm B Eerdmans, 2011).

Frank Uekötter is Reader in Environmental Humanities at the University of Birmingham. He has published widely on environmental history, agricultural and resource history, the history of science and technology and, most recently, memory studies. His publications include *The Green and the Brown. A History of Conservation in Nazi Germany* (Cambridge: Cambridge University Press, 2006), *The Age of Smoke. Environmental Policy in Germany and the United States, 1880–1970* (Pittsburgh, PA.: University of Pittsburgh Press, 2009) and *The Greenest Nation? A New History of German Environmentalism* (New York: MIT Press, 2014).

FOUNDING EDITOR'S INTRODUCTION

Just outside the International Cruise Terminal in the city of Nagasaki in Japan, there is a magnificent piece of bronze statuary. A man who looks distinctly Western and moustachioed sits in a rather grand chair. A woman, who looks Japanese, stands on the right, and a younger man stands on the left. The inscription on the plinth is entirely in Japanese, but there is no doubt for a non-Japanese speaker who these people are. The monument commemorates Thomas Blake Glover, the Scot who went to Nagasaki in 1859 and became its most famous resident in the Meiji era. The woman is his wife, Tsuru Yamamura, and the younger man is Tomisaburu, his son (though it is thought he may have been the son of Glover's concubine rather than of Tsuru). Across the road from this group of statuary are the surviving buildings of the foreign settlement of Nagasaki during treaty port days – the former British consulate, the customs house, and the original Hong Kong and Shanghai Bank. Further up the hill behind stands Glover's attractive home, now set in extensive grounds with many other surviving buildings moved to the same location. The 'Glover Garden', as it is now called, is one of the most popular attractions in Japan, thronged with Japanese visitors, although Westerners seem to have less interest in it. Images of Glover are everywhere, even in advertisements. A bronze bust outside his house has an inscription which clearly once referred to him as an Englishman, for it is apparent that the 'English' has been chipped off and the space inadequately filled with the replacement 'Scots'. It is one of the few hints of conflict, here over precise ethnicity (although in fact his father was English).

Why is this commemoration of a foreigner and his associates given so much prominence in Nagasaki and why are Japanese people so keen to see this site of memory? The answer seems to be that Glover symbolises not the informal imperialism of the Far Eastern treaty ports, but rather the strikingly successful industrialisation and modernisation of Japan in the Meiji era. He played with political fire, opposing the shogunate and supporting the royalist restoration. His house proudly displays the trap door to the attic where he used to hide such royalists when they were still outlaws. But it goes further. His hand was in any number of capitalist ventures, including the founding of the Mitsubishi Company, whose shipyards now dominate Nagasaki. In addition, all of this seems to overleap the period the Japanese wish to forget, the aggressive era of the 1930s, the horrors of the Second World

War, the loss of empire, the dropping of the atomic bomb on Nagasaki (amazingly missing the foreign settlement area), and the rigours of the post-war years. The whole site speaks of an era that was at the same time transformatory, positive and elegant (neatly illustrated by the manner in which young Japanese visitors dress up in costumes of the settlement period). And add to that the way in which his family life symbolised the hybridities of the time, not least through the genetic mixture of his children. Elsewhere, at the Sakamoto international cemetery, the graves of the Glovers and of many other Westerners, are also regularly visited.

Indeed, few cities are as full of sites of memory as Nagasaki. There is the striking cross-shaped monument to the 'Martyrdom of the 26 Saints', the Christians who were crucified in 1597 during the period when Christianity was banned in Japan. Twenty-six figures dressed in 'vestments' that could be either Japanese or Christian adorn this monument and it seems to be venerated in a country where Christians remain a minority. Then there is Dejima Island, the reconstruction of the Dutch trading post of 1636 where the Dutch, at the outer limits of their imperial exploration, were isolated to avoid the spread of Christianity, and where the Japanese kept contact with Western commerce, science and learning. Vast amounts of money have been expended on this remarkable reconstruction and there are plans afoot to return it to its status as an island (presently through land reclamation it is incorporated into the city), rebuild its bridge to the mainland, and restore six more buildings. Add to these the Atomic Bomb Museum (where a major display is devoted to the destruction of a Christian cathedral, perhaps pointing to the irony of its being destroyed by a Christian nation), the peace park with its immense statue dedicated to peace, and the separate Peace Museum, all of them heavily visited not least by large parties of schoolchildren. The Peace Statue is described in this way: its 'right hand pointing upward depicts the threat of the atomic bomb, the left hand stretching horizontally symbolises eternal world peace, and closed eyelids express the consolation for the war dead'.

Thus, Nagasaki's many sites of memory embrace its status as the southern city with its great natural harbour where the commercial empires of the West, Portuguese, Dutch, and then those of the settlement era in the later nineteenth century, stretched out their tentacles to Japan, drawing it into global trade, but ultimately into the industrialisation and modernisation that would enable it to become an imperial power itself in the Far East and South-east Asia. But this same southern location also placed it within the range of the American bombers which would seek to destroy the will of Japan to continue the war in August 1945. Japanese tourists and schoolchildren seem to flock to all of these.

The enquiring visitor cannot help feeling that collectively these many hybrid and complex sites of memory offer a variety of forms of consolatory success seized from the jaws of apparent disaster, potential and actual. The martyrs' memorial speaks to modern Japanese tolerance and respect for all religions. Dejima indicates the clever ways in which Japan succeeded in avoiding early modern commercial imperialism by keeping tight controls over the individuals who carried it from Europe. The ubiquity of ship models in Nagasaki (for they are truly everywhere, even in the reception areas of hotels) celebrates Japan's status as a maritime power and its adoption of marine innovation. The Glover Garden strikingly proclaims the great era of modernist response. The A-Bomb museum and all the associated peace institutions represent another symbolic triumph for the Japanese, the turning of a horrendously destructive defeat into a moral victory, the overcoming of adversity, the rebuilding of the city, and its emergence as one of the greatest shipbuilding ports of the world. What we have here are forms of empire, war, economic and social transformation, even religious complexity, all intertwining and conveyed through perhaps the most extraordinary complex of sites of memory to be found anywhere. They take highly conflictual periods of the Japanese past and smooth them out into what are perceived as the successful moral convictions of the present. They unite rather than divide, as other sites from the imperial period do, even carrying essentially similar messages to which both the Japanese and, to a certain extent at least, Westerners can subscribe.

Nagasaki is an important site of aspects of informal imperialism and war. This book deals more with formal modes of empires, strikingly engaging with the sites of memory that can be found in so many societies. Taking Nora's celebrated *Lieux de Mémoire* as its starting point, it ranges over the empires of Britain, France, the Netherlands, Austria-Hungary, Germany, Japan and Russia. It also examines individuals – of whom Glover is a notable example – as well as environmental institutions, like botanic gardens, and commodities like rubber. Sites of memory are everywhere, for many of us part of the fabric of our daily lives. In the past, I have written about such places in Glasgow as a significant imperial city, throughout East and Central Africa in my pursuit of David Livingstone, and in the statues, memorials and cemeteries of India. The analysis of the varied meaning of so many sites of memory will continue for a long time yet. This book constitutes a landmark study that will point the way to many more in the future.

John M. MacKenzie

ACKNOWLEDGEMENTS

The editors would like to record their gratitude to the individuals and institutions whose support made it possible to organise the conference which provided the starting point for this volume and who contributed to the completion of the final manuscript. We received financial assistance from the School of History at the University of St Andrews, the History Department at Bonn University, the German History Society, the Society for the Study of French History and the German Academic Exchange Service (DAAD). For research and editorial assistance we are indebted to Johannes Tröger, Nina Schnutz, Peter Beule, Jonas Klein, Benjamin Behschnitt and Juliane Clegg. We would also like to thank the two reviewers commissioned by Manchester University Press for their helpful comments on earlier drafts of this volume.

We dedicate this volume to the memory of Professor Hagen Schulze (1943–2014), who taught us both and who, through his 'German Sites of Memory' (*Deutsche Erinnerungsorte*), helped to inspire this volume.

Dominik Geppert and Frank Lorenz Müller
Bonn and St Andrews
September 2014

CHAPTER ONE

Beyond national memory. Nora's *Lieux de Mémoire* across an imperial world

Dominik Geppert and Frank Lorenz Müller

The imperial past is all around us. Decades have come and gone since the dissolution of Europe's great colonial empires, but the footprints they have left in the realm of memory all over the world are plain to see. Legacies of empire are present in the demarcations of state borders, in architecture and urban topographies, on the pedestals of monuments, in books, on cinema screens, in photo albums, on the internet, in public rituals and in political debates. Heroes from the age of empire – men such as Jan Pietersz Coen, Lord Clive, David Livingstone or Captain Marchand – have not been forgotten, even though their record may now appear in a much more ambivalent light. At the same time, Imam Shamil, the Mau Mau veterans and other erstwhile insurgents rebelling against the colonial order are now celebrated as freedom fighters. Imperial institutions such as the British and the Dutch East India Companies are familiar to every schoolchild – not just in Britain and the Netherlands, but in India and Indonesia as well. Even commodities of daily life, such as coffee or rubber, bear the deep imprint of their colonial histories. More than ever, troubling elements of the imperial past such as Britain's suppression of the Mau Mau uprising or the atrocities in the Belgian Congo are matters of public debate. This book ventures into these vast fields strewn with the debris of imperial memory. It analyses the genesis, shape and weight of some of the boulders left in these landscapes of memory and examines their function at different times and across different social, political, and cultural groups.

Ever since the end of the Cold War, Tony Judt and others have taught us, we have lived in an 'age of commemoration'. Naturally, this observation does not only apply to national memory. It also speaks to the commemoration of an imperial past. In 2011, for instance, a 60-member delegation travelled from Namibia to Berlin. The African delegates made the journey to collect and return to their home the skulls of twenty victims of the war Imperial Germany had waged against the Herero and Nama. More than a century had passed since these bones had been brought to the German capital where they were used for pseudoscientific race research.[1]

On more than one occasion, though, the imperial dimension has proved hard to accommodate within established national modes of interpreting and commemorating the past. By losing their empire, it has been quipped, the British were transformed from Romans into Italians in just a matter of years. How this transformation came to pass, however, and how it effected a lasting readjustment of the nation's identity (if it did), has not yet been fully explored or integrated into national historiography.[2] Until very recently, Stephen Howe has written, 'imperial and colonial history existed in an almost entirely separate sphere from the writing of "domestic" British history'.[3] There is thus no consensus as to how the British Empire should be remembered: as something to be ashamed of or as, on the whole, 'a good thing' that 'made the modern world', as Niall Ferguson provocatively put it.[4]

In the case of Germany, it is not even clear when imperial history ended: in 1919 when the Reich lost its colonies in Africa, Asia and the Pacific, or in 1945 when Hitler's attempt to establish a colonial and racialised empire in Eastern Europe was finally crushed?[5] This is one of the reasons why there has been a fierce debate about whether German colonial atrocities, particularly in Namibia from 1904 to 1907, could be interpreted as something of a precursor to the Holocaust.[6] The picture remains blurred when one moves on to a European perspective. The West European master narrative associated with 8 May 1945 tells a story of reconciliation and resurgence of the continent's nations in the wake of two devastating wars. On the former colonial periphery, though, 8 May 1945 loses its narrative coherence. In North Africa, for instance, the day is remembered primarily for the violent uprising in the Constantinois area and the subsequent massacres that French colonial troops committed there.[7]

Dan Diner's recent prediction does not merely apply to the Second World War: 'The Western, European image of history is being affected by a tendency towards pluralisation ... the experiences of other, hitherto neglected historical spaces will be considered: Arabic, South Asian, Far Eastern and Black African spaces of experience and memory'.[8] This development, Diner assumes, will make the already complex European picture even more difficult to fathom. A more globalised and pluralised view, it should be added, though, will also result in a better understanding of an intricate past and present.

[2]

Now seems to be an auspicious time to explore the historical spaces where 'empire' and 'memory' overlap. For a number of years both issues have been historiographical boom topics. Before its recent revival imperial history had been neglected as empires seemed politically obsolete; they corresponded neither to the nation-state nor to federally conceived supranational organisations such as the European Union. More recently, however, empires have assumed a central position in historical research. Our understanding of them has been greatly enhanced by a wealth of recent studies.[9] Some of this research has been explicitly comparative; other studies have analysed individual aspects of imperial rule on a more theoretical footing.[10] Questions such as the extent to which imperial concerns influenced the politics and political culture of the metropole, for instance, have triggered lively and searching controversies.[11] There is a growing interest in the 'colonisation of consciousness' concerning the white settlers and the indigenous inhabitants of the colonies as well as the domestic populations of the imperial powers.[12] Historians now compare methods of expansion, practices of rule, different (re)sources of legitimacy and the civilising missions of various empires,[13] and they contrast these phenomena with their functional equivalents at the level of the nation-state.[14]

Scholars are increasingly sceptical about a predominantly national perspective on the imperial phenomenon. Some prefer the notion of a common colonial culture: 'a shared European experience which in many ways transgresses the particular national outlooks'.[15] Others observe that among European colonial powers and their imitators in East and West, such as the United States or Japan, there was co-operation as well as conflict. Colonial forestry, scientific and technological developments, medicine, the promotion of museums, botanical gardens, and zoos are just a few areas characterised by close transnational collaboration and transfer. Although there was at times intense rivalry and conflict, their approach to the indigenous people they ruled was much the same, as John MacKenzie has noted: 'All constructed race and related natural historical and climatic studies in similar ways. All became involved in new disciplines, such as geo-politics or microbiology, and recognised their significance in respect of both dominance of the globe and rivalries and dangers within those patterns of dominance'.[16] The renewed interest in imperial history reflects a different understanding of empires: they are now conceptualised as transnational agglomerations of power, promoting cultural exchange as well as economic integration and channelling migration flows. As such they can be understood as prefiguring the globalised characteristics of the twenty-first-century world.[17]

The studies brought together in this volume point to the continued relevance and lasting emotive capacity of memory sites created under imperial conditions. Thus they point to the active legacies of empire in the making and remaking of our post-colonial world. Then as now, meaning and identity – as well as their expression and dissemination – had to be negotiated among different groups of agents, across shifting balances of power and with respect to the sensitivities and preferences of often disparate and far-flung audiences. That these imperial legacies of memory now work in both directions is powerfully illustrated by the call, published in a Berlin newspaper in December 2013, for the square in front of the reconstructed royal palace in Berlin to be named after Samuel Maherero (1856–1923). Forgotten in Germany but a celebrated hero in his native Namibia, this tribal chief led the unsuccessful Herero uprising against German rule in 1904 and managed to survive the colonisers' genocidal retaliation. Rather than picking the worthy but easy option 'Nelson Mandela Square', Germans should, the writer argued, confront a site evoking the memory of oppression and of the struggle for freedom in a more relevant and poignant fashion.[18] Memory, guilt and atonement, global brands and local adaptation, hero-worship and national amnesia: all tangled up in an idea that illuminates the reciprocal fertilisation of the twenty-first-century's globalised memory culture and the old imperial legacies it contains and re-evokes.

One of the chief results of recent research on imperial history has been to highlight the negotiated quality of a great deal of nineteenth-century imperial rule. The century witnessed an increased formalisation of colonies' ties to their mother countries, and this required increased representation. Alongside the hard power of military and institutional control, representation could ensure a certain degree of additional stability. Identity-forming symbols and rituals arguably played an even greater role for the maintenance of imperial cohesion than in the national context, because control through actual institutions was necessarily looser in geographically vast and multi-ethnic empires.[19] In some cases, symbols of integration had to 'serve as a functional equivalent of another, weak form of cohesion'.[20] It was not just the monarch or head of state at the apex of an imperial system who could assume such a role. As the studies assembled in this volume will demonstrate, historic events and persons, institutions, commodities and concepts from the spheres of politics, administration, economics and religion could also acquire symbolic sway within the different collective memories and thus function as sites of memory.

It is hardly surprising that recent research in imperial history has accorded such a prominent place to aspects of collective memory, since historical research into 'memory' has also flourished over the past decades. Questions of memory, it is true, have fascinated thinkers from Friedrich Nietzsche and Sigmund Freud to Henri Bergson and Émile Durkheim for much of the last 150 years or so. Ever since Maurice Halbwachs published his pioneering work on *Les cadres sociaux de la mémoire* in 1925 and then tested his ideas in *La Topographie légendaire des Évangiles en Terre Sainte*, there has been a strong under-current of scholarly interest in collective memory, not least in the *Annales* school of French historiography and its history of mentalities.[21]

It was, however, only in the late 1970s and 1980s that the under-current became dominant and resulted in a veritable 'memory boom'. Some observers have even diagnosed a 'surfeit of memory'.[22] The speeding-up of social and cultural change as well as the dwindling persuasiveness of theories of modernisation and progressive improvement in an age of *posthistoire* and economic crises contributed to this development. The increasing commodification of nostalgia and the waning of utopian visions caused by the stagnation and implosion of communism had a similar effect. In this context, Pierre Nora produced his monumental project on the French *lieux de mémoire* (published from 1984 to 1992), which was probably the single most successful outcome of the upsurge in memory studies.[23] Nora identified the importance of what he called 'Sites of Memory' against the background of what he perceived as the disappearance of traditional *milieux de mémoire*: he saw in the 'acceleration of history', in the ever-faster pace of change, the destruction of quasi-organic 'memory societies' and 'memory ideologies'.[24] This loss necessitated the conscious creation and maintenance of 'Sites of Memory' – physical and conceptual locations where specific memories, those of abiding relevance to nations and societies, could crystallise and negotiate identity.

Pierre Nora developed his research agenda, which would ultimately fill seven volumes, from the work of Maurice Halbwachs, who distinguished between the individual memory that receives its collective quality through social contexts, and the collective and no longer organic memory of a group that develops through communication. In the course of his work Nora eventually offered the following definition of his central analytical category, the *lieux de mémoire*: 'Any significant entity of ideal or material kind, which by intention or the work of time has come to be a symbolic element of the heritage of any community'.[25] It refers to the crucial element of symbolic significance within memory contexts.[26]

Nora's seminal work sparked a number of similar initiatives dedicated to studying the memory of national or other seemingly easily defined communities in Germany, Italy, Austria and the Netherlands.[27]

The most recent additions to this body of research include three volumes of European sites of memory as well as projects on bi-national (German–Polish), transnational and Christian sites of memory.[28] The adaptation of Nora's ideas by historians of countries other than France has often been informed by the specific needs of national historiographies. The lead researchers of the project *Deutsche Erinnerungsorte* ('German Sites of Memory'), for instance, stressed the procedural and malleable character of sites of memory. They did so by exploring these sites as pointers to the vicissitudes of their sometimes violent and disconnected histories rather than as expressions of the unchangeable character of a nation.[29] This adjustment to Nora's original notion posits that a site of memory is not static when it is fully developed. It can be forgotten again, or transformed through changes in the narratives which generated it in the first place. Other communities can overwrite it with their own meanings.

While the influence of the French connection from Bergson and Durkheim via Halbwachs to Nora has been strong, not all relevant studies have followed the path set by them – either closely or loosely. Nietzsche's claim that 'the past has to be forgotten if it is not to become the gravedigger of the present' inspired scholars to look into the role and the rules of forgetting as well as those of remembrance.[30] Freud's notion that repressed memories might not only haunt individuals but also collectives pointed to the importance of trauma.[31] Aby Warburg's emphasis on visuality stimulated research in the iconographic dimension of memory[32], while Jan Assmann's distinction between 'communicative' and 'cultural memory' helped to distinguish the ways in which images of the past are handed down over limited periods of time in smaller groups like families ('communicative memory') drawing on a 'body of reusable texts, images, and rituals specific to each society in each epoch whose cultivation serves to stabilise and convey that society's self-image' over longer time spans ('cultural memory').[33]

Much the same could be said about some investigations of a specific imperial memory. Bill Schwarz, in the first of three planned volumes on the lasting influence of Empire on the metropole, uses the notion of race to discover deep-seated connections. Like all memory, he claims, imperial memory is only partly grounded in actual history and is always shaped by the present and its needs. The perception of disorder in 1960s and 1970s Britain, which added to the development of the New Right, triggered a memory of the empire as a particularly ordered structure, as the times when the 'white man' was still in control.[34] In a different and more explicitly comparative approach, Dennis Walder, in his study of postcolonial literature, applies the notion of nostalgia. 'Exploring nostalgia', he finds, 'can and should open up a negotiation between the present and the past, leading to a fuller understanding of the past and how it has shaped the present, for good or bad, and how it has shaped the self in connection with others, as a task that may bring pain as well as pleasure'.[35] He thus dissolves overly simplistic divides between former colonial masters and former colonial subjects, showing how a nostalgic look back can be found on all sides.

Although the fingerprints of these useful approaches are clearly all over the contributions in this volume, the editors have nevertheless opted for Nora's notion of sites of memory as a unifying concept. They did so for a variety of reasons. First of all, the notion of 'sites' which forms the basis of Nora's approach works particularly well vis-à-vis imperial memory, which is by its very nature more complex, ambivalent and contradictory than national memory. By focusing on themes instead of narrative patterns Nora created a conceptual apparatus that makes it possible to appreciate the fragmented – rather than continuous and uniform – character of collective memory. It is open to a multitude of different forms of interpretation. Sites of memory offer a form of representation that concentrates on the specific context of each site or topos rather than on narrative linearity. In a field such as imperial history, with its necessarily tangled stories and intermingled diachronic and synchronic processes Nora's concept can develop its full potential even though Nora himself conspicuously omitted imperial topics from his inventory of France's memory sites.

Moreover, the analysis of imperial sites of memory can set out from the same theoretical foundations as those identified within national contexts, because Halbwachs's works on collective memory are by no means restricted to national memory. According to Halbwachs, historical perceptions and interpretational patterns evolve from an interaction between individual and collective memory.[36] The group cultivating a collective memory *may* be a nation, but could also be a different collective. All other social formations, such as families, cities, regions, generations, but also supranational communities such as 'the West' or 'Europe' can also become bearers of a group memory. In fact, they require one in order to function as a community at all. The symbolic bonds that are supposed to hold the diverse population of an empire together thus form one of many manifestations of memory communities.

Finally, there are already a number of studies concentrating on individual nations, or regions within nations, and examining the ways in which they remembered a specific colonial past, that clearly bear the imprint of Nora's influence. In his *Vestiges of the Colonial Empire in France*, for instance, Robert Aldrich focuses on topographical sites such as monuments, museums and exhibitions – one of the classic categories established by Nora.[37] In a similar attempt at filling the colonial void left by Nora, the contributors to a volume edited by Alec G. Hargreaves consider groups connected to French colonialism, such as the Acadians, descendants of French settlers in Canada, or Algerian immigrants and their peculiar memories.[38] Specialised studies have also started to address the memories of erstwhile imperial dominion in Italy, Portugal or China.[39] In her study of postcolonial India, K. E. Surpriya uses a geographical site of memory, Fort St George in Chennai, 'as both a compass and point of departure for following the ways in which Indian natives connect their lives across the pre-colonial and post-colonial frameworks'.[40]

A wealth of valuable recent work has thus been done on the dimension of memory within the context of empire. But it is striking that these issues have rarely been examined across a variety of historical experiences and contrasting categories. Moreover, research in this field has focused on the post-colonial era and has so far only seldom wondered which role memory might have played within existing empires. While the phenomenon of 'forgetting' has been identified as an important common denominator in the context of imperial memory and will receive further attention in this volume, other comparative and analytical potentials have not yet been fully gauged.

By utilising the conceptional tools provided by Pierre Nora's notion of *lieux de mémoire* and connecting this perspective with the history of empire this volume seeks to chart an important field. It presents imperial history as a history of interwoven, overlapping, partly contradictory memories in which non-European outlooks are considered on a more equal footing, alongside the recollections of former colonial masters. Moreover, by employing the new conceptual tools developed by recent adaptations of Nora's sites of memory paradigm, the contributors to this volume help to liberate the *lieux de mémoire* from their original, strictly national context and provide a new approach to the analysis of entangled memory cultures.

Exploring imperial history as a 'second-degree history', by which Nora meant a history not of the actual events but of the ways in which events were first perceived and subsequently remembered, requires making some adjustments to the concept of sites of memory. Three major considerations must be taken into account. First of all, imperial memory is now much more contested than national memory. To be sure, national memory is frequently embattled as well, but unlike imperial memory, it tends to enjoy the backing of effective government institutions and a greater degree of socio-political consensus among its memory community. Both factors – institutional backing and a social consensus – present themselves as more precarious in imperial contexts. From the start imperial sites of memory are characterised by a two-sided quality: depending on whether they are viewed from the perspective of the colonial masters (or their descendants) or of those colonised (or their descendants) they assume a fundamentally different meaning. To this day, the 'heroes' of imperial conquest have often remained the 'villains' of anti-colonial liberation movements, and vice versa. Issues such as varying intensity and duration as well as the symmetry or asymmetry of historical remembrance in the centre and on the periphery of colonial empires or their successor states are centrally important to the evaluation of imperial sites of memory.

Second, it would be too simplistic to assume that imperial sites of memory can merely be explained by the dichotomy between centre and periphery, between rulers and subjects, exploiters and those exploited. It is important to trace the memories of various types of social agents beyond the antagonism between the glorious narratives of imperial rule and the black legends of anti-colonial liberation myths. The contested character of imperial sites of memory guides attention towards the moment of their construction and reconstruction – and thus to the identifiable interests and intentions of their builders. For imperial sites of memory do not simply evolve, they are made, and continuously changed.

Third, unlike Nora's *lieux de mémoire*, the purpose of engaging analytically with imperial sites of memory is not to stabilise the nation or any other relevant memory community. Rather, it seeks to destabilise or undermine simplistic interpretations of the imperial past. The analysis of imperial sites of memory puts the perspectives of the colonised, which were rarely accorded an adequate role in traditional historiography, on a par with those of the colonisers. Forging a new conceptual apparatus for the study of memory cultures through a full consideration of the imperial dimension also requires a revisiting of the methodological framework of Nora's concept: sites of memory have to be understood as part of a dynamic of continuous remembering and forgetting. Developing Ernest Renan's insight that shared remembering as well as shared forgetting are constitutive elements of national identity, modern memory theories have highlighted the significance of forgetting.[41] Sites of memory point to events, persons, institutions, commodities or concepts into which symbolic capital has been invested at times. Yet the times when these sites have lain fallow or neglected are no less instructive: they point to deep-seated injuries or the need for concealment.

The interrelation between remembering and forgetting is not unknown for national sites of memory, but its importance is self-evident in the case of the asymmetrical imperial sites of memory. The creation of imperial memory communities often involved having to confront and make decisions about material that would invigorate the audience in the metropole but alienate the populations at the periphery: selecting, suppressing and forgetting was necessarily a part of this process. Conversely, to the states emerging after the end of the colonial era it frequently seemed to make sense to superimpose colonial memories with pre-colonial narratives. Omitting humiliating experiences from the colonial period and the development of alternative sites of memory have to be understood as a method of strengthening a possibly precarious memory community.[42]

Within an imperial context, individuals were frequently members of several memory communities. This volume locates such groups at four levels: imperial, national, sub-national and transnational. First, the respective British, Russian, French and Dutch empires are themselves memory communities. They were created, at least partially, through the attempts by imperial elites to generate a common identity by constructing sites of memory. Usually, only specific groups within the imperial territory, whether at the centre or on the periphery, are committed to these communities. Second, there are imperial sites of memory whose relevance rests on a controversy between two nations (for instance between the mother country and a national independence movement or, later on, the post-colonial state) or within a nation (such as the Mau Mau in post-independence Kenya or the *Monumento aos Combatentes do Ultramar* in 1990s Portugal[43]). Third, memory communities also exist below the level of the nation: parties, religious groups, political generations, occupational groups (such as military formations), mercantile elites or consumer groups. Finally, imperial sites of memory may also arise from transnational memory communities such as missionary and scholarly networks or those engaged in border-crossing commercial activities linked to photography, cinema or rubber.

Inverting the traditional sequence established by Nora, which begins its investigation with the defined memory community and sets out to locate its memory sites, this volume takes its cues from a number of identified sites of imperial memory. It does not set out from generalisations about colonial and post-colonial nations nor does it treat them as the most important, let alone the only relevant, memory communities. Rather, it considers sites of imperial memory as working hypotheses that can lead to the discovery of heterogeneous and unexpected memory groups. This approach may carry the risk of operating without the safety net of prior notions about the historical agents it analyses. At the same time, however, this conceptual openness avoids preconceived ideas about who drove imperial history. In the context of an imperial history as a history of entanglements, sites of memory highlight multifarious memories and their different connotations. They constitute a helpful means towards the end of a systematic, unbiased and open analysis.

The following studies illustrate powerfully how the application of the sites of memory approach to the history of empire yields a rich variety of concrete insights, empirical findings and fresh reinterpretations. Care has been taken to consider imperial experiences drawn from very different national contexts: Britain, France, the Netherlands, Germany, Russia, Japan, India, Kenya and Hungary. Such a wide geographic range makes it possible to test the hypothesis that all over the world and across very different systems of governance similar patterns of resistance to and appropriation of sites of imperial memory could and can be observed. This may have been the result of the broad similarity of the stimuli provided by the colonising powers, since 'European states engaged in similar practices and took hold of remarkably comparable ideas and sentiments in regard to their overseas empires', as Matthew G. Stanard recently concluded.[44] Much the same could be said with regard to the habits and thoughts of the colonised peoples towards their colonial masters.

In order to open up a number of comparative perspectives, case studies have been chosen that address three different thematic categories. A first group of studies take their cue from a classic category within the site of memory concept: *sculptural and architectural monuments and memorials*. At the heart of Xavier Guégan's comparative analysis of imperial monuments and architecture in nineteenth-century Algeria and India lies the notion of the duality of their existence. They were both concrete, fixed structures and 'transmissible' sites made mobile and accessible through the new and transnationally organised agency of commercial photography. These transportable sites, he points out, linked audiences at the periphery and in the metropole and enabled them to form larger communities of memory. 'Transmissible' sites thus facilitated the emergence of 'imagined' imperial communities. Staying with the theme of mobility, in this case the mobility of symbolic ownership, Shraddha Kumbhojkar charts the remarkable revalidation of the Koregaon obelisk. Originally erected to celebrate the military prowess of the East India Company, the monument has, over the centuries, changed to appeal to a very different memory community. Now morphed into a politico-religious site of pilgrimage for the low-caste neo-Buddhist community, the obelisk still honours martial valour and communicates, refracted through the prism of the politics of caste, a positive image of the British engagement in India. The monument commemorating the 'Thirteen Martyrs of Arad', discussed by James Koranyi, underwent a similarly dramatic process of relocation. Unveiled in 1890 to mark the sacrifices made in the Hungarians' national struggle against their imperial overlords in 1848, it was removed, stored, rebuilt and returned in line with the vagaries of the fall of various empires in twentieth-century Eastern Europe. Barak Kushner's study of Japan's fraught transition away from monuments celebrating the country's imperial and martial pride and towards a culture deemed more in line with the political and psychological needs of the post-1945 era concludes this section. His investigation shows how contradictory forces and unresolved issues within Japan's postwar society resulted in the creation of bland and perennially multivalent repositories of memories of war, empire, suffering and heroism.

The studies assembled in the second section of this volume investigate the memory generated by and in response to a number of outstanding individuals – the great *heroes and villains of the imperial piece*. Five essays explore how recollections of the deeds of so-called Great Men crystallised to form clearly delineated memory sites and show how these sites would change over time and influence their environments. Berny Sèbe discusses the mechanisms through which celebrated imperialists in Britain and France – men like Kitchener, Rhodes, Brazza and Marchand – acquired lasting status as containers and radiators of imperial memories. The other contributions examine individual case studies to illustrate how the memory sites that have emerged around notable individuals have engaged successive generations of memory communities in controversial processes of reevaluation and redefinition. Victor Enthoven charts the ups and downs in the public estimation experienced by the soldier and colonial governor Jan Pietersz Coen amongst Dutch audiences both at the colonial periphery and in the Netherlands themselves. How much the definition and redefinition of an erstwhile colonial agent's memory has, over the centuries, been a function of the needs of successive memory communities – both at the centre and the periphery – is highlighted by Richard Goebelt's discussion of Lord Clive, the victor of Plassey. John Stuart places his examination of the changing images of the explorer and missionary David Livingstone against the background of British missionary history. The many manifestations of the memory of Imam Shamil, the 'Lion of Dagestan', form the topic of Stefan Creuzberger's contribution. Shamil's resistance against the troops of Tsarist Russia became the stuff of legends and the function of his memory is explored not just against the background of the transitions from the imperial, Soviet and post-Soviet phases of Russian history, but also within the context of the political utilisation of this memory site for the intricate politics of the Caucasus region today.

The final group of studies is concerned with the fragility and precariousness of repositories of imperial memory. Four articles explore the roles played by processes such as *forgetting, discarding, ignoring or neglecting recollections of imperial dominion*. Maria Misra shows how in the development of India's post-independence identity the memory of the British Raj has not served as a straightforward and central negative point of reference generating a national consensus, but has instead been subjected to neglect, amnesia and – latterly – commercial commodification. Winfried Speitkamp's contribution focuses on the memory of the Mau Mau uprising to trace the cycles of obliviousness and remembrance, of suppression and political instrumentalisation that have accompanied the history of this event within Kenya ever since the Kenyatta era. Katja Kaiser explores a German site of imperial memory that – for some reason – dare not speak its name. The history of Berlin's Botanical Garden is intimately intertwined with Germany's colonial endeavours both during the German Empire and even during the Nazis' attempt at colonial revisionism, but this important aspect of the institution's history has remained all but suppressed. Frank Uekötter's discussion concludes the volume. Focusing on the imperial memory stored in a near-omnipresent commodity of daily use – rubber – he shows how the ubiquity of a staple can obscure the many layers of imperial history accrued in the course of its industrial utilisation, but also how easily these powerful connotations can be re-energised.

This volume represents a first foray into the wide field of a transnational and multi-perspectival exploration of imperial memory through the lens of Nora's *lieux de mémoire* paradigm. There are, naturally, glaring gaps in coverage and choice of angles. It would be fascinating to learn more about the experiences arising from the Italian, Ottoman, Portuguese, Spanish and Danish empires, to study literary landmarks or to tease out the layers of recollection imbricated in commercial organisations such as shipping lines, oil companies or financial institutions. Although the studies assembled here have asked how memory sites have changed over time, across castes, before and after defeats, among former colonial masters and their erstwhile subjects, at the periphery and in the metropole, there are other important changes of perspective that we have not been able to consider: differences between the old and the young, between urban and rural populations, or across social classes. Moreover, gender should surely be applied as a fruitful category of analysis. The sites of memory represented in this volume are still very male in outlook and all too few women appear in the story.[45] Our aim here, however, has been far less ambitious than striving for the encyclopaedic quality that marks many projects undertaken in the wake of Nora's monumental oeuvre. Rather than present a compendium of sites of imperial memory, this volume is an invitation to pursue this path further and to engage with the concluding observations it offers.

These conclusions are, of necessity, tentative and very much work-in-progress, but it appears that, regardless of when and by whom they were first established, sites of imperial memory have often tended not to become fossilized, but have remained relevant and topical thanks to a process of continuous reworking, re-creating and redefinition. Rather than fixing and illustrating old hierarchies and values, these sites – even the seemingly rigid ones carved in stone, cast in bronze or printed on photographic paper – have continued to reflect the needs and aspirations of ever new sets of contemporary colonial and post-colonial memory communities. The very ideal core of these sites – the victory at Plassey, the ruthless determination shown by Coen, the suffering of the thirteen 'martyrs' of Arad – has proved useful not just for those communities who first institutionalised the memory, but often became the buildings blocks of new and renewed versions of the past.

Perhaps even more surprisingly than for the inherently more open and symbolic monumental sites, this also appears to apply to sites of memory that have grown up around remarkable individuals. Even though the characteristics that first made them stand out as heroic or villainous may have been very much of their day, even though their black or golden legends may have sprung from imperial, Christian, male, martial and metropolitan mind-sets, once they had emerged as memory sites, these individuals could function in a variety of ways and for a variety of audiences. Former imperial heroes now also engage audiences in the former imperial metropoles who are critical of their country's past record and current attitude as well as groups at the former periphery seeking a powerful shorthand against which to define their own position.

The resilient versatility of imperial sites of memory appears to be linked to the great flexibility and unpredictability of the processes of their generation and maintenance. If, as the final group of our case studies suggests, even the Raj, the Mau Mau Rebellion or the spectacular imperial career of rubber can be subjected to neglect, amnesia or sporadic and opportunistic utilisation, then imperial memory sites appear to result from much more complex, multi-factorial and heterogeneous constellations than their national counterparts. When they did arise and managed to persist, they did so within a multi-polar imperial 'World System' which appears much more in tune with our situation in the twenty-first century than with an earlier world of homogenised memory communities located within assertive nation-states. Notwithstanding the end of Europe's empires and of the continent's erstwhile global predominance, this built-in topicality may well secure imperial sites of memory, the first beacons of a globalised memory culture, a good deal of fruitful mileage yet.

Notes

1 *Der Tagesspiegel* (28 Sept. 2011).
2 Gerhard Altmann, *Abschied vom Empire. Die innere Dekolonisation Grossbritanniens 1945–1985* (Göttingen, 2005).
3 Stephen Howe, 'Decolonisation and Imperial Aftershocks: The Thatcher Years', in Ben Jackson and Robert Saunders (eds), *Making Thatcher's Britain* (Cambridge: Cambridge University Press, 2012), pp. 234–51, p. 235.
4 Niall Ferguson, *Empire. How Britain Made the Modern World* (London: Penguin, 2004).
5 Philip Ther, 'Deutsche Geschichte als imperiale Geschichte. Polen, slawophone Minderheiten und das Kaiserreich als kontinentales Empire', in Sebastian Conrad and Jürgen Osterhammel (eds), *Das Kaiserreich transnational. Deutschland in der Welt 1871–1914* (Göttingen: Vandenhoek & Ruprecht, 2002), pp. 129–48.
6 Cf. Robert Gerwarth, Stephan Malinowski, 'Hannah Arendt's Ghosts: Reflections on the Disputable Path from Windhoek to Auschwitz,' in *Central European History* 42 (2009), pp. 279–300.
7 Dominik Geppert, '8. und 9. Mai 1945: Umkämpfte Erinnerungstage', in Etienne François and Uwe Puschner (eds), *Erinnerungstage. Wendepunkte der Geschichte von der Antike bis zur Gegenwart* (Munich: CH Beck, 2010), pp. 335–55, p. 354.
8 Dan Diner, 'Verstellte Wahrnehmungen', in D. Diner, *Gegenläufige Gedächtnisse. Über Geltung und Wirkung des Holocaust* (Göttingen: Vandenhoek & Ruprecht, 2007), pp. 14–8, p. 107.
9 Wm. Roger Louis (gen. ed.), *The Oxford History of the British Empire*, 5 vols. (Oxford: Oxford University Press, 1998–99); the 'Companion Series' to the Oxford History of the British Empire (addressing geographical foci [Australia, Canada, Ireland, Scotland] and key themes [migration, missions, gender, settlers, black history, environment etc.]) now numbers more than ten volumes and is ongoing; Dominic Lieven, *Empire. The Russian Empire and its Rivals from the Sixteenth Century to the Present* (London: Pimlico, 2002); Sebastian Conrad, *Deutsche Kolonialgeschichte* (Munich: CH Beck, 2008); John Darwin, *The Empire Project. The Rise and Fall of the British World System, 1830–1970* (Cambridge: Cambridge University Press, 2009); Odd Arne Westad, *The Restless Empire. China and the World since 1750* (New York: Basic Books, 2012).
10 See e.g. Marc Ferro, *Colonization. A Global History* (London: Taylor & Francis, 1997); Stephen Howe, *Empire. A Very Short Introduction* (Oxford: Oxford University Press, 2002); Hendrik L. Wesseling, *The European Colonial Empires 1815–1919* (Harlow: Pearson, 2004); Herfried Münkler, *Empires. The Logic of World Domination from Ancient Rome to the United States* (Cambridge: Polity Press, 2007); John Darwin, *After Tamerlane. The Global History of Empire* (London: Penguin, 2008); Timothy Parsons, *The Rule of Empires. Those Who Built Them, Those Who Endured Them, and Why They Always Fall* (New York: Oxford University Press, 2010); Jane Burbank/Frederick Cooper, *Empires in World History. Power and the Politics of Difference* (Princeton: Princeton University Press, 2010).

11 See e.g. Bernard Porter, *The Absent-Minded Imperialists* (Oxford: Oxford University Press, 2006) and Andrew S. Thompson, *The Empire Strikes Back? The Impact of Imperialism on Britain from the Mid-Nineteenth-Century* (Harlow: Routledge, 2005); for critical responses to Porter's stance see: *The Journal of Imperial and Commonwealth History* 36/4 (2008) ('Comfort' and Conviction: A Response to Bernard Porter, ed. by John M. MacKenzie).

12 Cf. J. and J. Comaroff, *Christianity, Colonialism, and Consciousness in South Africa*, 2 vols. (Chicago: Chicago University Press, 1991, 1997); J. MacKenzie (ed.), *European Empires and the People. Popular Responses to Imperialism in France, Britain, the Netherlands, Belgium, Germany and Italy* (Manchester: Manchester University Press, 2011), p. 1.

13 A. Lester, *Imperial Networks. Creating Identities in Nineteenth Century South Africa and Britain* (London: Routledge, 2001); Ulrike von Hirschhausen and Jörn Leonhard (eds), *Comparing Empires. Encounters and Transfers in the Long Nineteenth Century* (Göttingen: Vandenhoeck & Ruprecht, 2011); Boris Barth and Jürgen Osterhammel (eds), *Zivilisierungsmissionen. Imperiale Weltverbesserung seit dem 18. Jahrhundert* (Konstanz: UVK, 2005).

14 Jörn Leonhard and Ulrike von Hirschhausen, *Empires und Nationalstaaten im 19. Jahrhundert* (Göttingen: Vandenhoeck & Ruprecht, 2009).

15 Peo Hansen, 'European Integration, European Identity and the Colonial Connection', *European Journal of Social Theory* 5:4 (2002), p. 485.

16 J. MacKenzie (ed.), *European Empires and the People*, p. 7.

17 See e.g. Gary B. Magee and Andrew S. Thompson, *Empire and Globalisation. Networks of People, Goods and Capital in the British World, c. 1850–1914* (Cambridge: Cambridge University Press, 2010).

18 *Der Tagesspiegel* (16 Dec. 2013).

19 See e.g. David Cannadine, *Ornamentalism. How the British Saw their Empire* (London: Penguin, 2002).

20 See Jürgen Osterhammel, 'Expansion und Imperium', in Peter Burschel et al. (eds), *Historische Anstöße. Festschrift für Wolfgang Reinhard zum 65. Geburtstag* (Berlin: Akademie Verlag, 2002), pp. 371–92, p. 389.

21 Maurice Halbwachs, *Les Cadres sociaux de la mémoire* (Paris: Felix Alcan, 1925); *La Mémoire collective*, ed. by Jeanne Alexandre (Paris, 1950); *La Topographie légendaire des Èvangiles en Terre Sainte. Étude de mémoire collective*, (Paris: PUF, 2008).

22 Charles Maier, 'A Surfeit of Memory? Reflections on History, Melancholy and Denial,' *History and Memory* 5 (1992), pp. 137–51.

23 Pierre Nora (ed.), *Les lieux de mémoire*, 7 vols. (Paris, 1984–92). A selection of the volumes was published in English: Pierre Nora and Lawrence D. Kritzman (eds), *Realms of Memory. Rethinking the French Past*, 3 vols. (New York: Columbia University Press, 1996–98).

24 Pierre Nora, *Zwischen Geschichte und Gedächtnis* (Berlin: Wagenbach Klaus GmbH, 1997), p. 11.

25 Pierre Nora, 'Comment écrire l'histoire de France?' in P. Nora (ed.), *Les lieux de mémoire*, vol. 3: *Les Frances 1*, (Paris, 1992), pp. 9–32, p. 20 (our translation).

26 Indra Sengupta, 'Introduction. Locating *lieux de mémoire*: A (Post)colonial Perspective,' in I. Sengupta (ed.), *Memory, History, and Colonialism. Engaging with Pierre Nora in Colonial and Postcolonial Contexts*, German Historical Institute London Bulletin Supplement 1 (London, 2009), pp. 1–8, p. 1.

27 See e.g. Mario Isnenghi (ed.), *I luoghi della memoria*, 3 vols. (Rome: Laterza, 1996–97); Etienne François and Hagen Schulze (eds), *Deutsche Erinnerungsorte*, 3 vols. (Munich: CH Beck, 2001); Emil Brix, Ernst Bruckmüller and Hannes Stekl (eds.), *Memoria Austriae*, 3 vols. (Vienna and Munich: Verlag für Geschichte und Politik , 2004–05); Bert Bakker (ed.), *Plaatsen van Herinnering*, 4 vols. (Amsterdam: Bert Bakker, 2005–07).

28 Pim den Boer, Heinz Duchhardt, Georg Kreis and Wolfgang Schmale (eds), *Europäische Erinnerungsorte*, 3 vols. (Munich: Oldenburg Wissen Schaftsverlag, 2012); Hans-Henning Hahn (ed.), *Deutsch-polnische Erinnerungsorte*, 5 vols. (Paderborn: Ferdinand

Schöning, 2012); Bernd Henningsen, (ed.). *Transnationale Erinnerungsorte. Nord- und südeuropäische Perspektiven* (Berlin: Berliner-Wissenschaft, 2009); Christoph Markschies and Hubert Wolf (eds), *Erinnerungsorte des Christentums* (Munich: Beck, 2010).

29 Etienne François and Hagen Schulze, 'Einleitung', in E. François and H. Schulze (eds), *Deutsche Erinnerungsorte*, 3 vols. (Munich: CH Beck, 2001), vol. 1, pp. 9–24, p. 18.

30 Friedrich Nietzsche, 'On the Uses and Disadvantages of History for Life', in F. Nietzsche, *Untimely Meditations*, trans. R. J. Hollingdale (Cambridge: Cambridge University Press, 1997), p. 104.

31 Cf. Sigmund Freud, 'Totem and Taboo. Resemblances between the Psychic Lives of Savages and Neurotics', translated by Abraham Arden Brill (London: Routledge, 1919); Freud, *Moses and Monotheism*, translated by Katherine Jones, (New York: Vintage Books, 1967 [1939]).

32 Cf. Ernst H. Gombrich, *Aby Warburg. An Intellectual Biography* (London: Phaidon Press, 1986).

33 Jan Assmann, 'Collective Memory and Cultural Identity', *New German Critique* 65 (1995), pp. 125–33, p. 133.

34 Bill Schwarz, *Memories of Empire, Vol. 1: The White Man's World* (Oxford: Oxford University Press, 2011).

35 Dennis Walder, *Postcolonial Nostalgias. Writing, Representation, and Memory* (New York and London: Routledge, 2012), p. 9. For a comparative exploration of post-colonial nostalgia through the lens of women's writings see Patricia Lorcin, *Historicising Colonial Nostalgia. European Women's Narratives of Algeria and Kenya, 1900 to the Present* (Basingstoke and New York: Palgrave Macmillan, 2011).

36 Maurice Halbwachs, *Les cadres sociaux de la mémoire* (Paris: La Haye, 1976), p. 144.

37 Robert Aldrich, *Vestiges of the Colonial Empire in France. Monuments, Museums and Colonial Memories* (Basingstoke: Palgrave Macmillan, 2005).

38 Alec G. Hargreaves (ed.), *Memory, Empire, and Postcolonialism. Legacies of French Colonialism* (Oxford: Oxford University Press, 2005); see also Patricia Lorcin (ed.), *Algeria and France, 1800–2000: Identity, Memory, Nostalgia* (Syracuse: Syracuse University Press, 2006).

39 Krystyna von Henneberg, 'Monuments, Public Space, and the Memory of Empire in Modern Italy', *History and Memory* 16 (2004), pp. 37–85; Ellen W. Sapega, 'Remembering Empire/Forgetting the Colonies: Accretions of Memory and the Limits of Commemoration in a Lisbon Neighbourhood', *History and Memory* 20 (2008), pp. 18–38; James Flath, 'This is How the Chinese People Began Their Struggle: Humen and the Opium War as a Site of Memory', in Marc Andre Matten (ed.), *Places of Memory in Modern China. History, Politics, and Identity* (Leiden/Boston: Brill, 2012), pp. 167–92 and Hayan Lee, 'The Ruins of Yuanmingyuan: Or, How to Enjoy a National Wound', in Marc Andre Matten (ed.), *Places of Memory in Modern China*, pp. 193–231.

40 K. E. Surpriya, *Remembering Empire. Power, Memory, & Place in Postcolonial India* (New York: Peter Laing Publishing, 2004), p. 21.

41 Ernest Renan, 'What is a Nation?' in Geoff Eley and Ronald Grigor Suny (eds), *Becoming National. A Reader* (New York and Oxford: Oxford University Press, 1996), pp. 42–55, esp. p. 43; see also Paul Ricoeur, 'Memory – History – Forgetting', in Jörn Rüsen (ed.), *Meaning and Representation in History* (Oxford: Oxford University Press, 2006), pp. 9–19; Elena Esposito, *Soziales Vergessen. Formen und Medien des Gedächtnisses der Gesellschaft* (Frankfurt a. M.: Suhrkamp Verlag, 2002).

42 See Winfried Speitkamp, 'Grenzen der Hybridisierung? Symboltransfers in post-kolonialen Staaten Afrikas', in W. Speitkamp (ed.), *Kommunikationsräume – Erinnerungsräume. Beiträge zur transkulturellen Begegnung in Afrika*, (Munich: Meidenbauer, 2005), pp. 277–89.

[17]

43 Ellen W. Sapega, 'Remembering Empire/Forgetting the Colonies: Accretions of Memory and the Limits of Commemoration in a Lisbon Neighbourhood', *History and Memory* 20 (2008), pp. 30–2.
44 Matthew G. Stanard, 'Afterword', in J. MacKenzie (ed.), *European Empires and the People*, p. 231.
45 It would be intriguing, for instance, to learn more about the fashioning of Queen Victoria and the Dutch queens Wilhelmina, Juliana and Beatrix as imperial icons at home or at the periphery, or to study the figure of Rani Lakshmibai as a mythical heroine of indigenous resistance against the British during the Indian uprising of 1857.

PART I

Monuments

CHAPTER TWO

Transmissible sites: monuments, memorials and their visibility on the metropole and periphery

Xavier Guégan

In the mid-nineteenth century, British and French colonisation instituted distinct legislative and governmental models in India and Algeria. Following the defeat of the Sepoy Rebellion (1858) and the dismantling of the East India Company, Britain established direct rule in India. Similarly, in 1848, after several tumultuous decades of conquest and settlement, Algeria administratively became part of France. During this second wave of empire building (the first one finishing at the end of the eighteenth century) new justifications emerged to account for imperial motives and enterprises. In the nineteenth century, in post-Enlightenment and industrial France and Britain, political schemes and their related colonial discourses had to change in order to convince populations that there was a 'right' to colonise. The two imperial powers thus sought to legitimise their newly established colonial structures by different means: visual ones, the erection of monuments, statues and memorials, were part of this 'project'. Three practices of architectural visual politics were envisaged: firstly, the conservation and restoration of local buildings and monuments; secondly, the transformation of a number of indigenous monuments and buildings into colonial ones; and thirdly, the construction of new buildings to house the institutions of colonial administration. In addition to this, governments in both countries commissioned two types of memorial: statues honouring colonial rulers, and war memorials.

However, the creation of such colonial *lieux de mémoire* were not restricted to architecture and sculptural monuments. Visual representations (illustrations and photographs) of these artefacts were reproduced and disseminated by scholarly organisations, such as archaeological societies; by administrative bodies, such as city councils and town planners; and by commercial agents, such as photographic markets, manufacturers of postcards and organisers of exhibitions. This chapter will examine from a transnational and comparative perspective, the connection between the erection of monuments and memorials mainly at the colonial periphery – the *fixed* sites of imperial memory – and their political and cultural dissemination via photography in both the colonies and the metropoles – the *transmissible* sites. It highlights the multiform constitution of sites of memory during this formative moment in the establishment of colonial rule. During the period 1830–1914 the *transmissible* sites of imperial memory contributed to the institutionalisation of a colonial *mentalité* in both metropole and colony. Despite creating a sense of a common belonging, and thus a degree of successful cultural and political assimilation, these sites encountered very different readings and receptions. These varied according to the political and social principles connected to the rise of new social classes in both metropole and colony, and a growing political and social division between the subjects/citizens of the motherland and the inhabitants of the colonised lands. This study will first consider the establishment of monuments and memorials as sites of imperial memory and explore their photographic diffusion throughout metropoles and colonies. It will then focus on the image of indigenous and colonial monuments as examples of reconfiguration of meanings, and conclude by examining memorials and their representation as attempts at glorification of 'conquest' and 'pacification'.

Imperial monuments and the rise of photography

Pierre Nora claimed that 'the sites of memory are not what we remember but where the memory works; not the tradition itself but its laboratory.'[1] This is an essential element of the politics of what has been defined as the colonial discourse. When Nora wrote this in the general introduction to the seven volumes of his monumental 'Sites of Memory', his study focused on France as the Nation, Republic and State. The Republic denoted a symbolic order with monuments, education, and commemoration; the Nation encompassed representations of a distant heritage and the 'great' moments of redrafting; and finally the State produced the design of its greatness and glory – either military or civil, its heritage of monuments and arts, and its language.[2] All of these patterns were used to create a modern France. Yet, those patterns can also be used to understand the 'colonial moments' of the same period. The French colonial empire should naturally be included in this approach. Moreover, in the context of a memory-focused investigation a comparative analysis of the two colonial systems of France and Britain is most instructive.

In France and Britain, the transmission of the colonial affirmation, its commemoration and visual memorisation, was undertaken through the medium of visual artefacts of recognisable sites of memory or *souvenirs*. Colonial cities, adorned with monuments similar to the ones that could be admired at home, provided the nation with a sense of close connection with the metropole. They generated a sense of imperial coherence. This was possible because photography, which was becoming part of everyday life, made accessible the memorials and monuments erected in the periphery for home audiences. Photography emerged as a democratic form of the visual arts: initially the middle-class people buying photographic albums were the main audience[3], but towards the end of the century the market had grown, including working-class people who could afford postcards or, alternatively, see the photographs in exhibitions. The growing commodification of images created a bourgeoning trade in photographic souvenirs from the colonies. Rebecca DeRoo observes that at the turn of the century 'postcards became mass media of communication and collectible objects for the first time in French history' and that a 'significant portion of the millions of postcards produced yearly in France displayed Algerian tourist sites and ethnic types'.[4]

The sites of memory that contributed to the consolidation of French Algeria and British India as features in various landscapes of memory were thus rendered transmissible. They travelled within the great circuits of colonial trade. There, two new trends developed simultaneously, they interacted with and shaped the *transmissible* sites of imperial memory. One was that 'photography participated in the change to touristic consumption as a record and validation of leisure travel; it also created and amplified the desire to participate in leisure travel activities'.[5] The other trend was that both the consumption of travel photography and colonial *spaces* entered the middle-class (and later working-class) home in the metropole.[6] In this way, the sites were invested with a sense of immediacy and familiarity that connected the colonial (periphery) to metropolitan audiences.[7]

This bond does not mean, however, that the three main audiences – the indigenous, the colonists and the metropolitans – perceived, responded to, consumed and utilised the sites in the same manner. Reactions ranged from a sense of belonging to resentment. Indeed the subjective processes underpinning the construction of these imperial sites of memory varied according to where photographic images were purchased – in the cities in the colonised territory, where they were picked up by tourists, or at world exhibitions organised in the metropole. This subjectivity also varied according to whether observations were *direct*, usually by the indigenous and colonialist, or *indirect* through public exhibitions, private collections and in associated or administrative settings. Nora highlights that 'as soon as there are tracks, distance and mediation, we are not anymore in a memory that is "true", but in history.'[8] During the post-conquest period, the makers of empire tried to create the illusion of imperial eternity, of history.

In the making of a *souvenir* culture, there were two crucial moments. The first was the period of colonisation between 1830 and 1870, which was then followed by an even more pervasive imperialist culture between 1870 and 1914. This period, 1830–1914, will be the focus of this chapter. The second moment was the interwar era, replete with events like exhibitions and anniversaries, the promotion of intra-empire trade through nationalistic advertisement (the Empire Marketing Board) and by educating an 'imperial' youth in the classroom.[9] Basically both periods emerged when the colonial powers felt the need to emphasise their presence and reiterate their power.[10] Research has often focused on the second moment, particularly for France,[11] and has neglected the equally significant earlier one which will form the centre of this discussion.

During the first half of the nineteenth century public audiences in France and Britain already had some knowledge of Algeria and India. This was the result of popular writings and histories, paintings, engravings and the actions of prominent personalities. In the years from 1830 to 1870 the most successful travel writing came from the pens of officers, explorers and missionaries. The publication of their memoirs and adventures turned invasion and settlement into fascinating and exciting experiences. Explorers' diaries and novels were famous for their accounts of the discoveries of old palaces, and hidden temples. Amongst thinkers and politicians in France and Britain, there emerged a general consensus in favour of further colonisation and imperial control.[12]

During those decades, attitudes towards indigenous populations, their representation and the politics towards the annexed countries underwent a noticeable change.[13] With the Great Exhibition of 1851 and the popularisation of museums and galleries in the second half of the nineteenth century, the general public encountered a new dimension in the visual representation of India and Algeria. Anne Maxwell explains that colonised peoples, their environment, artefacts and monuments were now being displayed in response to a growing public interest in the concept of 'race'. They were organised into a hierarchy which could have been compared to botanical and zoological classifications.[14]

Moreover, the Great Exhibition of 1851 contributed to making photography attractive to the public. As well as presenting images of foreign cultures, the Exhibition also celebrated the achievements of modern science and technology, and photography brought these two together.[15] In the course of the following decades photography became ever more attractive. Responding to a strong demand for instruction, several institutions started teaching this new 'fashionable hobby,'[16] and numerous photographic societies – alongside geographical and archaeological associations – were founded in France and Britain. Photography was turning more and more into a commodity with the emergence of commercial photographic exhibitions. From the mid-1850s onwards, the market in photographic images reached different domains such as architecture, landscapes, city and countryside interests, topography, scenery, ethnology, portraits, and pictures from the wider world – both 'civilised' and 'non-civilised'.[17] In the decades following the Great Exhibition, international exhibitions in Paris (1855, 1867, 1878), London (1862 and 1871–73) and Philadelphia (1876) further developed the visual practices the Great Exhibition had pioneered, including the representation of foreign cultures and colonial commodities. Although these exhibitions principally sought to stimulate international trade, they also undeniably 'diffus[ed] the ideology of progress and the early forms of mass consumerism among the denizens of the west.'[18]

The creation of sites of imperial memory took several forms and resulted from different processes: through acts of self-promotion and propaganda on behalf of the state (exhibitions, games, anniversaries, school books, stamps, etc.) and via explorers, artists and commercial business and advertising. Alongside the building up of colonial cityscapes and the embellishment of an old indigenous *patrimoine* (heritage) there was also the rise of tourism, museums, and the growth of new markets at home. Colonial and travel photography enjoyed the same kind of success as photographs taken in Britain and France, and it was common to find both kinds of pictures in the same museums, exhibitions, shops and street sellers' stands. Photography played an ever increasing role both in these exhibiting practices and in their recording and commercial dissemination. It rapidly became a new site where colonial ideology and national memory fused with the myth of a Western *grandeur*.

Reconfiguration of meanings: from indigenous to colonial monuments and buildings

From the 1830s onwards, archaeologists and governments grew interested in the restoration of monuments from previous civilisations in Algeria and India. After the 1860s photographs of such restoration sites proliferated, creating a real boom in the 1880s. These pictures often represented the three phases of the process – the ruins, the restoration in progress, and the restored monument. The fact that such restoration projects were undertaken in both Algeria and India is not surprising. In those decades the formation of a new colonial discourse connected to Utilitarianism, Liberalism and Social Darwinism made it appear important that the need for British and French interventionist policies be made visible. The colonial rhetoric in France and Britain asserted that indigenous peoples were incapable of achieving modernity without the aid of newly industrialised Western European countries. Photography of the restoration was implicitly didactic, highlighting the benefits of colonial rule.

Archaeological sites, indigenous architecture and colonial new-builds were among the early topics that generated interest. Archaeologists welcomed photography as a fantastic medium to record the beauty of the past without the artist's 'imprecision'. Until the 1850s, the recording of Indian and Algerian sites was left to enthusiastic amateurs who first amassed collections of drawings, and then of photographs. These Orientalists were well known in European galleries, and 'the extraordinarily buoyant market of the nineteenth-century stimulated excess production', which involved 'extremes of admiration' for this group of artists.[19] Starting in 1847, the Governor General of India received orders from London to begin an inventory of historical monuments.[20] The programme aimed at composing 'a general, comprehensive, uniform, and effective plan of operations based on scientific principles'. The 'great object' was 'the preservation and illustration of the Monuments of India'.[21] Although this enormous enterprise soon faded, it initially gave a new impulse to the recording of architecture and archaeological subjects through photography. Something similar was also happening in French Algeria. The 'cult' of historical objects and monuments in Algeria started soon after the beginning of colonial rule. The French architects Amable Ravoisé (between 1840 and 1842) and Charles Texier (from 1846) embarked on the first inventories of historical monuments; this process was in line with the 'Commission des Monuments Historiques' that simultaneously conducted a similar mission in France.[22] Nearly every photographer who worked in Algeria and India in the nineteenth century took architectural pictures. In his *History of Indian and Eastern Architecture* of 1876, James Fergusson emphasised the importance of photographic works for history: 'For the purpose of such a work as this ... photography has probably done more than anything that has been written'.[23] Nevertheless his viewpoint, like that of the majority of scholars of the nineteenth century, was specifically focused on photography for purposes of documentation. He did not consider it as an aspect of a colonial and national enterprise.[24]

The *fixed* sites (the monuments and memorials themselves) and their *transmissible* counterparts (the photographs) were entangled with the political fashion for travelling and the official tours that emerged from the mid-nineteenth century onwards. Both Napoleon III's visit to Algeria in 1865 and the Prince of Wales's tour of India in 1875–76 connected the politics of colonisation to the ruling families and their entourages. The photographic albums created to record these trips portrayed both the indigenous environment and the changes wrought by colonial rule. Photography was thus used to record historical events, and also to witness 'noble' leisure pursuits and emphasise exotic pleasures.[25]

The volume of photography generated by nineteenth-century archaeological projects is astounding. The commercial photographic company Bourne and Shepherd took pictures of Indian temples for private clients and the Archaeological Survey of India. Their albums *General view of the Teli-ka-Mandir during restoration, Gwalior* (1883) and *Side view of the Small Sasbahu Temple, Gwalior* (1883) show temples from the eighteenth and eleventh century, and the photographs were taken during the restoration and after. In Algeria, the archaeological site of Djemila (near Sétif) was already an attraction in the early nineteenth century. During the July Monarchy, in 1839, King Louis-Philippe's son Ferdinand Philippe, the Duke of Orleans, wanted to transfer its Triumphal Arch to Paris. Although this relocation project was never realised, work to restore the ruins started in the 1860s. Pictures were then taken, one in 1861–62 (before the beginning of the work) and one in 1880 (once it was completed). The photographs were anonymous, exhibited and sold together in the 1880s with an added text as *Arc de Triomphe de Djemila (Algérie), avant et après restauration* (1880).

Archaeological sites were not the only large structures that were photographed. There were also depictions of new colonial buildings and of the transformation of indigenous monuments into colonial ones. These images documented the institutionalisation of the colonial administration. Built between 1878 and 1887, the Railway Station (Victoria Terminus) at Bombay became one of the most exuberant symbols of the British presence in India; again, photography was directly connected to the construction of a site of imperial memory.[26] This large Victorian Gothic building was often pictured but perhaps one of its most successful representations was James Ricalton's *The Most Magnificent Railway Station in the World, Bombay, India* (1903). Constructed out of two photographs to create a 3D effect it enabled the 'travellers' at home to imagine themselves on an Indian tour. This stereoscopic photograph from the Underwood Travel Library was one of a series of 100 photographs, designed to be viewed through a special binocular viewer, producing a 3D effect, sold together with a book of descriptions and a map with precise locations.[27] Félix Jacques Antoine Moulin's image *La Jenina, ancien palais des Deys* (1856) featured in an album entitled 'Souvenirs de l'Algérie. Province d'Alger' (1856–57), which belonged to General Daumas (1803–71). This Ottoman palace – previously a palace of the Deys – was used by the French administration, first for administrative services and then as a military depot. A fire broke out in 1844 and the building was demolished in 1856.[28] This picture was taken in the same year, just before La Jenina was dismantled. Here, the photograph is the testimony of both the precolonial rule and the beginning of colonisation, but now also of a time of change since this emblematic building has disappeared. By surviving the *fixed* site, this *transmissible* site became part of the preservation of the patrimony of French Algeria through the creation of a memory-image of a transcultural edifice. It established a rapport between this recent destroyed past with the history of a colonial–colonised nation under formation.[29]

Memorials and the glorification of 'conquest' and 'pacification'

During the period of the Indian Mutiny and the conquest of Algeria and in the two decades that followed, photography interacted with developments in imperial ideology. They were also linked to the emerging sites of imperial memory that were meant to consolidate the hold of Britain and France on their respective colonies. This was sought through the production of images of the peacemaking process following the annexations and the visual construction of a remembrance of the wars in France and Britain. A large number of photographs produced in mid-nineteenth-century India and Algeria came from official sources – the army or civilian administration – or from new commercial businesses. The use of photography had initially been spurred by the desire to obtain reliable information about British India and French Algeria, and the medium continued to contribute to the political, ideological and cultural reception of the British Raj and France's new departments. Foucault's concept of 'governmentality'[30] – the relationship between rationality and reality that articulates political knowledge, expressing how dominance operates through a wide range of control techniques – may be applied to the ways in which knowledge of the country, of its past, of its infrastructure and of its peoples were managed.

[28]

It is disputable to what extent the concept of photographic governmentality was only the result of organised political administration.
There was also the demand for 'views' of the exotic lands driven by
Western clients. As Peter Osborne has observed, explicitly governmental photography 'formed part of the practico-symbolic management
of the vast subcontinent which demanded the classifying, recording,
census-taking, mapping, displaying and licensing of everything, so
rendering it knowable, imaginable and controllable by means of
European systems and on British terms'.[31] This also applies to photography in French Algeria. It was through archaeological societies
and the military that photography started to develop in India and
Algeria. It was not only a tool to record campaigns and wars but it
also enabled Westerners to survey the country and people and explore
politically sensitive regions.

The meanings of visibility differed depending on whether the individual observer was experiencing the monuments in the colonised
country or in the metropole. In Algiers and Calcutta, for instance,
colonial settlers reshaped the cities in line with their memory of the
conquest of the territories – the Duke of Orleans's statue was erected
next to the Djemaa-Djeded mosque in Algiers (see Figure 2.1) and Lord
Hardinge's statue next to the Ochterlony monument in Calcutta (see
Figure 2.2). This confronted local populations with constant reminders of their colonial rulers. In the years and decades following the
formal annexations of Algeria and parts of India, both Britain and
France needed to establish their rule by asserting their colonial success and the pacification process that followed the military campaigns.
The sites of imperial memory created as part of this process were
connected to the twin celebrations of the 'conqueror' (MacMahon,
Victoria) and 'pacification' (war memorials).

Celebrations of the conqueror mainly took the form of sculptures
in honour of military officers and heads of state in Britain and France.
Postcards of the statue of Marshal MacMahon (1808–93) in Algiers
soon formed part of a canon of images of sites dedicated to this officer
and politician who, throughout most of the century, symbolically
connected the histories of Algeria and France.[32] The name MacMahon
was also given to streets in several cities and even to a town in Algeria
(in the Constantinois County). In India, it was Queen Victoria
(1819–1901) who became an emblem of the British Raj. Soon squares
and buildings bore her name. Samuel Bourne's image *Statue of the
Queen, Bombay* (1860s) was amongst many popular photographic representations of statues dedicated to the Queen (Empress after 1876).
Bourne showed an imposing sculpture representing Victoria sitting
on her throne within a neo-gothic church style. Outside the circular

2.1 A. Beglet, Statue du Duc d'Orléans et la Mosquée Djemaa-Djeded [or Alger, la Place du Gouvernement] (1890)

fences protecting the statue are six Indians facing the 'imposing' Queen.[33] Indeed, the Queen's 'providence' was also visible to her new subjects through numerous images, such as on rupee coins, and monuments throughout India. Ceremonials connected to the rulers and colonial administrators became more and more common from the 1870s. Durbars were used as a means of reasserting the role of the monarchy and its hierarchy on the subcontinent, and the message was then transmitted to remote audiences by means of photographic images like the ones contained in the album of the *Delhi Durbar* (1903). Festivities were organised to honour the Republican administrations of Algerian towns and cities – such as the Mayor of Bône, *M. Jonnart, Gouverneur Général prononce son discours* (unknown, 1907). Photographs of both events show massive crowds filling large public spaces.[34]

The conquerors were not only the rulers but also the officers on the fields of conquest. Marshal Bugeaud (1784–1849), for instance, was famous for his campaigns in Algeria which lasted from the early 1830s – when he fought local villagers and the national hero Abd-el-Kader

2.2 Samuel Bourne, *Lord Hardinge's Statue and the Ochterlony Monument, Calcutta* (1860s)

(1808–83) – until his appointment to the office of Governor General of Algeria (1840–48). He eventually acquired the nickname 'Père Bugeaud'. In colonial cities such as Algiers, main squares were given the names of such conquerors, and statues were erected to honour them. Again, photographs of this commemoration of 'glory' were taken, and the image *Place Bugeaud* (Unknown, Algiers – 1880s) uses the same visual rhetoric as Bourne's *Statue of the Queen, Bombay.* The photograph depicts the modernity of the Haussmannian buildings surrounding the square and the statue, the fences around it – a common feature of most of these statues – and the indigenous population marking a sharp contrast with this environment and the representation of Bugeaud.[35] Another famous name of the conquest, the Duke of Orleans, also featured as a statue in one of the main squares of Algiers. A. Beglet's image *Statue du Duc d'Orléans et la Mosquée Djemaa-Djeded* [or *Alger, la Place du Gouvernement*] (Figure 2.1) depicts the equestrian statue with the mosque in the background. The relationship between those statues and the buildings where political and administrative decisions were made is clear: the conqueror is exhibited, magnified, and visually directly connected to the colonial powerhouse.

The same system applied to Samuel Bourne's *Statue of Sir W. C. Bentinck and Government House, Calcutta* (1860s), and again this shows a similar colonial construction of sites in both French Algeria and British India.[36] The statue of the Duke of Orleans was cast in Paris from the melted bronze of cannons dating from the Regency of Algiers (Ottoman Algeria). It was unveiled on 28 October 1845 in the Place du Gouvernement – where La Jenina had previously stood. To the left of the picture, there is the minaret with a clock. The clock was installed in 1852 in order to match with the French fashion for clocks on city halls and churches – or any religious edifice.[37] At the time, the installation of the clocks was already perceived as the symbolic order of the colonial power because of its transformation of the indigenous societies, as mentioned by the French historian Louis de Baudicour in 1860 in his *Histoire de la colonisation de l'Algérie*.[38] From the 1830s numerous equestrian statues of conquerors were erected in Algeria and India. Samuel Bourne's *Lord Hardinge's Statue and the Ochterlony Monument, Calcutta* (Figure 2.2) shows Field Marshal Hardinge (1785–1856)[39] against the background of the Ochterlony monument. Hardinge personified the East India Company's growing administrative control over India, while the monument represented Major-General David Ochterlony's victories. Indeed this column had been unveiled by Ochterlony himself in 1825, in his capacity as Commander-in-chief of the army of the East India Company. It had been paid for from public funds[40] and would commemorate both his successful defence of Delhi against the Marathas in 1804 and the company's victory over the Gurkhas in the Anglo-Nepalese War in 1814–16.

It is striking that depictions of such sites were among the very first photographs in India, such as Frederick Fiebig's *Monument of Sir Thomas Munroe, Madras* (1851).[41] Often statues of this kind were erected to commemorate army officers who earned military honours from their exploits in the field or had died in battles which gained them the status of colonial 'hero'. This tendency of erecting numerous statues in cities and towns of all sizes was directly linked to a fashion that was increasingly popular in mid-nineteenth-century France and Britain.[42] Samuel Bourne's *Statue of Sir William Peel in the Eden Gardens, Calcutta* (1860s),[43] *Le Capitaine Lelièvre, Mazagran* (unknown, postcard – 1890s),[44] Ali Abbas's *General Havelock's Tomb, Lucknow* (1874)[45] and *Statue du Sergent Blandan, Boufarik* (unknown, postcard – 1887) and *Statue du Sergent Blandan, Lyon* (unknown, postcard – 1887) all fall into this category.[46] Statues in honour of Blandan, Lelièvre, Havelock and Peel were erected both in the metropole and at the colonial periphery. Their metropolitan monuments often linked these men to their local backgrounds, which highlight the imbrications of the French and British nation-making and the colonial discourse.

The end of the Sepoy Rebellion (Indian Mutiny) and the conquest of Algeria, as well as the pacification that followed were also captured and transported as photographic images. Felice Beato, in partnership with James Robertson (and then Charles Shepherd), photographed key places and scenes shortly after the Mutiny. Although Victorians perceived articles and accounts describing what happened as traumatising, photographic prints could undeniably evoke a more 'real' sense of what occurred. Thus, from the 1860s, photographers took pictures of military camps, officers and captains, and memorials in order to show their concern for the memory of the Mutiny but also to indicate and certainly reassure the British investors that India was then 'under control'; in the following decades, Lucknow and Cawnpore offered rich pickings for photographers. Commercial photographers and servicemen such as Captains T. Bigg and M. Clarke recorded the activities of the British army; for instance during the second Anglo-Afghan War in 1878–79 the firm Bourne & Shepherd sent one of their photographers, the former military surgeon Benjamin Simpson, to record the scenes.[47] Some photographers became famous or infamous for their professional extremism, such as Hooper, who asked a firing squad to synchronise the order to shoot with his own camera shutter to capture the exact moment of the execution of dacoits in Burma in 1885. Similar phenomena could be observed during the Algerian conquest. The Battle of Mazagran (1840) became famous amongst the French in the mid-nineteenth century. Newspapers related the news of the battle; paintings, lithographs, novels, history books and poems were published; and all kinds of merchandise – including medals – were produced to commemorate the event.[48]

Photographs also contributed to the creation of a trauma propaganda about indigenous violence. Felice Beato's *Interior of the Sikandar Bagh after the Slaughter of 2,200 Mutineers by the 93rd Highlanders and 4th Punjab Infantry* (1858) and Félix Jacques Antoine Moulin's *Cachrou, bureau d'Abd-el-Kader (ruines du château) (cercle de Mascara)* (1856) both show the battlefields, corpses (in Beato's *Interior*) and the shattered ruins of strategic places formerly held by colonial rebels. Samuel Bourne's *The Well, Cawnpore* (1860s) and *Memorial Garden, Cawnpore* (1860s), Félix Jacques Antoine Moulin's *Monument érigé en l'honneur de Saint-Augustin sur les ruines de l'ancienne église d'Hippône près de Bône* (1856) depict the sites of massacres, but only a few years after the pacification process and the building of memorials. The Memorial and the Well were built in order to commemorate the British victims, to represent the British victory and show the domestication of the event and place. These pictures recorded the locations of horrible episodes, but they were consumed amidst the reassuring feeling that by the time the photographs were taken, civilised colonisers had already restored order, peace and progress to formerly troublesome native societies.[49] Some of those memorials were built to commemorate the bravery and loss of British and French men during rebels' victories, as with the postcard *Monument Sidi Brahim, Oran* (unknown, postcard – 1900s).[50] Memorials in India and Algeria were also marked by surprising similarity featuring, as they did, an angel at their centre – for instance, Bourne's *The Well, Cawnpore* and the postcard *Monument Sidi Brahim* – and fences or encircling structures – for example, Abbas's *General Havelock's Tomb, Lucknow* and Moulin's *Monument érigé en l'honneur de Saint-Augustin sur les ruines de l'ancienne église d'Hippône près de Bône.*

Conclusion

Both *fixed* and *transmissible* sites of memory promoted British and French expansion. The commodification of colonial heroes, conquest, colonisation and pacification, archaeological sites and their restoration through photographic representations served several purposes: propaganda, tourism, narratives about ancient civilisations and the dominant modern West, nationalism, patriotism and unity as well as masculine enterprise. Thus those *transmissible* sites were material, symbolic and functional; and they implied imagination and rituals, growing into an ideological *cartography* of monuments and statues that represented the conqueror. Sites of memory in the shape of monuments and memorials could travel with the photographs depicting them, and this broadened their potential audiences.

In some cases, after the destruction of monuments and statues, the photographs remained the only testimonies and outlasted the original sites of memory. Gradually, throughout the nineteenth century, the role of *fixed* and *transmissible* sites enabled a connection via these dual cultural artefacts between different communities from diverse locations into an imperial 'imagined community'. They were part of, what Anderson has defined as 'the spontaneous distillation of a complex "crossing" of discrete historical forces; but that, once created, they became "modular", capable of being transplanted, with varying degrees of self-consciousness, to a great variety of social terrains, to merge and be merged with a correspondingly wide variety of political and ideological constellations'.[51] The availability of images of far-away and hard-to-imagine colonial places thus made them familiar and enabled home audiences to extend their 'imagined communities' from national communities to imperial ones. This system of physical and imaginary heritage developed into a visual language of modernity, continuity, unity and eternity serving an imaginary 'unified national language'[52] that was interlinked to an imperial idiom.

A comparison of India and Algeria as well as Britain and France in the nineteenth century makes evident that the modernity of the metropoles' cities was paralleled in the colonial cities, and photography was used to illustrate this practice. British and French imperialism are often differentiated because of the apparent ideological dissimilarities between direct and indirect rule systems; it is however clear that within both systems the connection between *fixed* and *transmissible* sites of imperial memory implemented memory-images of their colonies in very similar fashions. These memory-images coalesced into a colonial consciousness that connected the metropole to the periphery, which institutionalised the presence of France and Britain respectively in Algeria and India. Therefore the importance of this phenomenon highlights the similarity between both imperial systems demonstrating the formation of an imagined imperial community via trans-national and trans-imperial agents – such as governmental actors, modern urbanisation, markets for images, technical advance, public and private companies, communication and networks of suppliers, learned societies or tourist tours.

After Indian and Algerian independence, those *fixed* and *transmissible* sites of imperial memory remained but their meaning changed. First, many statues of the conquerors were repatriated and replaced with the symbols of fighters for independence and against colonial power. The Place Bugeaud is now the Place Abd-el-Kader. Secondly, the photographic representations of those anti-colonial heroes, such as *Statue équestre de l'Emir Abdelkader, Alger* (unknown, 2011) and *Lakshmibai, The Rani of Jhansi, Jhansi* (unknown, 2011), continue to be transmitted – now through the twenty-first century's defining new medium, the internet.[53]

Notes

1 P. Nora (ed.), *Les Lieux de Mémoire*, 3 vols. (Paris: Gallimard, 1984, edn 1997), vol. I, pp. 17–18.

2 *Ibid.*, pp.15–43.

3 For instance, among the famous albums bought during this period were Félix-Jacques-Antoine Moulin's *L'Algérie photographiée* (1856–57, under Emperor Napoleon III's patronage); J. F. Watson and J. W. Kaye's *The People of India* (1868–75, under Viceroy Lord Canning's patronage); James Fergusson's *History of Indian and Eastern Architecture* (1876); Samuel Bourne and Charles Shepherd's *Royal photographic album of scenes and personages connected with the progress of HRH the Prince of Wales through Bengal, the North West Provinces, the Punjab and Nepal with some descriptive letterpress* (1876), and the album of the *Delhi Durbar* (1903); Etienne and Antonin Neurdein's *Souvenirs d'Alger* (1890–99).

4 R. J. DeRoo, 'Colonial Collecting, French women and Algerian *cartes postales*', in G. D. Sampson and E. M. Hight (eds), *Colonialist Photography, Imag(in)ing Race and Place* (London: Routledge, 2002), p. 159.

5 K. S. Howe, 'Travel Photography', in J. Hannavy (ed.), *Encyclopedia of Nineteenth-Century Photography* (New York: Routledge, 2008), p. 1404.

6 See 'Worlds in a House: the Consumption of Travel Photography in the Victorian Middle-class Home' in P. D. Osborne, *Travelling Light: Photography, Travel and Visual Culture* (Manchester: Manchester University Press, 2000), pp. 52–69; G. Freund, *Photographie et Société* (Paris: Seuil, 1974), pp. 57–70 and 83–106. Also C. Hall and S. O. Rose (ed), *At Home with the Empire: Metropolitan Culture and the Imperial World* (Cambridge: Cambridge University Press, 2006).

7 See J. M. Schwartz, and J. R. Ryan (eds), *Picturing Place, Photography and the Geographical Imagination* (London, New York: I. B. Tauris, 2006, 2003); G. D. Sampson, and E. M. Hight (eds), *Colonialist Photography, Imag(in)ing Race and Place*; D. Crouch, and N. Lübbren (eds), *Visual Culture and Tourism* (Oxford: Berg, 2003); and Annette Kuhn, and Kirsten McAllister (eds), *Locating Memory: Photographic Acts* (Oxford: Berghahn Books, 2006).

8 P. Nora (ed.), *Les Lieux de Mémoire*, vol. I, p. 24.

9 J. M. MacKenzie, *Propaganda and Empire: The Manipulation of British Public Opinion, 1880–1960* (Manchester: Manchester University Press, 1984), chapters 7, 8 and 9; and T. G. August, *The Selling of the Empire: British and French Imperialist Propaganda, 1890–1940* (Westport CT: Greenwood Press, 1985), pp. 71–88 and 107–24.

10 J. M. MacKenzie (ed.), *European Empires and the People: Popular Responses to Imperialism in France, Britain, the Netherlands, Belgium, Germany and Italy* (Manchester: Manchester University Press, 2011), chapters 1 and 2.

11 See for instance J. Gosnell, *The Politics of Frenchness in Colonial Algeria, 1930–1954* (Woodbridge: Boydell & Brewer Ltd, 2002).

12 See J. Pitts, *A Turn to Empire: The Rise of Imperial Liberalism in Britain and France* (Princeton: Princeton University Press, 2008), parts 2 and 3.

13 Ideologies that championed Utilitarian reductionism, the beginning of social Darwinism, Republicanism and the Second Empire as dogmas in France, Conservatism and the modernisation of the monarchy in Britain, altogether used imperial knowledge as a practical frame for colonial policy and control.

14 A. Maxwell, *Colonial Photography and Exhibitions: Representations of the "Native" and the Making of European Identities* (London: Leicester University Press, 2000), p. 2.

15 R. R. Brettell, R. Flukinger, N. Keeler and S. M. Kilgore, *Paper and Light: The Calotype in France and Great Britain, 1839–1870* (Boston: David R. Godine and London: Kudos and Godine, 1984), pp. 35–7 deal with the importance of the Great Exhibition.

16 H. Gernsheim, *The Rise of Photography, 1850–1880: the Age of Collodion*, The History of Photography, vol. II (London: Thames & Hudson, 1988), pp. 19–34.

17 M. Warner Marien, *Photography: A Cultural History* (London: Laurence King Publishing Ltd, 2002), chapter 3, 'The Expanding Domain (1854–1880)'.

18 A. Maxwell, *Colonial Photography and Exhibitions*, p. 1.

19 J. M. MacKenzie, *Orientalism: History, Theory and the Arts* (Manchester: Manchester University Press, 1995), p. 44.

20 This programme started with Sir Henry Hardinge (1785–1856).

21 Public Despatches to Bengal, no.1 of 1847, 27 January 1847, IOR/L/P&J/3/1021 quoted by J. Falconer in *India: Pioneering Photographers 1850–1900* (London: The British Library, 2001), p. 16.

22 N. Oulebsir, *Les Usages du Patrimoine: Monuments, musées et politique coloniale en Algérie (1830–1930)* (Paris: Fondation de la Maison des Sciences de l'Homme, 2004), p. 14; see also chapters 1 and 2.

23 J. Fergusson, *History of Indian and Eastern Architecture* (London: Murray, 1876), preface.

24 Fergusson was a pioneering surveyor and scholar of Indian architecture who provided drawings, sketches and engravings of monuments. He collaborated with several photographers to publish their prints alongside his work. His main concern was to record historical monuments in order to aid the preservation and restoration of some perishing structures. See T. Guha-Thakurta's 'The Compulsions of Visual Representation in Colonial India', which is dedicated to Fergusson's work, in M. A. Pelizzari (ed.), *Traces of India: Photography, Architecture, and the Politics of*

Representation, 1850–1900 (Montréal, New Haven: Canadian Centre for Architecture, Yale Center for British Art, 2003), pp. 108–39.

25 Hunting was more than just a pastime; Ryan notes that 'the colonial hunter was one of the most striking figures of the Victorian and Edwardian imperial landscape.' [James R. Ryan, *Picturing Empire, Photography and the Visualization of the British Empire* (London: Reaktion, 1997), p. 99.] Killing a wild animal was considered as a sport and a scientific quest, but above all demonstrated the dominance of the British 'conquerors'. The master-photographers in this domain were Colonel W. W. Hooper and V. S. G. Western. From the 1850s to the 1880s, they photographed the jungle and its dangerous game with the artistic conventions of the time. This was captured photographically in the series *Tiger Shooting* (1870) – notably, the picture *Bagged*. In Algeria, the pictures were less concerned with hunting and more about eroticising local women. The brothers Etienne and Antonin Neurdein's *Femme mauresque* (Algiers, 1890s) epitomised the masculine colonial gaze of the photographer.

26 See J. M. Schwartz, and J. R. Ryan (eds), *Picturing Place, Photography and the Geographical Imagination*; C. E. Barton (ed.), *Sites of Memory: Perspectives on Architecture and Race* (New York: Princeton Architectural Press, 2001); T. R. Metcalf, *Forging the Raj: Essays on British India in the Heyday of Empire* (New Delhi: Oxford University Press, 2005); Part II: Architecture; and Z. Çelik, *Empire, Architecture, and the City: French-Ottoman Encounters, 1830–1914* (Seattle: University of Washington Press, 2008).

27 See information alongside Photo 181/(2) [British Library].

28 See information alongside FR ANOM 8Fi427/19 [Archives nationales d'outre-mer].

29 In connection to this argument, see M. C. Boyer, 'La Mission Héliographique: Architectural Photography, Collective Memory and the Patrimony of France, 1851', in J. M. Schwartz, and J. R. Ryan (eds), *Picturing Place, Photography and the Geographical Imagination* (London and New York: IB Tauris), pp. 21–54.

30 M. Foucault, *Discipline and Punish, the Birth of the Prison* (New York: Pantheon, 1975, 1977), p. 200. See also chapter 4 'Power/knowledge' in S. Mills, *Michel Foucault* (New York: Routledge, 2005, 2003).

31 P. D. Osborne, *Travelling Light*, pp. 39–40.

32 MacMahon first gained celebrity through his campaigns in Algeria (1830–54), then through the Crimean War and the Second Italian War of Independence. He served as Governor General of Algeria (1864–70), then went back to France to command an army unit during the Franco-Prussian War. He became Chief of State of France (1873–75) and the first President of the Third Republic (1875–79).

33 X. Guégan, *The Imperial Aesthetic: Photography, Samuel Bourne and the Indian Peoples in the post-Mutiny Era* (Aldershot: Ashgate, 2014), pp. 37–40.

34 For a general analysis of this kind of event see E. Hobsbawm and T. Ranger (eds), *The Invention of Tradition* (Cambridge: Cambridge University Press, 1983, 16th edition 2008), particularly chapters 5 and 7.

35 Since the nineteenth century, two new sites of memory have been created. In 1962 the statue was brought back to France and in 1967 erected in Excideuil. In 1999 Arnaud Le Guay (in charge of culture of the city of Périgueux) created 'l'année Bugeaud', a commemoration year around the nineteenth-century 'agricultural' man.

36 W. C. Bentinck was Governor General from 1828 to 1835.

37 N. Oulebsir, *Les Usages du Patrimoine*, p. 11.

38 *Ibid.*, p. 10.

39 Governor General of India between 1844 and 1848.

40 In 1969 it was renamed 'Shaheed Minar' (meaning 'martyrs monument') to the memory of the Indian Freedom Movement. 'Heritage Tour: Shaheed Minar' at www.bharatonline.com (accessed 22 January 2013).

41 Munroe (1779–1827) was Major-General and Governor of Madras from 1820 to 1827.

42 J. Hargrove, 'Les Statues de Paris', in P. Nora (ed.), *Les Lieux de Mémoire*, vol. II, pp. 1855–86.

43 Peel (1824–1858) was a Royal Navy officer who gained fame through his military exploits and received the Victoria Cross (the highest and most prestigious award

for gallantry in the face of the enemy that can be awarded to British forces), was made a Knight Commander of the Order of the Bath, and then became Sir William Peel. His two most famous campaigns were during the Crimean War – 1853–56 and the Sepoys Rebellion – 1857–58 (Indian Mutiny), where he died at Cawnpore of smallpox.

44 Lelièvre (unknown, 1851) went to Algeria in 1832 and was part of the conquest. Several visual representations (mainly paintings) of him during the Battle of Mazagran (1840) were made during that period. Because of his involvement in this battle, he was promoted to Captain in 1840 and received the Légion d'honneur.

45 Henry Havelock (1795–1857) was a Major-General, mainly remembered for his recapture of Cawnpore from the rebels during the Sepoy Rebellion where he died. Many representations of him during his last battle were popularised via plays, novels and paintings throughout the nineteenth century.

46 Jean Pierre Hippolyte Blandan (1819–42). Involved in the conquest of Algeria from 1837 at the young age of 17, he was promoted to Corporal in 1839 and Sergeant in 1842. He resisted a surprise attack, fought and won, but then died of his wounds at the age of 23. Because of his heroism and young age he was given a posthumous Légion d'honneur. The statue at Boufarik was repatriated to Nancy after Algerian Independence.

47 J. R. Ryan, *Picturing Empire*, p. 76.

48 Both la Bibliothèque nationale de France and les Archives nationales d'outre-mer have a large collection of all these artistic, literary and medals productions. It is interesting to see, however, that although this battle was highly related in the nineteenth century, it is nowadays nearly absent from most of the books dealing with French Algeria.

49 X. Guégan, *The Imperial Aesthetic*, pp. 172–3. See also G. D. Sampson and E. M. Hight (eds), *Colonialist Photography, Imag(in)ing Race and Place*.

50 The Battle of Sidi-Brahim (1845) was unplanned and poorly commanded by Lieutenant-Colonel de Montagnac, and within a few days the French were circled by Abd-el-Kader. Many French soldiers – including de Montagnac – died rather than surrender. The monument was built on the main square of Oran and inaugurated in 1898. After the Algerian Independence it was repatriated to Périssac.

51 B. Anderson, *Imagined Communities: Reflections on the Origins and Spread of Nationalism* (London: Verso, 1991), p. 4.

52 See Gramsci's use of the terms 'unified national language' and 'cultural hegemony' in his prison writings (1929–35), in D. Forgacs (ed.), *The Antonio Gramsci Reader: Selected Writings 1916–1935* (London: Lawrence and Wishart Ltd, 1999), pp. 356–7.

53 Those statues have become the emblems of a reconquered national history in post-colonial Algeria and India, and are still subject to polemics – for instance, see R. Ouahdi, 'Polémique autour de la statue «algéroise» de l'Emir Abdelkader', *Algérie Patriotique*, 17 August 2012, www.algeriepatriotique.com/article/polemique-autour-de-la-statue-algeroise-de-l-emir-abdelkader (accessed 10 April 2013). The Cyber-photographs are usually used within the frame of patriotic events or for the benefits of tourism – see for instance, 'Photos de la Place Emir Abdelkader à Alger' at www.alger-city.com/photos/photos-place-emir-abdelkader-alger.html (accessed 10 April 2013) and 'City of Brave Woman Rani Laxmi Bai – Jhansi' at http://members.virtualtourist.com/m/57987/10bb7a/ (accessed 10 April 2013). For a further assessment on the recent sites of memory and images of Abd-el-kader, see François Pouillon, 'Images d'Abd el-Kader: Pièces pour un Bicentenaire', in *La Fabrique de la Mémoire: Variations Maghrébines*, special volume of *L'Année du Maghreb* IV (2008), pp. 27–44.

CHAPTER THREE

Politics, caste and the remembrance of the Raj: the Obelisk at Koregaon

Shraddha Kumbhojkar

The commemorative history of the Obelisk at Koregaon is nothing if not surprising. A memorial commemorating a bloody encounter within an imperial war, this monument provides a case study which illustrates that contestations of memories often bear the imprint of contestations for hegemony that are played out in the present. The Obelisk at Koregaon in western India, built as a demonstration of empire build-ers' belief in their own power and military prowess, serves a similar function today, but for a different group of people: the former Untouchables who had collaborated with the colonisers against what they perceived as a tyrannical indigenous regime. The recently emerged tradition of an annual pilgrimage to the memorial[1] should be seen as an effort to create and popularise an alternative culture of the former Untouchables (*dalit*), now known as Neo-Buddhists. While Indian society grapples with the problem of accepting the equality of its various castes, one can witness different pathologies of memory sur-rounding the monument. Today, both amnesia and pseudomnesia are associated with the Koregaon Memorial, defying the locus of a person in the discourse on social justice in present-day India. The memorial had faded into oblivion from British public memory long before the end of the imperial rule. However, it has undergone a metamorphic rebirth of commemoration and now signifies something quite different from what was originally intended.

The battle of Koregaon and its memorial

The political ascendancy of the British East India Company in eastern and northern parts of India dates back to the battle of Plassey in 1757. From then on the Company gradually began extending its political hold to the other parts of India. During the same period, from their base in Pune in Western India, the Peshwa rulers (1707–1818) were also extending their political influence. Clashes between the Peshwas and the Company seemed inevitable. On 1 January 1818, a battalion of about 900 Company soldiers, led from Seroor to Pune by F. F. Staunton, was suddenly faced with a 20,000 strong army commanded by the Peshwa himself. The encounter took place at the village of Koregaon on the banks of the river Bheema.[2] In the words of Grant Duff, a contemporary official and historian, 'Captain Staunton was destitute of provisions, and this detachment, already fatigued from want of rest and a long night march, now, under a burning sun, without food or water, began a struggle as trying as ever was maintained by the British in India'.[3] The battle was not decisively won by either side, but in spite of heavy casualties, Staunton's outnumbered troops managed to recover their guns and carry their wounded officers and men back to Seroor.

As it was one of the last battles of the Anglo Maratha wars, which ended with a complete victory of the Company, the encounter quickly came to be remembered as a triumph. The East India Company wasted no time in showering recognition on its soldiers. While Staunton was promoted to the honorary post of *aide de camp* by the Governor General,[4] the battle received special mention in parliamentary debates in 1819.[5] A memorial was commissioned and a year later, Lieutenant Colonel Delamin, who was passing by the village, could already witness the construction of a 60-foot commemorative Obelisk (Figure 3.1).[6]

The Koregaon Memorial still stands intact today. It is supposed to commemorate the British and Indian soldiers who 'defended the village with so much success'[7] when the British East India Company confronted the Peshwa army in a 'desperate engagement'.[8] Marble plaques adorn the four sides of the Obelisk. The two plaques in English are mirrored by translations into the local Marathi language. The Memorial Plaque declares that the Obelisk is meant to mark the defence of Koregaon wherein Captain Staunton and his corps 'accomplished one of the proudest triumphs of the British army in the East'.[9] Soon after, the word 'Corregaum' and the Obelisk were chosen to adorn the official insignia of the regiment.[10] In the course of the parliamentary debates in March 1819, the achievements of the troops were described as follows: 'In the end, they not only secured an unmolested retreat, but they carried off their wounded!' In his 1844 study 'Our Indian Empire', Charles MacFarlane quoted from an official report to the Governor calling the engagement 'one of the most brilliant affairs ever achieved by any army in which the European and Native soldiers displayed the most noble devotion and the most romantic bravery'. MacFarlane praised the plucky Company force for displaying 'the most noble devotion and most romantic bravery under the pressure

3.1 The memorial Obelisk at Koregaon Bheema, erected in 1818
(author's photograph)

of thirst and hunger almost beyond human endurance'.[11] Twenty years
later, Henry Morris confidently added: 'Captain Staunton returned to
Seroor, which he entered with colours flying and drums beating, after
one of the most gallant actions ever fought by the English in India'.[12]
Later chroniclers of colonial rule continued to shower praise on the
soldiers and in 1885 even the *Grey River Argus*, a newspaper published
in far off New Zealand, described the battle in glowing terms.[13] After
the turn of the century, though, the lustre of the skirmish began to
fade and gradually the event slipped from Britain's public memory.[14]
The battle is now only mentioned in specialised literature on military
history as an example not of British martial capabilities, but of that
of the Sepoys (see Figure 3.2).[15]

Memories: 'ours' and 'theirs'

Today the memorial is just off a busy highway toll booth – a common
site in the post-globalisation Indian landscape. Every New Year's Day,
the urban middle classes who need to use the highway remind each

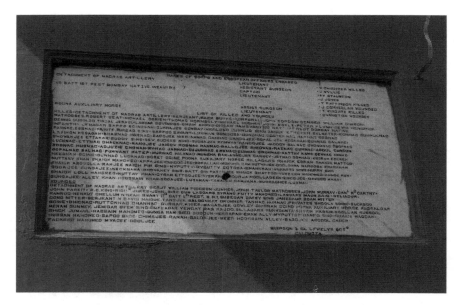

3.2 Plaque listing English and native casualties in the battle of Koregaon

other to avoid the particular stretch that passes by the memorial. Their reason for doing so is that '*those* people would be swarming *their* site at Koregaon'. Indeed, the memorial has become a site of pilgrimage attracting thousands of people who gather there every year on 1 January. If the pilgrims are asked what brings them together, there is a clear answer. 'We are here to remember that our *Mahar* forefathers fought bravely and brought down the unjust Peshwa rule. Dr Ambedkar[16] has started this pilgrimage. He asked us to fight injustice. We have come to take inspiration from the brave soldiers and Dr Ambedkar's memories'.[17]

Initially, one might be baffled by this admiration for the native soldiers who fought on the British side and lost their lives in a fight against their own countrymen. A careful scrutiny of the list of casualties inscribed on the memorial reveals, however, that twenty-two names from among the native casualties listed end with the suffix '-nac': Essnac, Rynac, Gunnac. The suffix '-nac' was used exclusively by the Untouchables of the *Mahar* caste who served as soldiers.[18] This observation becomes particularly relevant when considered within the context of the caste profile of the Peshwas, who were orthodox and high caste Brahmin rulers. The story of Koregaon is thus not just about a straightforward struggle between a colonial and a native power. There is another important but largely ignored dimension to it: caste.

The Peshwas, Brahmin rulers of western India, were infamous for their high caste orthodoxy and their persecution of the Untouchables. Numerous sources document in great detail that under the Peshwa rulers the 'untouchable' people who were born in certain so-called low castes were given harsher punishments than would be meted out to high caste people for the same crimes.[19] They were forbidden to move in public spaces in the mornings and evenings lest their long shadows defile high caste people on the streets. Besides physical mobility, occupational and social mobility were also denied to these people who formed a major part of the population. Human sacrifices of 'untouchable' people were not uncommon under these eighteenth century rulers who had framed elaborate rules and mechanisms to ensure that the Untouchables stayed just as their name suggests – untouchable. In 1855, Mukta Salave, a 15 year old girl from the untouchable Mang caste who attended the first native school for girls in Pune, wrote an animated piece about the atrocities faced by her caste:

> Let that religion, where only one person is privileged and the rest are deprived, perish from the earth and let it never enter our minds to be proud of such a religion. These people drove us, the poor mangs and mahars, away from our own lands, which they occupied to build large mansions. And that was not all. They regularly used to make the mangs and mahars drink oil mixed with red lead and then buried them in the foundations of their mansions, thus wiping out generation after generation of these poor people. Under Bajirao's rule, if any mang or mahar happened to pass in front of the gymnasium, they cut off his head and used it to play 'bat ball', with their swords as bats and his head as a ball, on the grounds.[20]

Peshwa atrocities against the low caste people have remained ingrained in public memory to this day.[21]

When the East India Company began recruiting soldiers for the Bombay Army, the Untouchables seized the opportunity and enlisted. Military service was perceived as a means to open the doors of economic as well as social emancipation. Political freedom and nationalism had little meaning for a population who had to choose between a life where the best meal on offer was a dead buffalo in the village and a life where their human dignity was respected – not to mention a decent monthly payment in cash.[22]

While the untouchable soldiers fought on the British side against their own countrymen, the valour they showed is not at all perceived as a shameful memory today. In fact, Koregaon has become an iconic site for the former Untouchables as it serves as a reminder of the bravery and strength shown by their ancestors – the very virtues that the caste system claimed they lacked. The memories related to the

Koregaon Memorial help to explain how a memorial of colonial victory built in the early nineteenth century has been adapted to serve as a site that gives inspiration to the formerly untouchable people of India.

Mahars and the military

Throughout much of the nineteenth century the battle of Koregaon and the memorial were warmly remembered amongst military, imperial and political circles in Britain. At the beginning of the twentieth century, though, British rule was firmly established all over India, and the Koregaon Memorial faded from mainstream commemorative practices. Neither Britain at the height of its colonial glory, nor India, which was beginning to receive small doses of independence, had occasion to commemorate the violent struggle of the days of the Honourable Company.[23] Other lines of tradition were broken, too. The Mahar regiment had continued to demonstrate its bravery and loyalty in the battles of Kathiawad (1826) and Multan (1846). But then, in spite of the low castes' long-standing military alliance with the British, some Sepoys from the Mahar Regiment, which formed a part of the Bombay Army, joined the 'Indian Mutiny' in 1857. This added to a certain reluctance the British had always shown with regard to the enlistment of Mahars.[24] Subsequently, they were declared to be a non-martial race and their recruitment was stopped in May 1892.[25]

When their recruitment was discontinued, the Mahars soon began to feel the pinch. Gopal Baba Valangkar, a retired army-man, founded a 'Society for Removing the Problems of Non-Aryans'.[26] In 1894 the members of this society sent a petition to the Governor of Bombay to remind him that the Mahars had fought for the British to acquire their present dominion over India and requested a reconsideration of the decision to exclude Mahars from the martial races, which deprived them of entry into the military service. The petition was rejected in 1896.[27]

Another leader of the Untouchables, Shivram Janba Kamble, made an even more sustained effort to achieve their emancipation. He had been involved in the work of the 'Depressed Classes Mission', which ran schools for untouchable children. In October 1910, R. A. Lamb of the Bombay Governor's Executive Council was invited as the chief guest for a prize-giving ceremony in one of these schools.[28] In his speech, Lamb mentioned his annual visits to the Koregaon Memorial. He drew attention to the 'many names of Mahars who fell wounded or dead fighting bravely side by side with Europeans and with Indians who were not outcastes' and regretted that 'one avenue to honourable work had been closed to these people'. It is not known whether it was Lamb's speech that put the Koregaon Memorial back into the limelight or whether it had remained in living memory. His words certainly lent weight to the argument that it was the Mahars who fought for the British and made them 'masters of Poona'.[29]

Within the first two decades of the twentieth century, Kamble organised a number of meetings of the Mahar people at the memorial site. In 1910, he arranged a grand Conference of the Deccan Mahars drawn from fifty-one villages in western India. The Conference sent an appeal to the Secretary of State demanding their 'inalienable rights as British subjects from the British Government'.[30] They made a strong case for letting Mahars re-enter the army and argued that the Mahars were 'not essentially inferior to any of our Indian fellow-subjects'.[31] Up until 1916 this request kept being repeated by various gatherings of Untouchables in western India. As the First World War gathered momentum, the Bombay government eventually issued orders in 1917 providing for the formation of two platoons of Mahars.[32]

The coming of Ambedkar

The happiness of the Mahars was, however, short-lived. Recruitment was stopped as soon as the war ended. This led to a renewed campaign for recognising the valour of the Untouchables. By then, the demand had long since assumed the level of a movement for the general emancipation of the Untouchables. Within this campaign the Koregaon Memorial had become a focal point. Various meetings were held at the Obelisk during which Kamble and other leaders invariably reminded the Untouchables of the valour and prowess exhibited by their forefathers. On the anniversary of the Koregaon battle on 1 January 1927, Kamble invited Dr Bhimrao Ramji Ambedkar to address the gathering of Untouchables.[33] Ambedkar was not merely another leader of the Untouchables. He was by now, as far as Indian politics was concerned, a force to be reckoned with.

Ambedkar was born in 1891, the son of a retired army *subhedar* from the Mahar caste. In spite of his first-hand experience of caste-based discrimination, he attained a doctorate from Columbia University, a D.Sc. from the London School of Economics and was called to the Bar at Gray's Inn by the age of 32. In 1926, he became a member of the Bombay Legislative Assembly. Ambedkar could not fail to appreciate the significance of the memorial for advancing the cause of the emancipation of the Untouchables. Not only did he make an inspiring speech at the gathering, he also supported the idea of reviving the memory of the valour of the forefathers through an annual pilgrimage to the site on the anniversary of the battle. As a representative of the Untouchables, he was invited by the British to the Round Table Conference in 1931 where the future of the Indian nation was to be decided. Based on his arguments at the conference, he wrote a small treatise called *The Untouchables and the Pax Britannica* in which he referred to the Koregaon battle to support his argument that the Untouchables had been instrumental in the establishment and con-solidation of British power in India.[34]

Indian mainstream politics from the 1920s until 1947 is recognised as the Gandhian era. Gandhi, having been born in the middle order caste of traders, had a different outlook on the systemic exploitation of the Untouchables on the basis of caste. He called the Untouchables *Harijans*, meaning people of God. Ambedkar and his followers resented both this name and what they perceived as the patronising attitude behind it. Underlying this surface issue, there were major ideological differences between Ambedkar and Gandhi. For the India represented by Gandhi and the Indian National Congress, the primary contradic-tion was that between colonial supremacy and Indians' aspirations for political freedom. For Ambedkar and the Untouchable masses he rep-resented, the oppression was not primarily located in the political system but arose from the socio-economic sphere. There was a clash of interests. The Indian National Congress under Gandhi sought to represent all Indians in a unified front against the colonial rule. Although Ambedkar was, unlike some 'sections of Dalits and non-Brahmans who believed that colonial rule had been an unambiguous liberating force',[35] by no means a staunch supporter of British rule, he had quite a different new India in mind. While Gandhi saw the ideal social order arising from a reformed Hinduism, Ambedkar sought 'political representation independent of the Hindu community'.[36] In 1930, Gandhi embarked upon the Civil Disobedience Movement against the systems and institutions of the colonial rule. Kamble and a few other representatives of the depressed classes retaliated by launching what they called the 'Indian National Anti-Revolutionary Party'. Its manifesto was quoted in *The Bombay Chronicle*.[37]

> In view of the fact that Mr Gandhi, Dictator of the Indian National Congress has declared a civil disobedience movement before doing his utmost to secure temple entry for the 'depressed' classes and the com-plete removal of 'untouchability', it has been decided to organise the Indian National Anti-Revolutionary Party in order to persuade Gandhiji and his followers to postpone their civil disobedience agitation and to join whole-heartedly the Anti-Untouchability movement as it is ... the root cause of India's downfall ... The Party will regard <u>British rule as absolutely necessary</u> until the complete removal of untouchability

[46]

Though this party did not attract much support in mainstream politics, it demonstrates that for the Untouchables, social and economic well-being was of greater and more immediate concern than political freedom, and hence colonial rule was regarded as a possibly necessary evil for the time being. It also shows that there were other and often contradictory voices in the independence movement of India. These have often been glossed over in nationalist rhetoric.

A new memory

India won her independence in 1947, and Ambedkar chaired the committee tasked with the drafting of the new constitution. The 'annihilation of caste',[38] however, remained a distant dream. The parliament did not accept the Hindu Code Bill proposed by Ambedkar in order to bring about extensive reforms in the Hindu socio-cultural scene. In 1951 a disillusioned Ambedkar resigned from the Cabinet. Five years later, under his leadership, millions of Untouchables converted *en masse* to Buddhism in a step towards attaining total freedom from exploitation. The same year, after Ambedkar's death, a political party, called the Republican Party of India, was formed to represent the interests of the low caste people.

The conversion opened the floodgates for cultural conflicts with the high castes. The immediate reaction of the Hindu right was one of denial. The strategy of cultural appropriation that has worked so well for Hinduism from the times of the Buddha is employed even today to project the Buddhists as just another sect within Hinduism.[39] For the neo-Buddhists, this necessitated the creation of new and different cultural practices. Among the neo-Buddhists in western India one of the invented cultural practices that emerged as a result is the pilgrimage to the Koregaon Memorial. Thousands of neo-Buddhists throng to the memorial every New Year's Day to commemorate the valour of the Mahars who helped to overthrow the high caste rule of the Peshwa. They also commemorate the visit to the site by their leader, Dr Ambedkar on 1 January 1927.

Unlike any Hindu pilgrimage site, the Koregaon Memorial is devoid of the tell-tale signs of a holy marketplace. No sellers of garlands and sweets and images of Gods are to be found here. It is a deserted place all through the year. However, come New Year, the place is dotted with little stalls selling books, cassettes and compact disks. Various publishers of Ambedkarite literature set up their stalls of books. Neo-Buddhist songs are played loudly in the stalls, extolling the greatness of Ambedkar and emphasising the need to change the world.[40] Leaders of the now numerous factions of the Republican Party of India address their followers. Neo-Buddhist families visit the memorial Obelisk. They offer flowers or light candles. An important part of the ritual is to offer a *Vandana*, a recital of verses from Buddhist texts.

An equally important element of their ritualised behaviour is the buying of books. Interviews with various booksellers have shown a surprising fact: whenever there is a gathering or a pilgrimage of the neo-Buddhists, the bookstalls do roaring business. The average length of books sold at these stalls is short – volumes of 30 to 70 pages priced between 10 to 50 rupees. It might be an indication of the fact that the readers may be neo-literate, have very little time to spend on reading and can only afford cheaper books. Many publishers of related literature have indicated that their daily sales figures at the Koregaon pilgrimage and other such important pilgrimages (e.g. Mumbai and Nagpur) often exceed their sales figures for the rest of the year.[41] It could be perceived as an indication of the belief in the emancipatory potential of education among the neo-Buddhists, especially of the former *Mahar* caste. Some of the bestselling titles include Marathi translations of books authored by Ambedkar himself, e.g. *Buddha and His Dhamma, Annihilation of Caste, Who Were the Shudras?* Other popular books include Dalit autobiographies. They also sell Dalit poetry and small biographies of Dalit leaders.

These books offer a Dalit perspective on Indian history wherein colonial rule is portrayed as instrumental for emancipation, even though it remained ignorant of the realities of caste exploitation. Jotirao Phule and Ambedkar are among the prominent Dalit writers who propounded this view of the colonial rule in which Gandhi and the movement for India's independence do not figure very positively.[42] The fact that Ambedkar chaired the Committee that created the Indian Constitution in 1950, however, is considered supremely important. Any attempt to criticise or seek a change in the Indian Constitution, therefore, provokes fierce opposition from the Dalit population. The anti-corruption movement led by Anna Hazare and his team in 2011 is a recent example. The extra-constitutional structure to create a powerful ombudsman (Lokpal) for resolving the issues of corruption was not welcomed by Dalit leaders and public.

The importance of forgetting

Although the Koregaon Memorial was constructed by the colonial rulers, it does not feature on the commemorative landscape of today's British public. This amnesia might be attributed to the fact that the colonial memories, especially of violent battles are no longer the object of pride in present-day Britain. This amnesia is matched by the high

THE OBELISK AT KOREGAON

castes in India. Poona, the capital of the Peshwas, has become a software and education city called Pune. When a sample of 130 members of the high caste, newly rich people (who have come to be nicknamed as Computer Coolies) were asked about the Koregaon Memorial, none of them knew what it was.[43]

Elite amnesia is not total, though. There are also what may be called conflicting memories. During the 1970s the western Indian state of Maharashtra witnessed a spate of popular (a)historical novels topping the bestseller lists in Marathi. Many of them dominate the historical understanding and perceptions of the Marathi-speaking middle classes even today. Two important novels from this genre, both authored by Brahmins, describe the battle of Koregaon in passing. *Mantravegla* by N. S. Inamdar is based on the life of the Last Peshwa. It claims that the battle was, in fact, won by the Peshwas.[44] Recently, this trend of creating alternative memories about the Peshwa battles has become even stronger. The battle of Panipat, which saw a complete defeat of the Peshwa armies in 1761, is commemorated today through high-sounding rallies.[45] The kind of rhetoric used during these rallies suggests that it was the Peshwa who won the battle.

The Koregaon Memorial occupies a very significant place in today's neo-Buddhist culture. The internet and other electronic media are used to document and commemorate the Koregaon battle and Ambedkar's visit to it. An image search for Koregaon Pillar yields hundreds of digital pictures of the Memorial Obelisk. Film clips are available on YouTube.[46] At least a dozen blogs in English and Marathi have entries related to the Koregaon Memorial. They describe the battle and the role of the Mahar soldiers and also remind the readers about what the Untouchables could achieve if they show the resolve.

Conclusions

The Obelisk of Koregaon Bheema is thus a site which has generated conflicting memories. These memories represent the divergent interests of the groups involved in their creation. Those wishing to commemorate the greatness of the Peshwa rule – the symbol of high caste supremacy – either choose to ignore the Koregaon battle, or create a pseudomnesia of Peshwa victory. While the Obelisk marks an imperial site of memory that is largely forgotten in the homeland of the empire, the monument has undergone a metamorphosis of commemoration in western India. It no longer reminds the public of imperial power, but for the former Untouchables whose forefathers fought at Koregaon it serves the purpose of providing 'historical evidence' of the ability of the Untouchables to overthrow the high caste oppression. Considering the fact that Indian society is still dominated by the system of caste hierarchy,[47] the Koregaon Memorial is also a reminder that present-day contestation for hegemony is often manifested in contesting memories.

Notes

1 J. Beltz, *Mahar, Buddhist and Dalit: Religious Conversion and Socio-Political Emancipation* (New Delhi: Manohar Publishers, 2005), pp. 173–4.
2 Variously spelt as Corigaum, Corregaum, Korygaom or Corygawm in contemporary English records. T. C. Hansard, *The Parliamentary Debates from the year 1803 to the present time*, vol. 39, p. 887 (House of Commons, 4 March 1819); Carnaticus, *Summary of the Mahratta and Pindarree campaign during 1817, 1818, and 1819 under direction of the Marquis of Hastings: chiefly embracing the operations of the army of the Deckan, under the command of His Excellency Lieut.-Gen. Sir T. Hislop, Bart. G.C.B.: With some particulars and remarks* (London: Williams, 1820), pp. 70, 75–6.
3 J. G. Duff, *A History of the Mahrattas*, vol. 3, (London: Longman, Rees, Orme, Brown and Green, 1826), p. 434.
4 C. MacFarlane, *Our Indian Empire: its History and Present State, from the Earliest Settlement of the British in Hindostan to the Close of the Year 1843*, vol. 2, (London: C. Knight & Co., 1844), p. 233.
5 Hansard, *The Parliamentary Debates* (n. 2, above).
6 Lieut. Col. Delamin, *Asiatic Journal and Monthly Miscellany* 5 (1831), p. 135.
7 *Ibid.*
8 G. N. Wright, *A New and Comprehensive Gazetteer of the Bombay Presidency*, vol. 2, (London: T. Kelly, 1835).
9 Inscription on the Memorial Obelisk, Koregaon Bheema 1822.
10 The second Battalion of the first Regiment of the Bombay Native Light Infantry that eventually came to be known as the Mahar Regiment.
11 C. MacFarlane, *Our Indian Empire*, p. 233.
12 H. Morris, *The History of India* (Madras: Madras School Book Society, fifth edn 1864), p. 207.
13 *Grey River Argus*, XXXI: 5202 (28 May 1885), p. 2.
14 The battle is usually not mentioned in the literature concerning British India. For example, see: J. Lawrence, *Raj: The Making and Unmaking of British India* (London: Little, Brown, 1997).
15 R. Holmes, *Sahib: The British Soldier in India 1750–1914* (London: HarperCollins, 2005), pp. 297–8.
16 Dr Bheemrao Ramji Ambedkar (1891–1956) is considered the greatest leader of modern India, who strove for emancipation and equality for all castes, especially the Untouchables, in India.
17 Interview with Mr Shankar Munoli (age 36, school teacher), who accompanied a group of sixty teenage schoolchildren to the memorial (1 January 2010).
18 D. L. Ramteke, *Revival of Buddhism in Modern India* (New Delhi: Deep & Deep Publications, 1983), p. 81.
19 H. G. Frank, *Panchyats Under the Peshwas: An original and detailed review of a very ancient system of local self-government, based entirely on discoveries made during research in the Poona Residency Daftar with the especial permission of the Govt. of Bombay* (Poona: Poona Star Press, 1900), p. 40.
20 Salave Mukta (transl. Maya Pandit) in S. Tharu and K. Lalita (eds), *Women Writing In India: 600 B.C. to the Present* (New York: The Feminist Press, 1991), p. 214.
21 For example, see G. P. Deshpande, *Selected Writings of Jotirao Phule* (New Delhi: Leftword Books, 2002); B. R. Ambedkar, *Annihilation of Caste* at http://ccnmtl.columbia.edu/projects/mmt/ambedkar/web/index.html (accessed 10 October 2011); R. O'Hanlon, *Caste, Conflict and Ideology* (Cambridge: Cambridge University Press,

2002); Vijay Tendulkar's 'Ghashiram Kotwal' is a popular and controversial play that has run on and off since 1972 and depicts the caste-based exploitation, downfall of the Peshwas and the ensuing power-struggle.

22 A number of autobiographies in Marathi language by Untouchable men describe the occasional 'feast' of dead buffalo meat. For example, see *Taraal Antaraal* by Kharat Shankarrao and *Baluta* by Daya Pawar. Also, see D. Arjun (ed.), *Poisoned Bread* (Mumbai: Sangam Books, 1992).

23 Various reforms and acts, especially Lord Ripon's resolution on local self-government in 1882 eventually led to self-government in a very limited sense. For details, see T. Hugh, *Foundations of Local Self-Government in India, Pakistan and Burma* (New York: Praeger, 1968), p. XII.

24 S. P. Cohen, 'The Untouchable Soldier: Caste, Politics, and the Indian Army', *Journal of Asian Studies* 28 (1969), pp. 453–68, 456; E. Zelliot, *From Untouchable to Dalit: Essays on the Ambedkar Movement* (New Delhi: Manohar, 1992), p. 58.

25 R. K. Kshirsagar, *Dalit Movement in India and its Leaders, 1857–1956* (New Delhi: M. D. Publications, 1994), pp. 137–8.

26 The original Marathi name is *Anarya Dosha Pariharak Mandali*.

27 The original English petition and the government resolution to make no change in the recruitment policy are quoted in C. B. Khairmode, *Dr. Bheemrao Ramji Ambedkar*, vol. VIII, (Pune: Sugawa Prakashan, 2010, first published 1987), pp. 228–50.

28 R. A. Lamb was an officer who had a long association with the Western Indian society. He had served as the collector of Ahmednagar and the chairman of the plague commission during the dreaded epidemic in Poona in 1897.

29 Text of the petition to the Secretary of State quoted in H. N. Navalkar, *The Life of Shivram Janba Kamble* (Pune, 1997, first published SJ Kamble, 1930), p. 149.

30 *Ibid.*, p. 154.

31 *Ibid.*, p. 153.

32 C. B. Khairmode, *Dr. Bheemrao Ramji Ambedkar*, p. 251.

33 A. Rao, *The Caste Question: Dalits and the Politics of Modern India* (Berkeley: University of California Press, 2009), p. 346.

34 B. R. Ambedkar, *The Untouchables and Pax Britannica*, www.ambedkar.org (accessed 19 August 2011).

35 G. Omvedt, *Dalits and the Democratic Revolution: Dr. Ambedkar and the Dalit Movement in Colonial India* (New Delhi: Sage, 1994), p. 82. *Dalit* is the widely used nomenclature for all the so-called low and Untouchable castes in India today, originating from the nineteenth century. It translates as suppressed or crushed. O. Mendelsohn and M. Vicziany, *The Untouchables: Subordination, Poverty, and the State in Modern India* (Cambridge: Cambridge University Press, 1998), p. 4.

36 J. Beltz, *Mahar, Buddhist and Dalit*, p. 49.

37 *The Bombay Chronicle* (2 April 1930). (Emphasis mine).

38 This is a title of a book by Ambedkar published in 1936.

39 For example, see the rightwing Hindu organisation RSS, which quotes from S. Radhakrishnan's *Indian Philosophy* on its webpage – 'Buddhism is an offshoot of Hinduism' at www.sanghparivar.org (accessed 1 March 2012).

40 A popular song by an Ambedkariate poet Annabhau Sathe goes 'Bheemrao (Ambedkar) has passed on the message to me. Strike the anvil and change the World'.

41 Interviews with publishers of Ambedkarite literature Mr Vilas Wagh and Dr Narayan Bhosle conducted in January 2010.

42 G. Omvedt, *Dalits and the Democratic Revolution*, pp. 169–77.

43 Spot interviews of approximately 120 people from software industry conducted in Pune, May–June 2011.

44 N. S. Inamdar, *Mantravegla* (Pune: Continental Prakashan, 1969), pp. 17, 461.

45 For example see this text message received by the researcher on 1 December 2011: '3rd January to 28 January 2012, a March towards Panipat on two-wheelers! 8 states, 76 districts, many forts, ancient temples and caves and holy places included. 7000 Kms of travel on bikes. The March begins from the historical palace of

Shrimant Sirdar Satyendraraje Dabhade Sirkar. Come one, Come all! Bring your friends along and join the Maratha forces. Yours Obediently, Prof. Pramod Borhade'.

46 For example, see www.youtube.com/watch?v=gSKRQ--1Pc4 (accessed 1 March 2012).
47 K. Shraddha and I. Devendra, 'Wither homo-hierarchus?' (unpublished paper presented at the Spalding Symposium on Indian Religions, University of Oxford, March 2008). One of the findings was that caste is the deciding factor when making choices of marriage and the location of housing, but not so much in the choice of friends and employers.

CHAPTER FOUR

The thirteen martyrs of Arad:
a monumental Hungarian history

James Koranyi

The monument which once dominated the central square of the town of Arad honoured the memory of thirteen *Honvéd* rebel generals, who had been executed there on the orders of the Austrian imperial government on 6 October 1849 following the failed Hungarian revolution of 1848–49.[1] The officers had been part of the *Honvédseg*, the Hungarian Army, which had struggled for the nation's independence – or freedom as they had called it – after March 1848. As part of the 'springtime of the peoples', Hungarian radicals and liberals strove for greater autonomy from Vienna, both political and cultural. At the beginning, the revolution registered some successes. Yet following a number of reversals at the hands of the imperial Austrian, Russian, Romanian and Croatian troops, most notably in Sighișoara and Timișoara, the defeat of the Hungarian Revolution was formally confirmed on 13 August 1849 in the Surrender of Világos (Șiria).[2]

The execution of the Arad Thirteen and of the former Prime Minister Lajos Batthyány on the same day marked the symbolic end of the revolution. The thirteen comprised a number of different nationalities, including six of Hungarian descent, three 'Germans', one Austrian, one of Serb descent, one of Armenian descent and one of Croatian descent. What all thirteen had in common was their service in the Hungarian Revolutionary Army fighting against what some perceived to be Habsburg imperial oppression and for a *liberal* cause. By 1890 all thirteen had become not fighters against oppression, but patriots, nationalists and above all Hungarians. Their execution and subsequent rather long-winded rehabilitation, and then renewed fall from grace, traced the development of liberalism from a contestation of empire into nationalism as a form of empire. Judging by the early, non-official commemorative rituals of the event, it becomes clear that it was primarily the juxtaposition of imperial oppression on the one hand and freedom – or *szabadság* – on the other that mattered. The legend of the Habsburg generals clinking their glasses as the thirteen generals were being executed allegedly led to the vow by Hungarians never to do so when toasting. The first commemoration on 6 October 1850 had therefore been primarily about remembering the executed generals while maintaining the 'cult of the revolution'.[3] In the foreground of such narratives and memories was the story of imperial oppression and cruelty.

As this chapter will demonstrate, with the nationalisation of the Arad Thirteen within the Hungarian Kingdom from 1867 onwards, the site and subsequent monument to the martyrs were transformed: the erstwhile symbols against empire were turned into symbols of empire. By exploring crucial moments in the history of the monument and its original and successive locations, it is possible to trace the changing meaning of this imperial site of memory. Indeed, spaces become sites of memory once they have been invested with meaning. As one of the leading pioneers on memory studies, Pierre Nora, maintained, 'We must deliberately create archives, maintain anniversaries, organise celebrations, pronounce eulogies [for] without commemorative vigilance, history would soon sweep them away'.[4] Therefore, it is in symbols that collective memory becomes 'crystallised',[5] and it is these symbols and narratives, as Roger Brubaker and Margit Feischmidt have contended, that are 'strikingly ethnicised' in Hungary, Romania and Slovakia.[6] Arad is a town which synthesises Hungarian, Romanian and indeed Austrian, German and Serbian narratives and symbols. Furthermore, borrowing from Jan Assmann's model of memory, we can see a shift from a communicative culture of mourning and remembrance to a (contested) cultural memory of imperial–nationalist legitimation towards the end of the nineteenth century.[7] The materiality of the monument built in 1890 certainly confirms that the memory surrounding the Arad Thirteen became a political and 'hard' memory and not one of mourning and personal remembrance.[8] What this case study will thus investigate is an imperial site of memory (and counter-memory), which became nationalised or 'ethnicised', as all groups recognised it as belonging to a particular imperial–national canon. It therefore breaks the mould of belonging to either imperial or national commemorative cultures, as it combines the two. As such, this contribution will focus on the altering perceptions during important phases such as 1867 to 1890 when the monument was planned and erected, the years from 1920 to 1925 during which the monument was removed from Romanian Arad, as well as the immediate period after the Second World War when the communists attempted to use the generals' legacy, and finally the post-communist period when various attempts were made to neutralise the imperial and antagonising aspects of the memory of the Arad Martyrs.

Copying Habsburg memory

Habsburg commemorative rituals, aesthetics and topography have certainly attracted a great deal of interest.[9] Scholars have investigated the meaning of monuments in east-central Europe in the nineteenth century as a way of ascertaining the processes of nation-building and the establishment of nationalism.[10] Yet what deserves more attention is the link between the imperial commemorative practices initiated in Vienna and their imitation by the emerging nationalisms in the regions. Romanians, for instance, excluded from official nationalist memory cultures, therefore perceived the Hungarian imitation to be imperial in nature, as it relegated local and emerging national cultural discourses to a position of inferiority.[11] In this sense, the imperial-nationalist memory cultures that arose towards the end of the nineteenth century were grounded in the imperial precedents rather than the liberal spirit of 1848.

Commemorative practices and rituals in the Habsburg Empire before the revolutions in 1848–49 did not enjoy the grandiose public attention they received under Emperor Franz Josef in the second half of the long nineteenth century. The imperial court and its celebrations of birthdays, marriages and anniversaries had been rather unspectacular and lacklustre affairs.[12] Indeed, the period from the late eighteenth century until 1848 witnessed very little change in the architecture of squares in the Habsburg Empire.[13] This changed under Emperor Franz Josef and with the end of the revolutions in 1849, though there was a brief hiatus between the end of revolutions and the emergence of 'overt political action'.[14] As others have demonstrated, commemorative practices became far more assertive and aggressive in the second half of the nineteenth century.[15] Daniel Unowsky ascribes this not only to the rise of nationalism, but also to the 'neoabsolutist' turn of the nineteenth century.[16] Bearing in mind this link between nationalism and empire, it seems obvious why later Hungarian *national* manifestations became so imbued with imperial ideas and connotations. The pomp and circumstance of Franz Josef's imperial court was echoed in future Hungarian nationalist rhetoric and practice. Access to court and imperial festivities was strictly limited.[17] In much the same way, the exclusive nature of the Hungarian commemoration of the Arad Thirteen, especially from 1890 onwards, served to remind minority groups of the reality of imperial rule. Although scholars have successfully revised the idea of the Habsburg Empire as a 'prison of nations', it is important to correct an entirely revisionist view of Habsburg as an antidote to nationalism.[18] The cornerstone of the imperial-nationalism associated with Hungarian memory politics had been laid in the aftermath of revolution as the undefeated empires sought to reassert themselves domestically through visual appearance.

Hungarian memory politics

The early and unofficial Hungarian commemorations of the martyrs of Arad focused on the remembrance of the thirteen individuals and on the revolutionary struggle for freedom.[19] As Margit Feischmidt and Zoltán Szabó have demonstrated, the story of the Arad Thirteen became highly important to popular Hungarian memory.[20] Indeed, even early attempts at reconstructing the events of the failed revolution quickly rendered all thirteen generals Hungarian.[21] This stood in stark contrast to the last letter written by Count Károly Leiningen-Westerburg to his wife on the eve of his execution. He made not a single mention of Hungary, the Hungarian nation, or his alleged Hungarianness.[22] On the whole, then, the memory of the Arad Thirteen in the early post-revolutionary phase was still centred on the ideas of remembrance and revolution rather than the nation.

With the Austro–Hungarian Compromise of 1867, however, the emphasis within the commemoration of these events began to shift. The relative autonomy enjoyed by Hungary in the dual monarchy helped shape an environment in which it was possible to create distance between Vienna and Budapest. Though formally united under the same monarch and sharing the same policies, especially in foreign affairs, Hungary was autonomous in many domestic issues. Calls for a monument in Arad had already been voiced in the immediate aftermath of execution.[23] Indeed, an obelisk was erected prior to the building of the great monument in 1881, but its abstract motif and peripheral location near Arad Fortress failed to inspire the outpouring of emotions and ceremony that the Freedom Monument would later accomplish. It was not until 16 June 1867 – a mere two and a half months after the Austro–Hungarian Compromise had come into effect – that a committee was set up in Arad under the leadership of mayor Peter Aczél in order to raise funds for a commemorative monument.[24]

Two decades later, the committee had raised enough money, some 120,000 Forint, for a so-called *Hungaria* statue (Figure 4.1). The design would depict – in the words of a contemporary newspaper from Timişoara – 'a tall, noble female figure whose youthful and beautiful traits represent the incarnation of the Hungarian type'.[25] She was to wear the crown of Matthias Corvinus, while the four bottom pillars were to be adorned with symbols representing 'the awakening of freedom', 'self-sacrifice', 'the dying soldier' and 'readiness to combat'.[26] While initial plans for this statue had focused solely on the figure of

4.1 The Hungaria Statue in Arad

Hungaria – later denounced in the *Temeswarer Zeitung* as a 'butcher's wife on her way to a costume ball' – the death of the original architect Adolf Huszár in 1885 enabled the young architect and designer György Zala to complete the project.[27] Praised for the 'combative readiness' of his work, Zala included the portraits of the thirteen generals around

[57]

the base of the monument.[28] The four allegories designed by Huszár remained in place, as did the female figure at the top, albeit in a somewhat altered fashion.

The opening ceremony for the statue on 6 October 1890 was, by all accounts, a spectacle to behold. It included General Damjanich's widow, remnants of the 48er *Honvéds* – including the surviving members of the skull-and-crossbones division who had once vowed never to surrender and instead fight to the death – the mayor of Arad, Julius Galacz, various clerics, György Zala himself, the statue committee, as well as representatives from the Hungarian Academy of Sciences, the Petőfi Society, the Hungarian Company of writers and artists and other relevant groups.[29] According to reports, the ceremony drew a crowd numbering many thousands.[30] However, the pomp and ceremony surrounding the event also presented difficulties to the Hungarian government. To be sure, successive Hungarian Prime Ministers had supported and encouraged this project, in particularly Kálmán Tisza (1875–90) and Count Gyula Szapáry (1890–92). Yet it had always been a balancing act between demonstrating assertive 'Hungarianness' and exhibiting loyalty to the Austro–Hungarian dual monarchy. In a note dated 16 July 1890, a mere three months before the event, the relatively new Prime Minister Szapáry explicitly asked for invitations not to be sent out to his government so as to avoid the embarrassment of being 'forced to deal with the issue'.[31]

In other words, the upper echelons of the Hungarian political class did not want to be seen acting disloyally towards the Habsburg Empire. Instead, in an attempt to downplay the importance of this event towards Vienna, only a single member of the House of Representatives was to be sent to Arad. Szapáry also emphasised the local nature of the event: the choir, the army representatives, and other attendees were to be from Arad County. Nonetheless, Szapáry called on the Sheriff of Arad County to respect the 'earnestness' (*komolysággal*) of the event.[32] He continued, '[k]nowing both the Sheriff's and mayor's composed, sober patriotism' (*Ismerve úgy a főispán mint a polgármester higgadt józan hazafiasságát*), the event should remain solemn without any overtly nationalist demonstrations.[33] This was demonstrated quite pointedly by officially labelling the big day a 'Festival of Reconciliation'.[34] While the unveiling of the statue had been much publicised in advance, during and after the event, heavyweight politicians had to keep enough distance so as not to antagonise the Austrian leadership too much.

In one sense, therefore, the opening ceremony nevertheless represented an anti-imperial event. The presence of the 48er *Honvéds* and relatives of the executed generals emphasised the fact that this was a counter-cultural, counter-political commemorative act vis-á-vis *imperial Habsburg* rule. Indeed, some parts of the ceremony still reflected the rhetoric of liberation of 1848. Ignoring the Sheriff's request to keep the speeches brief, Mayor Galacz spoke at great length and bemoaned the fact that Hungarians had been denied the chance to have a monument in honour of their fallen sons *for centuries*, thereby making a clear reference to the imperial regimes of the Habsburg and Ottoman Empires.[35] Women from all over the south of Hungary were dressed in mourning for the occasion, which marked it out as a moment commemorating imperial aggression and the failure of liberation. Furthermore, with the portraits of the thirteen generals engraved on the base of the statue, the site was clearly linked to a story of empire, resistance and defeat at the hands of the empire's military might.

Yet it was also a decidedly Hungarian and *national* affair. Prime Minster Szapáry, who was otherwise very cautious in embracing the overly public aspects of this event, ensured that the unveiling of the monument took place on the historically important and charged date of 6 October 1890.[36] Yet Szapáry was still constrained by his Prime Ministership. By contrast, from his exile in Turin, Lajos Kossuth – the erstwhile *de facto* President of Hungary during the revolutionary struggle of 1848–49 – recorded a rousing speech for the occasion.[37] Having gone into voluntary exile in 1849, he fell out with the architects of the 1867 compromise – most notably with Ferenc Deák – accusing them of 'selling out' and failing to pursue a purer form of *national* struggle.[38] In his speech, which was broadcast both in writing and by phonograph in a public booth in Arad, he appealed to his fellow Hungarian countrymen and women: 'Be unshakeably true to your Country, Magyar! Respect those who are worthy of respect, but true you should be only to your Country – do you understand this Magyar? – to your Country'.[39] Drawing an unmistakable parallel to his plea to European onlookers in the final stages of the defeat of the revolution on 27 June 1849, he no longer viewed the revolution as an international struggle but a decidedly national one. Back in 1849, Kossuth had insisted:

> You proud English nation . . . do you tolerate this assault on constitutional freedom? . . . You French Republic, have you forgotten the principles upon which your systems had been built? . . . Awake, O peoples and nations of Europe! Your freedom will be decided on the field of Hungary.[40]

Forty-one years later, on the occasion of the unveiling of the statue, Kossuth's call to remember and preserve the legacy of the martyred generals focused solely on Hungary and its representative figure, the Hungaria:

It is the sound of these appeals that I hear in the distance from the lips of the statue of Hungaria. I wonder if all those over there also hear it, and those close by, who came forth on the Hungarian Golgotha on that heart-rendingly woeful, never to be forgotten mournful 6 October, to bear witness before God and the world of the reverence that the Hungarian Nation held for the sacred memory of the Country's independence?[41]

The legacy of the generals had by now been transformed into a national, Hungarian story and was no longer primarily one of liberation from the Habsburg Empire. Their diverse backgrounds and motivations cast aside, the Arad Thirteen had now been united under Hungarian religious–national imagery. As Kossuth reminded his listeners and readers:

Their God is the God of freedom of the Hungarian country, and it is to his altar that they await the Magyar. . . . Let the sacred martyrs in their mortal remains be blessed, let them in their spirits be blessed with the best knowledge of the fatherland's God of liberty, through eternity. 6 October will find me, who is unable to throw myself down in the dust of the Hungarian Golgotha . . . and asking the God of the Magyars with ardent prayer to make victorious the appeal that searches the very marrow of the bone and sounds from the lips of Hungaria to the Hungarian Nation. So be it. Amen.[42]

The impact of this speech is not to be underestimated. At 88 years of age this elder statesman-cum-exile still wielded the power to electrify the crowds and incense his enemies, as would be demonstrated once again at his funeral only four years later in 1894.[43] The impression of hearing Kossuth on the new and surely remarkable technology of the phonograph would have certainly added to the importance of the occasion. It also marked the end of the communicative culture of the memory of the Arad Martyrs, as Kossuth's last public speech gave way to the hard, political memory of the monument. Listeners and readers alike were left in no doubt that the statue of the thirteen generals had become a story of Hungarian glory and no longer of international resistance against imperial rule.

The construction of the statue certainly fitted in with the monument craze that swept most of the Habsburg Lands during the late nineteenth and early twentieth centuries. It is important to note, however, that the Freedom Monument preceded many of the Hungarian imperial–nationalist monuments and statues both in its planning and construction. The Freedom Monument can therefore be viewed as a pioneering project for the ensuing public celebration of the Hungarian Kingdom. The Matthias Corvinus Statue in Cluj, which would later be the site of Romanian–Hungarian memory disputes in the 1990s, was commissioned in 1893 and inaugurated in 1902.[44] Similarly, the

Millennium Monuments, which sprang up in seven places across Hungary in 1896, had only been planned and signed off in 1890 and 1896 respectively.[45] Other examples include the Eötvös Statue and the Deák Monument, both designed by Huszár, the original architect of the Arad Monument. These statues became important national markers in Budapest's cityscape.[46] This was part of a Magyarisation enterprise in which a small number of architects and designers, including names such as Adolf Huszár, Albert Schickedanz, and György Zala, devised plans for statues and monuments across the Kingdom in order to nationalise space – in a cultural and physical sense. Yet this monument frenzy was not merely a Hungarian nationalist phenomenon. It mirrored a European pattern of publicly celebrating and glorifying individuals and moments central to an imperial view of the world. This was not just the case in the Habsburg Empire, but also elsewhere such as in the British Empire where ever-grander monuments were regarded as vital to portraying imperial power, especially vis-à-vis its rival empires.[47]

Thus, this one-time site of loss and imperial victory was converted into one of assertive, indeed aggressive Magyarisation, or in other words an exclusively Hungarian national site. Responses to the statue differed throughout the wider region. Austrian reactions were rather muted. On the days that followed the grand unveiling of the Arad Monument, Austrian newspapers mostly snubbed news of this event and instead focused on day-to-day politics. The Linz newspaper *Tagespost* chose to run a story on elections in Serbia.[48] The *Wiener Zeitung* also ignored the event altogether.[49] Only the radical Viennese newspaper *Neue Freie Presse* ran a sympathetic piece on the event in which it admonished the youth of Vienna not to forget the legacy of the thirteen martyrs. The article compared the commemoration in Arad to the enforced silence vis-à-vis the 48ers in Austria. It thereby not only maintained its oppositional stance towards government politics but also associated the legacy of the thirteen generals with its original anti-imperial connotation.[50]

Romanian perceptions of the meaning of this event, however, were more defensive. As Margit Feischmidt has pointed out, there was some resistance to the erection and unveiling of this statue. This, too, tended to be articulated through silence as well as general allusions to Magyarisation.[51] Feischmidt also outlines three categories into which the monuments erected in Hungary in the late nineteenth and early twentieth centuries could be divided: (a) those based on Habsburg-imperial themes, (b) those expressing Hungarian nationalist mythology, and (c) symbols of 'national-democratic', anti-Habsburg sentiment.[52] The Arad martyrology, however, points to a development of imperial-nationalism – one that mimicked the Habsburg-imperial mode of memorialisation while demoting the anti-imperial aspect to a peripheral role. Magyarisation was therefore not solely nationalist, but was in fact perceived as an imperial-national process. Amongst Hungarians the glorification of Magyar control was interpreted as a move towards reinstating former glory. Minorities, too, saw these processes as Hungarian attempts to create a Magyar empire.

In this milieu, rejection or silence was not the only response. The aggressive and all-pervasive nature of Magyarisation became evident in public avowals of Hungarian greatness by minorities. German-language newspapers such as the *Temeswarer Zeitung* or *Arader Zeitung* saw the unveiling of the statue as a true expression of Hungarian nationalist propaganda. On 5 October 1890 the *Temeswarer Zeitung*, a German-Swabian newspaper, glowed with Hungarian patriotism by pronouncing that 'finally, on 6 October [the day of the unveiling of the statue] every loyal Hungarian subject (*Untertan*) will be able to go on a pilgrimage to Arad with their heads held high'.[53] A day after the ceremonies the same newspaper proclaimed that 'yesterday every Hungarian heart was an altar . . . when the jewels of the Hungarian hearts united to form one big jewel, which was grafted by Hungarian artistry to shape an eternal monument . . . with blood for our fatherland.'[54] What such passages reveal is not a love for all things Hungarian by the Swabian minority, but rather the extent to which Magyarisation had become more and more assertive by constricting public space and public forums. The censored press thus relayed a Hungarian, nationalist narrative that surrounded not just this event, but politics in general. This site of defeated liberation against imperial rule, therefore, was itself turned into a site of new imperial rule.

Romanian Arad

This was most certainly understood as such by the minorities in the region and in particular by Romanians. Under Hungarian rule, Romanian political activists were spurred on in their pursuit of cultural autonomy and independence. Cultural movements such as *Astra* (*Transylvanian Association for Romanian Literature and Romanian's People Culture*) saw their future within Romania and understood their relationship with Hungarian cultural claims as one of oppression, rivalry and competition.[55] They did not have to wait for long to see their ambitions fulfilled. Following the break-up of the Austro–Hungarian Empire after the First World War, Arad became part of the newly unified Greater Romanian Kingdom. This fundamental change resulted in a rebranding of city space, the renaming of street names, and alterations to the commemorative landscape of the newly acquired Romanian territories. Indeed, the year 1918 was not just a moment of great change for former minorities in their new independent states, but also for the commemorative landscape within Hungary. The much-loathed monument of the Habsburg general Heinrich Hentzi in Budapest, for instance, was duly removed as part of the 'iconoclasm' that accompanied the end of the dual monarchy.[56]

The initial response by local and governmental authorities towards the memory landscape within Romania was uncoordinated and varied. Hence, it was not until 1929 that a Commission of Public Monuments was set up in Bucharest. This had been intended to comment solely on the artistic value of new projects for monuments. However, as Maria Bucur has demonstrated, the territories ceded to Romania after the First World War witnessed an upsurge in aggressively nationalistic local committees, which often took matters into their own hands.[57] Arad's commemorative restructuring was also quite a chaotic and, at times, local affair designed to rebalance the ethnic look of the city and to settle scores with Hungarians. A local committee in Arad, set up under the auspices of the Orthodox bishop of Arad, thus petitioned to erect a cross commemorating the 'massacre of almost 100 Romanians during the war'. The central commission reacted quite tepidly.[58] Romanian commemorative politics were by no means clear cut, but often erratic, contradictory, and parochial.

Other efforts at decolonising and Romanising space in Arad County were more successful. Both the commemorative plaque for the eccentric Romanian inventor and pilot Aurel Vlaicu in his hometown of Binţinţi and the Aurel Vlaicu fountain in Arad received great support from Bucharest, including from the future Prime Minister Octavian Goga.[59] Similarly, both local and central initiatives sought to rectify Arad's Hungarian appearance by addressing the issue of Hungarian monuments. In July 1922, the mayor of Arad, the prefect of the county, and central government in Bucharest sought to establish a quick solution to existing Hungarian edifices.[60] The Martyrs' Statue and a statue of Lajos Kossuth were duly earmarked for removal and the mayor of Arad dealt with the issue temporarily by erecting walls around them. Three years later, in July 1925, the Arad Thirteen were dismantled and moved from what was now called Avram Iancu Square – named after a Romanian hero of the 1848 revolution – to a warehouse deep inside Arad Fortress on the other side of the Mureş river.

Some Hungarians had fought against such a public purge and even liaised with the government in Budapest over the issues surrounding the statues on former Hungarian lands. In his memoirs the eminent politician Béla Barabás would carefully recall his efforts at protecting the monument.[61] Despite all the changes in connotation that this monument had undergone, Barabás still insisted in 1929 that it was a 'freedom monument'.[62] Romanians disagreed with such sentiments and praised the removal of the statue. Philosopher and sociologist Nicolae Petrescu celebrated this act of liberation from Hungarian jingoism in the newly established literary magazine *Tribuna Nouă*: 'The monument of the 13 martyrs has finally been removed from Avram Iancu Square. Everyone agrees that this chauvinist Hungarian monument had no place in Romanian Arad. It has gone forever'.[63]

To be sure, this was part of a new wave of Romanian nationalism, but it was targeted primarily at Hungarian imperial-nationalism. While Hungarian statues were in the process of being dislodged, the Swabian community constructed its own monuments to its dead. In Arad Nou, a Swabian war memorial, commemorating the Swabian dead of the First World War, was erected outside the Catholic Church in 1924–25 just as the statue of the Arad Thirteen was being demolished.[64] It thus cannot go unnoticed that it was precisely the presence of the Martyrs' Monument, which was perceived as a Hungarian imperial-nationalist statement, not merely the presence of non-Romanian monuments *per se*. It was a reminder of Hungary's yesteryear Magyarisation programmes, which – according to many commentators at the time – was still a danger and continued to hold back the Romanian nation. In a similar vein, another commentator claimed in *Tribuna Nouă* that '[f]or the past six years [since 1919], this monument has stood not only for *Hungarian* freedom but also for the chauvinism directed against us, in the centre of our town, defiant in the face of all things Romanian, and inspired by the naïve hope of foreigners for a future many of them had wanted'.[65] What many Hungarians wanted was a return to former Hungarian glory. The site of the statue had therefore gone from representing a space of imperial aggression and defeated liberty, to a site of nationalism, and by the interwar period back to a site of imperial aggression – this time, however, attributed to Hungary's position in the dual monarchy.

Epilogue: anti-imperialism, imperialism and reconciliation?

The 'Thirteen Martyrs' had not 'gone forever', as the writer in *Tribuna Nouă* had predicted. Deemed unsuited to the topography of *Romanian* Arad in 1925, the monument then embarked on an eighty-year journey. It remained in a warehouse in Arad Castle for twenty-five years before the communists reassembled it, albeit still within Arad Fortress, in 1949–50. Although the early communist period in both Romania and

Hungary was marked by a reinvention of commemorative practices and the toppling of statues,[66] the monument and the legacy of the generals remained curiously resilient to this challenge. There were in fact efforts to rehabilitate the thirteen generals as anti-imperialist fighters. Romania and Hungary appeared to be moving towards a rapprochement on the issue, but this was cut short by the Hungarian Revolution in October 1956.[67] For the remainder of the Cold War, the Arad Monument stayed out of sight, while the original site in the centre of Arad continued to be associated with the politically useful figure of Avram Iancu. In the meantime, the monument was entirely airbrushed from publications on the town of Arad.[68]

It was only at the end of the Cold War that the statue was rediscovered. It became the subject of much public debate when it was transferred to the courtyard of a monastery in 1999, after a first attempt at restoring the statue to the Arad topography in October 1999 had failed acrimoniously. Neither the Romanian Prime Minister Radu Vasile nor Hungarian Prime Minister Viktor Orbán took part in the scheduled opening ceremony of the newly designed Park of Hungarian–Romanian Friendship on the sesquicentennial of the execution of the Arad Martyrs on 6 October 1999. Vasile and other Romanian officials regarded the issue to be too Hungarian and did not want to clash with Arad municipal council or high-profile politicians such as Ion Iliescu who opposed and eventually scuppered the idea in 1999.[69] Orbán responded to this snub in kind by returning to Budapest to address the issue of Hungarians in Hungary's neighbouring countries. Four years later, in May 2003, under the new Romanian and Hungarian Prime Ministers Adrian Năstase and Péter Medgyessy, the statue was prepared for relocation to a place close to its original site in the city of Arad. This new square, previously designated as the Park of Hungarian–Romanian Friendship, was named Reconciliation Park.[70] In an echo of the 1890 opening ceremony, the belated sesquicentennial of the execution of the Arad Martyrs was marked by the unveiling of the statue. Some 7,000 Hungarians and a number of belligerent and booing Romanian nationalists attended the event.[71]

Yet in the spirit of the accession of both Hungary and Romania to the European Union (EU) in 2004 and 2007 respectively, the Romanian Minister for Culture and Religious Affairs, Răzvan Theodorescu, tried to defuse any tensions by stating that 'Hungarians and Romanians, Romanians and Hungarians, we can look together, definitely together, towards the future'.[72] Jonathan Scheele, the delegate of the European Commission, also emphasised the reconciliatory aspect of this new memory regime claiming that '[i]t is the only path for a common future of the two countries'.[73] Béla Markó, head of the Democratic

[65]

Union of Hungarians in Romania, agreed that the only path for both peoples was that of reconciliation within the EU.[74] The question of empire and nationalism was thus neutralised by introducing a rather ephemeral and unconvincing solution: under EU observation and using the euphemistic language of 'reconciliation', the two sides still face each other, as the Romanian 48ers continue to watch on from their Arch of Triumph and the Hungaria gazes beyond to a more glorious Hungarian past.

What has been played out on the site(s) of contention and over the monument are claims to space and territory. The monument and opposition to the monument quickly became part of a national and imperial power game. Oscillating between anti-imperial, imperial-national and chauvinist perceptions, the statue's biography tells a story of the complexity of changing memory cultures in the prism of empire, its subsequent break-up, and the vexed politicised and ideological debates thereafter. In this way, the commemoration of the 150th anniversary between 1999 and 2004 encapsulated the politics of memory that surrounded this site and statue: imperial in origin, national in recognition and political in its uses.

Notes

I wish to thank Gaëlle Fisher for her support in Arad.

1 These were Lajos Aulich, János Damjanich, Arisztid Deseffwy, Ernő Kiss, Károly Knezich, György Láhner, Valmos Lázár, Count Károly Leiningen-Westerburg, József Nagysándor, Ernő Pöltenberg, József Schweidel, Ignác Török and Count Károly Vécsey. The Magyarised names of the individuals have been used here.
2 I will use the present-day names of places unless otherwise stated.
3 M. Feischmidt, 'Die Verortung der Nation an den Peripherien: Ungarische Nationaldenkmäler in multiethnischen Gebieten der Monarchie', in W. Fischer and W. Heindl (eds), *Grenzen und Räume in Österreich-Ungarn 1867–1918* (Tübingen: A. Francke Verlag, 2010), p. 120.
4 P. Nora, 'Between Memory and History: Les Lieux de Mémoire', *Representations* 26 (1989), p. 12.
5 P. Nora, *Realms of Memory: Rethinking the French Past*, vol. I (New York: Columbia University Press, 1996), p. xv.
6 R. Brubaker and M. Feischmidt, '1848 in 1998: The Politics of Commemoration in Hungary, Romania, and Slovakia', *Comparative Study of Society and History* 44:4 (2002), pp. 725–6.
7 J. Assmann, 'Collective Memory and Cultural Identity', *New German Critique* 65 (1995), pp. 125–33.
8 See P. Connerton, *How Societies Remember* (Cambridge: Cambridge University Press, 1989).
9 See, for instance, P. Judson and M. Rozenblit (eds), *Constructing Nationalities in East Central Europe* (Cambridge, Mass.: Harvard University Press, 2005) or M. Bucur and N. Wingfield (eds), *Staging the Past: The Politics of Commemoration in Habsburg Central Europe* (West Lafayette: Purdue University Press, 2001).
10 See, for example, M. Bucur, *Heroes and Victims: Remembering War in Twentieth-Century Romania* (Bloomington: Indiana University Press, 2009).

11 Interpretations of the Habsburg period following the ideological turn in the second half of the twentieth century no longer saw this as imperial but as *imperialist*.
12 D. Unowsky, 'Reasserting Empire: Habsburg Imperial Celebrations after the Revolutions of 1848–1849', in M. Bucur and N. Wingfield, *Staging the Past*, pp. 13–16.
13 C. Corradi, 'Urbanism and Civilisation: The Making of City-Squares in Imperial Vienna (16th–20th Centuries)', in R. Jaworski and P. Stachel (eds), *Die Besetzung des öffentlichen Raumes: Politische Plätze, Denkmäler und Straßennamen im europäischen Vergleich* (Leipzig: Frank & Thimme, 2007), p. 69.
14 G. Szabad, *Hungarian Political Trends Between the Revolution and the Compromise (1849–1867)* (Budapest: Akadémio Kiadó, 1977), p. 41.
15 See, for example, M. Bucur and N. Wingfield, *Staging the Past*, P. Judson and M. Rozenblit, *Constructing Nationalities in East Central Europe*, N. Wingfield (ed.), *Creating the Other: Ethnic Conflict and Nationalism in Habsburg Central Europe* (New York: Berghahn, 2003) and R. Brubaker et al. (eds), *Nationalist Politics and Everyday Ethnicity in a Transylvanian Town* (Princeton: Princeton University Press, 2006), especially chapter one.
16 D. Unowsky, 'Reasserting Empire', p. 18.
17 *Ibid.*, p. 19.
18 See, for instance, J. Leonhard and U. von Hirschhausen, *Empires und Nationalstaaten im 19. Jahrhundert* (Göttingen: Vandenhoeck & Ruprecht, 2009), pp. 9–11.
19 Early memory cultures resembled far more closely the mourning practices described in Jay Winter's book on post-First World War memory. See J. Winter, *Sites of Memory, Sites of Mourning: The Great War in European Cultural History* (Cambridge: Cambridge University Press, 1995), as well as Feischmidt, 'Die Verortung der Nation', pp. 119–20.
20 *Ibid.*, p. 119 and Z. Szabó, 'Az aradi vértanúk emlékezete' at www.neprajz.hu/48/tanulmanyok/tan8.shtml (accessed 11 January 2012) quoted in M. Feischmidt, 'Die Verortung der Nation'.
21 A. Szilágyi, *Die letzten Tage der magyarischen Revolution. Enthüllung der Ereignisse in Ungarn und Siebenbürgen seit dem 1. Juli 1849* (Pest: Verlag Heckenast, 1850), p. 73.
22 C. Leiningen, 'Letter to his Wife Lisa Leiningen, 5–6 October 1849', in A. P. Petri, *Heimatbuch der Marktgemeinde Neuarad im Banat* (Marquartstein: T.H. Breit Verlag, 1985), pp. 200–1.
23 M. Feischmidt, 'Die Verortung der Nation', p. 119.
24 'Spezial-Telegram der "TZ"', *Temeswarer Zeitung* (7 October 1890), pp. 1–2.
25 *Ibid.*, p. 2.
26 *Ibid.*
27 See 'Georg Zala. (Der Schöpfer des Arader Märtyrer-Denkmals)', *Temeswarer Zeitung* (5 October 1890), pp. 2–3. I will be using the Hungarian form of Zala's name rather than the German form of his name, Georg Zala. Similarly, I will refer to Adolf Huszár in the Hungarian form of his name and not in the German form of Adolf Hußár.
28 *Ibid.*, p. 2.
29 Magyar Országos Levéltár, K26 2254. 16 July 1890.
30 'Die Arader Feier. Vom Spezial-Berichterstatter der "Tem. Zeitung"', *Temeswarer Zeitung* (7 October 1890), p. 1.
31 Magyar Országos Levéltár, K26 2254. 16 July 1890.
32 *Ibid.*
33 *Ibid.*
34 *Ibid.* This euphemistic language was echoed, perhaps unwittingly, 114 years later on, as the statue was reconstituted in Arad under the watchful eye of the EU.
35 'Spezial-Telegram der "TZ"', *Temeswarer Zeitung* (7 October 1890), p. 2.
36 Magyar Országos Levéltár, K26 2254. 16 July 1890. Curiously, this directive was issued in German, but the majority of inner-Hungarian state affairs were conducted in Hungarian.

37 For a transcript of the speech in English see 'Making Sound History: Lajos Kossuth's Speech on Phonographic Cylinders', OSzK at http://mek.oszk.hu/kiallitas/kossuthhangja/html/nyito_uk.htm (accessed 11 January 2012).

38 On the ambiguous role of Lajos Kossuth as both a nationalist and internationalist, see L. Deme, 'Nationalism and Cosmopolitanism among the Hungarian Radicals', *Austrian History Yearbook* 12:1 (1976), pp. 36–44.

39 'Making Sound History'.

40 Lajos Kossuth quoted in I. Deák, *The Lawful Revolution: Louis Kossuth and the Hungarians 1848–1849* (New York: Columbia University Press, 1979), pp. 292–3.

41 'Making Sound History'.

42 For both the English and the original Hungarian version see 'Making Sound History'.

43 D. Barenscroft, 'Trafficking in Photographs: Representational Power and the Case of Lajos Kossuth, Budapest 1894', *History & Memory* 22:22 (2010), pp. 34–67.

44 M. Feischmidt, *Ethnizität als Konstruktion und Erfahrung: Symbolstreit und Alltagskultur im siebenbürgischen Cluj* (Münster: LIT Verlag, 2003), pp. 68–9; see also Brubaker et al., *Nationalist Politics*, pp. 136–51.

45 M. Feischmidt, 'Die Verortung der Nation', pp. 113–15.

46 *Ibid.*, p. 121.

47 See, for instance, Tori Smith's study on the Victoria monument unveiled in London in 1911 and framed very much as a response to French grandeur: T. Smith, ' "A Grand Work of Noble Conception": The Victoria Memorial and Imperial London', in F. Driver and D. Gilbert (eds), *Imperial Cities: Landscape, Display and Identity* (Manchester: Manchester University Press, 2003), pp. 21–39.

48 'Die Wahlen in Serbien', *Tagespost* (7 October 1890), p. 1.

49 *Wiener Zeitung* (7–10 October 1890).

50 'Das Denkmal in Arad', *Neue Freie Presse* (7 October 1890), pp. 1–2.

51 Feischmidt cites newspapers from Braşov and Sibiu; see M. Feischmidt, 'Die Verortung der Nation', p. 123.

52 *Ibid.*, pp. 112–13.

53 'Zum 6 Oktober', *Temeswarer Zeitung* (5 October 1890), p. 2.

54 'Die Arader Feier', *Temeswarer Zeitung* (7 October 1890), p. 1.

55 J. P. Niessen, 'Museum, Nationality, and Public Research Libraries in Nineteenth Century Transylvania', *Libraries & the Cultural Record* 41:3 (2006), p. 306. For a good history of *Astra* see T. Dunlap, 'Astra and the Appeal of the Nation: Power and Autonomy in Late-Nineteenth Century Transylvania', *Austrian Yearbook* 34 (2003), pp. 215–46.

56 See D. Gamboni, *Iconoclasm and Vandalism since the French Revolution* (Chicago: Reaktion, 2007), pp. 25–50 for a general overview of iconoclasm in the late modern period. For a detailed study of the Hentzi monument, see M. L. Miller, 'A Monumental Debate in Budapest: The Hentzi Statue and the Limits of Austro-Hungarian Reconciliation, 1852–1918', *Austrian Yearbook* 40 (2009), pp. 215–37.

57 M. Bucur, *Heroes and Victims*, pp. 132–7.

58 *Ibid.*, p. 137.

59 Primaria Municipului Arad, Acte Administrative, 10–1924.

60 *Ibid.*, 21–1922.

61 See B. Barabás, *Emlékirataim* (Arad: Corvin, 1929).

62 Barabás quoted in Feischmidt, 'Die Verortung der Nation', p. 125.

63 N. Petrescu, 'Fântâna lui Avram Iancu', *Tribuna Nouă* (26 July 1925).

64 A. P. Petri, *Heimatbuch*, pp. 234–5.

65 P. Faur, 'Monumentul – fântână al lui Avram Iancu', *Tribuna Nouă* (23 July 1925).

66 Katalin Sinkó calls the processes of eviscerating the commemorative topography in the early communist period *Denkmalsturz*. See K. Sinkó, 'Zur Entstehung der staatlichen und nationalen Feiertage in Ungarn (1850–1991)', in E. Brix and H. Stekl (eds), *Der Kampf um das Gedächtnis: Öffentliche Gedenktage in Mitteleuropa* (Vienna: Böhlau, 1997), p. 266.

67 M. Feischmidt, 'Die Verortung der Nation', p. 126.

68 See, for instance, I. Niculescu (ed.), *Arad: Monografie* (Bucharest: Editura Sport-Turism, 1979), pp. 57–79 and V. Velcea, I. Velcea and O. Mîndruţ, *Judeţul Arad* (Bucharest: Editura Academiei, 1979), pp. 128–40. The latter only included censuses from 1930 on and omitted the category of ethnicity in an attempt to make Arad appear less Hungarian.
69 C. Lovatt and D. Lovatt, 'Romanian News Roundup', *Central Europe Review* 1:16 (1999) at www.ce-review.org/99/16/romanianews16.html (accessed 25 January 2012).
70 It is unclear whether this was a deliberate imitation of the Festival of Reconciliation in 1890.
71 'Hungarian Premier attends Inauguration of "Reconciliation Park" in Arad', *Newsline RFE/RL* (26 April 2004) at www.rferl.org/content/article/1143145.html (accessed 25 January 2012).
72 Official website of the Reconciliation Park at www.welcometoromania.ro/Arad/Arad_Parcul_Reconcilierii_r.htm (accessed 25 January 2012).
73 'Thousands of Persons at the Inauguration of Reconciliation Park in Arad', *Big News Magazine* (26 April 2004) at http://bignewsmagazine.com/2004/04/thousands-of-persons-at-the-inauguration-of-reconciliation-park-in-arad/ (accessed 25 January 2012).
74 *Ibid.*

CHAPTER FIVE

Heroes, victims and the quest for peace: war monuments and the contradictions of Japan's post-imperial commemoration

Barak Kushner

How do countries memorialise their defeat? More specifically: how did imperial Japan deal with the cultural legacy the war bequeathed to the nation in terms of shrines, monumental celebrations of martial victory and a myriad architectural structures that could not be simply erased overnight like words in textbooks? The shift in post-war Japan's attitudes towards the war can be traced by examining the construction of statues and the reconstruction of wartime monuments. These artefacts echoed a transition from a martial ideology to one that promoted an occasionally ambivalent variety of peace. These visual representations of the war often combined events and objects from the battles themselves, even though they occasionally did so in a completely repackaged fashion and they mirrored the extent to which wartime values remained contested in post-imperial Japan.

Monuments were erected to commemorate the war, but they were also the result of intersecting plans and policies that emerged within Japan's post-war society. They frequently arose from conflicts between political parties, war bereavement societies, associations supporting convicted war criminals and local groups opposing such plans. In this context it was the issue of Japanese war criminals, their trials, their fate and their place within the nation's public discourse which assumed a central role. The three categories of war crimes established at Nuremberg for dealing with Nazi atrocities also served as the template for trials of alleged Japanese perpetrators: 'crimes against peace', conventional war crimes, and 'crimes against humanity' – usually abbreviated as classes A, B and C. Class A war criminals were the men who planned and executed Japan's 'aggressive' war. Charges against them were pursued during the Tokyo War Crimes Trial.[1] The creation of the new C class of crimes allowed for the prosecution of citizens of one nation by another for acts of genocide against a third country and constituted a new departure in the practice of international law. Unlike the National Socialists the Japanese military did not pursue a genocidal policy, so its class B trials dealt with those in charge when conventional war crimes were committed, whereas the C category applied to individuals who actually carried out the crime. Usually, though, defendants were charged under the combined category 'BC class'.[2] Legal disputes and procedural issues that arose from these regulations and practices led many Japanese to believe, though, that the charges brought against their countrymen were unfair. After 1945, Japanese governments continually investigated the war criminals' issue, and their lasting dissatisfaction is reflected in post-war sites of imperial memory.

Within Japan's post-1945 commemoration of the recent past the two dimensions of war and empire are connected through a complex web of amnesia, suppression and distortion. This makes the task of disentangling the discrete elements in Japan's memory culture a challenging one. Several powerful factors have made it difficult for Japan to engage with its specifically imperial past in a candid and searching fashion. For one, there was a huge political effort – led by the Japan War-Bereaved Families Association (Nihon izokukai) and approved immediately after Japan regained sovereignty in 1952 – to grant pension benefits to Japanese war veterans and convicted war criminals. The focus on this measure shifted the nation's attention from memories of empire to a goal-oriented engagement with the topic of war.

Yet even this close attention paid to the actual conflict was characterised by remarkable blind spots. The Second World War, with all its ugliness and suffering, was amply depicted, but what led to the conflict in the first place was rarely addressed. When the issue was broached at all, this was done to decry that Japan had been compelled to protect itself against Western imperialism. The result, as public intellectual Kang Sang-jun has claimed, was that while Japan had suffered military defeat, which effectively de-militarised the country, the experience of occupation did not translate into the social recognition that Japan had also lost its colonies and had therefore ceased to be an empire. Essentially, even though Japan had been vanquished its people did not conceive of themselves as post-imperial. Kang is explicit that even though the Japanese people suffered defeat they did little in terms of considering what was actually taken from them – the empire. The empire was lost, but the consciousness that had once buttressed it, dissipated more slowly.[3] Moreover, since, from 1947 onwards, Japan was under the umbrella of American foreign policy and firmly located in the liberal capitalist camp opposed to world communism, there was little room for the Japanese themselves to consider their own imperial past. The dominant strain of thought was for Japan to rebuild and rejoin the Western world economy. The notion of 'empire' virtually disappeared as a topic from the Japanese media, replaced by discussions about democracy, United Nations-centred diplomacy and economic growth.

It was really only after the 1980s and 1990s that the Japanese began to confront their past. The country's economic bubble had burst, and a rising China and a democratised South Korea were coming forcefully onto the world stage. Faced with international pressure to come to terms with its voracious imperial past, Japan saw a new public debate emerging, albeit slowly. The legacies of the empire that had been buried now emerged in issues such as the politics of compensating 'comfort women', forced Chinese and Korean labour, as well as in continuing territorial issues over islands claimed by the USSR and then Russia.

Yet, the fact that so many elements of Japan's former empire have retained a symbolic presence in Japanese politics, including prime ministerial visits to the military Yasukuni Shrine, demonstrates that for many Japanese people memory is, to this day, limited to domestic concerns and their own role and does still not extend to a larger and more holistic consideration of Japan as an empire. This means that, in present-day Japan, few shrines or sites of remembrance mention the expanse of Japan's empire and link it to the memory of those who perished outside of Japan.[4] This absence signifies how the issue of a reflective memory of Japanese imperialism has remained confined to academic debates. It has not yet fully enmeshed itself into the wider public discourse on the war, and empire appears only in a deeply encoded form on the visual in sites of memory whose outward idiom is that of war and suffering.

In this chapter, four brief examples of constructed or reconstructed memorials of the war will be examined: a tower, a 'love statue', Japan's most important Shinto shrine, and a local council memorial. The aim is to investigate how venerating or denying aspects of Japan's imperial glory resulted in continued social tensions in the context of post-war Japan's diplomatic and constitutional commitment to the promotion of peace. A grand imperial tower was recommissioned to fit into the 'new democratic' post-war Japan – a goal both desired by the Japanese people and sanctioned by their American occupiers. After 1945, new structures were created to serve as *lieux de mémoire* that would replace an imperial, martial form of memory with a new representation of Japan as a victim of war. The iconic 'love statue' is a prominent example of such a site. But not all monuments were reupholstered or newly established. Japan's most important Shinto Shrine, Yasukuni, remained intact and to this day the imperial facades on several of its entrance pillars retain a legacy of the memory of Japan's empire. The last case study will explore a new memorial garden built by a local council on the edge of a busy urban street in northwest Tokyo. It demonstrates the deep divide that frequently separates official from unofficial memorial efforts. By way of conclusion the chapter will consider the way in which Japan's empire was perceived, celebrated and then remembered through these settings that were sculpted to provide an emotive and historical ideology.

In many ways, a study of both the sites of imperial remembrance themselves and of the public debates surrounding their production and maintenance underlines the continued centrality of the national discussion about memorialisation. Japan continues to commemorate the war in several ways: as the loss of empire with Japan retaining a sense of international victimisation; as a way of venerating old heroes who selflessly fought for the nation; and by mourning the Japanese loss of life in the war with a kind of grief that is unencumbered by shame. Ever since Imperial Japan's defeat in 1945 the reshaping and recreation of new forms of commemoration have expressed the nation's confusion and the lack of consensus about the meaning of the Second World War. Within the landscape of Japan's capital, Tokyo, and other urban areas throughout the former empire, monuments became the physical embodiment of this expression.

Empire redux

After Japan's Meiji Restoration in 1868 the country leapt on to the international stage, piling imperial victory upon victory. All over the country these glorious feats of arms were celebrated with massive and eye-catching military triumphal arches (*gaisenmon*). The visual splendour of these temporary features assisted in the production of imperial celebrations and later of historical memory.[5] Statues and monuments designed to depict national identity in public spaces were a relatively recent phenomenon in Japan. In the context of Japan's bid to be the first 'modern' East Asian nation, there emerged, however, a craze for fêting successful individuals, including military men. According to Sven Saalar, 'between 1880 and 1928, more than 800 of these statues were erected throughout Japan'.[6] In fact, the Japanese government did not only push this campaign during its imperial era. A large number of reconstructed or redacted sites of memory were also created during the post-war period, in a sense affirming that national identity is 'always being reconstructed in response to new needs, interests and perceptions', as noted by historian Anthony Smith.[7]

Other forms of memorisation flourished, too. As Kerry Smith explains, 'by the late 1990s, more than one hundred museums and exhibition sites in Japan reflected on the experiences of wartime, defeat, and the quest for world peace'.[8] There is, however, a marked difference between how the populace relates to academic textbooks and carefully designed exhibitions on the one hand, and their responses to public monuments and *lieux de mémoire* on the other. Statues and memorials rarely provide lengthy explanations. Thus, the decision to build and maintain such memorials remains fraught with uncertainty as to their precise meaning.

The so-called *Miyazaki Tower of Peace* is an example of such ambiguity and flexibility. This former imperial site visualises an imperious Japan – traditional yet shimmering with technological prowess. Officials in the capital of Miyazaki prefecture erected this thirty-seven metre tall stone monument in 1940 to celebrate the 2,600th anniversary of the mythic birth of Japan under the Emperor Jimmu. The *Hakkô Ichiu Tower* referred to an ambiguous propaganda slogan that supposedly meant bringing the 'Eight Corners of the World under One Roof'.[9] What that rhetoric really signified was open to wide and often opaque interpretations. Throughout most of Japan's war, few if any outside the inner Shinto sanctum and the academic confines of wartime philosophers had any true understanding of this phrase. In addition to its blurred propaganda implications, local and national officials pushed ahead with the construction of this massive monument to celebrate Japan's imperial expansion and to help compensate, in part, for the cancellation of what was to be Tokyo's crowning moment on the international stage: the opening of the first Olympic Games in East Asia.[10]

In order to 'maintain the country's will to fight, the 2,600th anniversary of Jimmu's achievement was exploited as a source of nationalistic inspiration', perhaps to compensate for the disappointing fact that even though the war in East Asia appeared to be going in Japan's favour there had still not been a major victory on the Chinese mainland.[11] To build the monument, stones as well as donations were collected from each prefecture on the four main home islands of Japan and also from areas around the empire. As Japan's international fortunes rose, officials hastened to celebrate such successes, but this would pose problems after the war when the nation finally had to face up to its imperial excesses.

In August 1945, a mere five years after its inauguration, 'defeat rendered the tower's expansionist ideology bankrupt, thereby transforming the monument into an example of "negative heritage", a site marked by undesirable or contradictory associations in the public memory'.[12] The determination of both the government and the population to avoid this 'negative heritage' became a key motif in the culture of post-war Japan. At the behest of occupation authorities and in line with public opposition to glorifying the memory of the Second World War, the monument had to change after the country's unconditional surrender. It was not destroyed, though, but relabelled. It started a new life as *Heiwa no tô*, or 'Peace Tower'. For the population the sudden reversal in Japan's fortunes of war was at first difficult to understand. What had previously been touted as the last push to secure Japan's ultimate victory, even at the cost of hundreds of thousands of lives, suddenly turned out to be a hollow promise. Historian Naoko Shimazu has illuminated that 'for the Japanese, it was [therefore] important to construct a clear demarcation between the pre-1945 and post-1945 Japan, because it needed to separate the "polluted" past from the new present, as a springboard to construct a new narrative of post-war Japan'.[13]

But this demarcation, as Shimazu observes, occurred very abruptly and turned into a taboo against the creation of popular representations of the war. That defeat in war coincided with the fall of its empire was a factor that crucially affected the identity of post-war Japan. This may appear to be a trivial point, but it set Japan apart from the experience of many European powers. The empires of Britain, France or even Belgium were not dismantled within the context of military defeat and thus the societies of the former colonial powers had time to adjust. In Japan, defeat hit suddenly and without warning. Consequently, post-war *lieux de mémoire* do not primarily emphasise the war and loss, but the idea of empire and sacrifice for the nation as a whole. Japan was defeated militarily, which led to its inevitable post-war demilitarisation, but, as political scientist Kang Sangjung explains, this experience did not translate into a social recognition that Japan had lost its colonies. The Japanese did not conceive of themselves as post-colonial or post-imperial and hardly considered how to re-establish relations with their Asian neighbours. The empire had fallen but the psychology that supported it lingered on.[14]

The memory of former imperial success survived even as its physical remnants were fading. Like popular clothing from the era, which was often emblazoned with repetitive emblems of victory over China and elsewhere, some of the wartime monuments were now heading for destruction.[15] As was demonstrated by the attempt to veil the imperial tower in a sacred post-war shroud of peace, not even famous wartime edifices were safe. The massive monument to the Imperial Japanese Navy Commander Hirose Takeo in Tokyo fared even worse than the Peace Tower. Hirose was killed in the line of duty during the Russo-Japanese War. In 1910 a tall and imposing statue was erected in his honour in front of the Manseibashi Station, right in the centre of Tokyo. After 1945 there were rumours that the American occupation authorities deemed the memorial both a traffic hazard and a glorification of war. As no effort was made to redeem or reinvent it as a paean to peace, the statue was promptly removed from its base, though who issued this directive – the American overseers or the Japanese themselves – has remained unclear.[16] This was not altogether unusual. Efforts to distance the Japanese nation from its immediate militarist and imperialist manifestations normally took the form of removing statues of a martial nature. While some of these removals were carried out at the behest of the Supreme Commander of the Allied Powers, the occupying rulers of Japan, at other times the plans appear to have been unilateral Japanese efforts to re-educate their own society toward democracy.

Post-war Japan made a concerted attempt to refashion its domestic and international image. In its famous Article 9 the nation's new 1947 constitution went so far as to outlaw war as a tool of diplomacy – in a bid to support peace in East Asia. After regaining its sovereignty in 1952, moves continued to propagate a new sort of Japan. Yet amid all the symbolic trappings there was no real development towards a supportive environment where actual peace policies could thrive. Built as late as 1975, the oddly named *Chiran Peace Museum for Kamikaze* in Kyushu, for instance, aims to bring solace to the families of those who died in the name of war. But extolling the virtues of young men who essentially died pointless deaths for a cause that did not warrant such devotion hardly makes a compelling case for peace. The list of prefectural or private museums that invoke peace in Japan is too long to enumerate here, but the salient point is that for the most part their exhibits concern war and not peace.[17]

The Japanese have been keen to erase vestiges of militarism in their society, but remain ambivalent about refusing to validate the idea of 'sacrifice for the nation' (*okuni no tame*) that was an integral part of that history. In his 2006 national manifesto *Toward a Beautiful Country* (Utsukushî kuni e), Japanese Prime Minister Abe Shinzô actually extolled the virtues of Japanese kamikaze pilots who 'were burdened with the destiny of dying for their country', because they believed in Japan's mission.[18] As a national leader Abe has been quoted many times to illustrate how central to Japanese memory was the sincerity of their wartime leaders' beliefs – yet he fails to recognise the consequences their actions wrought for Japan and Asia and that after 1945 many were considered war criminals. Abe and others remain fixated on the fact that these officials did have a set of convictions that drove them.[19]

Love statues and war criminals

Not long after Japan regained its sovereignty in 1952 and amid grow-ing public pressure to parole or release those still imprisoned as war criminals, the Japanese were already discussing how to memorialise their soldiers' sacrifice. In 1955, a decade after the embarrassing renam-ing of the 'Eight Corners of the World Under One Roof' Tower in Miyazaki prefecture, visitors and passers-by at one of the capital's main rail and subway stations would have noticed a new and unique landmark. Adjacent to its southern entrance, on a massive white pedestal stood a tall bronze statue. Several meters high and named *Agape* after the Greek word for love, the sculpture is better known as 'ai no zô' ('the statue of love'). The naked and muscular statue of the young man is poised athletically, his arms raised toward the heav-ens, as if praying for peace.[20] There are no tell-tale signs that the statue actually represented a country's mourning for those whom the Japanese believed were 'unfairly' or 'unjustly' executed following the post-1945 war crimes trials. The national grief may have been palpable and the statue may have mollified many, but it failed to open a wider debate about the actual nature of war crimes and what such legal procedures signified about the nature of Japan's war. Peace cannot be cherished without full disclosure of what preceded it.

The driving force behind the erection of the 'love statue' was Tajima Ryûjun, the senior Buddhist clergyman who served at Japan's Sugamo Prison. He offered spiritual guidance to BC class war criminals incar-cerated for lengthy terms or sentenced to death. Tajima propounded a particular philosophical view of the end of the war and of the Allies' aggressive attempts to find justice. His views on wartime culpability and responsibility were patently shaped by Buddhist beliefs concern-ing death and the afterlife. Tajima asserted that the conclusion of the Second World War, with its chaotic pursuit of justice and the subsequent commitment to peace, actually created a society that never found solace. In his memoirs of his time ministering at the Sugamo Prison he wrote, 'In the midst of the closure of the Second World War the omens portending the next world war were already apparent. The countries that are making efforts to attain "justice and peace" are actually, in effect, pushing the world toward the precipice of suicide through such action. It is, if one can put such a label on it, a great paradox'.[21] Tajima aimed to make the world aware of the suffering of Japanese war criminals at the hands of Cold War superpowers, including America and the European authorities. For him they were merely playing a game of political chess. Tajima never explicitly commented on the war itself, only on its ambiguous aftermath, and thus he avoided confronting the real issues at stake more directly.

Tajima served as the Buddhist chaplain at Sugamo Prison from 9 June 1949 and he was particularly committed to counselling lower ranking war criminals of the BC class who had been sentenced to death. He was also a professor at Taisho University in Tokyo. Soon after Japan regained its sovereignty, Tajima, supported by other luminaries in the world of Buddhist clergy, began a petition movement to assist the war criminals. He even made radio broadcasts imploring his listeners to feel compassion for the convicted. For his efforts he received a distinguished service award from the Minister of Justice in July 1952.[22]

It was the chaplain's belief that what the prisoners wrote in their last testaments was marked by a particular purity; that, in a sense, they had become true men, stripped down to their barest thoughts and emotions and were therefore worthy of respect in their final moments.[23] While it is easy to disagree with Tajima's philosophical assessment, his motives as a chaplain are hard to question. Yet his thoughts seem to consider the war criminals more than their victims, or even possibly their crimes, and he suggested the notion that their guilt was wiped away with their deaths. Tajima ardently espoused that people, and more specifically the Japanese nation, could use the horrors of the Second World War as a chance to renew its post-war society fundamentally. To achieve such a goal required finding in oneself that love for one's fellow men which the statue outside Tokyo Station was meant to express, a love seemingly absent from the decisions handed down in Allied courts which condemned former Japanese soldiers to death. The Buddhist clergyman maintained that Japanese war criminals were the products of a somewhat twisted world – which supposedly sought justice by killing the innocent. Tajima ultimately believed that in their deaths these men had a message of life and love to bequeath to the world.

After the end of Japan's domestic BC class trials, which were entirely managed by US officials, Tajima helped to publish a massive collection of the last wills and testaments of many of these war criminals – some of whom were, no doubt, wrongly convicted while others were guilty. He had collected these documents from throughout Japan and abroad, including China, sometimes by clandestine means. In Tajima's words, 'the goal of war is to attain the death of one's opponent, and in pursuit of such an aim we end up desiring our own deaths. In this manner, Japanese were taught that death was the most holy attainment of the soul'.[24] The initial chapter of this compilation brought together writings from soldiers who were executed in China. These showed that what many of the men hoped for, when they were penning their last diaries and testaments, was not to die in vain. Most maintained that the entire objective of Japan's war in East Asia had been to establish peace. The men who were executed in China often hoped that, 'our deaths serve as an opportunity for China and Japan to join together, stand as a human sacrifice to peace in East Asia. In this way I can be pleased that world peace will come about. No matter what I only pray that I do not die a dog's death and hope that my death will not be in vain. Long live China! Long live Japan! Long live the emperor!'[25]

Entitled *The Century's Last Will and Testaments*, the compilation became a bestseller and the profits, along with some further donations, paid for the construction of the 'love' statue. In his quest to translate these 'pure' thoughts into action, Tajima helped to commemorate the lost souls of these condemned BC class war criminals out of a conviction that their memory should not be forgotten amidst post-war animosity.[26] Instead of standing for hatred and war, the soldiers should be recalled in love, he hoped, a love that would aid in helping future Japanese generations find the true path toward fulfilment and better human understanding. A copy of *The Century's Last Will and Testaments* was placed in the stone foundation of the statue. On the pedestal Tajima himself wrote the calligraphy for the character *ai* ('love'), that is engraved into the statue base.

Tajima's monument was not hidden away in a peripheral location. It graced the front area of the major railway junction of Japan's capital city, and this demonstrates that his opinion on war criminals enjoyed wide support among the general public. Just before the occupation ended and after, groups like the Association to Help Those Sentenced For the War (Sensô jukeisha sewakai) formed. They worked for the construction of such memorials and a larger public discussion unfolded on the plight of convicted BC class war criminals and their legacy. Soon-to-be Prime Minister Kishi Nobusuke – arrested as a war criminal but later released and never charged – was on the association's executive board, as were many other wartime political and military luminaries: Ogata Taketora had been wartime head of the *Asahi* newspaper and later served as Minister of State in two of Prime Minister Yoshida Shigeru's Cabinets. Shigemitsu Mamoru had been convicted as a war criminal but later served as Foreign Minister. Arita Hachirô had been Foreign Minister during the war and Ayukawa Yoshisuke was a pre-war industrialist who had significant economic ties to Manchukuo. After the war he was arrested and imprisoned in Sugamo although he was never brought to trial. Eventually, Ayukawa became the executive director of the Association to Help Those Sentenced For the War and served in the upper house of the Diet.[27]

Mirroring Tajima's attitude, the Association to Help Those Sentenced For the War aimed to 'offer assistance and help to those convicted or executed for war crimes, as well as the families and relations of those affected, to promote the financial support of surviving families of those executed, and to pray for the spirits of the martyred'. The association's manifesto of April 1952 clarified its position on the whole issue of war crimes. War criminals, it seems, had no place in East Asia's post-war order because, as was shown by the so-called 'victor's justice' of the Tokyo War Crimes Trial, wartime propagandistic goals now melded almost seamlessly into the post-1945 period. The assistance group publicly stated that 'there are various opinions regarding war crimes but equally these men were following orders for the sake of the country. Due to the circumstances of the defeat these soldiers became victims of sorts'.[28]

The fact that Tajima's statue bore no real explanation of its meaning, except the Chinese character for 'love' and the Greek word for it carved on the front, is emblematic of post-war Japan's hazy understanding of the history of BC war criminals. Such an omission suggests historical equivocation or a belief that the historical chapter of the BC war criminals should help to energise the nation to rebuild and reconstruct a country virtually destroyed by the war. And in a sense the Japanese population supported such beliefs. Japan's economic white paper of 1956 used the phrase 'we are no longer in the post-war' (*mohaya sengo de wa nai*).

The 'love statue' thus epitomises the country's ambivalent reactions to the war crimes trials of average soldiers, of men who had followed orders on the ground and thus implemented Japan's policies throughout the empire.[29] An exploration of the ways in which the Japanese viewed war crimes and how this translated into monuments expressing lamentation but not empathy for others thus makes it possible to measure how intent post-war Japan was on pursuing a meaningful peace agenda in East Asia. How did the population deal with the post-war prosecutions of more than 5,000 individuals accused of war crimes? Cold War legal processes remained heavily laden with the baggage of wartime propaganda and the rhetorical legacy spilled into post-war history. The *longue durée* of the post-war period, the large number of venues across Asia where Japanese war crimes trials took place, and the fact that war criminals were being repatriated from across Asia to Japan right up until the 1960s, generated conflicting opinions on how the end of Japan's empire and the war in Asia could be judged in legal terms. Here, we can see the naked contours of post-war peace in Japan. Japan's sudden surrender in no way signified that the country would immediately disavow its extensive imperial ideology; such a move would be a long time in the making.

It is because of this disjunction between the goal of peace and the failure to pursue it in any meaningful manner in the immediate post-war period that there was such tension between the general discontent with Japan's predicament in the Cold War and the efforts to create a visual representation of empire. 1952 was a new dawn for Japan. The country felt ready to regain its sovereignty after the successful conclusion of the San Francisco Peace Treaty the previous year. To mark Japan's return as a sovereign nation and the reacquisition of authority over its own legal system, the government offered an amnesty to a variety of criminals. This was meant to be a benevolent gesture to honour the country's 'new' future. Most of these individuals had committed minor offences such as violating electoral laws, contravening the purge ordinances or failing to pay their taxes. But not everyone in Japan was pleased with these changes because there had been enormous expectations that as a result of the country's peaceful relations with its neighbours, war criminals would naturally be released. Japan's new status appeared to mean that some regular criminals were set free, but war criminals continued to languish in prison. Increasingly loud public voices thus began to interrogate the nature of the post-war peace that Japan had adopted.

As the circumstances of Japan's post-war fortunes changed, these suspicions gave rise to an internalised debate about the very nature of post-war peace and justice. On 2 June 1952 former Japanese naval military attaché Toyoda Kumao, now employed by the Ministry of Health and Welfare to collect material on the BC class war crimes trials, wrote a memo on the release of 'so-called war criminals' and emphasised the urgent need to reduce their sentences. Toyoda was an important figure in post-war Japan's efforts to protect its own leaders from war crimes trials. When Japan regained its independence, Toyoda wrote that the only problem left after the ratification of the peace treaty was to resolve the war criminal issue, but Article 11 of the San Francisco peace treaty made this a very thorny problem. This clause stipulated not only that Japan had to accept the judgments of the International Military Tribunal for the Far East and of other Allied War Crimes Courts both within and outside Japan, but more importantly that 'the power to grant clemency, to reduce sentences and to parole with respect to such prisoners may not be exercised except on the decision of the Government or Governments which imposed the sentence in each instance, and on recommendation of Japan. In the case of persons sentenced by the International Military Tribunal for the Far East, such power may not be exercised except on the decision of a majority of the Governments represented on the Tribunal, and on the recommendation of Japan'.[30] Fundamentally, even though Japan was sovereign by the letter of the law, it was not given full legal jurisdiction over its own post-war war criminals. Such stipulations further convinced the Japanese that they were being victimised.

In addition, Toyoda and his co-workers underscored other factors that stymied Japan's efforts at resolving the war crimes issues and thus impeded Japan's commitment to post-war peace: Japan possessed hardly any of the records of the BC class trials and therefore the Japanese government had no grounds on which to build a case to ask for reduced sentences. Toyoda's comments were not all off target. He wrote that there were even cases where fabricated evidence was presented but death sentences were nevertheless handed down and carried out. Because limits were imposed on defence teams, especially in trials outside of Japan, and defendants usually had limited access to effective legal defence, the trials were tainted. Testimony was often given years after the event and based on shaky memories. Toyoda asserted that the Japanese military was often defending itself or that the alleged crime had taken place during battles, but after 1945 this behaviour was judged a 'war crime'. Sentencing was varied and imposed without comparable standards, while some judges had previously been prisoners of war of the Japanese so they were biased, he claimed. Often translators were in short supply, his report highlighted.[31] The belief that post-war international law operated short-sighted justice ran deep in Japan.

All of these controversial and highly topical discussions would have been evoked – if only subconsciously – by the 'love statue', based, as it was – financially and literally – on the supposedly pure final words of convicted war criminals. The seemingly bland message of *Agape* delivered by the plaintive bronze in the centre of Tokyo was therefore much more than met the eye. In the context of a post-war society recovering only very slowly from the wounds of defeat and loss of empire, 'love' as well as 'peace' could mean many different things.

Enshrining heroic victims

Hope for an afterlife for the executed BC class war criminals links the 'love statue' to one of the most famous Shinto sanctuaries: Yasukuni Shrine.[32] If a historical dialogue exists between the dead and the world of the living, that portal is provided by the Yasukuni Shrine. Erected just after the Meiji Restoration in 1868 to honour men who had helped to restore the emperor to the throne and operated jointly by the imperial armed forces, it was deemed superior to other shrines. The issue of enshrinement involves deep introspection and is linked to Japanese religious and philosophical ideas about life and death. It is a relatively simple ritual that invites the spirit of the deceased to reside in a particular location, in this case in a national shrine. However, because Yasukuni is for those who died for the emperor or in his name and thus for the nation, enshrinement there takes on a much darker and more important political hue.[33] Yasukuni quickly became a tourist attraction as early as the 1870s and from 1874 onwards all soldiers who died for Japan's colonial expansion were enshrined there. The shrine's sacred mission was thus intimately linked to Japan's imperialism.[34] As historian Akazawa Shirô explains, the veneration and celebration of those lost in Japan's last war in this shrine makes Yasukuni an excellent yardstick with which to measure their position in Japanese society.[35]

In 1978, Japan's class A war criminals – those found guilty by an international court of law in the Tokyo War Crimes Trial – were commemorated at the Yasukuni Shrine. Many reacted with shock to this decision. It caused domestic outrage and triggered numerous, but ultimately unsuccessful, lawsuits. There were also complaints that this decision infringed on the post-war separation of religion and state. Beyond Japan, South Korean and Taiwanese groups launched separate legal objections. The historian Tanaka Nobumasa summed up such frustrations when he asked: 'To whom does the memory of the war dead belong?'[36] Because of their belief in the 'justness' of wartime actions, conservatives failed to see that these very actions had led to the ruin of the country. All that mattered then and now was the sincerity of the individual's belief. Progressive members of Japanese society were incensed by the move to memorialise war criminals in a sacred shrine. Adding weight to their cause Emperor Hirohito, who had visited the shrine since 1952, was later discovered to have stopped his yearly visits to the site in 1979 after he had learnt that the shrine had decided to pacify the spirits of convicted war criminals.[37]

Since the war criminals honoured in this way (A, B and C class) had often been convicted for their actions overseas, enshrinement also brought with it significant consequences for foreign policy and international relations. There were other contested issues, too. Having fought for their country and subsequently suffered death by execution, were these men different from other wartime dead? If Japan had won the war, would they not have been decorated? This popular counterfactual refrain completely avoids the fact that Japan actually suffered defeat. More importantly, this one-sided debate avoids the core issue of analysing war crimes themselves by implying that their nature only depended on subsequent developments. As an early post-war Japanese government summary of the matter proclaimed, these men 'happened to be saddled with the stigma of being labelled "war criminals" so therefore they differed from the average war soldier who died on the battlefield'. If they were not enshrined at the Yasukuni Shrine, their families and their spirits would remain in a state of limbo.[38]

This logic distorted to a certain extent the fundamental issue because it failed to address whether wartime behaviour was right or wrong – regardless of its perceived intentions. On 2 December 1965 the Tokyo *Asahi* newspaper ran a column entitled 'When will the spirits of those judged as war criminals make their way to Yasukuni Shrine?' The head priest at the time declared that there must be no bias. The war had created many who needed to be enshrined. For BC class war criminals the shrine completed this lengthy task in October 1966.[39] In this manner all the Japanese war criminals and some other nationalities were enshrined in a location whose entrance is still marked by two massive stone lanterns which bear bronze plaques glorifying Japan's imperial wars. The 'Enrich the Country and Draft Soldiers' Insurance Conglomerate donated these massive pillars in 1935 to celebrate the company's 10th anniversary at a cost of 300 million yen, a staggering sum at the time. One was to commemorate the battles of the Imperial Navy and the other honoured the Imperial Army. Interestingly, during the post-war occupation of Japan the bronze reliefs of imperial victories were cemented over. But these covers were removed and the images restored in April 1957 (Figure 5.1).[40] While the Miyazaki tower was reappropriated and Commander Hirose's statue destroyed, these visual representations of the empire survived.

Commemorating the convicted

The 'love statue' and the public art at imperial sites of memory such as the Yasukuni Shrine continue to engage the Japanese public in heated debates about the proper way to commemorate the war. They invite a much more morally ambivalent question: what did war criminals represent and should Japan conceive of them as victims or perpetrators?[41] A small monument on the former site of Sugamo Prison offers a third set of differing values surrounding this historical contestation.

Beginning in the 1960s, on the cusp of Japan's high speed economic growth and in the context of the massive reurbanisation programme that followed the 1964 Tokyo Olympics, the ground around where the Sugamo Prison once stood became the centre for one of Tokyo's main redevelopment zones, later called Sunshine City. On 3 July 1964 the *Yomiuri* newspaper reported that members of the Bereaved Families Group would like the execution site, where A class war criminals had been put to death, to be memorialised.[42] The national government had

5.1 The stone lantern and bronze reliefs at the entrance of
the Yasukuni Shrine

set aside 6,000 square meters of precious urban landscape to enable
the local council to create a 'peace park'. However, there was much
discord within Japanese society as to what form of monument was
acceptable. This stemmed primarily from local educational and religious groups opposed to such a memorialisation because in their
eyes this was tantamount to valorising Japan's historical militarism.
The local citizens protested that using public money to memorialise
imperial Japanese General Tôjô Hideki and the six other class A war

criminals who were tried in the International Military Tribunal for the Far East (colloquially known as the Tokyo War Crimes Trial) and later executed for pushing Japan into an 'aggressive and illegal' war was in itself illegal and immoral. The citizens filed lawsuits and requested that the money be returned. The plaintiffs observed that such a memorial blatantly glorified Japan's war and could lead to remilitarisation.[43]

It took more than a decade and a half until a compromise decision was finally reached, but even that seemed one-sided. Both progressives and conservatives hoped to create a *lieu de mémoire* in the garden but they failed to agree on the shape and tone of the memorial. The issue worked its way slowly through the Japanese bureaucracy until January 1980. The Toyoshima local council, a part of Tokyo, eventually received carte blanche and they intended to erect a memorial on the very site of the execution chamber.[44] The council organised numerous consultations in an attempt to move the process forward only to be continually stymied by residents who vehemently disagreed.

The monument that resulted from this tortuous process appears to satisfy nobody and fails to tally with any of the views on the meaning of the war and its victims (Figure 5.2). A boulder, just over five foot

5.2 The memorial at the site of the Sugamo Prison

tall and eight foot wide, was placed on the historic spot. The provenance and the designer of this rather bland memorial are not noted in the park nor was it explained in newspapers at the time. It was as if the local council had, unilaterally and under the cover of darkness, created a monument which they knew would displease some residents. The front facade of the rock facing the small area of the main park square bears the Japanese inscription 'Pray for Peace'. To see the inscription on the back visitors have to crouch down and hunch over while standing in the muddy area behind the monument. The text, missed by all but the most determined, reads: 'After the end of World War Two, on this spot the Military Tribunals for the Far East and other Allied military tribunals that adjudicated war crimes meted out executions. In order not to repeat the tragedy of war, we [Japanese] dedicate this spot to such memory and erect this monument'. The monument thus portrays – in a more or less clandestine way – the Japanese as passive recipients of fierce Allied 'justice' since the Japanese nation is accorded no agency in its own culpability or responsibility. Further strengthened by the fact that the Japanese population and government never pursued any of their own war criminals, justice concerning such matters appears as a sanction imposed from above, by an agency outside of Japan, in this case by the occupation forces and Allies in general.

Even after the erection of the monument, local residents continued to complain to the local council and to express their dissatisfaction to the courts, stipulating that their government had constructed a memorial that 'twisted the facts of history and gave the impression that war criminals were victims or martyrs for the country'. Along with other reasons the memorial was, in the words of the citizens' opposition, illegal.[45] In sum, the two sides were not necessarily antagonistic toward the idea of a monument in general, but some residents of the area stated they demanded a monument dedicated to remembering world peace rather than a monument dedicated to the war crimes trials, or the war criminals themselves, as the local government desired. The issue had grown from a local concern to a national debate and featured within a growing movement opposing a specific war crimes memorial.[46]

Conclusion

This discussion has focused on four sculptural representations of modern Japanese history: the Miyazaki Peace-War Tower, a wartime monument that was so large that removal would have been much harder than simply transposing it from a monument that glorified

Japan's empire to one that celebrated an often trumpeted yet rarely implemented vague idea of peace; an ill-defined anthropomorphic vision of peace in the shape of the 'love statue' which bears no inscription explaining its deeper meaning; the Yasukuni Shrine which ties Japan's executed war criminals into a revered continuity of imperial greatness and martial pride; and a former prison space turned into a thriving business district where the war is remembered on the back of a boulder with a vague reference to 'praying for peace'. To this could be added the many other monuments honouring executed war criminals that have been erected at Buddhist temples throughout Japan.

The legacy of war and subsequent peace reverberates in contemporary Japanese history, mirroring the social discord caused by differences over how to design Japan's war memorials. If one were to generalise, the hawkish side – most recently represented by Prime Minister Abe Shinzô – sees value in cherishing Japan's imperial past because soldiers showed pride in their dedication to their country and their values. The opposition asserts that Japan should not and cannot memorialise those who perished in the name of war because that only compounds Japan's feelings of victimisation and disregards the entire history of Japan's role in its own victimisation and in the suffering of others caused by the country's imperial aggression. The crux of the matter is that, ironically, both sides field their opinions under the banner of peace – even though neither is really promoting such an ideal.

The Japanese war criminal is both a victim, as sculpted into the bronze 'love statue', but simultaneously he is a hero, apotheosised at Yasukuni and other shrines around the country, dying for the sake of the Japanese nation. The historian M. G. Sheftall has analysed the similar pattern of the glorification of kamikaze pilots (officially known as *tokkôtai*) in post-war Japan. They have also been reborn as hero-victims. According to Sheftall the 'historical figure of the *tokkô* pilot offers the tantalising potential of being simultaneously dashing hero, sterling role model and victim of historical forces beyond his control (a qualification conveniently obfuscating the causality implications of Japan's decision to wage the war in the first place). He is both a lamb and a lion, a figure on whom little or no moral censure can be levied'.[47]

Tajima, the sympathetic and religiously driven clergyman at Sugamo, wished to assist the public in recalling the lamb side of this equation. It would be a disservice to the memory of the other victims, those with no voice, no family and no shrines to remember them, though, if this were the only form of memory carved into stone monuments and placed in front of rail stations or in public parks. Moreover, the love or lamb side barely recalls Japan's imperial history, using memorial

[88]

to reshape this era through monuments that often only comment on the end of war and not its origins. The narrative and memory of war crimes trials is a harsh but painful reminder of the legacy of the Japanese Empire. Rightly or sometimes wrongly managed and perhaps misguided, they still aimed to place the pursuit of justice over revenge or retribution and this should be reflected in the visual representation that succeeded the events. The question remains if Japanese memorial iconography reflects that necessary angle of the narrative.

The four commemorative sites discussed in this chapter emphatically demonstrate the intertwined and conflicted nature of even the most basic elements of post-imperial political and memorial culture in contemporary Japan. Each edifice specifically relates to Japan's domestic debate, in its association with shared perceptions of what the war meant for the nation. At the same time, these sites also house various physical embodiments of Japan's loss of empire. The two sides are, of course, intimately related and yet at times push the society in opposite directions in terms of producing sharply divided opinions regarding the fundamental question of the meaning of the war and the subsequent significance of the losses that followed.

Notes

1 Y. Totani, *The Tokyo War Crimes Trial: The Pursuit of Justice in the Wake of World War II* (Cambridge, Mass.: Harvard University Asia Center, 2008), and R. Minear, *Victors' Justice: the Tokyo War Crimes Trial* (Princeton: Princeton University Press, 1971). See also Y. Tanaka, T. McCormack and G. Simpson (eds), *Beyond Victor's Justice? The Tokyo War Crimes Trial Revisited* (Leiden: Brill, 2011).

2 H. Yoshinobu, *Tôkyô saiban*, Kôdansha, pp. 27–8; Y. Totani, *The Tokyo War Crimes Trials*, pp. 20–3.

3 Kang Sang-jun, *Ajia kara nihon o tou* (Iwanami bokkuretto no. 336, Iwanami shoten, 1994), pp. 12–13.

4 It should be noted, though, that the Hiroshima Peace Museum has adapted its exhibition to include references to Koreans and Western prisoners of war who died during the atomic bombing.

5 J. Tran, 'From Yokohama to Manchuria: a Photography Based Investigation of Nostalgia in the Construction of Japanese Landscape' (PhD thesis, University of the Arts London, 2005).

6 S. Saaler, 'Men in Metal: Representation of the Nation in Public Space in Meiji Japan, 1868–1912', *Comparativ* 19 (2009), p. 29.

7 See A. Smith, *Myths and Memories of the Nation* (Oxford: Oxford University Press, 2000), p. 17.

8 K. Smith, 'The Shôwa Hall: Memorializing Japan's War at Home', *The Public Historian* 24:4 (2002), p. 35.

9 For a full explanation of this slogan and the problems faced in explaining it, see B. Kushner, *The Thought War – Imperial Japanese Propaganda* (Honolulu: University of Hawaii Press, 2006), pp. 29–30.

10 B. Kushner, 'Going for the Gold – Health and Sports in Japan's Quest for Modernity' in W. Tsutsui and M. Baskett (eds), *The East Asian Olympiads, 1934–2008: Building Bodies and Nations in Japan, Korea, and China* (Folkestone: Global Oriental, 2011),

PART I: MONUMENTS

pp. 34–48; S. Collins, *The 1940 Tokyo Games: The Missing Olympics: Japan, the Asian Olympics and the Olympic Movement* (London: Routledge, 2007).

11 W. Edwards, 'Forging Tradition for a Holy War: The "Hakkō Ichiu" Tower in Miyazaki and Japanese Wartime Ideology', *Journal of Japanese Studies* 29:2 (2003), 289–324, p. 291. See also K. Ruoff, *Imperial Japan at Its Zenith: The Wartime Celebration of the Empire's 2,600th Anniversary* (Ithaca: Cornell University Press, 2010).

12 W. Edwards, 'Forging Tradition', p. 321.

13 N. Shimazu, 'Popular Representations of the Past: The Case of Postwar Japan', *Journal of Contemporary History* 38:1 (2003), 101–16, p. 101.

14 K. Sang-jung, *Ajia kara nihon o tou*, pp. 12–13.

15 B. Kushner, *Dreams of Empire: Japanese Propaganda Textiles* (Brussels: MHJ Collection, 2011); and I. Yoshiko, *Zusetsu kimonogara ni miru sensō* (Tokyo: Inpakutoshuppankai, 2007).

16 'Shōgun no dōzō – dō suru gunkoku no shōchō', *Yomiuri Shimbun* (10 June 1946); and 'Kieta Tokyo meibutsu', *Yomiuri shimbun* (23 July 1947).

17 I. Nish, 'Regaining Confidence – Japan after the Loss of Empire', *Journal of Contemporary History* 15:1, special issue on Imperial Hangovers (1980), 181–95, p. 190; A. Shinichi, *Sensō sekininron: gendaishi kara no toi* (Tokio: Iwanami shoten, 2005), p. 119.

18 A. Shinzô, *Utsukushii kuni e* (Tokio: Bunshun shinsho, 2006), p. 107.

19 *Ibid.*, p. 68.

20 The statue was removed in 2007 during the remodelling of the station and was slated to return. However, in January 2013 when I asked J. R. Rail, who manage the Tokyo Station, about a specific date they replied that currently the statue was in storage and it was unclear when and if it would return.

21 T. Shinyû (ed.), *Tajima Ryûjun no shôgai* (Ryûjunjizôsonhôsankai, 2006), from the preface.

22 *Ibid.*, p. 83.

23 *Ibid.*, p. 89.

24 S. I. Hensankai (ed.), *Seiki no isho* (Tokio: Shinkosha, 1953), Tajima Ryûjun, preface, p. 2.

25 *Ibid.*, p. 4.

26 *Mainichi Shimbun*, 20 April 2009.

27 National Archives of Japan, Tokyo, 4A-022-00, Hei 11 hômu 07314100, 'Saikin no senpan kankei jôkyô ni tsuite renraku kaisô'.

28 *Ibid.*

29 I elaborate more on this issue in my book *Men to Devils, Devils to Men: Japanese War Crimes and Chinese Justice* (forthcoming from Harvard University Press).

30 Treaty of Peace with Japan. www.taiwandocuments.org/sanfrancisco01.htm (accessed 26 November 2012).

31 'Iwayuru "zhanfan" no shakuhô, genkai nado ni taisuru ippan kankoku no jûyô kyûsei ni tuite no iken', National Archives Japan, Tokyo, hei11 – 4A. 21 5872, *Sensô saiban sankô shiryô*, 2 June 1952.

32 M. R. Mullins, 'How Yasukuni Shrine Survived the Occupation: A Critical Examination of Popular Claims', *Monumenta Nipponica* 65:1 (2010), pp. 89–136.

33 H. Ikuhiko, *Yasukuni jinja no saijintachi* (Tokio: Shinchôsha, 2010), pp. 13–15.

34 John Breen's edited volume analyses the complexities of the Yasukuni Shrine from a variety of angles. J. Breen (ed.), *Yasukuni – the War Dead and the Struggle for Japan's Past* (London: Hurst and Co., 2007).

35 A. Shirô, *Yasukuni jinja* (Tokio: Iwanami shoten, 2005), p. 60.

36 The full international and domestic reaction to the enshrinement is the focus of T. Nobumasa, *Dokyumento, yasukuni jinja soshô – senshisha no kioku wa dare no mono ka* (Tokio: Iwanami shoten, 2007).

37 'Yasukuni jinja A kyû senpan shôwa tennô gôshi fuyukai de bunshiron ni ikioi', *Yomiuri Shimbun* (20 July 2006, evening edition); A. Shimbunsha (ed.), *Shimbun to shōwa* (Tokio: Asahi shuppansha, 2010), pp. 462–3.

38 Yasukuni Archives, Tokyo, 393.4, Inoue Tadao shiryô, *Senpan shakuhôshiyô*, p. 755.
39 Yasukuni Archives, Tokyo, 393.4, Inoue Tadao shiryô, *Senpan shakuhôshiyô*, pp. 755–6.
40 Tokyoto rekishi kyôikusha kyôgikai (ed.), *Tokyo no sensô to heiwa o aruku* (Hiroshima: Heiwa bunka, 2008), p. 57.
41 See J. Orr, *The Victim as Hero: Ideologies of Peace and National Identity in Postwar Japan* (Honolulu: University of Hawai'i Press, 2001).
42 *Yomiuri Shimbun* (3 July 1964, morning edition).
43 *Yomiuri Shimbun* (29 May 1984, morning edition).
44 *Yomiuri Shimbun* (12 January 1980, morning edition). The problem with how to deal with images of the wartime that linger psychologically in post-1945 Japan but also in its former colonies that have since become tourism resorts, has also been poignantly analysed by Y. Makoto, *Guam to Nihonjin – sensô o umetate gakuen* (Tokio: Iwanami shoten, 2007).
45 *Yomiuri Shimbun* (16 August 1984).
46 *Yomiuri Shimbun* (12 January 1980, morning edition).
47 M. G. Sheftall, 'Tokkô Zaidan: A Case Study of Institutional Japanese War Memorialisation', in S. Saaler and W. Schwentker (eds), *The Power of Memory in Modern Japan* (London: Global Oriental, 2008), pp. 54–77, 61.

PART II

Heroes and villains

CHAPTER SIX

From the penny press to the plinth: British and French 'heroic imperialists' as sites of memory

Berny Sèbe

What could statues in London, Chatham, Gravesend and Melbourne; a commemorative service in Khartoum Cathedral; the cathedral itself; a stream of biographies published continuously since the mid-1880s; a secondary school in Woking; and an educational institution in the Anglo-Egyptian Sudan possibly have in common? What may appear to be a disorderly enumeration of motley elements reflects in fact the multi-faceted expressions of a phenomenon which left a deep imprint on late Victorian Britain: they all commemorated, either as their sole role or as an additional purpose, the memory of the imperial super-hero Charles George Gordon (1833–85), whose death at the hands of the Sudanese Mahdi's fighters received extensive media coverage at the time of the 'New Imperialism'. The imperial officer's name, character, achievements and even his face and dress became loaded with high symbolic value for many generations. The weight of this heroic reputation was sustained and developed through the repetition of a variety of occasional or permanent commemorative iterations. Taken together, these varied celebratory manifestations had the power to turn the reputations attached to prominent imperial heroes such as General Gordon into *imperial sites of memory*, often in the material sense, and always symbolically.

This chapter looks at a particular, but arguably influential, instance of the intertwining between imperial and national history: the figure of the 'heroic imperialist' who came to prominence against the back-drop of the 'New Imperialism'. These 'heroes' contributed to shape the mind-set of late-nineteenth-century British and French 'imagined communities' in ways which were long ignored, in spite of the fact that they came to embody the 'civilizing mission' which was routinely invoked to justify Britain's and France's overseas expansion.[1] Pierre Nora's concept of *site of memory* offers a useful way of encompassing the various means through which imperial heroes (who, taken together, created a new heroic model) became vectors of symbols and meaning in the collective memory of the two countries. The *lieu de mémoire* is not understood here as linked to a specific place (e.g. Versailles or Verdun), but rather as resulting from the accumulation over time and space of a variety of celebratory initiatives (mediated intellectually and physically), turning the reputations of these heroes into elements of national consciousness. The concept makes it possible to trace the translation of an individual existence into a *lieu de mémoire* of national significance, considering the modalities of this process which allowed a handful of conquerors to enter the Pantheon of 'public memory'.

The chapter begins with an attempt to historicise the development of these 'heroic reputations', exploring the influence of the mass-media, and the socio-cultural and political circumstances in nineteenth-century Britain and France. It was this context which made their rise to fame not only possible, but – from the point of view of a range of 'hero-makers' – positively desirable.[2] The concept of 'hero-maker' refers to a variety of cultural, economic or political intermediaries, often in a position of power within their own field, who contributed to the development of a heroic reputation. They did so for a number of reasons: for their own personal benefit, on behalf of an interest group or simply out of genuine admiration for the individual whom they were lionising. The chapter then considers long-term memorialisation processes which turned what could have been fleeting celebrity episodes into persistent commemorations. Remarkably, these reputations were not ephemeral: a variety of cultural productions (often state-sponsored, but also on other occasions reflecting specific interests) ensured their resilience over the following decades. Official celebrations in the urban space (street naming, commemorative monuments, statues, or the christening of institutions, to name but a few) echoed a variety of popular cultural products such as detailed reports of heroic deeds in newspapers and illustrated magazines, hagiographic books, postcards, cigarette and chocolate cards, and other forms of collectables. Later, there would even be full-length feature films. These phenomena deeply entrenched the reputations of imperial heroes in the imaginary landscape of the two nations. The chapter also looks beyond metropolitan and colonial perceptions: it considers the place of imperial heroism in the colonies before independence, and the post-colonial management of the symbolic and material legacy of these heroic reputations in newly independent countries as well as in the former metropoles.

Empirical evidence to illustrate these processes can be drawn from a range of case-studies, from individuals who rose to fame in the late nineteenth and early twentieth centuries: the explorer Pierre Savorgnan de Brazza (1852–1905), the imperialist entrepreneur Cecil Rhodes (1853–1902), the officers Charles George Gordon (1833–85), Horatio-Herbert Kitchener (1850–1916) and Jean-Baptiste Marchand (1853–1934), and the religious figures David Livingstone (1813–73) and Charles de Foucauld (1858–1916). Each of these exemplifies a particular aspect of imperial heroism. The object of a personality cult from the 1880s onwards, Brazza was celebrated as a peaceful conqueror championing freedom, the end of slavery, and France's national interest. The French public was fascinated by his single-handed conquest of the French Congo, against the wishes of his own government (which was reluctant to annex new possessions in Central Africa). There was also the much talked-about episode when Brazza's Senegalese sergeant, Malamine Kamara, repelled Stanley's attempt to annex the right bank of the Congo.

The architect of British paramountcy in southern Africa, the diamond magnate and South African political figure Rhodes epitomises the triumph of jingoism through aggressive imperialism. The other two heroes became noted sites of memory in the metropoles, though they did not leave any lasting legacy in Africa itself. In the wake of the Fashoda crisis that brought Britain and France to the brink of war over the control of the Upper Nile (1898), Captain Marchand and the Sirdar Kitchener 'of Khartoum' rose to prominence and quickly became, for different but equally potent reasons, major figures of the imperial imaginary of the two countries. Fashoda itself was an insignificant place, and following the *Entente Cordiale* the British were eager to bury any historical echo by discreetly renaming it 'Kodok'. However, the two heroes who had met there, each after an epic but under-publicised odyssey, and whose gentlemanly behaviour made it possible to avert open conflict, established themselves as household names in their home countries. They remained celebrities long after the dust had settled in the Upper Nile region. Lastly, David Livingstone and Charles de Foucauld exemplify the association of religious missionary work, exploration and national pursuit, in their respective periods and geographical areas of action (Southern and Central Africa in the mid-nineteenth-century for Livingstone, and the Sahara in the late nineteenth and early twentieth centuries for Foucauld). This combination of roles and corresponding support bases have allowed them to arouse sustained public interest up to the present. Taken together, these six case studies suggest how specific actions, which could have generated a fleeting form of celebrity, were actually the building blocks out of which durable heroic reputations were constructed and strengthened over time. In the process they gained the status of national symbols, embodying the greatness of their country.

[97]

Mediated figures: turning imperial heroes into sites of cultural memory

Nineteenth-century imperial heroes were products of their time and reflected the impact of rapidly changing societies undergoing the processes associated with rapid industrialisation: higher literacy rates and better wages, the rise of the consumer society and the concomitant development of the mass-media (facilitated by constant technological progress, from the telegraph to the printing press) multiplied the number of outlets through which reputations could be promoted.[3] At a time of sharp increase in the production of cultural artefacts, imperial heroes soon became multi-media sites of memory. The secret of their success and longevity lay in the multiple layers of celebratory material which durably entrenched their reputations in the collective memory of British and French societies.

At a time when the power and appeal of the media were constantly growing, the printed word was generally the first step in the development of the reputation of a 'heroic imperialist'. Each of these popular individuals was a 'mediated figure', gaining meaning and reality through the exposure which they were granted in the press. The wide press coverage of exceptional or remarkable achievements in the daily and illustrated newspapers made the heroes of the day. The combination of sensationalism, patriotism and escapism, which imperial heroes offered, made them valued topics for newspaper journalists and editors, who dedicated space to these stories out of commercial calculation or personal commitment to the cause of the empire or the hero (or both). The most emblematic of these instances where journalistic self-interest and imperial hero-making converged was certainly the publicity stunt that was H. M. Stanley's search for David Livingstone in the heart of Central Africa. The adventure propelled both the journalist and his subject to worldwide fame.[4] In France, news of the exploratory feats of Savorgnan de Brazza in Central Africa generated a high level of media interest: the press cuttings generated by his expeditions to the Congo fill no fewer than eight boxes of the Brazza papers.[5]

Brazza was well-connected with aristocratic and influential families, most of them based in the affluent areas of the Faubourg Saint-Honoré and the Faubourg Saint-Germain. For instance, he counted among his acquaintances the three brothers Charmes: Francis, a later director of the literary journal *Revue des deux mondes*, Xavier, who worked for the Ministry of Public Instruction, and Gabriel, a prominent colonial publicist.[6] This extended network of influential patrons certainly played a role in the wide media echo of his action in Africa. These early popular celebrations were triggered primarily by the news agenda (often promoted diligently by colonial publicists or friends of the hero who pulled media levers), and it was extended by the official honours bestowed upon the heroes upon their return. Such was the case when Kitchener came back to Britain in November 1898, or when Marchand returned to France in June–July 1899, as exemplified in the press coverage of the triumphant 'Marchand days' of early June 1899 (see Figure 6.1).[7] The rise to prominence of the hero in the press resulted

6.1 *Le Petit Parisien* (11 June 1899) covering the official celebrations for Major Marchand upon his return to France

primarily from media interest (frequently triggered by effective publicists), and it could also benefit from some form of official recognition
(with the ceremonies fuelling even more media interest). This was
usually the first level of the pyramid of celebrity: broad-based and
solid foundations on to which other levels would be built, each
strengthening the edifice. Yet, if no other layers were added, it faced
the risk of falling into oblivion, quickly covered by sand pushed by
the winds of time.

The decisive step needed in order to consolidate reputations came
in the shape of illustrated magazines and, above all, books. Because
their life-span was much longer than newspapers, these publications
had the power to entrench a legend. Book and magazine publishers
also benefited from the socio-economic and technical progress of
the period: they could count on a wider public. There were also im-
provements in printing techniques which increased the appeal and
affordability of books and illustrated magazines. Thus, within just
18 months, the publisher William Blackwood managed to sell about
240,000 copies of *With Kitchener to Khartoum* by the *Daily Mail*
reporter George Warrington Steevens. This book was crucial in establishing the long-term reputation of the Sirdar Kitchener.[8] The Rhodes
legend was also established by a group of admiring biographers who
not only sought to establish Rhodes's heroic image, but who also did
their best to counter more critical narratives. For most of the twentieth century, they retained the upper hand.[9] In addition, special features in illustrated magazines, such as the *Illustrated London News*
or *L'Illustration*, or in geographically orientated reviews such as *Tour
du Monde*, were instrumental in strengthening the status of imperial
heroes as figures of general interest in the long term. This was a crucial step to turn what could have been a fleeting heroic status into
an established place in a national Pantheon of celebrated figures. This
phase of consolidation stemmed primarily from private and individual
interest, with authors and publishers seeking financial and personal
profit. This was summarised rather bluntly by William Blackwood
when he confided to Steevens that he hoped that they would 'hit the
nail on the head [that] time.'[10]

Once the story of an imperial hero had become part of the national
epic, official, state-sanctioned publications such as school textbooks
would often strengthen it and ensured that it would transcend generations. Included in the national curriculum, imperial heroes were often
closely associated with national destiny, and they embodied the ideal-
ised values which the authorities sought to inculcate in schoolchildren.
For instance, a French primary school textbook of 1928 contained a
stereotypical image of Brazza ordering a group of passing-by slaves to

be stopped, before proclaiming 'Everywhere where France's flag flies, there shall be no slaves'. The caption concluded that 'this proves that France is good and generous to the people which it has subjected'.[11] Imperial heroes like Brazza became symbolic intermediaries who personified the supposed liberation which French rule bestowed on the colonisers, and as such were turned into *loci* of imperial memory for generations of pupils.

With further technical developments intervening over the years, the mediated nature of imperial heroes was diversified, in particular following the invention of the cinema (1895), which proved to be a powerful way of conveying heroic legends. The moving image granted some of them a new lease of life and recycled their reputations in more modern terms, as well as promoting a number of new legends. The relevance of the figure of the 'heroic imperialist' to national narratives was thus strengthened. In his own words, film-maker Léon Poirier produced his film on Charles de Foucauld, *L'Appel du Silence* (released in 1936) in order to contribute to what he saw as the necessary reinvigoration of France, which he argued would take place 'through the recovery of French conscience'.[12] Poirier's initiative reflected primarily the views and the agenda of practising Catholics as well as the French nationalists. It was an opportunity to develop Foucauld's legend at grassroots level. Foucauld had become a religious and national paragon. Having led a dissipated life in his youth, he converted to strict Catholicism in his late twenties, dedicated himself to the Sahara at a time when the French conquest of the territory was under way and was eventually assassinated in the middle of the desert during the Great War. All of this contributed to making him an exemplary figure in Poirier's eyes – especially at a time when France's decline was a constant preoccupation.

The film-maker sought to perpetuate and even expand the reputation of his hero through the new medium of the cinema; in order to collect funds to support his project, he gave eighty-two talks in France, Belgium and Switzerland, and his appeal was answered by around 100,000 people. This testifies to the success of this attempt to turn the legend of Charles de Foucauld into a deeply meaningful episode of recent French history.[13] The success of *L'Appel du Silence* allowed Poirier to move from Catholic and nationalist circles to a wider patronage base, which included official institutions. The committee of patronage of another of his films, this time looking at the role of Brazza in securing the Congo for France, included the Minister of the Colonies, a former Governor General of Madagascar and an admiral and member of the French Academy, who had held several ministerial posts, as well as the presidents of the *Société de Géographie* and of the *Académie des Sciences coloniales*.[14] The gradual and increased intertwining of individual, group-related and state-backed celebration reveals the complex channels through which this type of 'site of imperial memory' came into being.

Two closely intertwined factors ensured the success and longevity of heroic legends of empire: the plasticity of their symbolic meaning, which could be adapted to the teaching of various exemplary values at different times, and, closely linked to this adaptability, the suitability of these legends for perpetuation through repetition and recycling. This was summarised by Léon Poirier when he argued that 'a man of values like Charles de Foucauld deserve[s] to be cited as an example to the younger generation'.[15] The secret of how a heroic reputation could grow into an 'imperial site of memory' consisted of appealing to a variety of constituencies – especially those who valued national, geographical and religious achievements, which prompted the support of a range of influential groups in society. A case in point was that of David Livingstone, whose image and teachings were described along the following lines in 1940, by the *Life of Faith*:

> Among the great missionaries of the nineteenth century no name ranks higher than that of David Livingstone. Not only is his fame in all the Churches, but also far beyond their borders. He is one of our national heroes, whose memory is honoured by multitudes who own no Church allegiance. He was a great explorer, who did more than any other to 'blaze the trail' in the interior of the Dark Continent, and in that respect his labours and achievements were of national and international importance. He made contributions to geographical and ethnological knowledge the value of which was gratefully acknowledged by the learned societies of the civilised world.[16]

Being invested with a symbolic charge relevant to the national narrative was surely the greatest asset which any heroic reputation could boast. One of General Gordon's early biographers, Alfred Egmont Hake, underlined the posthumous national relevance of the general's story: 'Gordon is dead. We cannot bring him back to life. Yet from his death we may learn at least how fit he was to teach us while he lived, how fit to hold his country's honour in his hand, how fit to judge of what was right and what was wrong'.[17] Half a century later, a French journalist commenting upon Poirier's *Brazza ou l'épopée du Congo* referred to a similar feeling when he described it as 'a powerful *œuvre* in which the love of France and its pacifying mission find the noblest expression'.[18] The promotional mechanisms at work in the media world were significantly enhanced by the multiple meanings (and especially those with nationalist undertones) which could be attributed to heroic reputations linked to the empire. However, to become fully fledged 'imperial sites of memory', these heroes also needed to find a physical translation into the everyday landscape of the country where they were celebrated: this was what I call the 'ritualisation of celebration', a second and crucial step in the process.

From virtual to physical sites: the ritualisation of celebration

Once the reputation of a hero had been established through the variety of cultural artefacts mentioned above, a phase of consolidation was necessary to turn it into a lasting 'site of memory'. The mediated figure thus became a national symbol. This process required a physical translation of the celebration, moving from the intellectual or artistic realms (newspapers, books, films, etc.) to the public space – a translation that further strengthened its national relevance. More and more streets, avenues or districts, or official buildings in the metropole were named after imperial heroes, while in the colonies the celebration could go as far as naming new cities, fortresses or even new countries after them. Paid through public subscriptions (often launched by eminent patrons or newspapers) or the generosity of benefactors, statues were commissioned. Colonial exhibitions inevitably reminded visitors of the role played by empire builders. This represented a significant qualitative jump which increased the longevity and prestige of the individual's reputation. Though not all these activities were state-sanctioned (most of them were actually initiated at local level, only by town councils), investing public space with layers of commemorative meaning was a key step in the process of 'memorialisation' of the hero: it inscribed him into everyday life, giving his memory the benefit of familiarity and daily repetition, and turning him into a common, shared reference point. It also provided the heroic reputation with a convenient physical beacon around which all sorts of complementary celebratory initiatives, such as anniversaries or ceremonies of national homage, could be assembled: a commemorative monument in the public space was bound to become a natural symbolic 'home' for a hero, where a range of occasional or annual celebrations would naturally take place.

Numerous streets were named after imperial heroes in both Britain and France. At least eighty streets bearing the names of Brazza, Marchand, Lyautey and Foucauld can still be found in France, which reveals the extent to which their exemplary value attracted Gallic town councillors. In Britain, streets named after Livingstone, Stanley, Gordon, Rhodes or Kitchener are still commonplace in both major towns and small cities. Kitchener Avenues can be found in locations as diverse as Chatham, Derby, Dulwich, Gloucester, Gravesend, Leeds, Central London, Manchester and Salford, and Kitchener Streets appear on the maps of fourteen more places, ranging from the village of Oakenshaw (in County Durham) to York and Belfast. Birmingham alone has its Livingstone, Stanley, Gordon and Kitchener Roads (in addition to a Fashoda Road).[19]

Places of birth and death, or other sites associated with symbolically significant moments in the career of the hero frequently arranged ritualised commemorations of their local celebrity. For instance, the Duchess of York, herself a Scotswoman, opened the Blantyre memorial to 'Scotland's most famous explorer' (as a British Pathé newsreel described David Livingstone), and undated leaflets invited the public to 'visit Blantyre and see the most frequented personal shrine in Scotland'.[20] Marchand's birthplace, Thoissey (in the Ain department), commissioned a statue of its famous son by the locally renowned sculptor Jean Chorel (and the village also boasted a *Rue du Commandant Marchand*).

Dedicated memorials were the most significant way in which a hero could be turned into an 'imperial site of memory', as monuments created a focal point of attention and celebration.[21] They also counted among the most symbolically charged enterprises, as in most cases planning combined individual and collective initiatives. The Marchand monument in Paris resulted from the commitment of a small group of close supporters of the Marchand mission (especially the former expedition member, military doctor Jules Emily), but it was also backed by official or semi-official institutions: the headquarters of the *Comité pour l'érection d'un monument au Général Marchand* (Committee for the erection of a monument to General Marchand) were hosted by the Paris *Société de Géographie*, and it was presided over by the former Prime Minister Paul Reynaud. The President of the Republic of the time, Vincent Auriol, inaugurated the monument on 1 July 1949, giving the occasion the full weight of an official celebration. The speeches delivered on this day reveal the commemorative dimension of such an initiative. In his lyrical description of the purpose of the monument, Paul Reynaud unwittingly described what made the essence of a *lieu de mémoire* long before it was theorised:

> Marchand is dead. When the body of a great man goes down into the night of a vault, there remains among the living what makes its essence, namely his contribution to the collective soul of the nation. Marchand, Baratier, Mangin, France does not forget your heroic crossing of Africa, from the Congo to the Nile. This monument signifies our desire that future generations shall not lose its memory.[22]

The vice-president of the Municipal Council of Paris added: 'Paris, I can assure you, will faithfully keep [Marchand's] memory'. Representing the British side (he was one of the two members of the Anglo–Egyptian expedition to sit on the *comité d'honneur*), Admiral Sir Walter Cowan declared that the mission of the monument was 'to ensure the undying fame and memory of General Marchand'.[23]

Imperial heroes were also celebrated in the colonies themselves. There, in addition to their national or religious exemplary value, they could also be honoured as the 'modern' founders of the land. Rapid urban development along European standards offered many opportunities to name streets, squares or parks after imperial heroes. The adornment of new colonial cities was also an excellent opportunity to celebrate great men. The 'Gordon statue' which was on display at the symbolic centre of modern Khartoum (on Gordon Avenue, just behind the Palace in Khartoum) was a replica of a statue erected at Chatham (a town to which the General was closely linked through the Royal Engineers). The replica had first been displayed at St Martin's Place, London, before being shipped to Khartoum in 1902 to honour Kitchener's efforts in the Anglo–Egyptian Sudan.[24] At some distance, an equestrian statue of Kitchener, standing on an equally high plinth, reminded passers-by of the architect of the reconquest of the Sudan. The Gordon statue quickly established itself as the usual place in Khartoum where the nation's symbolic gratitude towards General Gordon was formally expressed. On the anniversary of his death, 'his statue was decorated as usual with a simple laurel wreath' (and, reportedly, on the following Sunday evening 'his favourite hymn was sung and his example referred to in the Service at the Palace Chapel').[25] The combination of street naming, statues and often plaques made colonial cities powerful *loci* of heroic reputations in an imperial context.

The commemoration of the conquerors often gave rise to the construction of what was literally a *lieu de mémoire*: a commemorative building invested with practical value alongside its celebratory purpose. The Kitchener School of Medicine and Gordon Memorial College in Khartoum, or the *Lycée Lyautey* in Casablanca and the *Lycée Savorgnan de Brazza* in Brazzaville all matched the role of the Gordon Memorial College, as described by a journalist in 1904: to be 'an educational institution which commemorates the work and fulfils the ideals connected so intimately with the late hero'.[26] A former warden of Gordon College, Nicholas R. Udal, asserted in 1952 that the Memorial College had been built and endowed 'as a pledge that the memory of Gordon was still alive', and, in his view, this institution had been worthy 'not only of its illustrious founder but of the great Christian whom

[105]

it commemorates' and that his example was 'still alive among us and that his aspirations are at length to be realised'.[27]

Religious buildings erected as a result of the conquest were also ideal sites to celebrate colonial heroes. Overlooking the Bay of Algiers, a statue of Cardinal Lavigerie, Bible in hand and standing high on an imposing plinth, decorated the forecourt to the cathedral, *Our Lady of Africa*. In Khartoum, the Anglican Cathedral was consecrated on the 27th anniversary of the death of General Gordon, which made it a site of memory for the British and Christian community in Sudan. It bore a memorial inscription commemorating the name of Gordon.[28] The cathedral was indeed a major landmark in the colonial landscape of Khartoum. The diocesan magazine hoped 'that this Memorial will appeal to all who honour the name of Gordon and are proud to see his work maintained and strengthened by those who come after him'.[29] The cathedral was clearly intended as a site of memory, encapsulating the ideals of the British colonial community in Khartoum and reasserting the values which united it. This is exactly what a preacher emphasised to his parishioners on the occasion of the Gordon Anniversary Sunday service (which coincided with the 35th anniversary of the consecration of the cathedral): 'To the old generation and to the new, the complete building is a constant reminder of the ideals of our race, and of the faith, not only of General Gordon, but of the many other lives of service which have been given since his day to bring prosperity and peace to the Sudan'.[30]

The period of decolonisation

The reordering of world affairs which was triggered during the Second World War amounted to an earthquake of considerable magnitude for many of these heroic reputations. Standard-bearers of the colonial ethos, imperial heroes were not immune to the radical re-evaluation of the 'white man's burden' which took place everywhere. In many cases this led to a significant reconfiguration of the landscape of these 'imperial sites of memory', not only in the colonies as could be easily anticipated, but also in the former metropoles themselves, where the triumphant values of imperialism became increasingly incompatible with a growing feeling of guilt towards colonialism.[31]

In the former colonies where there was a clear governmental drive to emancipate official culture from the former colonial power, what could be 'recycled' of these sites was often kept in use (under a new name), and what could not be made to fit another purpose was either disposed of or 'returned to sender'. The removal of statues was certainly among the most symbolic changes in the latter category. The

Gordon and Kitchener statues in Khartoum were taken down in 1958, shortly after the independence of the Sudan, while the Bugeaud statue suffered the same fate in 1962 as soon as French rule ended in Algeria. As a clear sign that the wheel of time had turned, it was replaced by an equestrian statue of Emir Abd-el-Kader, who had resisted the French conquest of the country. The Sudanese quickly buried memories of Gordon and Kitchener. While Kitchener is still sometimes remembered – but clearly as a villain responsible for the destruction of the Mahdi's tomb and the subjugation of the country to an external power – Gordon has disappeared from the symbolic map of post-colonial Sudan. The Khartoum Cathedral was turned into the Republican Palace Museum, complete with a section on the Sudanese struggle for independence, and the Gordon Memorial College (which merged with the Kitchener School of Medicine in 1951) became the University of Khartoum. Memorial institutions which had some sort of practical relevance survived at the price of the loss of the symbolic message that they had once carried.

By contrast, those 'sites of imperial memory' which were only celebratory and 'ornamental' were generally swiftly dismantled after independence. When the old statues were not left rotting in some obscure backyard, they were repatriated to the metropoles, where they were taken charge of by local associations who had their own agendas. The place these imperial heroes had once enjoyed in national history was generally used as an argument to justify the effort needed to relocate these remnants of a bygone age with dignity. Thus Kitchener and his horse now stand in the gardens of the School of Military Engineers at Chatham and the Gordon statue has found a new home in Gordon's School in Woking (the school was founded in 1886 at the behest of Queen Victoria as a National Memorial to the General and still bears his name).[32] Bugeaud's statue from Algiers eventually found a new home in 1999, in the village of Excideuil (Dordogne), thanks to a committee made up of military men and repatriated settlers.[33]

Private subscription and volunteering sustained the financial and logistical effort needed to find a new suitable park or public space, to build a new plinth and to cover the cost of transport and installation. In a striking repetition of the funding strategies which allowed them to be produced in the first place, the statues were therefore given a new lease of life thanks to an association between private initiative and some sort of official backing – at least at a local level. Metropolitan statues have generally remained where they were installed in the first place, or were relocated when necessary, as was the case with Sir Hamo Thornycroft's statue of Gordon which was removed from Trafalgar Square for 'Wings of Victory' week in March 1943, before being returned to Victoria Embankment a decade later (where it still stands today; Figure 6.2).[34] In spite of constant pressure for the recognition of new figures, streets named after imperial heroes have not been renamed. However, the low level of public engagement with these outdated celebratory fragments and figments (apart from a few exceptions, such as the David Livingstone Centre in Blantyre), as well as the absence of regular commemorative events in most cases, means that they have gradually lost their status as 'imperial sites of memory',

6.2 The present-day site of Sir Hamo Thornycroft's statue of General Gordon, cast in 1887 and relocated to Victoria Embankment in 1953

to become mere objects of curiosity (at best) or to face the indifference or even hostility of the public (at worst).

Yet the reputations of some heroes have managed to survive or even, in some cases, to experience phoenix-like rebirths, in some countries of sub-Saharan Africa. Countries which had a peaceful and negotiated path to independence, and retained strong cultural and political links with the former metropoles through organisations such as the *Commonwealth* or the *Francophonie*, often felt it unnecessary to erase even the most obvious traces of their colonial past. Capital cities such as Dakar or Brazzaville still have streets named after colonial heroes (Brazza, Faidherbe, Marchand, etc.), as do Dar es Salaam or Pretoria (with Livingstone or Rhodes). The largest city of Malawi is still named after Livingstone's birthplace, and Livingstone has remained one of the important cities in Zambia; Brazzaville is still the capital of the Republic of the Congo. Although Cecil Rhodes's restless imperial designs and racially inspired imperialism are no longer seen as politically correct, and his critics now have more clout than his hagiographers, the physical remains of his celebration by the white community in South Africa have survived even the end of apartheid: the name of Rhodes University remains unchanged in Grahamstown, the Rhodes Memorial overlooks Cape Town undisturbed, and even Rhodes's final resting place in Zimbabwe has resisted President Mugabe's attempts to target and eliminate symbols which perpetuate colonial memories. Ironically, one of the very few 'sites of imperial memory' beyond the metropoles to have remained undisturbed since colonial times, the Rhodes Matopos National Park, lies in a territory known for its increasing hostility towards the descendants of white settlers.[35]

In a few cases, when the narrative surrounding imperial heroes was liberal enough, post-colonial independent countries have ended up recycling these 'imperial sites of memory' into their own. Brazza's reputation lost relevance in Central Africa with independence, but it was revived when Congolese president Denis Sassou Neguesso decided to turn him into the founding father of his country (known as 'Congo-Brazzaville' in French), and ploughed at least ten billion CFA francs into building a lavish memorial in the centre of a capital city still named after him. His case illustrates how post-colonial governments can be tempted to invest old colonial legends with new meanings, especially in the absence of any major and consensual pre-colonial narrative to tap into.[36] Brazza's reputation as a peaceful conqueror, keen to end the slave trade and willing to collaborate with indigenous rulers and populations, whilst refraining from violence, made him an ideal 'site of memory' for such a new life in a post-colonial African context. In Anglophone Africa, the equivalent was David Livingstone, who has remained an acceptable reference point in the new national narratives, to such an extent that he has often been referred to as 'Africa's first freedom fighter'.[37] In 2013, Malawi president Joyce Banda seized the occasion of the 200th anniversary of Livingstone's birth to issue, from the Blantyre memorial and in the company of Scotland's First Minister Alex Salmond, a call for increased cooperation with the United Kingdom.[38] In her speech to the members of the Scottish Parliament she movingly described how 'you can still sit under the tree where Dr Livingstone negotiated with slave traders to set people free'.[39] Though President Banda has also decided to return to the independence-era flag (which had been abandoned by her predecessor), she seems to be using the reputation of David Livingstone as a way of fostering bilateral links.

The 'heroic imperialist' as a 'site of imperial memory' – a hybrid type?

The 'heroic imperialist' as an ideal-type seems a peculiar but powerful 'site of imperial memory'. It owes its singularity to its nature as a hero of the 'in-betweens'. Geographically and culturally, it brought into symbolic contact different regions of the world, cultural practices and value systems. From a purely functional perspective, its reputation rested on a variety of promotional means – often of considerable heterogeneity. It was their combination which lifted the celebrated individual to the rank of an exemplary figure with national relevance. It is powerful precisely because of its multi-faceted aspect, which ensured its popularity and resilience. The plasticity of these reputations explains that they could easily be turned into national symbols in the nineteenth and twentieth centuries, playing a unifying role in societies which sought to overcome their internal divisions of politics, class and religion. The 'heroic imperialist' symbolically linked metropolitan cultures and overseas conquest, the centre and the periphery, and tied the coloniser and the colonised into a hierarchical relationship; it appealed to a variety of overlapping constituencies who saw in the imperial hero an exemplary figure for different reasons. These 'heroic imperialists' were multi-media figures *avant la lettre*, as demonstrated when Poirier tried to promote his film about Charles de Foucauld by referring to biographies published about his hero, and by arguing that 'his memory belongs to the national heritage [*patrimoine*]', before adding, to strengthen his point, that the Paris Town Council had decided to name a street after him and that 'a liner already [bore] his name', as if this celebration under various guises was the ultimate proof of the worthiness of his initiative.[40]

Even though the specificities of each political and imperial context influenced the modalities of how 'sites of imperial memory' developed in Britain and France, the mechanisms through which they came into being were similar on both sides of the Channel. French heroic imperialists often had national relevance (like Brazza), or appealed more precisely to a particular constituency of the national community (like Foucauld to the Catholics, or Marchand to the Nationalists). By contrast, British imperial heroes tended to combine various aspects more effectively, making them less factional (the emblematic example being David Livingstone). The unique ability of the British Empire to create a new 'Anglo-world' was also reflected at the heroic level.[41] Heroic reputations clearly had the power to expand successfully beyond the limits of the metropole and appeal to large constituencies of colonial settlers. Subscriptions for the Gordon Memorial College in Khartoum came not only from Great Britain, but also significantly from around the British Empire, with Reginald Wingate reporting that 'subscriptions poured in' from Canada, Australia, New Zealand, Cape Town, the United States, India, Egypt and other parts of the empire.[42] Lord Kitchener's visit to Australia in 1910 was widely covered in the Australian press, with more than sixty press articles published during his visit.[43] When news of the death of Lord Kitchener broke, his private secretary received testimonials of his popularity in Canada ('Truly we all love him over here', stated a correspondent), as well as from India (with 843 messages of condolence received from the sub-continent).[44] By contrast, French heroic reputations could not count on such a large reservoir of overseas supporters.

The memorialisation of 'great men of empire' was a complex process involving a variety of media, celebratory strategies and hero-makers. As a result, they can be seen as a 'hybrid' type of imperial site of memory associating material and virtual celebration in a unique way – relating to symbols, ideas and physical commemoration at the same time. The plasticity of these reputations, which has allowed some of them to survive into the post-colonial period, made them potentially appealing to large constituencies of the public, and as such they offer a rare insight into the cultural and political consequences of 'new imperialism', while demonstrating the strength of the multiple processes which turned them into symbols of national greatness. With decolonisation, the growing rift between national and imperial ideals turned them into contested sites of collective memory, especially in the former colonies where reactions oscillated between outright rejection and recycling.

Notes

1 The concept of 'imagined community' is taken from B. Anderson, *Imagined Communities* (London: Verso, 1983). For a Europe-wide consideration of the phenomenon of popular imperialism, see J. M. MacKenzie (ed.), *European Empires and the People* (Manchester: Manchester University Press, 2011). The importance of imperial heroes in metropolitan cultures was first identified in J. M. MacKenzie, 'Heroic Myths of Empire', in J. M. MacKenzie (ed.), *Popular Imperialism and the Military* (Manchester: Manchester University Press, 1992), pp. 109–38, and gave rise to several subject-specific studies: B. Singer and J. Langdon, *Cultured Force* (London and Madison: University of Wisconsin Press, 2004); E. Berenson, *Heroes of Empire* (Berkeley: University of California Press, 2011); B. Taithe, *The Killer Trail* (Oxford: Oxford University Press, 2011); B. Sèbe, *Heroic Imperialists in Africa* (Manchester: Manchester University Press, 2013).
2 There is now a significant historiography on heroes and heroism and their meaning in the societies where they developed: see in particular G. Cubitt and A. Warren (eds), *Heroic Reputations and Exemplary Lives* (Manchester: Manchester University Press, 2000); M. Jones, 'What Should Historians do with Heroes? Reflections on Nineteenth- and Twentieth-century Britain', *History Compass* 5:2 (2007), pp. 439–54; G. Dawson, *Soldier Heroes: British Adventure, Empire and the Imagining of Masculinities* (London: Routledge, 1994), in addition to the pioneering W. E. Houghton, *The Victorian Frame of Mind* (New Haven, CT: Yale University Press, 1957), pp. 305–40. For a wider historiographical consideration of the theme, see Sèbe, *Heroic Imperialists in Africa*, pp. 1–24, and M. Jones, B. Sèbe, J. Strachan, B. Taithe, P. Yeandle, 'Decolonising Imperial Heroes: Britain and France', special issue of the *Journal of Imperial and Commonwealth History* [forthcoming: November 2014].
3 The history of the mass-media has lately attracted plenty of scholarly attention; see J. Theobald, *The Media and the Making of History* (Aldershot: Ashgate, 2004); J. Curran, 'Media and the Making of British Society, c. 1700–2000', *Media History* 8:2 (2002), pp. 135–54; F. d'Almeida and C. Delporte, *Histoire des médias en France* (Paris: Flammarion, 2003), J.-N. Jeanneney, *Une histoire des médias des origines à nos jours* (Paris: Seuil, 1996), J.-P. Rioux and J.-F. Sirinelli (eds), *La culture de masse en France de la Belle Epoque à aujourd'hui* (Paris: Fayard, 2002); D. Kalifa, *La Culture de masse en France. 1/1860–1930* (Paris: La Découverte, 2001).
4 On the Stanley–Livingstone media context, see C. Pettitt, *'Dr. Livingstone, I Presume?' Missionaries, Journalists, Empire* (London: Profile Books, 2007).
5 Archives nationales d'Outre-Mer, Aix-en-Provence, Brazza Papers, PA 16 VI (8 boxes).
6 R. E. Nwoye, *The Public Image of Pierre Savorgnan de Brazza and the Establishment of French Imperialism in the Congo* (Aberdeen: Aberdeen University, 1981), p. 29.
7 On Marchand's return to France in the summer of 1899, see B. Sèbe, 'From Thoissey to the Capital via Fashoda: Major Marchand, Partisan Icon of the Right in Paris', in J. Wardhaugh (ed.), *Paris and the Right in the Twentieth Century* (Cambridge: Cambridge Scholars Publishing, 2007), pp. 18–42.
8 National Library of Scotland, Blackwood papers, MS 30864, Sales ledger, pp. 347 & 395. See also K. Surridge, 'More than a Great Poster: Lord Kitchener and the Image of the Military Hero', *Historical Research* 74:185 (2001), pp. 298–313 and Sèbe, *Heroic Imperialists in Africa*, ch. 7.
9 P. Maylam, *The Cult of Rhodes* (Claremont: Philip, 2005), pp. 1–30.
10 National Library of Scotland, Blackwood papers, MS 30386, Private Letter Book, p. 220, William Blackwood to Christina Steevens, 29 September 1898.
11 E. Lavisse, *Histoire de France, cours élémentaire* (Paris: Hachette, 21st edn, 1928), pp. 166–7.
12 L. Poirier, *Pourquoi et comment je vais réaliser l'Appel du Silence* (Tours: Comité d'action Charles de Foucauld, 1935), p. 38. On *L'Appel du Silence* and French imperialism, see S. Ungar, 'Léon Poirier's L'Appel du Silence and the Cult of Imperial France', *Journal of Film Preservation* 63 (Oct. 2001), pp. 41–6.

13 L. Poirier, *Charles de Foucauld et l'Appel du Silence, photographies du film* (Tours: Maison Mame, 1937), p. 64.
14 Programme of the first showing of *Brazza* at the Cinéma Marignan, Paris, 30 January 1940. Private collection, *Les Documents cinématographiques*, Paris.
15 L. Poirier, *Pourquoi et comment*, p. 12.
16 'David Livingstone: Centenary of Great Missionary's Ordination', *The Life of Faith* (20 November 1940), p. 643.
17 A. Egmont Hake (ed.), *The Journals of Major-Gen. C. G. Gordon, C. B., at Kartoum* (London: K. Paul, Trench & Co., 1885), p. ix.
18 *Le Jour* (1 February 1940).
19 On streets named after imperial heroes, see R. Aldrich, 'Putting the Colonies on the Map: Colonial Names in Paris Streets', in A. Sackur and T. Chafer (eds), *Promoting the Colonial Idea: Propaganda and Visions of Empire in France* (Houndmills; Basingstoke; Hampshire; New York: Palgrave, 2002), pp. 211–23 and Sèbe, *Heroic Imperialists in Africa*, pp. 33–5.
20 British Pathé Newsreel, 7 October 1929: www.britishpathe.com/video/scotlands-famous-missionary-explorer (accessed 10 November 2012). Undated leaflet: National Library of Scotland, Edinburgh, MS20318, f. 47.
21 See M. Agulhon, 'La "Statuomanie" et l'histoire', *Ethnologie française* 8 (1978), pp. 145–72. Indeed, statues feature among Nora's *Lieux de mémoire*: J. Hargrove, 'Les statues de Paris', in P. Nora (ed.), *Les lieux de mémoire*, vol. 2 (Paris, 1986), pp. 1855–86.
22 Anon., *Au Commandant Marchand, chef de la mission Congo-Nil et aux membres de l'expédition* (leaflet produced on the occasion of the inauguration of the Marchand memorial) (Paris, 1949).
23 Both quotations taken from Anon., *Au Commandant Marchand*.
24 Durham University Library, Sudan Archive, 714/10/22. (The statue was unveiled in Khartoum in 1903.)
25 *Sudan Church Notes* (15 February 1911), p. 67.
26 Durham University Library, Sudan Archive, SAD 817/1, Udal papers, press cutting from *The Graphic* (12 November 1904).
27 Durham University Library, Sudan Archive, SAD 817/1, Udal papers, address on the history of the Gordon Memorial College (1952).
28 Durham University Library, Sudan Archive, SAD 830/8, Khartoum Cathedral.
29 *The Diocese of Egypt and the Sudan* (December 1922), p. 26.
30 Durham University Library, Sudan Archive, SudA PK1602 khA.
31 See M. Kahler, *Decolonization in Britain and France: The Domestic Consequences of International Relations* (Princeton, NJ: Princeton University Press, 1984); J. Darwin, *Britain and Decolonization* (Basingstoke: Macmillan Education, 1988), pp. 1–33.
32 Hansard Lords Debate, 22 January 1959, vol. 213, c. 707.
33 Dordogne libre. http://excideuil.blogs.dordognelibre.fr/tag/statue+bugeaud (accessed 20 March 2013).
34 C. Hibbert, B. Weinreb, J. Keay, J. Keay, M. Weinreb, *The London Encyclopedia* (London: Macmillian, 1983, c2010), p. 871.
35 P. Maylam, 'Monuments, Memorials and the Mystique of Empire: The Immortalisation of Cecil Rhodes in the Twentieth Century', *African Sociological Review* 6:1 (2002), pp. 138–47.
36 L. Atondi-Monmondjo, 'Pouvoir congolais et révisionnisme postcolonial: le cas Pierre Savorgnan de Brazza' (2006), www.congopage.com/IMG/Revisionnisme_P_nial_Atondi.pdf; J. Tonda, 'Le Mausolée Brazza, corps mystique de l'État congolais ou corps du «négatif»', *Cahier d'études africaines* 198-199-200 (2010), pp. 799–821; F. Bernault, 'Colonial Bones: The 2006 Burial of Savorgnan de Brazza in the Congo', *African Affairs*, 109:436 (2010), pp. 367–390 and 'Quelque chose de pourri dans le post-empire: Le fétiche, le corps et la marchandise dans le Mémorial de Brazza au Congo', *Cahiers d'études africaines* 198-199-200 (2010), pp. 171–98.
37 M. Barrett, 'Presumed Innocent: Michael Barrett on the Contentious Life and Work of David Livingstone, "the First African Freedom Fighter"', *New Statesman* (1 July 2002).

38 'Malawi President Joyce Banda Marks David Livingstone birth', BBC News website, www.bbc.co.uk/news/uk-scotland-scotland-politics-21820886 (accessed 23 March 2013).

39 S. Carrell, 'David Livingstone's Bicentenary Marked by Appeal from Malawi', www. guardian.co.uk/world/2013/mar/19/david-livingstone-bicentenary-appeal-malawi (accessed 23 March 2013).

40 L. Poirier, *Pourquoi et comment je vais réaliser l'Appel du Silence* (1935), p. 10.

41 The concept of Anglo-World comes from J. Belich, *Replenishing the Earth. The Settler Revolution and the Rise of the Anglo-World, 1783–1939* (Oxford: Oxford University Press, 2009).

42 Durham University Library, Sudan Archive, SAD 272/8/40, Wingate papers, speech on the occasion of the opening of the Gordon Memorial College.

43 National Archives, Kew, PRO 30/57, Kitchener papers, piece 40 (Visit to Australia 1910: Newspaper cuttings).

44 National Archives, Kew, PRO 30/57, Kitchener papers, PA 17/16b.

CHAPTER SEVEN

Jan Pietersz Coen: a man they love to hate. The first Governor General of the Dutch East Indies as an imperial site of memory

Victor Enthoven

On 30 May 1893, a large crowd gathered in the Roode Steen, the square in the centre of Hoorn, a sleepy fishing town on the Zuiderzee. People had assembled to witness the unveiling of the statue of Jan Pietersz Coen, the first Governor General of the Dutch East Indies. The initiative to erect a statue had been launched five years earlier, in the run-up to the tercentenary of Coen's birthday. Over 100 years later, in 2012, a people's court found this national hero guilty of genocide and Hoorn City Council decided to alter the text on the plaque accompanying the statue.

This study addresses the Dutch East India Company, better known as the VOC, in general and, especially, its most famous servant: Jan Pietersz Coen, who will be treated as a representation and maybe even as a metaphor for values and images associated with the VOC. In 2006, during a debate in Parliament, his voice cracking with excitement, Prime Minister Jan-Peter Balkenende summed up the Dutch view of what the VOC stands for: 'This VOC-mentality, looking across borders, dynamic! . . . Right?' For Balkenende, the VOC represented business acumen, decisiveness and courage.[1]

Despite the fact, that the VOC has formed part of the Dutch collective memory for a long time, no site of memory associated with it has ever emerged. This is partly explained by the company's decentralised structure: it was scattered all over Holland, without a central location. Its branches, called *kamer* (chamber), were located in five different port cities. Despite the fact that many remains still exist today, they never developed into sites of memory.[2] The commemoration of the 300th anniversary of the founding of the VOC in 1902, for instance, was a very small affair indeed. In that year, just one booklet saw the light of day.[3] On 20 March 1902, several newspapers paid attention to the signing, three centuries earlier, of the Company's charter[4] and just two colonial associations, Oost en West and Moederland en Koloniën, organised a meeting in the club Dilligentia in The Hague. The historian Jan E. Heeres gave a lecture, actor Willem Boyaards recited some poems and Miss O. Munniks sang Malayan songs. While Heeres emphasised the importance of the VOC, he was puzzled by the fact that in Holland the public at large was barely aware of this. On the other hand, he mentioned the awful atrocities committed by the Company's servants, in particular by Coen.[5] Yet on another occasion in the spring of 1902, the historian Hendrik Brugmans remarked:

> After careful historical research, much of the VOC history captivates us more, than repels us. And yet – at a distance, when we try to capture its history, much of it charms us. Here we find again the best qualities of our people in its best times and placed under the golden brilliance of the Southern solar goddess. Our colonial history is a manifestation of national strength, which always remains attractive.[6]

In a socialist weekly, lawyer and later colonial administrator J. C. Kielstra, was less flattering: 'Is March 20, a day to celebrate? I do not think so. The acts of the Company are not such that our people can be proud of it; on the contrary many black pages blotted its history'.[7]

The commemorations that took place in 2002 to mark the VOC's 400th anniversary were intended to be a very different affair. A budget of 4.5 million Euros was made available by the government. A nation-wide celebration including exhibitions, festivities, street parties and books was organised. But in the course of the year the mood changed. From several different sides, including Indonesia, the Moluccan community in Holland, and the political left, critical voices grew louder and louder. The festive year ended on a low.[8]

In the wake of the 2002 anniversary year, two monuments were dedicated to the VOC: one in Middelburg (2003) and one in Amsterdam (2004).[9] Neither has succeeded in acquiring the status of an imperial site of memory. Between 2005 and 2007, publisher Bert Bakker published *Plaatsen van Herinneirng* (sites of memory), a four-volume series modelled on Pierre Nora's *Lieux de mémoire*. Only three of the eight colonial sites discussed in this work deal with the VOC, and none of these are located in the Netherlands![10]

Yet while the VOC lacks a site of memory in its home country, Jan Pietersz Coen is faring much better. Coen was the founder of Batavia, today's Jakarta, in Indonesia, the headquarters of the VOC in the East Indies. The Dutch possessions in the Archipelago were only opened for private investors and entrepreneurs in the second half of the nineteenth century. The new class of planters who flocked to Indonesia chose to identify with self-made man Coen and his alleged motto 'dispereert niet' (do not despair) rather than with the institution of the Company. As a consequence, the tradition of commemorating Coen is now much stronger and runs more deeply than the commemoration of the VOC.[11]

After a short biographical sketch, outlining Coen's careers as a merchant, a soldier and a colonial administrator, this chapter will focus on how Coen has been remembered through the ages. First it will consider his commemorations at the colonial periphery during the seventeenth and eighteenth centuries. Then we will turn to the history of the statue erected in his honour in Batavia in 1876. After this the focus will turn to the Dutch metropolis – especially to the Hoorn statue of 1893. The fifth and final section will address the critical re-evaluation of Coen's role which started in the 1930s and still continues.

Jan Pietersz Coen (1587–1629): merchant, soldier, colonial administrator

Jan Pietersz Coen was born on 8 January 1587 in the Dutch town of Hoorn. He died on 21 September 1629, during a siege of Batavia. As Governor General (1618–23 and 1627–29) of the Dutch East India Company (VOC) he forcefully established the Company in Asia.[12] Having been apprenticed to a merchant in Rome, this ambitious young man, now a junior merchant, sailed to the East Indies in December 1607 on board the *Hoorn*. The main objective of the expedition, led by Admiral Pieter Verhoeff, was to enforce a monopoly in the nutmeg trade.[13] The monopoly was to be effected by contracts between the VOC and the *orangkaya*, the Bandanese elite. Because of growing competition from English and Portuguese traders the balance of options was beginning to tilt in favour of military options. Verhoeff planned to build a fort on one of the islands. The local inhabitants were rather reserved about this plan and when a small party including Verhoeff and Coen went ashore to negotiate, they were ambushed; forty-six Dutch, including Verhoeff, were killed. Coen survived the attack.

In 1612, Coen, now a senior merchant, sailed to the East Indies for a second time. Two years later he outlined a strategy for the VOC: oppose European competitors; monopolise the spice trade by subduing local rulers; establish European settlements; and participate in the intra-Asiatic trade, the proceeds from which could finance the commodities for the European market. In 1615 the Dutch tried to conquer Pulau Ai in the Banda Sea for the first time, but they were repulsed. A year later they managed to conquer the island, but suffered the loss of many inhabitants who tried to flee to nearby Pulau Run, which was administered by the English. In the meantime the islands of Banda Neira and Lonthor traded with the Dutch, English, Portuguese and Javanese.

In 1617, Coen was appointed Governor General and found himself in the position to execute his plans. His first act was to establish a forward base of operation. He conquered Jakarta on the island of Java (1619). Renamed Batavia, the town became the administrative, commercial and maritime centre for the VOC in the Far East. In January 1621 Coen arrived with a strong fleet off the Banda Islands. What followed is one of the darkest pages of Dutch colonial history. In a ruthless and bloody campaign Coen and his men brought the main island of Lonthor under Dutch control. After swift initial successes, the *orangkaya* approached Coen to bargain for a new contract that would have given in completely to Dutch demands. However, the leaders were imprisoned and tried; foty-eight of them were beheaded. The families of the *orangkaya* (some 789 old men, women and children) were deported; some of them were put to work as slaves in Batavia, others were sent away as far as Sri Lanka. The remainder of the islanders fled into the mountains, but the Dutch still pursued them. In the end, many Lonthoirese, including women and children jumped to their death off the cliffs near Selamma or chose to starve, rather than surrender. Only a few escaped. The population of Pulau Rosingain was deported to other islands to work on the nutmeg plantations. In the end the Banda Islands were more or less ethnically cleansed: only about 1,000 of the original population of some 15,000 inhabitants remained. Pulau Run was not affected, because of the English presence. Lacking effective protection, however, the inhabitants of Run had all sorts of obligations forced upon them by Coen. After this, VOC authority over the Banda Islands was virtually complete.[14]

By these brutal means Coen established a monopoly in the production and trade in nutmeg and mace for the Company. The islands were repopulated by European planters and their slaves. Under his direction the VOC entered the intra-Asiatic trade. By attacking Portuguese Macao and Spanish Manila he also tried to direct the Chinese junk trade to Batavia. Although the Company's China policy had failed, Coen had laid the foundations on which the Company would thrive for nearly 200 years.

During the 1620s, however, it became clear that the Company had overstretched itself. The directors in Holland were more interested in cash and dividend, than in Coen's ambitions. Several of the Company's factories were in trouble. On Java the sultanate of Mataram opposed the Company and, by 1625, had become the dominant force on the island. In 1628, Sultan Agung besieged Batavia. The town was abandoned and burned down, while the Dutch withdrew to the fort. Lack of rice, however, eventually forced Agung's troops to end the siege. A year later a second siege followed, but the Dutch again succeeded in repelling the attackers. Coen, however, became ill with dysentery on 20 September 1629 and died the following day.

Commemorations at the colonial periphery: burial and early ceremonies

The governor's body was laid to rest in style. On 22 September 1629, while the fighting was still going on and the air was filled with screaming and gunshots, the funeral procession passed through the fort. The cortege consisted of Company soldiers, followed by Coen's horse draped in black velvet; high-ranking VOC officials followed, carrying Coen's sword, helmet, gloves and decorations. His remains were carried by senior merchants and officers of the militia, and members of his family and invited guests marched at the end of the procession. The late governor was buried in the town hall, because the church had been burned down the year before. A week after the funeral, the Dutch launched a decisive attack, which finally defeated the Matarans. A few months later the news reached Holland that Batavia was saved, but that Coen had perished.[15]

Batavia was rebuilt after the second siege. While the so-called Oude Hollandsche Kerk (old Dutch church) or Kruiskerk was still under construction, the remains of Coen were re-buried in the floor of the church on the south side on 4 August 1634. After the completion of the church in 1640, his coat of arms, sword, gloves and other relics were hung above the pews reserved for the wives of the Councillors of India. During the 1730s the cruciform church was replaced with a domed octagonal building. In 1733, the remains interred in the old church were transferred to the new building, but the precise location of Coen's grave is unclear. In 1808 the octagonal church was demolished and fifty years later the plot was sold to the firm Geo Wehry, who built a warehouse there.

In the late 1920s lawyer and genealogist P. C. Bloys van Treslong Prins began a campaign for the founder of Batavia to be given a more dignified final resting place than the Geo Wehry warehouse. In 1934, Bloys van Treslong Prins excavated the foundations, and on 20 June, a headline in the newspaper *Het nieuws van den dag voor*

Nederlandsch-Indië announced that the 'Remains of Jan Pietersz Coen are probably found'.[16] Only two days later, the Dutch Government appointed a formal Coen Grave Commission to scrutinise Bloys van Treslong's findings, but the investigations were carried out rather unsatisfactorily and the remains of Coen could not be positively identified. A year later, however, to mark the 350th anniversary of Coen's birthday, the warehouse was converted into the historical museum Oud Batavia. In the courtyard a sober monument was unveiled: a large white plaque cemented into a wall to mark the location of the Oude Hollandsche Kerk or Kruiskerk (1640–1732) and the Nieuwe Hollandsche Kerk (1736–1808) where the grave of the founder of Batavia Jan Pietersz Coen in 1634 was located.[17] In 1975, a museum dedicated to the Indonesian art of Wayang puppetry was opened in this location, but the colonial past still casts a long shadow: one of the puppets displayed there depicts Coen.

As long as the VOC ruled the Dutch East Indies Coen and his accomplishments for the Company were not forgotten, and his achievements were actively commemorated in Batavia and on the Banda Islands. For over 150 years, the siege and conquest of the *desa* Jakarta was marked every year on 30 May.[18] The first mention of any commemoration dates to 1633, when a thanksgiving service was held. Over time the festivities developed into a sort of festival. On May 30, at sunset, banners were hoisted at the four strongholds of the fort and the gates and all sort of trophies of the Company were erected. All the cannons in the fort, in the city and on ships fired a salute. In 1745 the number of rounds fired had to be reduced, because the houses and warehouses in the fort were so dilapidated that they threatened to collapse. A few hours later, the church bells rang out to gather the congregations. A service in Dutch, Malayan and Portuguese was held first in the Kruiskerk and later the Nieuwe Hollandse Kerk, during which the story of the conquest was told replete with numerous references to the Old and New Testament and with expressions of gratitude to God for all the good fortune experienced since then.

After the service, the three European companies of the militia, comprising free burghers and Company personnel, and the seven *mardijker* companies would assemble,[19] flying their colours and fully armed. More than once, the flying of the colours led to riots and even killings, and in 1724 the practice was prohibited. Four years earlier, slaves were forbidden to join the parade, because the government feared that they would riot. At the time of the Coen commemoration, the Governor General and Council would assemble in the main hall of the fort, where they were joined by the Aldermen of the city. A meeting would then be held during which a new Council was appointed. The proceedings would conclude with a large banquet. The template for these festivities remained rigidly fixed, because the VOC officials feared that any change would cause discontent among the Javanese. It appears that these festivities and commemorations of Coen's conquest of Jakarta were abandoned around 1800 when the British temporarily took over the rule of the Dutch East Indies.

The Batavia playhouse opened in 1757. Five years later, the play 'Jan Pietersz Coen: Advocate of Batavian Freedom, a War Game' was performed. The play had been written by P. de Vries, based on notes by Johannes Camphuys (1634–95), Governor General (1684–91), who had carried out some research using Coen's private papers. By 1762 these papers were lost. The play is set in newly founded Batavia during the siege of the fort by Javanese warriors in 1618–19. The hero of the play was, of course, Coen. Apparently, the play was performed only once and it provides the only entry on Coen in the Short Title Catalogue Netherlands, a catalogue listing all Dutch publications before 1800. It appears, therefore, that before the nineteenth century Coen was anything but a well-known figure in the Dutch Republic. He was still a figure of the colonial periphery.[20]

The festivities on Banda are less well known than those in Batavia, but the German soldier Ernst Christopher Barchewitz, who stayed on Banda Neira between February 1712 and August 1714, described vividly how the Dutch commemorated the conquest of the island. In the early morning, banners once captured by Coen were planted on the walls of fort Nassau. After more than 100 years they were just rags. Then, a sermon was read twice: first in Dutch, and then in Malay. Afterwards, the garrison paraded inside the fort, while the militia, comprising free burghers, VOC personnel, *mardijkers*, and their (European) officers assembled at the house of the Captain. From there, in full dress uniform and with the band playing, they marched to the fort. According to local traditions, some *voorvechters* (rangers), armed with shields, swords and lances headed the procession: dancing, jumping and grimacing. While entering the fort, the garrison presented their arms, and the militia took up positions alongside the garrison. Then, the Governor General and Council would appear on the balcony. The secretary then read the treaty between the VOC and the Bandanese in Malayan. Afterwards he asked the local people present if they were still willing to uphold the treaty. In response they shouted 'yes'.

They were not, of course, the descendants of the Bandanese who had signed the treaty, because their ancestors had migrated to the island. Furthermore, it is unclear which text was read. Coen had probably never concluded a treaty, because the islands were largely depopulated by the end of the conquest. The text was almost certainly a later fabrication produced specifically for this purpose. When the treaty had been read and acclaimed, the soldiers of the garrison and the militia fired their weapons in salute three times, and this was answered by the guns of Fort Belgica. The militia then marched back to the Captain's house, and high-ranking VOC officials would sit down to a banquet. It is unclear when this annual event on Banda Neira started and ended. Another German, Johann Sigmund Wurssbain, who visited the island in the 1630s, does not mention the festivities, and it seems likely that it was discontinued around 1800 when British rule was established.[21]

Figurehead of free enterprise: the Batavia statue

Thus, by the beginning of the nineteenth century not much was left to remind the world of Coen. His grave was lost, and the commemorations in Batavia and Banda were forgotten. After the middle of the century, however, this changed. Following the bankruptcy of the VOC in 1795, all the Company's assets and liabilities were handed over to the Dutch state. After the Napoleonic era, the Kingdom of the Netherlands was in dire financial straits and the overseas possessions had to support the metropolis. In the East Indies a two track policy was implemented. First, the archipelago should come under Dutch rule – by diplomatic negotiation, if possible, otherwise by force. Almost a century of conflict and war now took place in an attempt to subject the indigenous populations. Second, in 1830 the Dutch colonial government enforced a so-called 'culture system' in the subjected territories. Under this system, indigenous farmers were forced to put aside one-fifth of their rice fields for the cultivation of export crops such as sugar, coffee, indigo, tobacco and pepper. Alternatively, if they had no land of their own, they had to work in a government field for one-fifth of a year (sixty-six days), so that they could pay their land tax to the colonial government. These crops were purchased at low prices or appropriated in lieu of land rent owed to the Dutch East Indies government and sold on markets in Holland. The net proceeds went to the Exchequer, after deduction of costs of the government in the East Indies: this led to a rapid decrease of the Dutch public debt.[22]

Over time, despite the huge success for the Exchequer, the system attracted criticism, especially from the emerging liberal party. First, there was concern about the atrocious conditions under which the farmers had to work. The harmful effects of the system became manifest after 1845, when the price of rice rose dramatically and there was famine in Java. Second, private enterprise was excluded. The whole system, with the exception of sugar refinery, was controlled by the government, which meant that, by the middle of the nineteenth century, only a very small number of private citizens actually lived in the Dutch East Indies. Both in Holland and in Batavia a polemic developed over the *cultuurstelsel*.[23]

In Batavia the advocates of abolition of the 'culture system' seized the 250 year anniversary of the founding of the city in 1869 to make their point. Coen quickly emerged as a powerful symbol and soon there were plans for a Coen statute. In 1869, Coen's founding of Batavia was celebrated with an elaborate festival. On Saturday 29 May, the first stone was laid for the Coen monument; the ceremony took place to the sound of music including 'Neêrlands Volkslied' by Thollens, then the country's national anthem. In the evening, there was a concert in the play house. The cantata 'Batavia founded' was performed, in which Coen's voice rang out:

Dutch sons
will throne
in the flowering heart of the East!
new sources will flow,
new flows spraying prosperity,
and the country's own fruit will grow,
by a new sun blushed.

Could anyone imagine a better rallying cry for new opportunities and private enterprise?[24]

The Coen statute was sculpted in Holland by Eugène de Plyn, cast in bronze by L. J. S. van Kempen, and shipped to Batavia in early 1874 (Figure 7.1). In its left hand the figure of Coen holds a map of Batavia, while the right hand points to where Jakarta once stood. The heroic figure was probably modelled after King Gustavus II Adolfus of Sweden (1594–1632). The statue was unveiled in 1876. By that time the *cultuurstelsel* had been abolished, private entrepreneurs flooded the archipelago and *tempoe doeloe* (the easy times) had begun.[25]

Metropolitan commemorations: Hoorn's great son

Today, Hoorn is a sleepy provincial town on the shores of the IJsselmeer, home to a large number of sailing yachts. During the so-called Dutch Golden Age, Hoorn was a thriving port city in the vicinity of Amsterdam, with direct access to the North Sea. In 1602, when the Dutch East India Company was founded, Hoorn was allocated one of the *kamers*. More accurately, together with another port city, Enkhuizen, it hosted the branch of the Noorderkwartier, the northern county of Holland. Hoorn was a maritime centre with a global reach.

7.1 Statue of Jan Pietersz Coen in Batavia/Jakarta

The southernmost tip of Latin America, Cape Hoorn, for instance, was named after the port city. During the eighteenth century the maritime activities shifted to Amsterdam, and Hoorn entered a long decline. By the nineteenth century it was a small fishing town, and in 1905 a mere thirty or so coastal fishing vessels were moored there. Now only a small community, Hoorn remained fiercely proud of its maritime and colonial history.[26]

Many remnants of the VOC are still present in Hoorn, including the East India House (Oostindisch Huis) office building and several warehouses. In 1950, the VOC shipyard and slipways were excavated. The large impressive townhouse Foreesthuis, on Grote Markt no. 43, was built by VOC director Naaning van Foreest (1682–1745), heer van Petten–Nolmerban. The Westfries Museum is housed in the former Oostindisch Huis and the warehouses on the Oude Doelenkade and Onder de Boompjes no. 21–22 have now been converted into condominiums.[27] At a crossroads in the main high street, a more than life-size VOC logo is cut into the pavement. The town of Hoorn clearly identifies itself with the VOC. In that respect, one could say the town centre is a colonial site of memory with the statue of Coen in the middle of the town square at its very heart.

On 9 January 1884, the Hoorn Vereeniging voor Volksvermaken (the Hoorn Association for Public Entertainment), chaired by physician J. J. Aghina, held their annual meeting in the playhouse. Probably inspired by a plaster statue of Coen that had been prominently displayed at a colonial trade exhibition in Amsterdam the previous year, teacher P. Bakker noted that it was three years until the 300th anniversary of J. P. Coen's birthday. Would it not be a splendid idea for the town to create a lasting monument for its most famous son? Aghina promised to look into the matter. It took two years before any action was taken, though. On 10 February 1886, Aghina and Mayor Willem Karel Baron van Dedem organised a meeting with the local elite. The Bakker idea was warmly received. However, what would be an appropriate monument? A pump or fountain maybe? Teacher Vorderman rejected these ideas. A pump was not appropriate for this great man; and a fountain would run dry too frequently. Vorderman preferred a column and one with a height of at least 15 meters! Aghina begged to differ: 'A column is more a site of memory of a fact, than of a great person'. In the end, an Executive Committee was formed to realise a monument. The committee included local dignitaries like Mayor Van Dedem and physician Aghina, but also national figures like the banker, philanthropist and Senator A.C. Wertheim and the historian H.J.A.M. Schaepman MP. They gave the initiative the national status that would put Hoorn back on the map.[28]

By now Coen had risen to the rank of a national figure. That his birthday, 8 January, had become a day of great significance for the Dutch people, can be gleaned from a circular that was issued by the Executive Committee, which stated that 140 people from all over the country should come together to form a National Committee. In the circular national symbols, including the slogan of the house of Orange 'je maintiendrai', which fits well with Coen's 'dispereert niet', were connected to the founder of Batavia. A few days later the National Committee met in Amsterdam's Odéon club. During the meeting local subcommittees were set up to raise money in their communities, not only in Holland, but as far away as Assen in the northeast of Holland.

In the end, the Executive Committee settled for a statue. Sculptor F. K. A. C. Leenhoff (1840–1914) received the commission. Leenhoff was a pupil of Joseph Mezzara in Paris. During the 1890s he was professor at the Amsterdam Rijksakademie van Beeldende Kunsten, the national academy of visual arts. Other statues by him included those of Johan Rudolph Thorbecke in Amsterdam (1867), and the bust of Queen Wilhelmina in front of the Academiegebouw in Utrecht (1892). The Executive Committee proposed to erect the statue on the Roode Steen, the large square in the city centre. There Coen would be surrounded by historical buildings like the Waag and the former Oostindisch Huis. The Mayor and Aldermen had a different site in mind: a park in front of the railway station, but their proposal was rejected by the City Council. The council also decided to unveil the statue on 30 May 1893 – the anniversary of the day, when, in 1619, Coen had conquered Jakarta.[29]

To emphasise the national character of the commemoration, Queen-Mother Emma and the young Princess Wilhelmina were invited to attend the celebrations. There was widespread disappointment when both had to decline, because of a trip abroad.[30] Among the guests who did attend were cabinet ministers Johannes Tak van Poortvliet, Cornelis Lely and Baron van Dedem, the Minister for the Colonies.

The festivities started on the evening of Monday 29 May 1893. The Hoorn Vereeniging voor Volksvermaken had organised a soiree in the playhouse Het Park. The following day, all schools and public buildings were closed. Many people had raised the national flag. A special train transported the dignitaries from Amsterdam to Hoorn. Mayor August Eduard Zimmerman welcomed the excellencies in the Town Hall, and then a long procession moved to the Roode Steen, where a huge crowd had gathered underneath countless flags fluttering in the wind. Van Dedem was the first speaker. Having welcomed everybody he declared: 'Coen's statue in this town amongst his people is safe. As long as Hoorn, as long as West-Friesland, and as long as the Netherlands will not forget its history, this will be holy ground'. Then historian Schaepam reminded the audience of Coen's accomplishments in the East Indies, and their importance for the nation. Finally Aghina thanked the Dutch people for their gifts, which had enabled the town to create this national symbol. During the unveiling a loud cheer filled the square and war ships in the harbour fired a salute. All sorts of festivities were organised for the rest of the day, such as a horse race and a matinee concert in the park. In the evening the Vereeniging voor Volksvermaken organised an illuminated cruise on the canals, which concluded with fireworks at the Kaperkuil. The festivities ended with a soiree in the park. Leenhoff and Aghina were honoured with a royal citation.[31]

Over the years many festivities and commemorations took place at the Hoorn statue. In 1919, for instance, a national ceremony was held to commemorate the 400th anniversary of the founding of Batavia by Coen. Prime Minister C. J. M. Ruys de Beerenbrouck and Minister for the Colonies A. W. F. Idenburg were present. Queen Wilhelmina laid a wreath.[32] The financial crisis meant that the 300th anniversary of Coen's death in 1929 was marked very modestly, but his 350th birthday was a cause for big celebrations.[33] On 1 February 1937, Prime Minister Colijn delivered a memorial speech in the Noorderkerk. He choose Coen's motto 'Dispereert niet' as the title and praised Coen elaborately, calling him a light amidst much darkness, and an example to follow because of his sacrifice and wisdom.[34] For Mayor H. C. Leemhorst Coen was a great citizen of Hoorn.[35]

The summer of that year was dominated by a week-long Coen-festival in Hoorn. The town wanted to show what it had in store for tourists. Just outside the city centre the open air play 'Onze Groote Zoon' (Our Great Son) was staged, which involved 500 actors. The playhouse hosted a colonial exhibition. The Doelenplein Square was transformed into a *passar malam* (Indonesian market) and a historical procession was organised.

In 1987, the Coen statue was the centre of a festive commemoration for the last time, and now included a Coen exhibition in the Westfries Museum. By then, however, the mood had changed completely.[36]

Re-evaluations: Coen on trial

Coen had been controversial for a long time. Could he be the right choice for a site of imperial memory? During the debate on the 'culture system' and the planning for the Batavia statue in the 1860s, former soldier, sugar refiner, colonial administrator and publicist J. Hageman published a vicious pamphlet under the title 'The Projected Statue of Jan Pietersz Coen in Batavia, in historical perspective'.[37] It is a curious booklet because Hageman was a radical supporter of private enterprise and advocated opening the *cultuurstelsel*, but for him Coen represented government, mercantilism, and monopoly trade. In his view, Coen stood for the very opposite of free trade, private enterprise and competition.[38] In 1869, J.K.J. de Jonge, author of the multi-volume *De Opkomst van het Nederlandsch Gezag in Oost-Indië* (The Rise of Dutch Rule in the East Indies), concluded that Coen 'had tainted his own reputation and that of the Dutch nation with an almost indelible bloodstain'.[39] In a similar vein, F. W. van Eeden, the director of the Koloniaal Museum (Colonial Museum) in Haarlem was not impressed with the plaster statue of Coen which took pride of place outside the colonial pavilion at the 1883 World Fair at Amsterdam. In his opinion there was really only one Dutch military leader – Stadholder Maurits, Prince of Orange – and certainly not Coen.[40]

When the statue of Coen at Hoorn was planned, several historians pointed out that the Governor General was hardly a suitable figure for a local, let alone a national site of memory. In the mid-1880s librarian P.A. Tiele noted that 'for the sake of monopoly, the affluent population of a beautiful archipelago . . . was murdered in a cold-blooded manner'. Two years later the head archivist of the Algemeen Rijks Archief (National Archives), J. A. van der Chijs remarked: 'If a statue for Coen had not already been erected [in Batavia], I doubt whether one would rise now. His name is covered with blood'.[41] He was proved to be wrong.

In the run-up to the 1937 festivities, Coen was, in a manner of speaking, completely dragged from his pedestal. The famous writer and poet Jan Jacob Slauerhoff worked on Coen in 1930. He never completed his planned biography, but in 1931, Slauerhoff's only play was published 'Jan Pieterszoon Coen. Drama in Eleven Tableaux'. Slauerhoff completely stripped Coen of his hero status. To cite author and novelist Menno ter Braak: 'Just because of his vulgarity Coen becomes a fully formed personality, just because there is no attempt to idealise and there is no romantic cover-up, Slauerhoff's hero is real'. But most critics were shocked. The text remained so scandalous that performances planned in 1937, 1943, 1948 and 1961 were cancelled. The first two attempts failed, because of the vicious content. Political sensitiveness prevented the latter two: Indonesia's independence in 1948 and the conflict between Indonesia and the Netherlands over New Guinea in 1961. Eventually the play was shown for the first time on national television in 1969. The first time the play was performed on stage was 6 February 1986, fifty years after Slauerhoff's death.[42]

The unmasking of Coen was completed in 1933 when R. A. M. Bergman published a so-called psychograph. Based on Ernst Kretschmer's theory of pathological psychology, Bergman created a so-called constitutional type. As sources, Bergman used Coen's extensive correspondence. From this he concluded that Coen was a person characterised by great activity, but he had little to praise where his emotions and character were concerned. For Bergmann, Coen fell between the two groups of Anaesthetic and Hypomaniac characters. Emotionally, Coen struck him as phlegmatic: 'Cold we call a man who walks over dead bodies, without much feeling'. Pointing to Coen's own complaints about his physical and mental state, the historian Willem Coolhaas suggested in 1944 that here was a case of *tropenkoller* – of insanity induced by life in the tropics.[43]

The first visible protest against the glorification of Jan Pietersz Coen as a national hero occurred at the Hoorn statue during the celebrations in 1937. Just before the arrival of Prime Minister Colijn the Revolutionary Socialist Workers Party issued leaflets with the text: 'Monday the Dutch upper class will applaud in grandiloquent terms the exploitation of the Indonesian people'. The Summer festival was also criticised: 'Over the years the Indonesian people have, through Coen's intervention, been degraded to *koelievolk* [coolies] and currently live in utmost poverty. And Hoorn celebrates this!!!'[44]

Fifty years on, the protests were fiercer. Protest posters went up in the town, a collection of protest poems was published, and the statue was smeared with paint. Dirk Beemster, poet and one of the protesters, declared: 'I knew about the atrocities conducted by Coen on the Banda Island. I had read Slauerhoff. This kind of deeds should never happen again, things had to change. Festivities were not appropriate'. One of his poems started with:

Exploit
He was actually a miserable person,
so I read in the local newspaper.
A murderer, bitter to death,
a pirate, a bad husband.

Now we know:
Coen was only interested in money,
but then, some eighty years ago
he was worshipped.

The Moluccan community in Holland seized the opening of an exhibition on Coen in the Westfries Museum to air their grievances. This led to fierce riots and intervention by the riot police. Moluccan artist Willy Nanlohy presented the Queen's husband, Prince Claus, with a black book on the atrocities carried out by Coen. The message is clear: Coen stands for oppression and colonialism, and that does not deserve a tribute.[45]

In 2011, a group of citizens petitioned the local government. They advocated the removal of the Coen statue from the Roode Steen. After all, he was guilty of genocide. For the Westfries Museum the reopened debate on the Coen statue just outside its doors provided an incentive for an exhibition. The exhibition was presented in the form of a trial. The accused was Jan Pietersz Coen. The charges were: Coen does not deserve a statue. There were witnesses to speak for and against the indictment and there was 'evidence', including objects, video and sound clips that supported or refuted the charge. The historian Maarten van Rossem acted as judge. The visitors assumed the role of jurors, and were asked, after hearing the witnesses and viewing all the evidence, to decide for or against the statue.[46] A majority of 60% would eventually vote in favour of retaining the statue.[47]

On 13 March 2012, the Hoorn City Council considered the citizens' initiative and decided not to remove the statue, but to alter the text of the plaque on the base. It used to read:[48]

Jan Pieterszoon Coen (1587–1629)
Born in Hoorn, Governor General of the VOC
and founder of Batavia, nowadays Jakarta.

Now it carries the following wording:

Jan Pieterszoon Coen (Hoorn, 1587 – Batavia, 1629)

Merchant, Director-General and Governor-General of the Dutch East India Company (VOC).

Architect of the VOC's successful trading empire in Asia. Founder of the city of Batavia, currently known as Jakarta.

Coen was praised as a vigorous and visionary administrator. But he was also criticised for the violent means by which he built up trade monopolies in the East Indies.

In 1621 Coen led a punitive expedition against one of the Banda Islands, as the local population was selling nutmeg to the English in disregard of a VOC ban. Thousands of Bandanese lost their lives during the assault and the survivors were deported to Batavia.

By the end of the nineteenth century Coen had grown into a national hero and was honoured with a statue in his home town. A national committee headed by Mayor of Hoorn, Baron van Dedem, collected money to realise this. The bronze work which was designed by Ferdinand Leenhoff (1841–1914), an instructor at the National Academy of Visual Arts in Amsterdam, was unveiled during a festive ceremony in 1893.

This statue is controversial. According to critics, Coen's violent mercantilism in the East Indian archipelago does not deserve to be honoured.

Ironically, in August 2011, in the middle of the debate on what to do with Coen, the statue was hit by a van and Coen fell – literally – off his plinth.

Conclusion

All over the world objects refer to the VOC in general and Coen in particular. In Amsterdam alone, for instance, there are several small statues of Coen, most on façades including the Beurs van Berlage (1906), the Scheepvaarthuis (1913–16), the Nederlandsche Handel-Maatschappij (1925), and the Koloniaal Instituut voor de Tropen (1926). All were created during *tempoe doeloe*, when many private persons made a living in the Dutch East Indies.[49] None of these, however, developed into an imperial site of memory. Despite the fact that the figure of Coen has been contested for a long time, Coen gave rise to sites of memory at three different locations: his grave in Batavia, the Batavia statue and the Hoorn statue. Each with their own function and meanings as sites of imperial memory.

During the seventeenth and eighteenth centuries Coen was a figure of the periphery. His grave symbolised VOC rule of Batavia and its surroundings. From 1633 onwards, every year on 30 May a thanksgiving service was held in the church housing his remains. Worshippers remembered the conquest of Jakarta and thanked God for all the good fortune since. In due course this commemoration developed into elaborate festivities, for both VOC officials and the local population, including the slaves. Shortly after the demise of the Company in 1795, the grave was lost and Coen nearly slipped into oblivion.

In the metropolis Coen had no profile at all. During the seventeenth and eighteenth centuries not a single publication about him saw the light of day in the Dutch Republic. There was no need for him. As a maritime nation the Dutch had an extensive pantheon of forty or fifty *zeehelden*, naval heroes, like Piet Heyn and Michiel de Ruyter. They loved and worshipped these national heroes, who had perished at sea. In the Dutch maritime cultural identity there was no room for a landlubber like Coen.[50]

In the 1860s, during the debate surrounding the opening of the 'culture system', there was a Coen revival, and again it happened at the periphery. He became the figurehead of private enterprise. The Batavia statue symbolised *tempoe doeloe*; the period when private citizens and private enterprises dominated the Dutch East Indies. The Japanese occupation of the archipelago ended the easy times. The Japanese, in conjunction with Indonesian nationalists, removed and destroyed the statue in 1942.

In the metropolis Coen had to wait until the end of the nineteenth century to emerge as a national figure. The Hoorn statue was a local, a national and an imperial symbol. For the people of Hoorn, and especially the local elite, the Coen statue symbolised the once glorious past of their sleepy fishing town. Furthermore, the Kingdom of the Netherlands, as a unified nation-state, was a creation of the early nineteenth century. In the course of that century, Dutch citizens sought to celebrate their cultural heritage with statues, painting, literature, music and art festivals, expressing their new national identity. The Coen statue strengthened the sense of national unity and fitted nicely into the current world politics of modern imperialism. Holland was a small country, surrounded by mighty neighbours, but with a large overseas empire. Fear of losing prestige and wealth forced the kingdom to maintain and defend its empire. A vision, not only designed, but actually executed with force by Coen two and a half centuries ago.[51]

During the twentieth century Coen and his legacy became more and more contested, especially in the metropolis. This started in the 1930s, the zenith of *tempoe doeloe*. And the debate about his legacy and what he stands for, is still on-going today. Over the centuries Coen's profile as a site of memory has followed a curve: starting high (burial and early ceremonies in the East Indies), then declining (late eighteenth and early nineteenth centuries) and then rising again: first as a positive figure (for private enterprise and for reasons of national identity and pride); then as a negative figure (with growing awareness of the problematic nature of some of Coen's legacies). In short: Jan Pietersz Coen was a man they loved to hate.

Notes

1 To watch his tirade go to www.youtube.com/watch?v=mBN8xJby2b8 (accessed 22 April 2013).
2 R. van Gelder and L. Wagenaar, *Sporen van de Compagnie. De VOC in Nederland* (Amsterdam: De Bataafsche Leeuw, 1988).
3 M. Nijhoff [sic], *A list of the best books relating to Dutch East India made up in commemoration of the third centenary of the foundation of the East India Company (20 March 1602)* (The Hague: Nijhoff, 1902).
4 *De locomotief* (20 March 1902); *Nieuwsblad van het Noorden* (21 March 1902); *Nieuwsblad van Friesland* (22 March 1902). All newspapers cited in this essay are available on the webpage of the Koninklijke Bibliotheek, http://kranten.kb.nl.
5 *Algemeen Handelsblad* (17 March 1902); *Het Nieuws van den dag voor Nederlansch Indië* (22 March 1902).
6 *Onze Eeuw* (April 1902); *Het Nieuws van den dag voor Nederlansch Indië* (7 May 1902).
7 *Leeuwarder Courant* (21 March 1902).
8 B. Funnekotter, 'Jongensboekenromantiek en sluwe koopmansgeest', *Mare* (21 March 2002); R. Meijer, 'Niet louter jubel bij 400 jaar VOC', *De Volkskrant* (20 March 2002); 'Viering 400 jaar VOC' (4 April 2005), available on the webpage of the VNO-NCW, www.vno-ncw.nl; M. Maas, 'Herdenking VOC is Indonesiërs wat al te feestelijk', *De Volkskrant* (21 March 2002); S. van Walsum, 'Uitzuiger en grondlegger van de Archipel', *De Volkskrant* (21 March 2002); Harry Westerink, 'Hollandse koopmansgeest geen reden tot feest', *De Fabel van de illegaal* 52/3 (2002), available on the webpage of Gebladerte Archief, www.doorbraak.eu/gebladerte; F. Gaastra, 'De neerslag van een jubileumjaar: VOC 2002', *Bijdragen en Mededelingen betreffende de Geschiedenis der Nederlanden* 120:4 (2005), pp. 546–61; R. Raben, 'VOC-Herdenking ontloopt iedere controverse', *Historisch Nieuwsblad* 11 (December 2002), pp. 26–30; G. Oostindie, 'Squaring the Circle: Commemoratong the VOC after 400 Years', *Bijdragen tot de Taal-, Land- en Volkenkunde* 159:1 (2003), pp. 135–61.

9 G. Oostindie, H. S- Nordholt and F. Steijlen, *Postkoloniale Monumenten in Nederland* (Leiden: KITLV Press, 2011).

10 The three VOC sites are located in Ambon (Indonesia), Cape Town (South Africa), and Jakarta (Indonesia). M. Prak (ed.), *Plaatsen van Herinnering. Nederland in de zeventiende en achttiende eeuw* (Amsterdam: Bert Bakker, 2006).

11 *Coen! Geroemd en vergruisd* (Hoorn: West-Fries Museum, 2012).

12 V. Enthoven, 'Coen', in J. J. McCusker (ed.), *History of World Trade since 1450* (London: Macmillan 2006); F. S. Gaastra, 'The Organization of the VOC', in, M. A. P. Meilink-Roelofsz, R. Raben and H. Spijkerman (eds), *De Archieven van de Verenigde Oostindische Compagnie/The Archives of the Dutch East India Company, 1602–1795* (The Hague: SDU, 1992); H. T. Colenbrander, *Jan Pietersz Coen. Levensbeschrijving* (The Hague: Nijhoff, 1934).

13 Els M. Jacobs, *Koopman in Azië. De handel van de Verenigde Oost-Indische Compagnie tijdens de 18de eeuw* (Zutphen: Walburg Pers, 2000), pp. 24–7; Andrew Dalby, *Dangerous Tastes. The Story of Spices* (London: British Museum Press, 2000), pp. 53–4.

14 V. C. Loth, 'Pioneers and Perkeniers: The Banda Islands in the 17th Century', *Cakele* 6 (1995), pp. 13–35, special 18; V. C. Loth, 'Armed Incidents and Unpaid Bills: Anglo-Dutch Rivalry in the Banda Islands in the Seventeenth Century', *Modern Asian Studies* 29:4 (1995), pp. 705–40.

15 H. T. Colenbrander, *Jan Pietersz Coen. Levensbeschrijving*, pp. 441–2.

16 *Het nieuws van den dag voor Nederlandsch-Indië* (20 June 1934).

17 *Om het graf van Coen. Het graf van Jan Pietersz. Coen. Verslag der commissie, ingesteld bij gouvernementsbesluit van 23 Juni 1934* (Batavia: Noordhoff-Kolff, 1936); W. Ph. Coolhaas, 'Over karakter en daden van Jan Pietersz Coen', *Bijdragen voor Vaderlandsche Geschiedenis en Oudheidkunde* (1943), pp. 201–37, esp. p. 203.

18 J. A. van der Chijs, *De Nederlanders te Jakarta. Uit de bronnen, zoo uitgegevene als niet uitgegevene* (Amsterdam: Frederik Muller, 1860), pp. 258–64.

19 The *Mardijker*, descendants of freed slaves, were mostly Christian of Indian or Portuguese origin, and spoke a Portuguese *patois*.

20 J. Kamphuys [sic], *Jan Pietersz: Coen, voorstander der Bataviase vryheid, bly-eyndent oorlog-spel* (Batavia: F. Tetsch, 1762); N. P. van den Berg, 'Het toneel te Batavia in vroegeren tijd', *Tijdschrift voor Indische taal-, land- en volkenkunde* 26 (1881), pp. 313–411, esp. p. 333, available on the KITLV-webpage, www.kitlv.nl/documents.

21 J. A. van der Chijs 'Banda's veroverings-dag,' *Tijdschrift voor Indische Taal-, Land-en Volkenkunde* 26 (1881), pp. 195–8, available on the KITLV-webpage, www.kitlv.nl/documents. For Ernst Christopher Barchewitz, see R. van Gelder, *Het Oos-Indisch avonduur. Duitsers in dienst van de VOC* (Nijmegen: SUN, 1997).

22 P. Silaen and C. J. Smark, 'The "Culture System" in Dutch Indonesia 1830–1870: How Rawls's Original Position Ethics were Violated' (2006) available on the webpage of University of Wollongong, http://ro.uow.edu.au; S. Chandral and T. J. Vogelsang, 'Change and Involution in Sugar Production in Cultivation-System Java, 1840–1870', *The Journal of Economic History* 59:4 (1999), pp. 885–911.

23 C. Fasseur, *Kultuurstelsel en koloniale baten. De Nederlandse exploitatie van Java, 1840–1860* (Leiden: Universitaire Pers Leiden, 1975); U. Bosma, 'Het cultuurstelsel en zijn buitenlandse ondernemer. Java tussen oud en nieuw kolonialisme', *Tijdschrift voor Sociale en Economische Geschiedenis* 2 (2005), pp. 23–8, available on the IISG webpage, www.iisg.nl/hsn/documents/109-bosma.pdf; G. R. Knight, 'Descrying the bourgeoisie Sugar, Capital and State in the Netherlands Indies, circa 1840–1884', *Bijdragen tot de Taal-, Land- en Volkenkunde* 163 (2007), pp. 34–66, available on the KITLV webpage, www.kitlv-journals.nl.

24 *Gids van de Feestviering ter gelegenheid van het 250-jarig bestaan van Batavia* (Batavia: H. M. van Dorp, 1869) available on the webpage of the Koninklijke Bibliotheek, http://boeken1.kb.nl.

25 E. Snijders, 'Coen monumenten', in *Coen! Geroemd en vergruisd* (Hoorn: West-Fries Museum, 2012), pp. 66–9; Ulbe Bosma and Kees Mandenmakers, 'Indiëgangers: sociale herkomst en migratiemotieven, 1830–1950. Een onderzoek op basis van de Historische

Steekproef Nederlandse bevolking (HSN)', *Bijdragen en Mededelingen betreffende de Geschiedenis der Nederlanden* 123 (2008), pp. 162–84.

26 C. M. Lesger, *Hoorn als stedelijk knooppunt. Stedensystemen tijdens de late middeleeuwen en vroegmoderne tijd* (Hilversum: Verloren, 1990); P. Dorleijn, *Van gaand en staand want, I. De zeilvisserij voor en na de afsluiting van de Zuiderzee* (Amsterdam: VK&Z, 1982), p. 184.

27 R. van Gelder and L. Wagenaar, *Sporen van de Compagnie*, pp. 42–59.

28 E. Snijders, 'Een nationalistische onthulling', in *Coen! Geroemd en vergruisd*, p. 58; H.J.A.M. Schaepman, 'Een standbeeld voor Jan Pietersz. Coen, te Hoorn', *Verslagen der algemeene vergaderingen van het Indisch genootschap* (1887), pp. 120–1.

29 [Circulaire tot herdenking van den 300-jarigen geboortedag van Jan Pietersz. Coen] (s.l., s.n.), available in the KITLV library, no. M dd 263; for Leenhoff, see: http://nl.wikipedia.org; E. Snijders, 'Een nationalistische onthulling', p. 60.

30 E. Snijders, 'De mythe van de Koninklijke afwezigheid', in *Coen! Geroemd en vergruisd*, pp. 62–3.

31 A. E. Zimmerman, *De onthulling van het standbeeld van Jan Pietersz Coen te Hoorn op 30 mei 1893* (Hoorn: Kapteijn, 1893), KITLV library no. M dd 286; E. Snijders, 'Een nationalistische onthulling', p. 61; *Algemeen Handelsblad* (18 May, 21 May, 30 May, 31 May, 1 June 1893); *Het nieuws van den dag: kleine courant* (30 May 1893); *De Tijd: godsdienstig-staatkundig dagblad* (31 May, 1893).

32 *Coen! Geroemd en vergruisd*, p. 104.

33 *Nieuwe Rotterdamsche Courant* (26 May 1929).

34 H. Colijn, *Dispereert niet ..... Rede ter herdenking van den 350sten geboortedag van Jan Pietersz. Coen uitgesproken te Hoorn den 1sten Februari 1937* (Amsterdam: W. ten Have, 1937).

35 H. C. Leemhorst, *Plechtige herdenking van Jan Pieterszoon Coen in de Groote Kerk van zijn vaderstad Hoorn, 350 jaren na zijn geboorte: openingsrede* (Hoorn: Edecea, 1937), p. 3.

36 'De Coen zomerfeesten van 1937', in *Coen! Geroemd en vergruisd*, pp. 102–3; www.coenstandbeeld.blogspot.nl/2012/04/coenfeesten.html#more.

37 Koninklijk Instituut voor Taal-, Land- en Volkenkunde, Leiden, Collectie H. J. de Graaf [H 1055] no. 12, Aantekeningen en opstellen over J. Hageman Jcz. (1817–1871), c. 1970.

38 W. Ph. Coolhaas, 'Over het karakter en daden van Jan Pietersz Coen', p. 201; J. Hageman, *Het ontworpen standbeeld voor Jan Pieterszoon Koen te Batavia tegenover de geschiedenis* (Batavia: Ogilvie & Co., 1868) available on the webpage of the Staatsbibliothek Berlin, http://digital.staatsbibliothek-berlin.de.

39 E. Snijders, 'Een nationalistische onthulling', p. 6; P. J. Veth, 'Levensbericht J.K.J. de Jonge', in *Jaarboek* (1880), pp. 22–68, available on the webpage of the Huygens Institute, www.dwc.knaw.nl.

40 *Het Nieuws van de Dag* (10 September 1883); M. Bloembergen, *Koloniale vertoningen*, pp. 53 and 80.

41 W. Ph. Coolhaas, 'Over het karakter en daden van Jan Pietersz Coen', p. 202; E. Scnijders, 'Een nationalistische onthulling', p. 60.

42 J. J. Slauerhoff, *Jan Pieterszoon Coen. Drama in elf taferelen* (Maastricht and Brussels: A. A. M. Stols, 1931); Menno ter Braak, 'Een nieuwe Rembrandt en een nieuwe Coen', *Forum* 1 (1932), pp. 124–5, available on the DBNL webpage, www.dbnl.org; *Friese Koerier* (24 October 1961); *De Waarheid* (7 October 1961); C. Koenjer, 'Dubieuze hoofdrol. Het toneelstuk van Slauerhoff over Jan Pieterszoon Coen', in *Coen! Geroemd en vergruisd*, pp. 80–1.

43 R. A. M. Bergman, 'Jan Pieterszoon Coen. Een psychografie. Bijdrage tot de leer der constitutietypen', *Tijdschrift voor Indische Taal-, Land- en Volkenkunde* 73 (1933), pp. 1–56, available on the KITLV webpage, www.kitlv.nl/documents; W.Ph. Coolhaas, 'Over het karakter en daden van Jan Pietersz Coen', pp. 207–8; W.Ph. Coolhaas, 'Over karakter en daden van Jan Pietersz Coen (slot)', *Bijdragen voor Vaderlandsche Geschiedenis en Oudheidkunde* (1944), pp. 60–74, esp. p. 60.

44 www.coenstandbeeld.blogspot.nl/2012/04/kritiek.html#more (accessed 22 April 2013).
45 'Heldenverering niet op zijn plaats', *De Waarheid* (17 January 1987); *Limburgsch Dagblad* (20 May 1987); S. Kingma, 'J. P. Coen: meedogenloze grondlegger overzees wereldrijk', *Leeuwarder Courant* (20 May 1987); D. Beemster, 'De laatste der hekeldichten', in *Coen! Geroemd en vergruisd*, pp. 100–1; www.coenstandbeeld.blogspot. nl/2012/04/kritiek.html#more.
46 *Coen! Geroemd en vergruisd*, p. 3; B. Funnekotter, 'Eerst de 'Maarten' nu de 'Coen', *NRC-Handelsblad* (14 April 2012), p. 26.
47 'J. P. Coen verdient zijn standbeeld', *De Telegraaf* (2 July 2012).
48 Hoorn City Council minutes are available on the city's webpage, www.hoorn.nl; 'Hoorn geeft J. P. Coen na veel gediscussieer een genuanceerde sokkel', *NRC-Handelsblad* (11 March 2012).
49 E. Snijders, 'Coen monumenten', pp. 67–9.
50 *Het leven en de daden van Nederlands meest beroemde Zeehelden en Vlootvoogden* (Amsterdam: Erven Hendriuk van Munster en Johannes van der Hey, 1841); S. de Vries, *De lucht in gevlogen, de hemel in geprezen. Eerbewijzen voor Van Speyk* (Haarlem: Joh. Enschedé en Zoonen, 1988); Ronald Prud'homme van Reine, *Zeehelden* (Amsterdam: De Arbeiderspers, 2005); G. G. Hellinga, *Zeehelden uit de Gouden Eeuw* (Zutphen: Walburg Pers, 2006); A. Zuidhoek, *Held of schurk. Dertien zeerovers uit de Lage Landen* (Utrecht: Omniboek, 2011).
51 J. Bank, *Het roemrijk vaderland. Cultureel nationalisme in Nederland in de negentiende eeuw* (The Hague: SDU, 1989); E. Snijders, 'Een nationalistische onthulling', p. 58. The Van Heutsz monument in Amsterdam is another example of expressing Dutch colonial power. In 1935, the largest colonial memorial in the Netherlands was unveiled in Amsterdam. It paid tribute to General J. B. van Heutsz (1851–1924), who embodied Dutch colonial expansion and power in the East Indies. The memorial was controversial from the start. G. Oostindie, H. S. Nordholt, F. Steijlen, *Postkoloniale Monumenten in the Nederland* (Leiden: KITLV Press, 2011), pp. 20–1.

[135]

CHAPTER EIGHT

The memory of Lord Clive in Britain and beyond: imperial hero and villain

Richard Goebelt

From the late eighteenth century onwards, and well into our own post-colonial times, 'Clive of India' has been a household name in much of the 'British world'. Statues dedicated to Robert Clive (1725–74), military leader and governor of Bengal, adorn both Shrewsbury, the county town of his native Shropshire, and King Charles Street in central London, near St James's Park. In 1935, a Hollywood movie entitled *Clive of India* was released in the US, and later shown both in Britain and France. A Senior Girls House at the Duke of York's Royal Military School is still named after Clive, as is a settlement in the Hawke's Bay province of New Zealand. Intrepid Australians who enjoy their food hot can still spice it up by adding a good dose of 'Clive of India Authentic Hot Madras Curry Powder'. When, in 2006, a 250-year-old giant tortoise died in the Kolkata zoo, headlines in the British press proclaimed the demise of 'Clive of India's pet'.[1] And the 250th anniversary of Clive's famous victory in the battle of Plassey in northern India led to nationalistic demonstrations on the battlefield in 2007.

Robert Clive has doubtless played an important role within the memory cultures of both Britain and India. Seen from an Indian nationalist perspective, his success at Plassey (1757) was won by foul means and marked the beginning of India's loss of freedom.[2] To British imperialists Clive was the hero who laid the foundations for and provided a legitimisation of British rule in India. As late as 1975 an article in *The Times* stated that, 'Clive has been exciting English passions, sometimes patriotic pride, more often envy or sanctimonious indignation. He was a popular ogre in his own time, a *Boy's Own* hero in the imperial heyday, a figure of obloquy in all those commentaries which have, into our own day, successfully persuaded the English how wicked they used to be.'[3]

Notions about Robert Clive have been created and disseminated by different media. Newspaper articles, official and unofficial histories, novels, photography and film: they all helped to transform Clive into a personalised site of memory – shared by Britons and Indians and contested for two and a half centuries. At least three distinct periods can be identified in the history of Clive's memory. In the middle of the eighteenth century, when British rule in India was being established, Lord Clive was seen as an archetypical nabob – a ruthless and wealthy servant of the East India Company. In the nineteenth century, when the British Empire had to struggle to maintain its position, he morphed into a national hero. In the early twentieth century, when the empire was engaged in the suppression of rising nationalism in British India, Clive emerged as an imperial apotheosis.

This chapter seeks to deal with the fluidity of Lord Clive's image by placing him into the context of a symbolic transnational intersection of India and Great Britain – neighbouring countries in historical and political terms even though geographically they are separated by thousands of miles. Transnational sites of memory can be as important to the memory culture of the states and societies participating in them as national ones. Whereas national *lieux de mémoire* serve to unify collective memory, sites of imperial memory tend to be divisive. They have a two-sided character because the versions that are prominent in the minds of the colonial masters (or their descendants) are often radically different from the perspective of the colonised (or their descendants).[4]

This study will first explore eighteenth-century perceptions of Clive: the lavishly wealthy 'nabob' who threatened English morality by importing Asian decadence and luxury to the British Isles. It will then proceed to analyse his transformation into an icon of the British Empire in the nineteenth and early twentieth centuries, which owed a great deal to Macaulay's seminal essay on Lord Clive. Finally, it will examine the alternative readings of Clive as a symbol of oppression and exploitation pioneered by Thomas Paine in America and later adopted and elaborated by Indian writers and historians.

Perceptions in eighteenth-century Britain: nabob and hero

Clive's career illustrates both the changing realities of British society in the second half of the eighteenth century and the new challenges the country faced at its imperial periphery. His arrival in India on 1 June 1744 did not appear to anyone, least of all to Clive himself, to be an event of great importance. Financially self-serving, unpopular and plagued by suicidal moods, Clive hardly looked like the typical founder of an empire. He first rose to prominence when he defended the Carnatic's capital of Arcot against the French in October 1751. According to Macaulay, this feat moved Prime Minister Pitt the Elder (1708–78) to describe Clive, who had received no formal military training, as a 'heaven-born general [. . .] a military genius which might excite the admiration of the King of Prussia'.[5] As a lieutenant-colonel Clive was then put in command of the expedition sent to recover Calcutta from the Bengal prince *nawab* Siraj ud Daulah (1733–57) in December 1756. Within the following year, Clive would enter into two secret treaties (replete with false promises) with the Bengal merchant bankers Jagah Seth and Omichand, which secured him the funds to defeat Siraj ud Daulah's army at the battle of Plassey on 23 June 1757.[6] Mir Jafar (1691–1765), who had thrown in his lot with the East India Company before the battle, was appointed *nawab* by Clive, but remained little more than a puppet ruler of the British.[7]

Clive's victory in a corner of eastern India, coupled with the Company's defeat of French forces in the Battle of Wandiwash in 1760, the battle of Buxar and the granting of Diwani (1765) consolidated the British position in South Asia and revolutionised the nature of British power on the subcontinent. Within the next 100 years, the East India Company brought the entire subcontinent under its military control.[8] The new *nawab* granted Clive an assignment of revenues as a kind of salary (*jagir*) and this would form the basis of his great wealth.[9]

In Great Britain, Clive emerged as the most popular, the wealthiest and probably the most politically ruthless of eighteenth-century 'nabobs'. What marked him out as the exemplary 'nabob' was his explicit and transparent ambition to amass wealth and gain a reputation in the metropole. This was not an aim in itself, though, but served the ulterior purpose of influencing the course of political events in India. In 1761 he acquired a seat as the Tory Member of Parliament for his hometown of Shrewsbury; he was created Baron Clive of Plassey in the Kingdom of Ireland and received a knighthood.[10]

In line with the growing influence in society and policy enjoyed by men like Clive, a resistance to them developed among Britain's political élite. It was feared that they might bring about a subversion of the familiar political order in the United Kingdom.[11] Plays like Samuel Foote's *The Nabob*[12] or poems such as Swift's 'The East India Culprits'[13] captured a widespread feeling: 'Nabobs' with their 'ill-gotten' imperial gains were destroying the carefully established stability of British social life. Growing levels of wealth and increased living standards would lead to a loss of individual freedoms and to a cossetting of the political class. 'The riches of Asia', as William Pitt put it, 'have been poured in upon us, and have brought with them not only Asiatic luxury, but, I fear, Asiatic principles of government'.[14]

In an important sense, Indian culture and wealth as much as the nabob himself were perceived as sources of corruption. The moral and legal probity of the new Asian possessions were finally thrown into doubt, when information leaked out about malpractice within the East India Company – along with charges of oppression and plunder of the people of Bengal. The British Empire was regarded with mistrust, because it appeared questionable how the extension of executive power at the colonial periphery could be combined with the freedom of the British nation.

This kind of perception was still very much present during the impeachment of Warren Hastings and corrupt 'nabobs' initiated by Burke and the Whig alliance after 1786.[15] The two decades that followed the battle of Plassey were years of instability of the United Kingdom. The political system first had to accommodate the social disturbance evoked by returning nabobs like Clive. Second, ways had to be found to cope with the financial and political transformations which arose from the riches of Bengal. As a consequence, Britons had to rework entirely their ideas of empire, governance, rule and supremacy.[16] The special committee set up by the House of Commons in 1773 to examine charges of corruption and greed against Clive, as well as his subsequent defence were thus dramatic pieces in a theatre of public disapproval. Accused of having 'set an evil example to all the rest . . . to the dishonour and detriment of the state'[17], Clive responded: 'By God, at this moment do I stand astonished at my own moderation'.[18] On another occasion he exclaimed: 'Leave my honour, take away my fortune'[19] – and then left Parliament in tears. In the end, he was acquitted for lack of evidence.

Nineteenth-century imperial icon

No one has done more to elevate Robert Clive to the status of an imperial hero than Thomas Babington Macaulay. His 'Speech on the Government of India' (1833)[20] portrayed the British Raj in India as characterised by moral selflessness and generous paternalism. There was no doubt that Britons, as God's chosen people, were acting with benevolence, compassion and charity, and hence their imperial efforts could be productive of nothing but favourable consequences for the Indians.[21] In fact, the empire itself began to be justified in largely moral terms, as an enterprise intended to bring civilisation to the less advanced. Macaulay wrote his essay on Lord Clive in 1840, after his return from a three and a half year stay in India.[22] He portrayed the victor of Plassey as a pioneer, who had both inaugurated the policy of annexation and initiated methods of government by which the advance of British arms might be made beneficial to the subjected races. The superiority of English civilisation is one of the determining themes of the essay.[23]

Macaulay offered a generous estimate of Clive's character, who 'seems to us to have been constitutionally the very opposite of a knave; bold even to temerity; sincere even to indiscretion; hearty in friendship; open in enmity'.[24] He accorded Clive an honourable place among the great statesmen of all time, because he was among the first to recommend that the conquests of the East India Company be taken under the protection of the British crown. Macaulay put it succinctly: 'From his first visit to India dates the renown of the English arms in the East. [. . .] From Clive's second visit to India dates the political ascendancy of the English in that country. [. . .] From Clive's third visit to India dates the purity of the administration of our Eastern empire. When he landed in Calcutta in 1765, [. . . he] first made dauntless and unsparing war on the gigantic system of oppression, extortion, and corruption'.[25]

Clive's third visit to India, as Macaulay should have known, was not undertaken to realise a lofty vision of statesmanship or to restore law and order. For years Clive had been fighting a high-stakes battle to retain the wealth he had acquired in India. He finally returned to India to settle some of the problems facing the East India Company on the condition that his *jagir* would continue to be paid to him. Macaulay omitted the most important fact from his essay: the underlying continuity of Clive's concern for his own personal interests.[26] While Macaulay did concede that 'Clive committed great faults',[27] and, on occasion, displayed behaviour which, 'if not in itself evil, was yet of evil example',[28] there was no room for fundamental doubt. 'But his faults, when weighed against his merits, and viewed in connection with his temptations, do not appear to us to deprive him of his right to an honourable place in the estimation of posterity', he concluded.[29] In doing so, he painted the portrait of a new kind of hero: a great policy maker, who accomplishes great undertakings.[30]

Macaulay's essay contributed to a change in the perception, reception and popularisation of Robert Clive. On 23 June 1857 a group of notables met in Willis's Room on St James's Street in London to celebrate the centenary of the battle of Plassey.[31] The principal purpose of the gathering, which was chaired by the Lord Edwin Hill, a Conservative Member of Parliament, had been to plan the erection of a statue 'of the great Lord Clive'[32] in his hometown of Shrewsbury.

The meeting took place against the backdrop of the escalation of the so-called Indian Mutiny in May 1857. This rebellion among Sepoy soldiers appeared to be an attack on both the belief that the British were generally recognised as benefactors and on British ideals of free-dom.[33] The propaganda which described the British response to the Indian Mutiny as a heroic fight put Clive in a new light. This new dynamic of commemorating him reached a first climax with this call for a worthy monument in his honour, because, in the words of the Earl of Stanhope, 'it was unnecessary to say a word of the transcendent merits of Lord Clive who was the founder of our Eastern empire'.[34] By erecting a monument to Clive in his hometown the initiators sought 'to stimulate and to excite the moral principles of the rising generation'.[35]

All of a sudden Clive appeared to be the very antidote to the cur-rent problems. The 'late defection in the Indian Army', *The Times* observed, had resulted from a 'departure from the principles laid down by Lord Clive, which was to treat the Sepoys not with severity, but with kindness'. The article would have its readers believe that Clive had promoted 'social and kindly intercourse' between the Sepoys and their officers – 'thereby stabilizing the Empire in the East'.[36] If only his policy to let the Indians attain wealth had been adhered to, it was supposed, the rebellion of the Indian officers would never have occurred.

As a side effect, Clive's perception as a national hero also served to elevate the British Army, which seemed the only institution cap-able of defending the empire in emergencies such as the Indian Mutiny.[37] Before the Crimean War (1853–56) and the Indian Mutiny, the military had been seen in a much more equivocal light. The events of 1857–58 led to substantial political and military reforms, the most significant being the replacement of the East India Company with a more formal colonial administration, and the strengthening of the British Army in India.[38] As befitted an imperial nation, British officers and soldiers serving in the subcontinent should behave in a chivalrous manner and it was Lord Clive who emerged as the paragon to provide the British with a sense of orientation and self-assurance in the light of the Indian challenges. By winning against the odds at Arcot (1751) and Plassey (1757), Clive had proved Britain's military superiority. According to Macaulay '[e]very person who takes a fair and enlightened view of his whole career, must admit that our island, so fertile in heroes and statesmen, has scarcely ever produced a man more truly great, either in arms or in council'.[39]

A century after Plassey, Clive had emerged as the finest example of a military man and empire-builder. As was purportedly demonstrated by his sympathy for vanquished enemies and indigenous people alike, he was also a man of feeling and justice.[40] As the founding hero of the empire, the erstwhile nabob had morphed into a sensitive human being. Masculinity was no longer exclusively defined by military success, but also by compassion and mildness.[41] Using this new palette of colours, the Victorian myth-maker Macaulay drew a picture of Clive as a just hero protecting allegedly British values and fighting against the reign of terror associated with his opponent Siraj ud Daulah.[42]

Macaulay's myth was largely based on John Holwell's dubious eyewitness account of the massacre that had gained notoriety under the gruesome name of 'Black Hole of Calcutta'.[43] According to Macaulay the atrocious experience of more than 140 British and Anglo-Indian soldiers being left to suffocate in a dungeon was crucial for the East India Company's decision to conquer Bengal: 'The cry of the whole settlement [Ft. William] was for vengeance. . . . Within forty-eight hours after the arrival of the intelligence it was determined that an expedition should be sent to the Hoogley, and that Clive should be at the head of forces'.[44] The retelling of the Black Hole story by Macaulay impacted directly on the refashioning of the public memory of Clive. The massacre justified military intervention in Indian politics. Clive's decisive action was portrayed as an outstanding example of self-sacrifice.

The narrative of Plassey as an illustration of Clive's military genius was still promoted in 1905 when S. C. Hill published his monumental *Bengal in 1756–1757*, and six years later a widely read *School History of England* claimed that 'Clive, who began life as a clerk, was the real founder of our Indian Empire'.[45] Eventually, even the colourful commodities of popular mass culture – such as collectors' cards in cigarette packets – proclaimed the story of Clive as the gallant imperial hero.[46]

Imperial apotheosis

In April 1907, 150 years after the battle of Plassey, *The Times* published a letter it had received from a former viceroy of India. Lord Curzon of Kedleston deplored the fact that the City of London still lacked a memorial to honour Lord Clive. Clive, Curzon argued, 'was the man who at the age of thirty-one laid the foundations of an Empire more enduring than Alexander's, more splendid than Caesar's'.[47] The newspaper's editors added to Curzon's paean of praise by pointing out that after Plassey 'the Natives everywhere had turned their eyes away from the fallen fortunes of France to the actual and incontestable might of England'.[48] Some weeks later Lord Curzon elaborated on further aspects of Clive's life which he deemed worthy of commemoration. In a speech at the Merchant Taylor's School, which Clive had attended between 1737 and 1739,[49] the former viceroy argued that 'Clive was one of the master spirits of the English race. Behind everything lay a high ideal of duty, and a passionate love for the country from which he had sprung. He was one of those forces that seem to be put into the world to shape the destinies of mankind'.[50] By July 1908, more than £5,000 of public donations had poured into the Clive Memorial Fund, set up by Curzon to finance both a bronze sculpture for the capital and a marble statue for the as yet unfinished Victoria Hall in Calcutta.[51]

Curzon's contributions fitted smoothly into a contemporary feeling of national pride and of jingoist superiority over the native populations of the subcontinent. Denied their own sovereignty, Indians were defined as subjects of the 'greatest governing race that the world has ever seen'.[52] The context of the renewed celebration of Clive was a sense of historical mission and of a collective act of national self-affirmation. It revolved around legitimising historical patterns of thought and communicating the notion of an 'imperial nationality of British subjecthood', that is, of a concept of general citizenship of all those accepting their subjection under the British Crown.[53]

On 24 August 1912 John Tweed's statue 'Clive of India' was finally unveiled 'without ceremony' in the garden in front of Gwydyr House, overlooking Whitehall.[54] Notwithstanding the austere nature of this event Clive's reputation as the founder of the British Empire in the East had reached its climax. The bronze statue in London and its marble counterpart in Calcutta invited onlookers to make amends for the hostility Clive had to endure during his lifetime.[55] Four years on, the London monument was relocated to a more prominent position on the steps of Charles Street, a spot originally chosen for it by King Edward VII in 1907 (Figure 8.1).[56]

It was again Lord Curzon, as head of the Clive Memorial Fund, who wrote to the Dean and Chapter of Westminster in November 1913 to request that a memorial for Clive be installed in the Abbey. Early in 1915 the Dean eventually provided a costing for erecting it. The Great War caused a delay, though, and it was not until 1919 that a memorial tablet was finally placed in the south choir aisle.[57] It is not without deeper meaning that even a religious setting was deemed suitable for honouring the memory of Clive. Macaulay had already made clear that Clive's record as the founder of Britain's rule in India did not constitute his central virtue. It was crucial that he possessed an unblemished character. The decency and morality of those wielding Britain's military and political might were seen as the pillars supporting the country's rule over her far-flung empire. A British imperial hero was thus marked by archetypical characteristics such as energy, fortitude, self-control, readiness to serve and an imperturbable sense of duty towards the greater good.[58] Clive's image therefore changed to

8.1 Statue of Robert Clive, London located at the end of King Charles Street, overlooking St James's Park

fit this new matrix: only those facets of his biography remained which marked him out as a keen and faithful paladin of the British Empire.[59] Unsuitable aspects of his life disappeared from the public view.

This process was clearly in evidence when military historian John William Fortescue (1859–1933) considered the bicentenary of Clive's birth in 1925. 'We are', he maintained, 'still too much influenced by the prejudices of Clive's enemies to estimate him aright'. True, he had 'accepted between two and three hundred thousand pounds' from Mir Jaffar, but this was only because he appreciated money 'as a means to power and to the benefit of those whom he loved. . . . He was, in fact, far too great to care for opulences'. Faced with a 'system [that] was built up on corruption', Clive sought 'to place India under the crown'. Even Clive's suicide was evidence of his superiority: 'Human stupidity and physical pain had beaten him at last. . . . A "nameless and inscrutable disease" hung always about him'. Just like Arthur Wellesley – the later 'Iron Duke' of Wellington – Clive defined a 'standard of duty and integrity which, if sometimes for a time abandoned, has never been wholly lost'.[60]

Clive's dictum, 'I stand astonished at my own moderation' would occupy an especially precious place in the minds of the following generations. When addressing the Primrose League in 1919, Lord Curzon could think of no phrase that would be more apt to characterise Britain's attitude to defeated Germany: 'Gentlemen, I stand aghast at my own moderation'.[61]

Indian readings

Clive's apotheosis in the imperial metropolis was matched by his vilification at the colonial and ex-colonial peripheries of the British Empire. On the eve of the American War of Independence, in 1775, Thomas Paine published *Reflections on the Life and Death of Robert Clive* in the Pennsylvania Magazine.[62] The famous Radical launched a fierce attack on the inhumanity of Britain's imperial conquest in the East, the corruption of the Westminster system and the decline in moral values amongst the British citizens. For Paine, Robert Clive was the archetypical beneficiary of this negative development. 'But, oh India! Thou loud proclaimer of European cruelties, thou bloody monument of unnecessary deaths, be tender in the day of enquiry, and shew a Christian world thou canst suffer and forgive', he implored.[63] Clive's lust for power, Paine explained, had struck the people of Bengal like a storm. Wherever Clive and the East India Company had ventured, 'murder and rapine' had followed, with 'famine and wretchedness' not far behind.[64]

Several decades later, on the eve on the Indian Mutiny, Paine's writings were to exercise a significant influence on the formation of the political discourse in India. Anti-British Brahman teachers used his texts to instruct their students – among them the polymath and social reformer Mahatma Jyotiba Phule (1827–90) – that nothing but a coming together of India's castes could bring about the regaining of political control over the subcontinent. It was from his reading of Paine that Phule derived his argument that all human beings – including British subjects – possessed natural and inalienable rights.[65] The context within which this discourse unfolded was a memory not just of Clive but of the Raj more widely, which, for many Indians, remained a painful one. 'Whenever I read or hear the phrase colonial India', Ramachandra Guha remarked in 1998, 'it hurts me. It hurts like an injury that has healed and yet has retained somehow a trace of the original pain linked to many different things – memories, values, sentiments'.[66]

Indian historiography in a Western sense of the word developed in the second half of the nineteenth century. At the time, Bengal saw the publication of two literary works that evoked immense excitement among the educated classes.[67] The first of these publications was a poem by the Bengali poet and writer Nabinchandra Sen (1847–1909) entitled 'Palashir Yuddha' ('Battle of Plassey'), which was performed as a play in 1875, but was not made available in print until twenty years later.[68] 'Palashir Yuddha' combined real events of the year 1757 with literary additions which triggered several controversies both in literary circles and within the British government in Calcutta.[69] A more scholarly and focused attempt to correct the historical accounts disseminated through the available histories and textbooks was made by the Bengali historian and social worker Akshaykumar Maitreya (1861–1930).[70] In his book *Sirajuddaula*, published in 1897, he sought to defend the character of the nawab Siraj ud Daulah by contradicting the common narrative of a depraved king who lost his kingdom as a result of his own evil character. Moreover, he challenged the story of the Black Hole of Calcutta ('Andhakoop-kahini'), which, he argued, required careful investigation 'according to the well-established system of modern critical method, which is a method of Science'.[71] In light of the growing political tensions after 1905–06, the British government prohibited 'Palashir Yuddha' as well as *Sirajauddaula* alongside a number of other plays. 'Palashir Yuddha', the government claimed, was 'of an objectionable nature and likely to excite feelings of disaffection to the Government established by law in British India'.[72]

The rewriting of the British period by Indian historians began in earnest with the publication, in 1946, of Jawaharlal Nehru's *The Discovery of India*, where Clive was characterised as having won the battle of Plassey 'by promoting treason and forgery'.[73] What followed amounted to a recasting of Clive and a reciprocal re-evaluation of his enemy Siraj ud Daulah. In 1963, the writer and historian Ram Gopal questioned the entirety of the British interpretation of Clive's life as an 'empire builder, and as such a hero to history' and thus challenged the legitimacy of British domination of India. 'It is to urge the necessity that history of the British period must be rewritten', he explained. In his interpretation, Gopal focused on the endeavours of Siraj ud Daulah to maintain the independence of Bengal, and rejected British accounts that vilified him as 'a heartless monster who had pregnant women ripped open to gratify his curiosity and had boatloads of people upset in the Ganges to watch the agonies of the drowning'.[74]

For the Indian historian, Siraj ud Daulah was 'a tragic hero, who was the only one of the principal actors in the tragic drama who did not attempt to deceive, [who wanted to assert the authority of his government and consequently] stands higher in the scale of honour than does the name of Clive'.[75] At the same time B. K. Gupta exposed inconsistencies in the eyewitness account underpinning the story of the 'Black Hole' and claimed that Siraj ud Daulah had not intended to kill the prisoners in Calcutta.[76] The Bengali historian Kalikinkar Datta portrayed Siraj ud Daulah as an Anti-Clive, who did not fall back on collusions and fraud, but trusted his subjects. Indian historiography even cast doubt on Clive's military abilities: 'Clive won the battle of Plassey in spite of himself. In the war council held at Katwah, only two days before, he gave his vote in favour of retreat'.[77] *The History of Asia* by Beldona Vittal Rao reduces Clive's victory in the battle of Plassey to nothing more than a conspiracy with the merchant bankers Jagat Seth and Omichand, who in turn conspired with Siraj ud Daulah's disloyal general Mir Jafar to dethrone the nawab. The British victory was thus the result of treachery by the nawab's generals and officers.[78]

Even today, the battle site at Plassey evokes strong nationalist sentiments. During the 250th anniversary of the battle in 2007 Indian politicians such as Debrata Biswas, general secretary of the Forward Bloc, a party set up by India's independence war hero, Subhas Chandra Bose, used it to promote nationalist visions. In their view, Siraj ud Daulah embodied a warning to future generations that collaboration with foreign powers and discord among Indians were signs of political immaturity and would always lead to the loss of freedom. At this occasion, the BBC reported, local leftists displayed huge cut-outs of Siraj and Clive alongside Iraq's hanged leader Saddam Hussein and US President George W Bush. Cut-outs of Subhas Bose and Bangladesh's first leader, Sheikh Mujib, could also be seen.[79]

A bronze bust of Siraj ud Daulah was installed in front of the white memorial erected by the British at Plassey 100 years ago to commemorate their victory. 'Both monuments will remain', Biswas of the nationalist 'Forward Bloc' predicted; 'one to remind us of the price for loss of freedom, the other to remind us of Siraj and his uncompromising stance against the British. . . . Plassey will help us emphasise the need for Asian unity against Western imperialism again'. West-Bengal politician and deputy for the Indian National Congress Adhir Choudhury explained that Siraj ud Daulah 'is now seen as a victim of British guile and conspiracy, and as the last independent ruler of undivided Bengal, he provokes much warm sentiment in both West Bengal and Bangladesh'.[80]

Conclusion

In the United Kingdom the transition from the British Empire to the Commonwealth has coincided with a gradual waning of the interest in 'overseas' issues. Freed from the pressure of public preconceptions, modern research has been able to debunk much of the heroic narrative of the nineteenth and early twentieth centuries, even though some of them have proved hard to shift. With regard to 'Clive of India' the process of de-mystification was speeded up in 1960 when a previously unknown account of the battle of Plassey was found. It came from the pen of the officer John Wood, who had been present on the battle-field. On 6 July 1757, Wood had sent a report to his superiors.[81] He had hoped to learn about the art of generalship but he left disappointed. 'Such was this great and decisive battle by which a kingdom was conquered without there ever having been a general assault', he concluded sarcastically.[82] There was no praise of Clive as a 'heaven-born general', no legend about the events of the day. According to Wood's report, nothing had happened at Plassey that would justify calling Clive a military hero.[83]

Since the discovery of Wood's report, historical research on Clive has gone a long way and has left behind the pattern of the heroic school of interpretation. Instead of uncritically praising Clive's genius and outstanding military qualities, modern historians now emphasise the very 'conventionality' of his early career in the East India Company.[84] The attack against Siraj ud Daulah, they stress, was neither carried out to exact revenge for the capture of Fort William nor was it motivated by Bengal merchants who feared losing attractive trading partners, if the British were to withdraw from Bengal. The real reason for British military involvement in Plassey was the defence of their trading monopoly, which was persistently threatened by the nawab.

The perceptions of Robert Clive that have been generated over the past 250 years have manifested the typical characteristics of a site of memory. Several layers of written, oral and medial traditions have contributed to a permanently shifting construction of the meaning of Clive's life and record. As a site of memory, Robert Clive has been relevant, above all, to audiences in Britain and India. On the erstwhile colonial periphery, the manifold traditions stand in stark contrast to Macaulay's seminal essay and cast doubt on the mid-nineteenth-century lionising of Robert Clive. For Indians, it was the policy of the East India Company, established by Clive, that first de-industrialised their country and then empowered Britain to its own industrial revolution. In essence, 'Asia played a great role in civilizing Europe'.[85]

The permanent reshaping of Clive as a site of memory is a process that is still ongoing. One can find allusions and – often contradictory – references to him in current political debates in Southeast Asia as well as in Britain. During the 2013 general election campaign in Bangladesh, for instance, the opposition party claimed the government suffered from the 'Lord-Clive-syndrome' of shamelessly enriching itself.[86] In Britain, on the other hand, in the search for causes of the current banking and financial crisis in the Western world, Clive has recently, and rather surprisingly, resurfaced as a pioneer of anti-corruption policies.[87] In this vein, even the embodiment of the venal nabob of the eighteenth century could turn into an icon of fair financial dealings in the early twenty-first century. These most recent reconfigurations thus highlight how much notions of the past are influenced by the challenges of the present.[88]

Notes

1 See *Daily Mail* (24 March 2006).
2 S. Bandyopadhyay, *From Plassey to Partition: A History of Modern India* (Hyderabad: Orient Longman, 2004), p. 44.
3 *The Times* (16 October 1975), p. 12.
4 E. François, 'Europäische lieux de mémoire', in: G. Budde, S. Conrad and O. Janz (eds), *Transnationale Geschichte: Themen, Tendenzen und Theorien* (Göttingen: Vandenhoeck & Ruprecht, 2008), pp. 290–304, 296–7.
5 V. D. Scudder (ed.), *Macaulay's Essay on Lord Clive* (Honolulu: University Press of the Pacific, 2002), p. 86.
6 R. Travers, *Ideology and Empire in Eighteenth-Century India: The British in Bengal* (Cambridge: Cambridge University Press, 2007), p. 4. T. W. Nechtmann, 'Nabobs Revisited. A Cultural History of British Imperialism and the Indian Question in Late-Eighteenth-Century Britain', *History Compass* 4/4 (2006), pp. 645–67, 648 and P. Lawson, *A Taste for Empire and Glory: Studies in British Overseas Expansion, 1660–1800* (Aldershot: Variorum, 1997).
7 P. Lawson, *A Taste for Empire*, p. 803. N. Ferguson, *Empire: How Britain made the Modern World* (London: Penguin Books, 2004), p. 36.
8 M. Fisher, 'Asians in Britain: Negotiations of Identity Through Self-representation', in K. Wilson, *A New Imperial History; Culture, Identity, and Modernity in Britain and the Empire, 1660–1840* (Cambridge: Cambridge University Press, 2004), p. 99.
9 For a brief report of the battle of Plassey: J. Wood, 'Regarding Colonel Cleve's victory in Bengal over the Nabob of Moxeadabath', in H. Furber and K. Glamann, 'Plassey: A New Account from the Danish Archives', *The Journal of Asian Studies* 2 (1960), pp. 177–87.
10 P. Lawson, *A Taste for Empire*, p. 228.
11 T. W. Nechtmann, 'Nabobs Revisited', pp. 655–6.
12 S. Foote, *The Nabob. A Comedy in Three Acts* (London: W. Lowndes and S. Bladon, 1795).
13 'The East Indian Culprits'. A poem [electronic resource Public Library New York City]. In imitations of Swift's 'Legion Club' (By an officer, who was present at the battle of Plassey.) Imprint [London]: London for G. Kearsly, no. 46, Fleet-Street, 1773.
14 P. Lawson and J. Phillips , '"Our Execrable Banditti": Perceptions of Nabobs in Mid-Eighteenth Century Britain', *Albion* 16 (1984), p. 238.
15 M. Mukherjee, *India in the Shadows of Empire: A Legal and Political History, 1774–1950* (New Delhi: Oxford University Press, 2010), pp. 1, 11.
16 *Ibid.*, p. 11.
17 *The Annual Register of the Year 1773* (London: J. Dodsley 1774), p. 106.
18 J. Malcolm, *The Life of Robert, Lord Clive: Collected from the Family papers. Communicated by The Earl of Powis Vol. 3* (London: John Murray, 1836), pp. 349–50.
19 *Ibid.*
20 T. B. Macaulay, 'Speech on the Government of India [July 1833]', in *The Complete Works of Lord Macaulay, XII vols.* (London: Longman, Green and Co., 1898), vol. XI, pp. 543–86.

PART II: HEROES AND VILLAINS

21 T. B. Macaulay, *The Works, vol. XI, Speeches, Poems & Miscellaneous Writings, vol.1* (Port Chester: Adamant Media Corp., 2006), p. 423.

22 V. D. Scudder (ed.), *Macaulay's Essay on Lord Clive* (Honolulu: University Press of the Pacific, 2002).

23 U. S. Rau, 'The National/imperial Subject in T. B. Macaulay's Historiography', *Nineteenth-Century Contexts: An Interdisciplinary Journal* 23:1 (2001), 89–119, p. 98.

24 *Ibid*, p. 60–6.

25 V. D. Scudder, *Macaulay's Essay on Lord Clive*, p. 127.

26 J. Nigel, 'Robert Clive and Imperial Modernity', *Comparative Literature and Culture* 12:2 (2010).

27 V. D. Scudder, *Macaulay's Essay on Lord Clive*, p. 126.

28 *Ibid.*, p. 77.

29 *Ibid.*

30 U. S. Rau, 'The National/imperial Subject', p. 108.

31 *The Times* (24 June 1857), p. 12.

32 *Ibid.*

33 For a history of British and Indian memories of the 'Indian Mutiny' from 1857 to the present see A. Erll, *Prämediation – Remediation: Repräsentationen des indischen Aufstands in imperialen und post-kolonialen Medienkulturen von 1857 bis zur Gegenwart* (Trier: Wissenschaftlicher Verlag Trier, 2007); P. J. Cain and A. G. Hopkins, *British Imperialism: 1688-2000* (London: Pearson Education, 2002), pp. 300–2.

34 *The Times* (24 June 1857), p. 12. Like Stanhope in his speech on 23 June 1857, Macaulay also stressed parallels to the Duke of Wellington (1769–1852), Macaulay's *Essay on Lord Clive*, p. 78. The analogy to the Duke of Wellington was re-enacted in a solemn article honouring the bicentary of Clive's death by the President of the Royal Historical Society John William Fortescue. *The Times of London* (29 September 1925), pp. 15–16.

35 *The Times* (24 June 1857), p. 12.

36 *Ibid.*

37 V. Nünning, 'Daß Jeder seine Pflicht thue'. Die Bedeutung der Indian Mutiny für das nationale britische Verständnis', *Archiv für Kulturgeschichte* 78 (1996), pp. 363–91, p. 381.

38 S. Heathorn, 'The Absent Site of Memory', in I. Sengupta, *Memory, History and Colonialism. Engaging with Pierre Nora in Colonial and Postcolonial Context* (London: German Historical Institute, 2009), pp. 73–117, p. 81.

39 V. D. Scudder, *Macaulay's Essay on Lord Clive*, p. 68.

40 V. Nünning, 'Daß Jeder seine Pflicht thue', p. 381.

41 K. Wilson, 'Empire, Gender, and Modernity in the Eighteenth Century', in P. Levine (ed.), *Gender and Empire* (Oxford: Oxford University Press, 2007), pp. 14–45, p. 22.

42 V. D. Scudder, *Macaulay's Essay on Lord Clive*, p. 54.

43 R. Travers, 'Death and the Nabob. Imperialism and Commemoration in Eighteenth Century India', *Past and Present* 196 (2007), pp. 84–121, p. 98; J. Dalley, *The Black Hole. Money, Myth and Empire* (London: Fig Tree, 2006).

44 V. D. Scudder, *Macaulay's Essay on Lord Clive*, p. 58.

45 S. C. Hill, *Bengal in 1756-1757: A Selection of Public and Private Papers Dealing with the Affairs of the British in Bengal During the Reign of Siraj-uddaula* (London: John Murray, Albemarle Street, 1905); C. R. I. Flechter and R. Kipling, *A School History of England* (Oxford: At the Clarendon Press, 1911), p. 193.

46 Copy available: The National Library of Australia, Digital Collections, PIC P/2225/230 LOC Album 1004, http://nla.gov.au/nla.pic-vn3891223 (accessed 23 November 2012).

47 *The Times* (8 April 1907), p. 6.

48 *Ibid.*

49 *The Times* (13 June 1907), p. 16.

50 *The Times* (14 December 1907), p. 14.

51 *The Times* (19 April 1907), p. 4; (15 July 1908), p. 12 and (15 June 1909), p. 11.

52 Joseph Chamberlain on the Australian Colonies, *The Times of London* (12 November 1895), p. 6.
53 J. Osterhammel, 'Symbolpolitik und imperiale Integration: Das Britische Empire im 19. und 20. Jahrhundert', in B. Giesen, J. Osterhammel and R. Schlögl (eds), *Die Wirklichkeit der Symbole* (Konstanz: Universitätsverlag Konstanz 2004), pp. 395–421, p. 409.
54 *The Times* (24 August 1912), p. 8.
55 Lord Curzon, *The Times* (8 April 1907), p. 6.
56 P. Ward-Jackson, *Public Sculpture of Historic Westminster: Volume I* (Liverpool: Liverpool University Press, 2011), pp. 108–11, p. 110. and J. L. Tweed, *Sculptur. A memoir* (L. Dickson, 1936), p. 152.
57 Oral communication of information provided by a clerk of Westminster Abbey, 11 May 2013.
58 L. Goodlad, *Victorian Literature and the Victorian State: Character and Governance in a Liberal Society* (Baltimore: Johns Hopkins University Press, 2004), p. 263.
59 J. MacKenzie, 'Heroic Myths of Empire', in J. MacKenzie (ed.), *Popular Imperialism and the Military 1850–1950* (Manchester: Manchester University Press: 1992), p. 115.
60 *The Times* (29 September 1925), pp. 15–16.
61 *The Times* (17 May 1919), p. 10.
62 T. Paine, 'Reflections on the Life and Death of Robert Clive', *Pennsylvania Magazine* (1775).
63 *Ibid.*, p. 57.
64 *Ibid.*, p. 58.
65 R. O'Hanlon, *Caste, Conflict and Ideology. Mahatma Jotirao Phule and Low Caste Protest in Nineteenth-Century Western India* (Cambridge: Cambridge University Press, 1985), pp. 111, 195.
66 R. Guha, 'A Conquest Foretold', *Social Text* 54, 16:1 (1998), pp. 85–99, 85.
67 P. Chatterjee, *The Black Hole of Empire: History of a Global Practise of Power* (Princeton: Princeton University Press, 2012), p. 222.
68 R. Chaudhuri, 'History in Poetry: Nabinchandra Sen's Palashir Yuddha [Battle of Palashi] (1875) and the Question of Truth', *Centre of South Asian Studies Occasional Paper* 1 (2005), p. 1.
69 *Ibid.*, p. 2.
70 *Ibid.*
71 *Ibid.*, pp. 5/6.
72 P. Chatterjee, *The Black Hole of Empire*, p. 263.
73 J. Nehru, *The Discovery of India* (London: Penguin Books, 2004), p. 297.
74 R. Gopal, *How the British Occupied Bengal* (Bombay: Asia Publishing House, 1963), p. 3.
75 K. Datta, *Siraj-ud-Daulah* (Bombay: Orient Longman, 1971) p. 106.
76 B. K. Gupta, *Sirajuddaulah and the East India Company, 1756–1757: Background to the Foundation of British Power in India* (Leiden: E.J. Brill, 1966). P. Chatterjee, *The Black Hole of Empire*, p. 19, 20.
77 R. C. Majundar, H. C. Raychaudhuri and K. Datta, *An Advanced History of India* (New York: Macmillan, 1967), p. 657.
78 B. V. Rao, *History of Asia. From Early times to the Present* (Elgin: New Dawn Press, 2005), p. 307; Mihir Bose, 'Tell us the truth of the Empire', *Observer* (6 October 2002).
79 S. Bhaumik, 'Plassey rekindles Indian anti-imperialism', BBC News, 29 June 2007; http://news.bbc.co.uk/2/hi/south_asia/6242346.stm (accessed 24 June 2013).
80 *Ibid.*
81 J. Wood, 'Regarding Colonel Cleve's', pp. 177–87.
82 *Ibid.*, p. 181.
83 See also D. Rothermund, *Geschichte Indiens: Vom Mittelalter bis zur Gegenwart* (München: C. H. Beck, 2006), p. 49; M. Mann, *Bengalen im Umbruch: Die Herausbildung des britischen Kolonialstaates* (Stuttgart: Franz Steiner Verlag, 2000),

p. 64. Although the source was already published as early as 1960, the document did not enjoy wide circulation. The story of Britain's expansion in Bengal still often consists of a retelling of the story of 'Plassey'; for example in G. K. McGilvary, *Guardian of the East India Company: The Life of Extraordinary Lawrence Sulivan* (London: Tauris Academic Studies, 2006).

84 E.g., Philip Lawson, *The East India Company. A History* (London: Longman, 1993), p. 87.

85 N. Robbins, 'Loot: In Search of the East India Company, the World's First Transnational Corporation', *Environmental & Urbanization* 14:1 (April 2002), pp. 79–88, p. 82.

86 Raja, Brig Asif Haroon, India schemed for East Bengal since 1947, 17 April 2013; www.opinion-maker.org/2013/04/india-and-bangladesh/ (accessed 22 December 2013); M. T. Hussain, *Patriot-Traitor Question: Bangladesh Syndrome: A Collection of Some Published & Unpublished Essays of the Author Produced Between 1988–2005* (Dhaka: Nehal Publication, 2006), p. 8.

87 Michael Smith, 'Leaders with Good Ethics are the Key to Changing Irresponsible Banking', *The Times* (2 December 2010).

88 Cf. L. A. Coser (ed.), *Maurice Halbwachs: On Collective Memory* (Chicago: University of Chicago Press, 1992), p. 34.

CHAPTER NINE

David Livingstone, British Protestant missions, memory and empire

John Stuart

In December 2010 Cain Mathema, governor of Bulawayo, Zimbabwe (formerly Southern Rhodesia), called for the exhumation and repatriation to Britain of the remains of Cecil Rhodes, buried for more than a century in the Matopos Hills in southern Zimbabwe. He also called for the destruction of a statue at Victoria Falls erected in 1934 to commemorate the missionary and explorer David Livingstone. 'All over the country', Mathema stated, 'you find schools named after colonialists, statues erected to celebrate colonialism. I am struck and baffled by the attitude of our people to continually embrace a bygone system that worked tirelessly to thwart their energy and aspirations'.[1] Rhodes's grave has long been a site of dispute as well as of pilgrimage and remembrance.[2] The government of Zimbabwe did not hesitate after independence in 1980 to remove statues of Rhodes from prominent locations in Bulawayo and Harare.[3] That of Livingstone remained in place. In 2001 supporters of the ruling Zanu-PF party attacked and damaged it. Three years later local leaders near the town of Livingstone across the border in Zambia (formerly Northern Rhodesia) expressed interest in appropriating it from Zimbabwe, ostensibly to facilitate its relocation to a more hospitable environment. According to Chief Siloka Mukuni, 'Zambians have a great deal of affection for Livingstone's memory, unlike the Zimbabweans . . . we have kept the name of Livingstone out of a deep respect'.[4]

In the event, Zambians commissioned a new statue and had it installed on their side of the Falls. If Zambians regard Livingstone's legacy as bound up with their country's colonial past, many have perceived it as also influencing their transition to statehood. For President Kenneth Kaunda, Livingstone was nothing less than the 'first freedom fighter'.[5] Kaunda made this assertion in 1973 at a ceremony in Chitambo, in north central Zambia, to mark the centenary of Livingstone's death. For seventy years there has been an obelisk at

Chitambo, denoting the location of a tree under which Livingstone's heart may have been buried. Like the Victoria Falls, Chitambo is one of many sites of memory in Africa associated with Livingstone. Not all are marked by statues or other monuments. Chitambo Hospital (some distance away) was founded by Livingstone's nephew, Malcolm Moffat, a missionary of the Free Church of Scotland, in memory of his uncle, and two Livingstone grandchildren would later undertake nursing and medical work there. As a rule, missionaries eschewed the overtly political. Livingstone was neither colonialist nor freedom fighter; and while monuments to him had their place, his memory might best be served and maintained through Christian service to Africa, colonial and independent.

Protestant missionaries, being Protestants, disagreed with each other about many things, but as to the importance of Livingstone and his posthumous legacy they were unanimous. They chose to remember him in a variety of ways. They sometimes did so in denominational terms, because Livingstone had links with Anglicanism, with Scottish Presbyterianism and with Congregationalism. At other times missionaries were ecumenical in their remembering. In what might seem un-Protestant fashion they came to value relics associated with Livingstone, provided by his family and others. They also participated in national acts of commemoration, secular as well as religious, and in public memorialisation of Livingstone by geographers and explorers. This participation endured for a century and more after Livingstone's death, vicissitudes of mission – and of empire – notwithstanding. It may have become commonplace now for historians to regard memory as invariably 'negotiated' and 'contested'.[6] Livingstone's memory still has the capacity to incite controversy within Zimbabwe, but this may have as much to do with local and regional politics as with popular or official attitudes to empire and colonialism.[7] More widely, since his death in 1873 Livingstone has been and is still largely revered, less now as a missionary than as a humanitarian, as an opponent of the slave trade and an explorer. But mission was a vitally important part of Livingstone's life, and for British Protestant missionaries the memory of him was exceptionally important. Rarely was it a matter of significant contestation or dispute.[8]

Missionary attitudes towards and links with British imperialism were complicated, fluid and subject to change over time. Missionaries were variously supportive of, ambivalent about and critical towards empire.[9] Their memory of it, like that of other Britons, was linked to race.[10] For them, however, Livingstone became the embodiment of Christian dedication and compassion, his commitment to mission transcending categories such as 'race', 'nation' and 'empire'. Livingstone himself had written of mission as the means 'by which God was bringing all His dealings with man to a glorious consummation'.[11] Missions felt a special connection with Livingstone, for many reasons – not least theological. They were determined to preserve a religious memory of him. Religious memory has been described as powerful and with the potential to be conflictual, a characteristic to which theology may help bring order and even harmony.[12]

As a young man Livingstone (and his father Neil) had taken an important doctrinal and theological decision: to reject the Presbyterianism of the Church of Scotland for Congregationalism, which vested ecclesiastical authority not in a priesthood (much less an episcopacy) or in select laypeople but in each congregation. The only missionary society to which Livingstone became affiliated was the London Missionary Society (LMS), avowedly interdenominational but in practice Congregational and with close links to Congregational churches throughout the British Isles and further afield. In 1840, aged twenty-seven, Livingstone began a period of seventeen years' service with the Society, having that year also obtained his medical qualifications and been ordained. Among many custodians and promoters of Livingstone's memory in religious terms, the LMS would prove to be the most dedicated and assiduous. While taking account of Livingstone's links with Scottish missions and churches, this contribution mainly focuses on less well-known aspects of the posthumous connections between Livingstone, Congregationalism and the LMS. In three chronologically arranged sections, each culminating in a year of remembrance, it addresses the first century after Livingstone's death.

1873–1913

In a real sense Livingstone was already a legend by the time of his death, through his remarkably successful writings, through accounts by others of his exploits and through the publicity surrounding the search for him by H. M. Stanley. That status was confirmed through his funeral and burial in Westminster Abbey in February 1874. In Scotland, as elsewhere in Britain, missionary discussion focused on how he might be remembered and his work continued and extended. His friend James Stewart was in no doubt: a mission in Central Africa would be 'the truest memorial to Livingstone'.[13] The Free Church of Scotland (which had been unresponsive to earlier appeals from Livingstone) established the Livingstonia mission. The Church of Scotland then set up a mission, named after Livingstone's birthplace of Blantyre. Located in what later became the British colony of Nyasaland (later still Malawi), these institutions, with their strong focus on education, would eventually exert an influence not anticipated by their founders – on mid-twentieth-century African nationalism. The missions were also important in the forging of a strong (if not always unproblematic) relationship between Scotland and Malawi that continues to the present day.

Anglicans had reacted with greatest alacrity to Livingstone's calls for Africa to be opened up to commerce and Christianity. For members of the high church party of the Church of England, his speech at Cambridge University in 1857 was extremely significant. It inspired the subsequent formation of the Anglo-Catholic Universities' Mission to Central Africa (UMCA). A disastrous initial foray into the African interior reflected badly not only on the mission but also on Livingstone (whose reputation in life was by no means always secure). Some fifty years later that seemed less important in the light of subsequent progress and in the glow of Livingstone's posthumous reputation. At a memorial meeting at Senate House, Cambridge, in December 1907 Archbishop of Canterbury Randall Davidson spoke effusively of Livingstone as a missionary and crusader against slavery, his influence in that latter respect comparable to that of William Wilberforce and Abraham Lincoln.[14] Celebration was not confined to Cambridge. The mission also held religious services at its outpost in Zanzibar, with African priests and deacons in attendance.

The Protestant organisation most actively committed to Livingstone's memory during the imperial period was neither Scottish nor Anglican. The LMS, founded in 1795, was experienced in the art and practice of commemoration. It had run a successful fundraising campaign after the martyrdom in 1839 of the missionary John Williams, in Vanuatu. Like others before and after him Williams collected ethnographic objects. These, together with missionaries' personal effects, formed the basis of a museum collection, located at LMS headquarters from 1815. In time, and especially after missionaries' deaths, these effects might assume the status of relics. So it proved in relation to Livingstone. The Society loaned objects associated with him for display by other organisations. It also included them in its own exhibitions.[15] Like those of other missionary societies these could be very large in scale and scope.[16] The biggest LMS event ran for five weeks in London in the summer of 1908. Opened by president of the Board of Trade Winston Churchill, it promoted every aspect of the Society's current and past work, with due emphasis on relics of Livingstone, Williams and other missionaries. The Livingstone legend was central to the exhibition's most extraordinary aspect: a combination of miracle play and oratorio entitled 'The Pageant of Darkness and Light'. Accompanied by an orchestra and 600-strong choir, this re-enacted the Stanley–Livingstone meeting against a background of Arab slave trading and church-building. Such was its musical and theatrical power that the pageant acquired an extended life, being subsequently performed in whole and in part by amateurs and by professionals in various parts of the British Empire and in the United States.

It is difficult to ascertain the impact that exhibitions (and pageants) may have had on support for missions or on public awareness of Livingstone. One historian has suggested that the 'feverishness' of such activity in the early twentieth century was indicative of difficulty in maintaining interest in mission whether through personal service or financial contribution.[17] There was undoubtedly missionary (and wider popular) interest in late nineteenth-century imperial expansion, although missionaries interested in sharing resources and promoting evangelism also became more ecumenically minded.[18] A world missionary conference was held in Edinburgh, in 1910. More importantly where Livingstone was concerned, the centenary of his birth three years later offered a unique opportunity to celebrate his achievements and his memory. Of this opportunity the LMS was above all other organisations determined to take full advantage.

During 1913 Livingstone was celebrated as a missionary, as a humanitarian and as an explorer. He was celebrated in 'national' terms, as a Scot and a Briton.[19] He was also fêted as a progenitor of empire. At the Royal Geographical Society Lord Curzon described him as the 'unconscious parent' of many of Cecil Rhodes's ideals.[20] Very many people and places laid claim to association with Livingstone. At only a few major events were members of his family and descendants present, such as memorial services at St Giles's Cathedral, Edinburgh, and at Westminster Abbey. In countless other churches of every denomination (including St Paul's Cathedral) Livingstone was remembered, in prayers and through sermons. Clergymen invoked him as a religious and moral exemplar and as a stimulus to missionary service and to giving in support of mission. They ascribed to his writings a value and status that was almost Scriptural.[21]

Among all this, the approach of the LMS to the centenary was both thorough and thoroughly distinctive. Its aims were, variously, denominational and interdenominational, national and international, 'cosmopolitan' and 'interracial'. They owed nothing to empire. Primarily focused on Livingstone, the centenary celebrations would also constitute a reaffirmation of Congregationalism as a vital element in Livingstone's life and as a still vibrant part of British and world Christianity. Committed to overseas mission, the Society was also attuned to the necessity of mission at home, especially in urban Britain. And its officials well knew the extent of their reliance on the

Congregational churches and the importance of sympathetic lay organ-isations such as the National Brotherhood Movement.[22] Above all, their celebrations would be inclusive; and for their largest event they hired a suitably large venue: the Albert Hall.

The audience on the evening of 19 March 1913 heard a specially composed cantata, 'Livingstone the Pilgrim', as well as addresses from Archbishop Davidson and other civil and religious dignitaries. Absent invitees sent tributes, which were read out. These came from Prime Minister Asquith, US President Wilson and Khama, king of the Bangwato in what is now Botswana. Booker T. Washington, the African-American activist whose educational institution at Tuskegee, Alabama, was of great interest to missions, also sent a message in which he expressed 'the gratitude of my race' for Livingstone's service to Africa.[23] The event fulfilled all expectations, in terms of celebration, publicity and even fundraising: the sale of tickets for the best seats (other seats were free of charge) helped offset costs, and a Livingstone Memorial Fund was launched, for mission in Africa.

Important as this and other events were, they represented but part of a broader LMS strategy for memorialising Livingstone. By 1913 there had already been many biographies. That year the LMS published four, aimed at children and adolescents. The most popular, by editor-ial secretary Basil Mathews, was *Livingstone the Pathfinder*. Vividly written and illustrated, it sold 30,000 copies in its first year of publi-cation. It was translated into many other languages including Welsh, Danish and Tamil. A consignment of the German-language version, produced in Switzerland by Basel Missionsbuchhandlung, was des-patched to the US for sale to the 'Teutonic population' there.[24] Book publication was complemented by large-scale production of publicity, educational and fundraising material: there were colouring sets and dioramas for children, lantern slides for hire, helpful hints for Livingstone-related sermons and addresses and customised envelopes for donations to the memorial fund. The Society's board of directors was in no doubt that 'the virile, aggressive and broad-minded mission-ary advocacy associated with the name of Livingstone has its appeal to those often regarded as beyond our reach'.[25]

1914–40

Its missionaries, officials and supporters could not know at the time that 1913 was in many ways the end of an era, for Congregationalism and for the LMS. Ahead lay chronic decline, in terms of church and missionary society finances, support and recruits. Never again would the LMS attempt anything on the scale of the centenary celebrations;

but the memory of Livingstone would remain a vital part of its identity. The inter-war period was notable for a number of initiatives. Some had important religious aspects linked to Congregationalism and thereby to the LMS. Others, not connected with missions, had an imperial aspect. The most notable initiative in any sense, the Scottish National Memorial to David Livingstone, opened at Blantyre in Lanarkshire in 1929 and was largely the outcome of one remarkable man's vision. That man was a lowland Scot, like Livingstone. And also like Livingstone he was a Congregationalist with close links to the LMS, in his case twenty-six years' service in south India. His name was James Irvine Macnair, born into some prosperity in Glasgow in 1869. The family owned the Dalmarnock Hair Factory, at Bridgeton. There was also an office at Finsbury in London, and the young Macnair worked there for five years. In his twenties he developed (gradually, he would later admit) a strong interest in religion and theology. He undertook study at the Theological Hall (later the Scottish Congregational College) and, briefly, in Germany.[26] Caught up in the end-of-century fervour for overseas evangelism generated by the Student Volunteer Missionary Union, he volunteered for service with the LMS and was accepted.[27] After ordination at his local church in Hillhead, he sailed for the Telugu mission in December 1898. His fiancée, Jessie Longbottom, joined him in 1900. They married in Madras that same year.

Macnair retired as a missionary in 1924. Indefatigably industrious, he then devoted his energies to committee, educational and other work in the service of Congregationalism and the LMS. Following a visit to Livingstone's birthplace, a room in a tenement threatened with demolition, he envisaged the building's reconstitution as a memorial. With others, he formed a trust and drove the project forward in the face of considerable difficulty. The emphasis of Macnair's appeal for support and funds was necessarily broad; and it appears to have evoked the desired response in almost every case. The memory of Livingstone resonated with many people, especially Scots at home and overseas and also with geographical, humanitarian and religious societies. Scottish churches and missions were enthusiastic; so too was the LMS, keen to assert Livingstone's Congregationalism (in effect his non-sectarianism) and thus ensure that his unarguable Scottishness was not incorrectly equated with Presbyterianism.[28] While the mid-1920s indeed saw an increase of Scottish nationalist sentiment, there was also an upsurge of Scottish Congregational interest in overseas mission: in June 1925 Olympic champion Eric Liddell set off from Edinburgh for north China, and service with the LMS.[29]

For Macnair, this Scottish national memorial was to have religious, moral and educative purpose. His main emphasis, like that of the

LMS, was firmly on the young. The room where Livingstone was born would become 'a place of pilgrimage, a shrine in which the great tradition should remain firmly founded, where the generous heart of Scots youth would fire to the thrill of his story and respond to his noble inspiration'.[30] Enormous care was taken with restoration of room and building, and with layout and design. The trust commissioned and was also gifted sculptures, tableaux and murals, which were arranged to facilitate an imaginative journey or rather pilgrimage through the various stages of Livingstone's life. There was extensive deployment of relics. Only some were of an overtly religious nature, but there was no escaping the religious emphasis of the memorial as a whole. The visitor's pilgrimage ended at a space denoted as a shrine, with a cross on the wall. Here was their opportunity for contemplation and reflection, and not merely on Livingstone. Macnair speculated 'that if the traveller had had a say in the form of his own memorial, he would have wished that the last thought should not be of him but of the saviour whose fellowship was the deep secret of his life'.[31] The Duchess of York, accompanied by Macnair, opened the memorial on 5 October 1929 (Figure 9.1). Representatives of family, churches, missions and the state attended, along with 12,000 other people. The memorial became a successful visitor attraction.

Macnair's networking, widespread press reports and newsreel coverage all boosted awareness of the memorial. It influenced a decision by Caledonian and other Scottish voluntary organisations in southern Africa to raise funds not for mission but for their own memorial to Livingstone. They were sufficiently successful to be able to commission the eminent Scottish sculptor William Reid Dick. He reconnoitred the site at Victoria Falls, which the government of Southern Rhodesia had agreed to make available. Deciding on a form that would harmonise with its surroundings, Reid Dick sculpted a three-metre statue of Livingstone in bronze. On a granite base was inscribed the legend 'Missionary, Explorer, Liberator'. Howard Unwin Moffatt, a nephew of Livingstone's wife Mary and a former prime minister of Southern Rhodesia, performed the unveiling to the accompaniment of bagpipes on 5 August 1934. Among the project's patrons had been imperial statesman Jan Smuts. Five years earlier he had publicly described Livingstone as Scotland's 'gift' to South Africa.[32] The statue was primarily an affirmation of Scottishness imperial, Rhodesian and South African, created by white settlers for white settlers. The ceremonies did include religious elements: prayers and an address by Presbyterian minister Reverend James Gray comparing Livingstone's influence on Africa to that of Rhodes, albeit in different spheres of activity.[33]

9.1 James Macnair with the Duchess of York at the opening of the Scottish National Memorial to David Livingstone, Blantyre, 5 October 1929

Two representatives of the LMS attended, from the Society's teacher training institute at Tiger Kloof in the Northern Cape.

The 1920s and 1930s were marked by settler assertiveness. This was also a period in which Britain sought to redefine its imperial commitment to Africa in terms of 'trusteeship', whereby the potentially harmful impact of settler communities on indigenous peoples in colonial territories might be ameliorated. This idea was of considerable interest to missionaries. For the clergyman and theologian R. J. Campbell, whose denominational affiliation encompassed (at different times) both Congregationalism and Anglicanism, trusteeship owed more to Livingstone than to any other person. It was Livingstone's example that had made possible and practical that 'moral trusteeship of the advanced over the backward races which is now a principle of the League of Nations ... this was Livingstone's vision'.[34] For missionaries involved through evangelism and increasingly also through education among Africans, trusteeship spoke to modern-day realities, and colonial problems. Macnair concurred with this interpretation. The only type of imperialism that deserved to continue, he wrote, 'is that of David Livingstone – an Imperialism that is prepared to accept responsibility for undeveloped races, and to do so in a spirit of unselfishness that steadily keeps their interests in view'.[35]

Unwilling to pass up any opportunity for public remembrance of Livingstone, Macnair organised a celebration of another centenary – that of Livingstone's initial departure from Britain in December 1840. He enlisted the assistance of churches and universities in Scotland, and of the Royal Scottish Geographical Society. He persuaded Secretary of State for Colonies Lord Lloyd to give a centenary address in Glasgow. This posed the question 'What would Livingstone bid us do in Africa?' The answer, Lloyd averred, must come in Christian terms and also by means of colonial welfare and development.[36] Earlier that year, Lloyd had delivered a similarly themed address to Protestant missionary societies in London.[37] This explicit equation of Christianity with empire was indicative of Lloyd's personal faith, not of government policy. Missionaries found it reassuring but they would derive no benefit from it. The LMS organised its own celebrations in memory of 1840, receiving endorsement both from monarch and from government.[38] But in 1940 the concerns of missionaries were of little significance to a country at war. To that larger struggle Livingstone's memory might also be enlisted, as *The Times* noted: Livingstone's 'conception of liberty' would help arm an empire 'fighting to destroy the evil doctrine of the *Herrenvolk* and its right to exploit and tyrannise over a subject race'.[39]

1941–73

Missionaries hoped that in the aftermath of the Second World War a new age of overseas evangelism would dawn. In this hope they were to be disappointed. Colonial welfare and development policies meanwhile meant attenuation of missionary influence on colonial policymaking. To that was now added the challenge of nationalism, in every part of Africa. It came not only from black Africans but also from Afrikaners and Rhodesians. Shocked, even stunned by South African legislation in support of apartheid, missionaries were uncertain how to respond. The LMS, like other missionary societies, struggled in this new environment. Its officials sought inspiration in the achievements of their 'notable predecessors' of the nineteenth century.[40] That was of little help: but British imperial policy seemed to offer reassurance. Government in London had replaced the rhetoric of 'trusteeship' with that of 'partnership', between black and white in Africa. It supposedly underpinned an important imperial initiative: the Central African Federation, comprising the Rhodesias and Nyasaland, set up in 1953.

The idea of racial 'partnership' appealed to missionaries committed to a similar 'partnership', with the indigenous Church in Africa.

White settlers, no less than missionaries, venerated their past. The Voortrekker Monument, unveiled in 1949, was a national shrine for Afrikaners. In 1953 Rhodesians extravagantly celebrated the centenary of Rhodes, their 'founder'.[41] Two years later came a celebratory opportunity for the town in Northern Rhodesia named after David Livingstone: 100 years since his 'discovery' of the Victoria Falls. The organisers invited the LMS to participate. Initially enthusiastic, the Society's response was ultimately ambivalent. British Protestant churches and missionary societies had recently issued a 'call for Christian action in Africa'. This was an ecumenical response to the Bantu Education Act, which had come into effect in South Africa the previous year to the detriment of mission schools. In such circumstances, it seemed to the LMS, reasserting Livingstone's ideals might be a means of bearing witness, even from afar, to the iniquity of apartheid.[42] It sent two representatives to the celebrations, clergyman Cecil Northcott and evangelist Aaron Mwenya. Neither was inclined to controversy. Mwenya contributed prayer, Northcott a rambling address on Livingstone's legacy and its relevance to 'partnership' in Central Africa.[43]

Both consciously and unconsciously, the commemoration was almost entirely a celebration of whiteness. Much of it centred on the statue of Livingstone in Southern Rhodesia. There, Dr Hubert Wilson, Livingstone's grandson, unveiled a commemorative plaque. He had already done much to help maintain Livingstone's memory, and would continue to do so into the era of decolonisation and beyond. He was in that respect an unofficial successor to James Macnair, who had died three months earlier, in August 1955. Born at Kendal, Cumbria, in 1884 Wilson was the son of Anna Mary, Livingstone's youngest child, and her husband Frank Wilson. Having studied medicine at the University of Glasgow he, together with his sister Ruth, took up a post at Chitambo mission hospital.[44] Mindful of her father's legacy, Anna Mary (like her sister Agnes) had retained some of his papers and belongings. Many of these she and Wilson made available to Macnair. Living in Northern Rhodesia, Wilson got to know J. Desmond Clark, curator of the Livingstone Museum, which had opened in 1934, in the town of Livingstone. Its original aims were broadly ethnological and archaeological. It would become subsumed into the Rhodes-Livingstone Institute, the contradictory-sounding name of which inspired a nickname: 'the Saint and the Sinner Institute'.[45] From Wilson, Clark obtained material about Livingstone, for display in the museum. Exhibitions sponsored by the colonial authorities did not, however, emphasise the religious nature of Livingstone's work. Rather they portrayed Livingstone, like Rhodes, as a bringer of civilisation and commerce to Africa.[46]

In a Britain entering its 'second Elizabethan age', explorers, whether historic or contemporary, might feature more prominently than missionaries in public celebrations.[47] Livingstone of course was both. But it was primarily as explorer that he was commemorated in London in October 1953. Secretary of State for Colonies Oliver Lyttelton unveiled a statue of him, at the Royal Geographical Society. For those currently engaged in helping the people of Africa in their 'forward march' to nationhood, Lyttelton said, Livingstone's example was both inspirational and humbling. Also present was Reverend Maxwell Janes, general secretary of the LMS, who reminded the audience that though undoubtedly a great explorer and discoverer Livingstone was 'even more a great missionary'. As on other similar occasions at this time and after, Hubert Wilson provided a living link to the past; in a short address on behalf of the Scottish National Memorial to David Livingstone Trust he informed those present how Africans still spoke of Livingstone.[48] Wilson would continue in a quiet, understated way to promote awareness of Livingstone especially among children and young people (he had written a short biography, published in 1923). At a children's church service in Glasgow in 1958, he advised those present that if they some day wished to work in Africa, they should live among the local people 'in a manner worthy of the great missionary'.[49]

Like many Europeans with experience of British colonial Africa Wilson anticipated that over time Africans would acquire greater responsibility and greater autonomy in political as in church affairs. He believed in the ideal of 'partnership' between the races in Central Africa. By the late 1950s, however, African dissatisfaction with Rhodesian racism was being expressed in ever more radical political terms. Long-standing African dissatisfaction with mission Christianity meanwhile found increasing expression through independent churches and Pentecostal movements. This was the context in which Livingstone ultimately became 'a patron saint of African nationalism', perhaps for Scottish missionaries as much as for African nationalists.[50] It is nevertheless unclear precisely what influence Livingstone's work and writings much less the memory of him may have had on these developments; but Africans had already played important roles in the perpetuation by missionaries and others of Livingstone's memory, none more so than those who knew him and had carried his remains on the nine-month journey to Zanzibar in 1873–74. Only one, Jacob Wainwright, attended the funeral at Westminster Abbey. The testimony of two others, Abdullah Susi and James Chumah, was vital to

Horace Waller in editing Livingstone's last journals – and in helping to mythologise Livingstone.[51]

In 1913, during the UMCA centenary celebrations at Zanzibar, the bishop created 'an enormous sensation' by introducing to participants the gardener at the local theological college: this was Tom Peter Sudi, believed to have seen Livingstone die and to have helped embalm his remains and carry them to the coast.[52] The last living African link with Livingstone was sundered only in 1935, with the death of his acquaintance Matthew Wellington. His residual fame ensured him respite (if not complete relief) from destitution in old age.[53] Missionaries continued to value their own memories of Africans' oral testimony about Livingstone. As late as 1940 one retired Scottish missionary was relating stories about Livingstone he had learned at the 1913 celebrations at Livingstonia from Africans who had known him.[54] By the late 1950s missionaries had begun to assign Africans more formal, participatory roles in memorial services to Livingstone.[55] In the 1960s Africans played roles equal to those of missionaries, as at a commemorative service in Westminster Abbey in 1963 where the South African priest D. G. S. M'timkulu preached the sermon.

By 1973, 100 years after Livingstone's death, Britain's formal empire in Africa was extinct. Rhodesia (as Southern Rhodesia had become in 1965) was both exception and anomaly. Many missionary societies had reconstituted themselves as part of worldwide partnerships in evangelism. From the mid-nineteenth century onward missionaries articulated the possibility and indeed the desirability in theological terms of self-government for indigenous churches. This objective they termed 'euthanasia', to mean the death, as it were, of missions and their succession by indigenous churches, prepared by missions for this transition.[56] But missionaries were far from consistent in their commitment to the ideal. Their often contradictory impulses were evident within the LMS even in the celebratory year of 1913. As well as remembering Livingstone the LMS recorded its view that 'the real ambition of a missionary society is to extinguish itself; to create in the field so powerful a Church as shall make the foreign missionary an unnecessary agency'. Always tempering that impulse, however, was an accompanying anxiety: about 'the perils attending a too early departure'.[57] By the 1960s the need for unprecedented change could no longer be avoided. By the centenary year of 1973 the LMS no longer existed as an autonomous agency.

Conclusion

As historians have debated missions' links with empire, so also have they debated those of Livingstone. John M. MacKenzie has written

[165]

that Livingstone may be regarded as 'a complex apostle for empire'.[58] For Andrew C. Ross, he was, conversely, 'a consistent opponent of white rule in Africa'.[59] In a centenary assessment George Shepperson commented on the impossibility of doing full justice to Livingstone's complex personality and protean character. 'Each age', Shepperson noted, 'makes its own David Livingstone'.[60] That same year, Tim Jeal published what is regarded by many as the first truly revisionist biography, a more critical interpretation of Livingstone than had previously been attempted. Jeal would subsequently acknowledge in greater detail his debt to Hubert Wilson among others, for making publicly available letters and other material written by Livingstone.[61]

Jeal contended that although he was a great man, Livingstone was a failure as a missionary: he only ever made one convert. Even if they had been completely aware of this, other missionaries who followed Livingstone may not have been willing to bear too much in mind the shortcomings of 'Saint David'.[62] The memory of Livingstone exerted a powerful hold upon them. It was not for them a source of contention. Rather, it was something to be cherished and celebrated. This was true of Protestant missionary societies generally and Scottish ones particularly; but the LMS made special claim to Livingstone, and to his memory. It would name its headquarters for him, and its publishing imprint. A representation of Livingstone's image prefaced every LMS promotional film, of which there were many.[63] On his birthday the Society's officials would visit the grave at Westminster Abbey, to give thanks for his life. Given the attenuation of Congregationalism's distinctive presence in the UK and the eventual demise of the LMS, it is worth noting the extent to which the memory of Livingstone meant so much for one particular Protestant denomination. Though the LMS did not define itself in terms of Livingstone alone, the memory of him after 1873 suffused its activities, its image and its identity as empire never did.

For missions, Christian work and Christian institutions in Africa were Livingstone's legacy, a phenomenon that could neither be encapsulated nor adequately represented by memorials such as statues. The statue at Victoria Falls has been the subject of controversy, however. It was not a mission initiative, but Livingstone was indisputably a missionary. 'His heroic figure looms over the dark continent', Smuts wrote, 'showing to dark Africa the shining example of a Christian gentleman'.[64] That this missionary, venerated by whites, should also be regarded by some Africans as a freedom fighter and as their liberator not only from slavery but from colonialism might seem to some other Africans a denial of their own agency. In the Livingstone centenary year of 1973 Zambians were free; the people yet to become Zimbabweans were at war, with each other. Just as Zambians currently embrace Livingstone's memory, so may Zimbabweans resist that embrace, but perhaps only up to a point. The name of Livingstone continues to resonate, in new ways. His bicentenary in 2013 gave reason for celebration and hope for much-needed economic benefit, on both sides of the Victoria Falls: the town of Livingstone hosted bicentennial commemorative events, with Zambia and Zimbabwe also acting as joint hosts to the general assembly of the United Nations World Tourism Organisation.

Notes

1 P. Thornycroft, 'Cecil John Rhodes' Body should be Exhumed and Sent back to Britain', 15 December 2010, www.telegraph.co.uk/news/worldnews/africaandindianocean/zimbabwe/8203863/Cecil-John-Rhodes-body-should-be-exhumed-and-sent-back-to-Britain.html (accessed 12 November 2012).

2 Terence Ranger, *Voices from the Rocks: Nature, Culture and History in the Matopos Hills of Zimbabwe* (Bloomington: Indiana University Press, 1999).

3 P. Maylam, *The Cult of Rhodes: Remembering an Imperialist in Africa* (Cape Town: David Philip, 2005), p. 45.

4 D. L. Robert, *Christian Mission: How Christianity became a World Religion* (Malden, MA, and Oxford: Wiley-Blackwell, 2009), p. 87.

5 A. C. Ross, *David Livingstone: Mission and Empire* (London and New York: Hambledon Continuum, 2006), p. 239.

6 A. Confino, *Germany as a Culture of Remembrance: Promises and Limits of Writing History* (Chapel Hill: University of North Carolina Press, 2006), pp. 154–6.

7 J. L. Fisher, *Pioneers, Settlers, Aliens, Exiles: The Decolonisation of White Identity in Zimbabwe* (Canberra: ANU E Press, 2010), pp. 64–6.

8 On the potential for dispute, J. D. Livingstone, 'A "Body" of Evidence: The Posthumous Presentation of David Livingstone', *Victorian Literature and Culture* 40:1 (2012), pp. 10–11.

9 B. Stanley, *The Bible and the Flag: Protestant Missions and British Imperialism in the Nineteenth and Twentieth Centuries* (Leicester: Apollos, 1990); A. Porter, *Religion versus Empire? British Protestant Missionaries and Overseas Expansion, 1700–1914* (Manchester: Manchester University Press, 2004); J. Cox, *The British Missionary Enterprise since 1700* (New York and London: Routledge, 2008).

10 B. Schwarz, *Memories of Empire, Volume I: The White Man's World* (Oxford: Oxford University Press, 2011). The subject of missions and the memory of empire awaits fuller treatment.

11 D. Livingstone, *Missionary Travels and Researches in South Africa* (London: John Murray, 1857), pp. 673–4.

12 D. Hervieu-Léger, *Religion as a Chain of Memory* (Cambridge: Polity Press, 2000), pp. 124–7.

13 Cited in H. J. Sindima, *The Legacy of Scottish Missionaries in Malawi* (Lampeter: Edwin Mellen Press, 1992), p. 19.

14 'The Universities' Mission: Livingstone Memorial Meeting at Cambridge', *The Times*, 5 December 1907, p. 4.

15 I am grateful to Dr Chris Wingfield for this information.

16 A. E. Coombes, *Reinventing Africa: Museums, Material Culture and Popular Imagination* (New Haven, CT: Yale University Press, 1994), pp. 162–5.

17 R. Tudur Jones, *Congregationalism in England, 1662–1962* (London: Independent Press, 1962), p. 385.

18 B. Stanley, *Bible and the Flag*, pp. 111–32; J. G. Greenlee and C. M. Johnston, *Good Citizens: British Missionaries and Imperial States, 1870–1918* (Montreal: McGill-Queen's University Press, 1999).

19 E. Breitenbach, *Empire and Scottish Society: The Impact of Foreign Missions at Home, c. 1790 to c. 1914* (Edinburgh: Edinburgh University Press, 2009), pp. 158–61.

20 'Livingstone Centenary: Lord Curzon's Panegyric', *The Times*, 18 March 1913, p. 11.

21 'The Anniversary', Universities' Mission to Central Africa, *Central Africa* 31: 366 (1913), pp. 147–8.

22 School of African and Oriental Studies, London (SOAS), London Missionary Society papers, Council for World Mission archive (CWM), Home, Livingstone pictures, 2, 15, circular letter by Basil Mathews and Nelson Bitton, no date, but c. March 1913. On the National Brotherhood Movement, S. Thorne, *Congregational Missions and the Making of an Imperial Culture in Nineteenth Century England* (Stanford, CA: Stanford University Press, 1999), pp. 108–13.

23 'London Missionary Society (hereafter LMS)', *Chronicle* (April 1913), p. 83.

24 *Ibid.*

25 LMS, *The Hundred and Eighteenth Report of the London Missionary Society for the Year ending March 1913* (London: LMS, 1913), p. 39.

26 SOAS, CWM, home candidates' papers, 11, James Irvine Macnair to Dr Ralph Wardlaw Thompson, 5 November 1896.

27 SOAS, CWM, home candidates' papers, 11, Macnair to LMS, 25 May 1898.

28 J. I. Macnair, *The Story of the Scottish National Memorial to David Livingstone* (Blantyre: Scottish National Memorial to David Livingstone Trust, 1944), pp. 25–6.

29 H. Escott, *A History of Scottish Congregationalism* (Glasgow: Congregational Union of Scotland, 1960), pp. 209–11.

30 J. I. Macnair, *Story of the Scottish National Memorial*, p. 15.

31 J. I. Macnair, 'The Scottish National Memorial to David Livingstone', *International Review of Missions* 20:79 (1931), p. 454.

32 General J. C. Smuts, *Africa and Some World Problems* (Oxford: Clarendon Press, 1930), p. 4.

33 Rev. J. Gray, LLD, 'Address on the Occasion of the Unveiling of the Livingstone Memorial', *Heritage of Zimbabwe* 9 (1990), pp. 103–7.

34 R. J. Campbell, DD, *Livingstone* (London: Ernest Benn Ltd, 1929), p. 20.

35 J. I. Macnair, *Livingstone the Liberator: A Study of a Dynamic Personality* (London and Glasgow: Collins, 1940), p. 363.

36 Lord Lloyd, *What would Livingstone bid us do in Africa?* (Blantyre: Scottish National Memorial to David Livingstone Trust, 1940). Macnair had the address printed as a pamphlet.

37 The National Archives of the UK: Public Record Office, INF/1/408, Lord Lloyd, address to Conference of British Missionary Societies, 14 June 1940.

38 'David Livingstone: The Centenary Commemoration in London, December 11th, 1940', *Journal of the Royal African Society* 40:159 (1941), pp. 108–20; J. Reason, 'Colonial Policy since Livingstone: A Forward Move in War-Time', LMS, *Chronicle* (December 1940), p. 157.

39 'Livingstone', *The Times* (9 December 1940), p. 5.

40 SOAS, CWM, AF26/17A, Rev. Ronald K. Orchard to Rev. Alfred J. Haile, 25 July 1951.

41 A. K. Shutt and T. King, 'Imperial Rhodesians: The 1953 Rhodes Centenary Exhibition in Southern Rhodesia', *Journal of Southern African Studies* 31:2 (2005), pp. 357–79.

42 SOAS, CWM, AF/2D, Barnes correspondence, Orchard to Rev. Harold J. Barnes, 17 January; Central Africa district committee meeting, minutes, 2 May 1955.

43 J. Lewis, 'Rivers of White: David Livingstone and the 1955 Commemorations in the Lost "Henley-upon-Thames of Central Africa"', in J.-B. Gewald, M. Hinfelaar and G. Macola (eds), *Living the End of Empire: Politics and Society in Late Colonial Zambia* (Leiden: Brill, 2011), pp. 196–203.

44 M. A. Currie, *Livingstone's Hospital: The Story of Chitambo* (Bloomington, IN: AuthorHouse, 2011), pp. 74–92. Wilson lived until 1976.

[168]

45 L. Schumaker, *Africanizing Anthropology: Fieldwork, Networks, and the Making of Cultural Knowledge in Central Africa* (Durham, NC, and London: Duke University Press, 2001), p. 52.
46 F. Mufuzi, 'Establishment of the Livingstone Museum and its role in colonial Zambia', *Historia*, 56:1 (2011), pp. 33–9.
47 J. Littler, ' "Festering Britain": the 1951 Festival of Britain, Decolonisation and the Representation of the Commonwealth', in S. Faulkner and A. Ramamurthy (eds), *Visual Culture and Decolonisation in Britain* (Aldershot: Ashgate, 2006), p. 16.
48 'The Unveiling of the Livingstone Statue', *Geographical Journal* 120:1 (1954), pp. 15–20.
49 'Sunday Schools' Procession: David Livingstone Anniversary', *Glasgow Herald* (17 March 1958), p. 3.
50 A. C. Ross, *David Livingstone*, p. 239.
51 D. O. Helly, *Livingstone's Legacy: Horace Waller and Victorian Mythmaking* (Athens: Ohio University Press, 1987).
52 J. Tengatenga, *The UMCA in Malawi: A History of the Anglican Church, 1861–2010* (Zomba: Kachere Books, 2010), pp. 154–5.
53 Rev. W. J. Rampley, *Matthew Wellington: Sole Surviving Link with Dr Livingstone* (London: SPCK, 1930). Anna Mary Wilson, another surviving link with Livingstone, lived until 1939.
54 'Honouring Famous Missionary: Livingstone Memorial Sunday', *Glasgow Herald* (4 December 1940), p. 9.
55 J. Tengatenga, *UMCA in Malawi*, pp. 411–13.
56 C. P. Williams, *The Ideal of the Self-Governing Church: A Study in Victorian Missionary Strategy* (Leiden: Brill, 1990).
57 LMS, *The Hundred and Eighteenth Report*, p. 35.
58 J. M. MacKenzie, 'David Livingstone and the Worldly After-Life: Imperialism and Nationalism in Africa', in J. M. MacKenzie (ed.), *David Livingstone and the Victorian Encounter with Africa* (London: National Portrait Gallery Publications, 1996), p. 215.
59 A. C. Ross, *David Livingstone*, p. 243.
60 G. Shepperson, 'David Livingstone 1813–1873: A Centenary Assessment', *Geographical Journal* 139:2 (1973), p. 217.
61 T. Jeal, *Livingstone* (New Haven, CT: Yale University Press, 2001), pp. xiv–xv.
62 D. Crawford, *Back to the Long Grass: My Link with Livingstone* (London: Hodder & Stoughton, 1922), p. 12. Crawford (1870–1926) was a missionary of the Plymouth Brethren.
63 My thanks to Dr Francis Gooding for this information.
64 Cited in 'David Livingstone: The Centenary Commemoration', p. 110.

CHAPTER TEN

Freedom fighter and anti-Tsarist rebel: Imam Shamil and imperial memory in Russia

Stefan Creuzberger

The collapse of the Soviet Union has put an end to the Communist Party's former prerogative to interpret the past. In post-Soviet Russia it is not only Russian historians, but even more so those of the different nations and ethnicities within the Russian Federation, who have used their new freedom to reconstruct their identity by reshaping their collective memory and rewriting their history. Prominent among those are the official national political leaders and historians of the Autonomous Republics of Dagestan and Chechnya. After nearly a century and a half of Russian and Soviet imperial predominance in this region, they can now, for the first time, create new historical narratives without any direct external interference from St Petersburg or Moscow.

The nineteenth-century Caucasus war occupies a central place within recent research and continuing public debates. Above all, it is Imam Shamil who dominates the list of 'national heroes' in Dagestan and Chechnya (Figure 10.1).[1] He is deeply connected with the legendary resistance of the Miurids, followers of a militant form of Islam, who were drawn from the mountain tribes under his command. For twenty-five years, between 1834 and 1859, the so-called 'Lion of Dagestan' entangled the Tsarist army in a fierce guerrilla war, inflicting heavy casualties on his Russian enemies.[2]

Shamil left a lasting impression on his contemporaries. Evidence for this can be found in an 1842 diary entry by a Russian officer who was serving on the North Caucasus front. In the midst of a difficult military situation, he contemplated his opponent with palpable respect and asserted without malice:

> If we bear in mind the fact that, over the course of just a few years we
> have regularly sacrificed more people in this bloody war than were ever

10.1 Contemporary photograph of Imam Shamil (1797–1871)

under Shamil's command, then we must look with admiration to this brilliant field commander. He stands at the head of a small heap of rag-tag warriors, ready to do battle with an utterly superior power such as ours, ready not just to hold his ground but year after year to expand his reputation and his power, and to emerge from each new encounter even more fearsome than before.[3]

Shamil was not only a respected military leader, but a charismatic personality. His fellow fighters referred to him as the prophet. Countless Dagestani folksongs praised his legendary reputation.[4] Even West Europeans travelling to the Caucasus in the nineteenth century, such as the Frenchman Alexandre Dumas or the German Friedrich Bodenstedt, sought a personal audience with Shamil. They eagerly collected the exotic tales that were woven around the persona of the rebel leader.[5] In 1848, following many years of residence in Russia, Bodenstedt published his cultural history *The Peoples of the Caucasus and Their Battles for Freedom against the Russians*. The author was clearly taken with Shamil's image of sovereign self-mastery:

His appearance is utterly noble and full of dignity. He is the absolute master of himself and exercises a quiet hegemony over all those who approach him. An unshakeable marble stillness, which persists even in moments of extreme danger, hovers around his visage. He pronounces a death sentence with the same calm that characterizes his bestowing of an honorary sword, following a bloody battle, to his bravest Miurid. He converses with traitors or criminals, whose deaths he has just determined, without expressing the least sign of anger or revenge. At the same time, he regards himself only as an instrument in the hands of a higher being, considering all his ideas and decisions – in according with Sufi teaching – as the direct result of divine inspiration.[6]

Reports such as these spread Shamil's fame beyond the borders of the Tsarist Empire. Between 1854 and 1856 some twenty-eight books, including translated works, were published in Western Europe and the United States about Imam Shamil and the Caucasus. By the time of his military defeat and imprisonment there were a further ten publications.[7]

In the Northern Caucasus area Shamil is not only revered for his military achievements and his extraordinary personality, but also for his ability to form a regular army. For a quarter of a century he even developed a regular state based on Islamic law. Given that traditional organisational structures predominated in this area, this was an extraordinary achievement. What is more: the commonwealth which Shamil established by sheer skill, persistence and personal power of persuasion, possessed a complexity altogether uncommon for its time and place. At the same time, Shamil's state represented 'the culmination of the anti-colonial movement', and both local patterns and broad elements of Middle Eastern statecraft were united within it. To be sure, Sharia provided the legal foundation for these institutions, but notwithstanding theoretical claims to the contrary, Sharia was by no means applied consistently in practice. In the end, Shamil's Imamate served as the operational basis for further Islamisation. His unification of a multitude of tribal communities – the first example of this in a region famous for its multi-ethnicity and its distinctive clan structures – indisputably counts as one of the most extraordinary achievements of his era. This applies particularly to the Chechens. By allowing themselves to be integrated into Shamil's state, they accepted far-ranging changes in their traditional social structure and everyday life. At the same time, these changes signified an important prerequisite for what would become the Chechens' enduring participation in the anti-colonial resistance against the Russian occupying forces. The fact that the tsar's army found itself entangled in a devastating colonial war lasting several decades had much to do with these circumstances.[8]

What were the effects of this episode at the southeastern periphery of the nineteenth-century Russian Empire for imperial memory in Tsarist, Soviet and – above all – post-Soviet society? This chapter will mainly focus on the first decade of the post-Soviet Russian Federation and in particular on the legacy of events in Dagestan. In this regard, the official celebrations of Imam Shamil's bicentennial in 1997 shed light on the extent to which he became a symbol of resistance, defeat and/or victory in Russia's collective memory. Attention will also be devoted to the impact of the *longue durée*, bearing in mind that the Russian Empire has undergone three distinctive regime changes since the nineteenth century. Only by tracing their evolution across this history, it will be argued, can one begin to make sense of the various Shamil narratives, and with them, of the identity formation, memory politics and historical legitimation deployed by contemporary state actors.

'The Lion of Dagestan' in Tsarist Russia

In view of the lively debates during the Soviet and post-Soviet eras, it is striking that neither Shamil nor his political–religious Miurid resistance movement were ever of central importance to Russia's pre-revolutionary historians. '[T]he main interest of Russian historiography', Moshe Gammer, the Israeli expert on Shamil's resistance to the tsar, argues, 'was in the Russian conquest of the Caucasus and in allocating responsibilities for success and failures during this lengthy war'.[9] For the majority of pre-1917 historians the military campaign against Shamil was a just war. Because it was part of Russia's imperial civilising mission, no one doubted the necessity to pacify and subdue the 'wild' backward mountain tribes.[10]

Even though historians paid him scant attention, Shamil and his Miurid warriors nevertheless left a lasting impression on the late Tsarist public sphere. In the first half of the nineteenth century only a minority regarded him as a religious fanatic and a 'wild beast'.[11] At the same time a handful of Russian writers described him as a 'noble savage'.[12] Similar attitudes could still be found as late as 1856, although they were clearly in decline by then. A good example of this genre was *Shamil's Prisoners* by Evgenii A. Verderevskii, a writer and editor working for the *Kavkaz* (*Caucasus*) newspaper. The book was based on a variety of interviews and described the fate of two Georgian princesses who, between 1854 and 1855, spent eight months as Shamil's prisoners. The text proved an enormous success among the Russian elites. Verderevskii portrayed the abduction of the two aristocratic Christian women by mountain people (gortsy) as violent and brutal, but as soon as they had reached Shamil's residence in Vedeno, in eastern Chechnya, and were in the custody of the Imam, the situation changed completely. In stark contrast to the raw and primitive world of the North Caucasian mountains, there appeared to them, in almost poetic fashion, the figure of the Imam Shamil: an honourable fighter, a hostage-taker full of humanity, and even a loving father and loyal husband.[13]

Descriptions of this kind were also found among the Tsarist military elite. As early as the 1840s Russian military men had shown respect for Shamil. General Golovin for instance called him an 'unusually "crafty" opponent' and stated that the Imam had become 'by now a virtually historical personage'.[14] Russia's general response to Shamil's defeat in 1859 was marked by overwhelming respect and adoration for the former anti-Tsarist rebel due to his exceptional qualifications as military commander, political leader and administrator.

At the same time, the empire could not resist the urge to celebrate the victory over Russia's arch-enemy with lavish military parades, balls, and fireworks in St Petersburg, Moscow and many important provincial cities.[15] Equally remarkable, though, is the fact that the tsar's most prominent prisoner of war became an important element of imperial representation. This did not happen in a demeaning way; on the contrary – the tsar and various imperial dignitaries gave Shamil an honourable reception as a hero. In a tour lasting several weeks he was shown the achievements of Russian civilisation. In Tula, south of Moscow, he was proudly led through the local munitions factory. During his sojourn in Moscow and St Petersburg, Shamil took in the cultural highlights: visiting the theatre, the ballet and the opera; touring the Kremlin, various museums, and public libraries; during his visit to the military printing facility, he was presented with a large-scale map of the Caucasus.

At the time, veritable 'Shamil-mania' swept the country. Countless photographs and portraits showing him in North-Caucasian uniform, looking like a worthy and dignified Field Commander, appeared in illustrated periodicals. Newspapers waxed lyrical about the 'Lion of Dagestan'; bookstores were awash with enthusiastic works about Shamil. Thus it is hardly surprising that, at his departure from St Petersburg, Shamil received a grand and thoroughly heartfelt farewell. Captain Apollon Runovskii, who for the next two and a half years was charged by the Tsarist government to ensure Shamil's wellbeing in Kaluga, captured that stirring moment:

> There is no doubt that Znamenskii Square had not seen such a conflu-
> ence of people since the opening of the railroad. Indeed, the procession
> of Shamil looked like a festival. How many kisses were thrown through
> the air by pretty hands! How many cried, 'Good-bye Shamil! Good-bye
> Shamil! Stay with us! Stay a while longer with us ... Good-bye! Come
> back and visit us! Tell him that we love him very much! Tell him that
> we wish him the very best!'[16]

Even his exile was honourable: in Kaluga Shamil and his family were provided with an imposing house, complete with its own private mosque. Twenty-two servants were at the family's beck and call. Moreover, Shamil received an annual stipend of 20,000 roubles from the Russian government.[17] Behind this extraordinary generosity to a former military foe and the strikingly positive place he occupied – in his own lifetime – in Russia's public culture of memory, there lay, of course, a sober stratagem. The Tsarist Empire thereby presented itself not only as a culture- and civilisation-bearing colonial power. By elevating the status of the anti-Tsarist rebels the empire simultaneously heightened the prestige of its victory over Imam Shamil and his Miurid resistance movement.[18] Indeed, Shamil and the battle against the mountain tribes had become a favourite motif of contemporary Russian painting, even during the war itself.[19]

Ambivalent figure in the Soviet era

As might be expected, the Bolshevik revolution and the associated break with Russian imperial culture brought important consequences for the perception of Shamil and his resistance against Tsarist colonial power. To be sure, when the young Soviet power was under threat – in the civil war era, for example, or during critical phases of the Second World War, official Soviet memory culture was notably mute about historical themes with anti-Russian or anti-Soviet character.[20] But in the 1920s, when, under the watchword 'Friendship of the Peoples', the state busily sought to fashion a new Soviet identity for the multinational Soviet Empire, the Caucasian war and the resistance by the mountain peoples gradually made their way on to the agenda of local historians. Initially, Shamil was hardly the centre of attention. Eager to employ the ideological tool-kit of Marxism–Leninism, Soviet historiography was less interested in outstanding historical personalities than in allegedly history-making socio-economic structures and questions of class struggle. Mikhail N. Pokrovskii, then the Nestor of Soviet historiography, provided the interpretive template: under its religious guise, the resistance of the mountain peoples was revealed as an anti-colonial liberation movement driven by class struggle, an attack on both Tsarist oppression and exploitation by local feudal lords and khans. Citing Marx and Engels, Pokrovskii described Imam Shamil as the capable leader of a 'democratic movement'. Since the odds were so heavily weighted against it, though, the movement was doomed. In the long run it had to suffer defeat by the tsar's colonial army.[21] Thanks to the countless historical investigations that were undertaken in this spirit, Caucasian documents were gathered and edited in Russian-language publications for the first time.[22]

[175]

With the Stalinist reorganisation of the USSR and the associated Russification of the historical profession, Soviet historians who wished to avoid official repression were forced to invent new modes of historical legitimation for the regime. Shamil was transformed, almost overnight, into the leader of a reactionary feudal religious revolt against a more highly civilised Russia. By the 1930s, scholars who failed to toe the line of this Stalinist interpretation of Shamil would meet with considerable obstacles. This was the experience of the young historian Nikolai I. Pokrovskii. His 1934 dissertation on the Caucasus wars and the Shamil Imamate was eventually published after a sixty-six-year delay.[23] The research of his colleague A. B. Zaks was completely suppressed.[24] By contrast, those who produced studies that were neutral or hostile to Shamil and his Miurid movement received favourable attention from the state and their careers developed accordingly.

This trend not only continued but intensified when, in connection with the 1944 deportations of the Chechens and other peoples from the North Caucasus, the Stalin regime systematically sought to erase their past and their culture of memory. It was hardly an auspicious time to study national heroes who had distinguished themselves by resisting the Russians. Not surprisingly, between 1944 and 1949 only a single published work touched on the topic of Shamil – a Russian-language edition of an Arabic chronicle. Even this text remained truncated, since a promised companion volume with commentary and annotations never appeared. The few Dagestani historians who had remained undaunted and who, notwithstanding the difficult circumstances, continued to explore Shamil and the themes associated with him, had to content themselves with a niche apart from all official institutions. As private individuals they were able to gather manuscripts and mostly Arabic-language materials which addressed Shamil and the Caucasus wars, but only to a very limited extent. Insofar as scholarly manuscripts emerged from their work, they remained for the most part in desk drawers, coming to light only in post-Soviet Russia.[25]

The early 1950s represented the high-watermark of Stalinist stigmatisation and falsification generally. Official Soviet memory culture now presented the Imam as a fanatical, anti-democratic religious leader. The cliché of the anti-Tsarist rebel was once more revived to reveal a movement not of national liberation but of conspiracy against Russia in the service of British colonialism and Ottoman imperialism, or as Mir Dzhafar Bagirov, the Stalinist party boss of Azerbaijan and close protegé of Lavrenti Beriia, argued:

[Shamil] wanted to tear the Caucasus away from Russia ... [and] he attracted a huge number of Russian troops, thus assisting her military opponents – Britain, France and Turkey – and creating opportunities for them in the Crimea. [... Insofar as the integration to Russia was] the only way for the Caucasian peoples to develop their culture and economy [since] the choice before them was either to be swallowed by feudal Persia and Turkey or to join Russia.[26]

The era of the 'Thaw' and of de-Stalinisation under Nikita Khrushchev also left clear traces in the evolution of the historical image of Shamil and his resistance movement. Important stimuli emerged from a conference organised by the Dagestani branch of the Soviet Academy of Sciences in October 1956 in Makhachkala. Young Dagestani historians such as V. G. Gadzhiev and D. D. Daniialov, supported by their local Communist Party leaders, worked tirelessly towards a revision of the dominant interpretation. There was a notable decline in attacks against Shamil and his resistance movement for allegedly collaborating with enemy powers – accusations levelled as recently as the early 1950s. The conference concluded that:

the participants of the Dagestani session supported the necessity to reject the point of view asserted after 1950 as if the movement of the mountaineers of the Caucasus were reactionary and anti-popular, and its leaders agents of Turkey and England. The joining of Dagestan to Russia had an objectively progressive historic significance. However, the [Tsarist] autocracy pursued in the Caucasus, as in other peripheral territories, was a brutal colonizing policy and supported the yoke of feudal lords, which aroused the resistance of the popular masses. Although Powers hostile to Russia tried to use the movement of the Caucasian mountaineers, it grew in the socio-economic soil of the North-eastern Caucasus. The movement of the mountaineers under the leadership of Shamil aimed its spearhead at the colonizing policy of tsarism and was a struggle for national independence. The religious cloak of this movement, however, was reactionary: Miurdism kindled religious fanaticism, [and] provoked hatred of peoples professing Christianity.[27]

This gesture, aimed at Imam Shamil's rehabilitation, was all the more effective in light of the fact that, one month later, a conference of historians in the Soviet capital also embarked upon a search for new methods and interpretations. They sought to free themselves from ossified Stalinist positions and to find a moderate stance vis-à-vis the Shamil question. A complete rehabilitation of the Imam was unthinkable, though. According to the compromise position, which the Dagestani historians offered to the orthodox hardliners in Moscow and especially to non-Muslims in the Caucasus region, Shamil was to be understood as the leader of a progressive anti-colonial movement that attempted to stand up to reactionary tsarism. The Russian annexation of the Caucasus was not to be condemned, though. Rather, it was to be praised, since it brought the region into the sphere of influence of Russia's more highly developed culture and civilisation. After vigorous debates, the various sides arrived at a formula that was politically and ideologically acceptable for the Soviet regime, and that would remain more or less in force until the end of the USSR. From now on Imam Shamil would be honoured as the spiritual and military leader of a progressive, popular, anti-colonial, national liberation movement. However – and here one recognises a concession to the orthodox interpretation – in the course of time all these progressive commitments came to be undermined by anti-popular, clerical and feudal interest groups and finally turned in a reactionary direction.[28]

Conciliator and freedom fighter in post-Soviet Dagestan and Chechnya

Given these developments, it is hardly surprising that during the final years of perestroika and especially the first post-Soviet decade, memory politics regarding Shamil took on a distinctively post-colonial hue. Following the collapse of the USSR the former imperial peripheries enjoyed a greatly expanded field for debate. As previously mentioned, the search for new identity-fostering historical narratives was especially pronounced in Dagestan, Shamil's birthplace, as well as in Chechnya. But even in the Russian heartland, representatives of the state responsible for official versions of history considered it necessary to distance themselves from former Soviet interpretations of Shamil. This was all the more true given Dagestan's and Chechnya's geopolitical importance as Autonomous Republics within the Russian Federation, and in view of the local separatist tendencies that helped to spark two bloody wars between Chechnya and the central powers in Moscow between 1994 and 2009.

Shamil's gradual rehabilitation began in 1990–91, especially in Dagestan, not least because he himself was a Dagestani, or more precisely, an ethnic Avar. Thanks to the initiative of various public organisations and intelligentsia circles, including representatives of the Avar national movement, a Shamil Foundation was established in the Dagestani capital of Makhachkala. Even before the demise of the USSR, pressure from below had forced the Dagestani authorities to name a newly built urban centre 'Shamilka' in honour of the Imam. The Shamil Foundation, which cultivated close informal ties to the Dagestani branch of the Academy of Sciences of the USSR (and today, of the Russian Federation), established itself thanks to an energetic publication programme, lectures' series, scholarly conferences, the financing of folklore celebrations, films, and various theatre and music festivals. By these means the Foundation has contributed significantly to the process of identity formation and in no small measure to anchoring the legendary Shamil in the memory culture of present-day Dagestan.[29] The official commemoration of Imam Shamil's 200th birthday in October 1997 marked a high-point in this development. The ceremonies gained special importance in light of the engagement of the Russian central government in Moscow. On 18 August 1997, the then Russian Prime Minister Viktor Chernomyrdin established a high-level commission to organise the bicentennial festivities on a Federation-wide level.[30]

In Dagestan itself this event surpassed all previous efforts to rehabilitate Shamil and his legacy. Planning had begun as far back as 1994.[31] In addition to official bodies, a striking number of non-governmental social and cultural organisations, academic societies, and not least the Dagestani media took part in preparations for the festivities.[32] Well in advance, but especially during the jubilee itself, a large number of scholarly, popular and also literary publications flooded the market – frequently financed by the Shamil Foundation. Extensive Shamil bibliographies, relevant archival documents and contemporary memoirist accounts were published. The media made Shamil a central theme of its reportage, and regularly sought out the judgments and appraisals of historians, political scientists and sociologists.[33] In order to lend these efforts additional gravitas, on 21 and 22 October 1997 a large international conference, attended by Western as well as Russian historians, was convened in Makhachkala. The results and recommendations of this prominent gathering of Shamil experts were communicated to the public.[34]

The main celebratory event, which was accompanied by an official holiday for the entire Autonomous Republic, took place in the Dagestani capital at the end of October. Along with commemorative processions in historical costumes, folklore performances and street festivals, the ceremonies climaxed with the renaming of Makhachkala's longest street, the former Kirov Avenue, in honour of the Imam. The National Library, newly reopened on that day, was also named after him. The Dagestani State Council ratified an official act of commemoration, at which numerous delegations from other countries in the Commonwealth of Independent States were present. The cultural aspect of the celebration culminated with the premiere of the play 'Shamil in Kaluga', regarding the Imam's exile in Russia, by the young Avar playwright Shapi Kaziev.[35]

What were the central narratives, the historical and political messages and implications that emerged from this commemorative event on the former periphery of the Russian and Soviet Empire? What position did the central authorities, the government of the Russian Federation, take vis-à-vis this process of political memory formation?

On the whole, the commemoration conveyed an image of Shamil that clearly diverged from previous interpretations from the Tsarist and Soviet eras. It was impossible to miss the sense of restorative justice in Dagestan: Shamil and his Miurid movement finally received historical justice. The central Russian government even permitted that Shamil was honoured in Moscow, St Petersburg and other large Russian cities. On 30 October 1997 Moscow mayor Yuri Luzhkov used the central commemorative space of the Hall of Columns in Moscow's House of Labour Unions to praise Shamil as a talented military leader, outstanding politician and statesman. He paid special tribute to Shamil's accomplishments as a reformer. These, according to Luzhkov, had made it possible to fashion stable governing institutions for the multi-ethnic, multi-national, and multi-religious North Caucasus, which culminated in the establishment of the Imamate. In this, Luzhkov recognised the admirable life's work of a man who, among other things, was a bearer of religious tolerance.[36]

In his opening remarks, which were published on 7 August 1997 in the newspaper *Dagestani Pravda*, Razman G. Abdulatipov, Russia's Minister for Nationality Policies, offered similar praise. For him Shamil was neither a fanatical nationalist nor a separatist, let alone a person who – in contrast to his falsified image in the Soviet era – served the interests of the Ottoman Empire. Instead, Abdulatipov described Shamil as a historical personality who deserved to be mentioned in the same breath as such exalted figures in Russian history as the famous patriotic military leaders 'Minin, Pozharskii, Suvorov, Kutuzov, Zhukov'.[37]

The driving force behind all this were historical and political motives, aimed less at the Russian than at the Dagestani and Chechen populations of the Russian Federation. The political message of the central government in Moscow was clear. It is to be understood against the background of separatist tendencies especially in Chechnya, which local nationalists repeatedly justified by invoking Shamil and his struggle for liberation from the Russians. By the end of the Soviet Union, probably even earlier, this position had emerged as dominant. Imam Shamil was the object of public veneration. As early as 1992 authorities in Grozny, Chechnya's capital, released a special set of commemorative stamps, which honoured the outstanding leaders of Chechen resistance against Russia. Shamil's portrait adorned these stamps along the images of Imam Mansur, the first resistance fighter against the Russian Empire in the years between 1785 and 1791, and General Dzhokhar M. Dudaev, who, as president of the Autonomous

Chechen Republic since 1991, had led a campaign for independence from the Russian Federation. Shamil's bicentennial was especially marked in the Vedeno region of Chechnya, which had served as the capital of Shamil's Imamate between 1845 and 1859. It was there that Chechnya's president, Aslan A. Maskhadov, dedicated an architectural ensemble in memory of the great Imam on 21 July 1997. Along with the ramparts of the old fortress, which had been destroyed by Russian artillery, the ensemble included a school for Islamic study, i.e., a madrasa, as well as a mosque, whose 25-metre minarette symbolised the quarter century of Shamil's reign.[38]

Although Chechens of the post-Soviet period have stylised Shamil as a defender of local separatism, such arguments were absent from Dagestan's official memory culture. In order to preserve the unity of the state within the Russian Federation, Moscow regarded the preservation of the Dagestani Shamil-narrative and Shamil's installation as a historical figure within the pantheon of Russian heroes as useful for its own purposes.[39] The politically inspired comments by Abdulatipov, Russia's Minister of Nationalities, mentioned above, should be seen against this background.

In Dagestan itself, the Russian stance reinforced the reception of Shamil that had expressed itself in the 1997 official commemoration ceremonies. The Imam was cast as a great national hero; all the qualities of a charismatic leader were dutifully ascribed to him. He served as a central figure generating a sense of collective identity. Through him the new Dagestani polity could find historical legitimacy within the Russian Federation. Shamil and the Imamate he created symbolised not only unity, cooperation, mutual understanding and peace in the North Caucasus, but because the Imam had begun to take an interest in Russia during his exile there and eventually pledged his loyalty to the tsar, his legacy served as a call to maintain the alliance with Russia. From this perspective, the fact that a decades-long anti-colonial people's war of liberation had preceded the exile changed nothing. This was not the least of the reasons why in 1997 Chechen separatism found little sympathy in Dagestan – especially as the official Dagestani reading of Shamil rejected the misuse of his legacy for such purposes.

In the official Dagestani memory culture of 1997 Shamil embodied, and continues to embody, the overcoming of cultural backwardness. In contrast to the stereotypes dating from the Soviet and pre-revolutionary eras, the political, financial, and organisational structures of Shamil's Imamate were now considered entirely progressive, anti-feudal and even democratic. His social, political and legislative measures – not least among them the abolition of slavery – appeared as exemplary acts, far ahead of their time and thus celebrated as a barometer of an exceptional civilising capacity.[40]

The resulting self-confidence for the Dagestani state persists even today. Imam Shamil is very much alive in twenty-first-century Dagestan. It is thus hardly surprising that in 2011 local newspapers commented on literary–musical evenings in Shamil's honour, that in June 2011 the theatre season in Makhachkala concluded with a play about the national hero, or that at the beginning of August 2011 a notice in the press described how the winners of a school competition shone by demonstrating – how could it be otherwise? – their knowledge of Dagestan's great son.[41] Shamil the freedom fighter is thus always present, and one can only conclude that he will remain so for the foreseeable future. The domestic situation in today's multi-ethnic autonomous republic has done little to alter this situation – which is hardly reassuring. While in the mid-1990s one eagerly awaited economic prosperity and – with reference to Shamil – the capacity of the Dagestanis to manage their own state, now such hopes are threatened by the chaos of unchecked corruption, persistent crime and growing Islamic fundamentalism.[42] All that remains is the certainty of possessing, in the person of the Imam, a prominent historical representative of Dagestan. At least in hindsight, Shamil and his nineteenth-century achievements in temporarily overcoming backwardness represent the civilisational legacy of the North Caucasus Republic on Russia's periphery.

Notes

1 To get a sense of the liveliness of the field, see R. M. Magomedov, *Shamil'. Illiustrirovannaia entsiklopediia* (Moskva: Regional'nyj Fond Poddershkei Gosudarstvennoj Nacional'noj Politiki 'Sodrushestvo', 2005), pp. 416–24. *Imam Shamil na vesakh istorii: K 200-letiiu so dnia roshdeniia. Bibliograficheskii ukazatel'* (Makhachkala: Fundamental'naia biblioteka Dagestanskogo gos. pedagog. univ., 1997).
2 For further operational aspects of the Caucasus war and Shamil see M. Gammer, *Muslim Resistance to the Tsar: Shamil and the Conquest of Chechnia and Daghestan* (London: Cass, 1994). J. F. Baddeley, *The Russian Conquest of the Caucasus* (London: 1908, Reprint: RoutledgeCurzon, 2003).
3 As recorded in F. Bodenstedt, *Die Völker des Kaukasus und ihre Freiheitskämpfe: Ein Beitrag zur neuesten Geschichte des Orients* (Frankfurt and London: Keßler, 1848), pp. 411–12.
4 *Ibid.*, p. 412.
5 For Dumas see e.g. A. Dumas, *Gefährliche Reise durch den wilden Kaukasus: 1858–1859* (Stuttgart and Vienna: Ed. Erdmann in K. Thienemanns Verlag, 1995), pp. 158–70.
6 F. Bodenstedt, *Völker*, pp. 415–16.
7 T. M. Barrett, 'The Remaking of the Lion of Dagestan: Shamil in Captivity', *The Russian Review* 53 (1994), pp. 358–9.
8 M. Gammer, 'Collective Memory and Politics: Remarks on Some Competing Historical Narratives in the Caucasus and Russia in their Use of a "National Hero"',

Caucasian Regional Studies 4:1 (1999), pp. 1–15, here: online version: http://proxy. library.upenn.edu:6064/olj/crs/crs_1999/crs99_gam01.html (accessed 20 August 2011); C. P. Sidorko, *Dschihad im Kaukasus: Antikolonialer Widerstand der Dagestaner und Tschetschenen gegen das Zarenreich (18. Jahrhundert bis 1859)* (Wiesbaden: Reichert, 2007), pp. 183–404, 433–6.

9 M. Gammer, 'Shamil in Soviet Historiography', *Middle Eastern Studies* 28:4 (1992), pp. 729–77, here: 730.

10 A. E. Save'lev, 'Kavkazskaia voina 1817–1864 gg. V istoricheskoi nauke', *Voprosy istorii* 2 (2001), p. 161. R. M. Magomedov, *Shamil' v otechestvennoi istorii* (Makhachkala, 1990), pp. 6, 37.

11 *Ibid.*, p. 38. M. Gammer, 'Shamil in Soviet Historiography', p. 730.

12 S. Layton, 'Primitive Despot and Noble Savage: the Two Faces of Shamil in Russian Literature', *Central Asian Survey* 10:4 (1991), pp. 31–45, here: 32–3.

13 E. A. Verderevskii, *Plen u Shamilia* (St Petersburg: V tip. Koroleva, 1856). Layton, 'Primitive Despot', pp. 34–5. S. Layton, *Russian Literature and Empire: Conquest of the Caucasus from Pushkin to Tolstoy* (Cambridge: Cambridge University Press, 1994), pp. 153–4. One year later an English-speaking version had already been published in London: 'Captivity of Two Russian Princesses in the Caucasus: Including a Seven Months' Residence in Shamil's Seraglio'.

14 General Golovin quoted in: *Akty sobrannye kavkazskoiu arkheograficheskoiu kommissieu*, vol. 9 (Tiflis: Tipogr. Glavnogo Upravlenija Namestnika Kavkazskogo, 1884), p. 230.

15 For more information see T. M. Barrett, 'Remaking', pp. 353–66. M. N. Chichagova, *Shamil' na Kavkaze i v Rossii: Biograficheskii ocherk* (St Petersburg: Tip. i Litografiia S. Muller i I. Bogel'ma, 1889), pp. 108–21.

16 A. Runovskii, *Zapiski o Shamile* (St Petersburg: V Tip. Karla Vul'fa, 1860), pp. 30–1.

17 G. Omarov, 'Shamil' v Rossii', in *Shamil': Illiustrirovannaia entsiklopediia*, p. 339.

18 Savel'ev, 'Kavkazskaia voina', pp. 161–2.

19 P. Ganzatova, 'Russkaia zhivopisis', in *Shamil': Illiustrirovannaia entsiklopediia*, pp. 392–7.

20 M. Gammer, 'Shamil in Soviet Historiography', p. 731.

21 Savel'ev, 'Kavkazskaia voina', p. 162. M. N. Prolerovskii, *Diplomatiia i voiny tsarskoi Rossii XIX veke* (Moskva: Krasnaia nov, 1923), pp. 211–29. The views of Marx and Engels are summarised in Magomedov, *Otechestvennoi istorii*, pp. 54–8.

22 C. P. Sidorko, *Dschihad*, p. XIII.

23 N. I. Pokrovskii, *Kavkazskie voiny i Imamat Shamilia* (Moskva: ROSSPEN, 2000).

24 For further information see A. B. Zaks, 'Kak ia zashishchala dissertatsiiu i probovala ee opublikovat', *Voprosy istorii* 6 (1989), pp. 164–7.

25 C. P. Sidorko, *Dschihad*, p. XIV.

26 This new anti-Shamil campaign began in 1950 with a series of articles by M. D. Bagirov, the Stalinist party chief of Azerbaijan. See e.g. M. D. Bagirov, 'K voprosu o kharaktere dvizheniia Shamilia', *Bol'shevik* 13 (1950), pp. 21–37, and M. D. Bagirov, 'Starshii brat v sem'e sovetskikh narodov', *Kommunist* 3 (1953), pp. 64–8.

27 'Obsuzhdenie voprosa o kharaktere dvizhenii gorskikh narodov severnogo Kavkaza v 20–50 kh godakh XIX veka', *Voprosy istorii* 12 (1956), p. 191.

28 For more detailed information on the post-Stalinist debates see: M. Gammer, 'Shamil in Soviet Historiography', pp. 731–65.

29 D. Magomedov and G. Mentesh, 'Fondy Shamilia', in *Shamil': Illiustrirovannaia entsiklopediia*, pp. 402–3. M. Gammer, 'Collective Memory', p. 3. R. Chenciner, *Daghestan: Tradition and Survival* (London and New York: St. Martin's Press, 1997), pp. 17, 19.

30 *Pravitel'stvo Rossiiskoi Federatsii: Razporiazhenie ot 18 avgusta 1997 goda N 1166-r [Ob obrazovanii organizatsionnogo komiteta po podgotovke i provedeniiu iubileinikh meropriiatii, posviashchennikh 200-letiiu so dnia rozhdeniia Imama Shamilia]*, in http://docs.kodeks.ru/document/9047552 (accessed 20 August 2011).

31 D. M. Magomedov, 'Vydaiushchiisia gosudarstvennyi deiatel', ubezhdennyi gumanist i demokrat', in G. G. Gamzatov (ed.), *Istoricheskie, dukhovnye i nravstvennye*

uroki Shamilia: Slovo k 200-letiu imama Dagestana i Chechni (Makhachkala: DNTS RA, 2000), p. 149.

32 M. M. Magomedov, 'Ob itogakh prazdnovaniia iubileia 200-letiia imama Shamilia', in *ibid.*, p. 168.

33 'Nauchnye i nravstvennye masshtaby shamilevskogo iubileia', in *ibid.*, p. 8. For the special Shamil bibliography see: *Shamil': Illiustrirovannaia entsiklopediia.* For popular Shamil biographies and brochures see, e.g.: R. M. Magomedov, *Dva stoletiia c Shamiliem* (Makhachkala: Biblioteka fonda Shamilia, 1997).

34 'Osnovnye vyvody i rekomendacii mezhdunarodnoi nauchnoi konferentsii "Narodno-osvobozhditel'naia voina na Severnom Kavkaze pod predvoditel'stom Shamilia i ee mezhdunarodnoe znachenie", posviashchennoi 200-letiu so dnia rozhdeniia imama Shamilia', in G. G. Gamzatov, *Istoricheskie, dukhovnye i nravstvennye uroki Shamilia*, pp. 156–62.

35 M. Gammer, 'Collective Memory', pp. 4, 12.

36 Iu. M. Luzhkov, 'Vydaiushchaiasia lichnost'', in G. G. Gamzatov, *Istoricheskie, dukhovnye i nravstvennye uroki Shamilia*, pp. 55–6.

37 R. G. Abdulatipov, 'Takim on byl, imam Shamil'', in *ibid.*, pp. 61, 64.

38 M. Gammer, 'Collective Memory', pp. 5–6.

39 *Ibid.*, p. 4.

40 For further details see, e.g. the following contributions in G. G. Gamzatov, *Istoricheskie, dukhovnye i nravstvennye uroki Shamilia*: 'Nauchnye i nravstvennye masshtaby', pp. 7–10; M. M. Magomedov, '200-letie imama Shamilia i uroki istorii', pp. 11–26; Kh. I. Shkhailov, 'Shamil' byl i ostaetsia sovremennikom vsekh pokolenii liudei', pp. 44–6; R. M. Magomedov, 'Triumf i tragediia Shamilia: uroki i predosterezheniia istorii', pp. 71–87; R. M. Magomedov, 'Vydaiushchiisia gosudarstvennyi deiatel'', pp. 149–55; 'Osnovnye vyvody', pp. 156–62; 'Obrashchenie uchastnikov torzhestvennogo gosudarstvennogo soveta, narodnogo sobraniia, pravitel'stva respublik Dagestan i predstavitelei obshchestvennosti k narodam Dagestana', pp. 163–5; R. M. Magomedov, 'Ob itogach', pp. 166–9. 'Imamat', in: *Shamil': Illiustrirovannaia entsiklopediia*, pp. 83–120.

41 'An Evening in Memory of Imam Shamil Takes Place in Makhachkala', *Republic Information Agency (RIA Dagestana)*, (11 April 2011), www.riadagestan.com/print.php?new=6255&page_index= (accessed 20 August 2011). 'Dagestanskii teatr opery i baleta zakryl sezon spektaklem "Imam Shamil'", *Respublikanskoe Informatsionnoe Agenstvo (RIA Dagestana)*, (4 July 2011), www.riadagestan.ru/print.php?new=116322&page_index=, (accessed 20 August 2011). 'God imama Shamilia', (5 August 2011), www.islamnews.ru/news-print-75041.htm (accessed 20 August 2011).

42 'Kaukasus. "Tragt Chaos in ihre Reihen"', *Der Spiegel* 30 (2010), pp. 94–7.

PART III

Remembering and forgetting

CHAPTER ELEVEN

From Nehruvian neglect to Bollywood heroes: the memory of the Raj in post-war India

Maria Misra

In 1863 the British government in India built the 'Mutiny Memorial' to commemorate those lost in the so-called 'Indian Mutiny' (or 'Rebellion') of 1857–58 – an uprising of Indian peasants, soldiers and aristocrats that seriously challenged British power in north India. Built to evoke the gothic medievalism of a European church spire, the tapering octagonal sandstone edifice is punctuated by marble niches in which is recorded a somewhat selective narrative of the 'Mutiny'. Also inscribed are the numbers and regiments of all those killed on the British side, but of the 1,029 slain on the British side only the forty-seven white British officers are actually named.[1] Looming over the ridge in Delhi, which had been one of the epicentres of the 'Mutiny', it was a brutal reminder in what was to become India's capital of Britain's triumphalism. Appropriately enough it quickly became known by Indians as *Fatehgarh*, or Victory Fort.[2]

It might be felt that such a challenge to Indian sensitivities would be an early victim of independence, and yet it was not until August 1972, that is, a full quarter century after Independence, that this British memorial was officially converted into a memorial for the 'Indian martyrs of the Mutiny'.[3] This conversion involved nothing more than the erection of a small stone plaque stating that 'the "enemy" of the inscriptions on this monument were those who rose against colonial rule'.[4] This seems a rather perfunctory gesture, aimed less at commemorating Indian freedom fighters, than at 'correcting' the hitherto excessively pro-British perspective. There is no separate memorial in India to honour the rebels of 1857, nor is there any major monument (bar one, as we shall see later) to the victims of other traumas of the Raj, such as the 17 million estimated dead either in famines, or as casualties of Partition. And unlike other ex-colonial Asian states, there has been very little demolition or removal of the omnipresent physical remains of the Raj – its cityscapes, its civic amenities and even, in a surprising number of cases, its statuary.

This peculiar lack of interest in memorialising the trauma of colonial rule and its martyrs or opponents has not gone without comment, and various explanations have been advanced in both popular and academic writing. Some, such as Pavan Varma, suggest that India's elites have focused primarily on contemporary concerns, and not on the political and cultural ramifications of India's colonial heritage.[5] For the art historian Tapati Guha-Thakurta, a prevailing apathy accounts for this forgetfulness. She writes of Curzon's grandiose edifice, 'The Victoria Memorial', which still dominates Kolkata (Calcutta), 'for the Calcuttans it has prevailed for many years now as a memorial to a dead Raj, whose memories, like its representations, have long lost their edge'.[6] Others suggest that the lack of concern for the Mutiny Memorial is simply a special case: its traumatic associations are local Delhi memories, and have been overshadowed by the city's role as India's national capital.[7] A more radical explanation, however, has been proffered by post-colonial historians, such as Ann Laura Stoler and Karen Strassler, who suggest that post-colonial society's apparent indifference to the colonial past should be seen as an example of willed neglect and deliberate 'forgetting' – an essentially 'subaltern' rejection, which is not merely apathy or indifference.[8]

Some of these explanations are more convincing than others. The particular place of the Mutiny/Rebellion in Delhi is clearly important, whereas, as I shall show, Varma's and Guha-Thakurta's emphasis on elite apathy is less persuasive. However, none of these interpretations explains why the memory of the Raj is so different in India compared with other formerly colonial Asian states. This article will argue that far from being indicative of apathy and indifference, the absence of major physical memorials to colonial trauma and victims and the preservation of much of the physical cityscapes of empire is actually a sign not of forgetting, but of the politicisation and deeply contested nature of memory. Because there is no agreement on the meaning of empire in India, it has proved difficult to create cults of victimhood, villainy or heroism that might command common assent and thus facilitate memorialisation. Paradoxically, therefore, empire as memory seems to be absent because empire as politics is too present. I shall also argue that we cannot understand the real place of empire in memory if we treat the 'Raj' as if it were one thing which its successors might simply remember or forget – as some writers assume. The British Empire was a complex phenomenon, experienced differently at different times. To understand memory of the Raj, we need to disentangle these varied elements and comprehend their often contrasting resonances in the context of post-independence Indian political and cultural conflicts. These very specific associations help to explain why India's memory of colonialism contrasts so strikingly with that of China and South-east Asian states.

British memorialisation of the Raj

The British Empire has been open to a number of meanings and interpretations for Indians, reflecting the fact that British imperial strategy and culture changed over time. We can identify three broad understandings of empire. Firstly, imperialism was often seen as a largely commercial project. This interpretation was most suited to the East India Company era, particularly in the late eighteenth century, when parts of India were governed by a hybrid commercial-cum-military formation, whose goal could be seen as largely profit-seeking rather than state-building. Secondly, British imperialists could be seen as modernisers and bureaucratic state-builders. This interpretation focused particularly on the so-called 'reforming period' between 1800 and the 1830s, and the post-First World War era of real, if limited, economic developmentalism. Thirdly, imperialists could be seen as essentially the authors of an ideology and style of rule based on hierarchy – both aristocratic and racial. This could plausibly be said to describe the period of 'high imperialism' of c. 1860–1914, when the Raj embarked on what some have seen as a 'Durbar' style (courtly) of governance, involving minutely calibrated hierarchies of race, class and culture.

The contrasts between these distinctive views of empire can be seen in British memorialisations of their own rule. The most resonant monuments of the commercial Company period must be the commemorative obelisks or pillars to victims of what were seen as cruel massacres by Indian rulers. Most notorious was that erected to mark the so-called 'Black Hole of Calcutta' of 1756; another was placed at the site of the so-called Patna Massacre of 1763 – where East India Company men were imprisoned and then killed by the Nawab of Bengal and Bihar. Both monuments supposedly marked the precise spot where British bodies had been discarded – a ditch in the case of the Black Hole and a well for Patna. Strikingly, though both massacres had in fact occurred in the context of war and their victims were soldiers, the monuments presented the British as peaceful and commercial martyrs of irrational and militaristic oriental rule.[9] By contrast, 'modernising' imperialists tended to favour self-commemoration in the form of monumental civic architecture, the most striking examples of which are Calcutta's Government House (1803) and the Lutyens' New Delhi complex, built in the 1920s, both evoking in different ways a neo-classical style.[10] But it was the third imperialist project, the hierarchical, that produced the most flamboyant monuments, with the development of the Indo-Saracenic style, blending medieval Hindu, Islamic and European gothic to signify, in the eyes of its builders at least, the indigenisation of the British within an organic Indian aristocratic-cum-racial hierarchy. This style was enthusiastically emulated by the high Raj's closest collaborators, the Indian princes.[11]

Since Independence, then, India's urban citizens have been reminded of all three imperial projects, and understandably India's political leaders and movements have 'remembered' different aspects of the Raj, depending on their ideological views and policy objectives. At the same time, of course, the broad parameters of political debate have changed over time, and when analysing attitudes to the Raj it makes sense to divide the post-colonial era into three broad periods – that of Congress hegemony (1947–67), the breakdown of Congress's dominance and the emergence of powerful regional parties (1967–85), and the era of neo-liberalism and the rise of the Hindu right (late 1980s to the 2000s).

Nehruvian neglect (1947–67)

Jawaharlal Nehru, the first Prime Minister of Independent India, had a notably ambivalent attitude towards the Raj, but it becomes more explicable if we appreciate that he distinguished between the different aspects of the British imperial project. In particular, Nehru valorised its 'modernising' characteristics, while denigrating its commercial and aristocratic-hierarchical aspects. At times, it seemed that Nehru was rejecting the British legacy *tout court* seeking an indigenous genealogy for modernity in the example of the supposedly Buddhist Emperor of second century BCE India, Ashoka. A number of studies of this period had been published in inter-war India, all emphasising the period's supposed 'rationality', economic developmentalism and republicanism.[12] It was therefore not surprising that in choosing an iconography for the new Indian republic, Nehru should have alighted on the famous ancient Ashokan column and its three-headed lion capital, which were adopted as emblems of the state. Meanwhile, the Ashokan wheel, symbolising universal law, was incorporated into the Indian national flag.[13] It seemed, then, that Ashoka, not the British, had become the historical legitimator of bureaucratic modernity in Nehru's India.

However, beyond the realms of the symbolic, a great deal of Nehru's bureaucratic modernity was in fact derived from British precedents. He was close to the British Fabian left and the Attlee government that presided over Indian independence; he viewed aspects of the

British governing apparatus quite positively, most notably the elite Indian Civil Service (ICS), which underwent a reasonably smooth transition into the fully Indianised Indian Administrative Service (IAS), and India's constitution incorporated 75% of the 1935 Raj Government of India Act. Nehru was also an enthusiastic supporter of the economic developmentalism of the late colonial period. Some have even argued that his models for planning owe as much to British examples as those of Soviet Russia.[14] It is therefore unsurprising that he saw no problem in taking over wholesale the grandiose 1920s neo-classical government buildings of New Delhi, even occupying the residence of the former Commander-in-Chief of the British Army in India (having renamed it Teen Murti Bhavan).

This sympathetic attitude towards the modernising elements of the British legacy help to explain why Nehru did not do more to erase the visual traces of the Raj or to seek to demonise it. However, there were aspects of the Raj Nehru was willing to denounce in monumental form: its racist, hierarchical and aristocratic elements. Apart from memorials to Gandhi and nationalist-era heroes and changes in street names, the only notable condemnation of the Raj in monumental form is the Jallianwala Bagh Martyrs Memorial and Garden of Remembrance – built to remember the victims of the 1919 Amritsar Massacre, when British forces, commanded by the controversial General Dyer, killed 379 unarmed Indians (Figure 11.1). Here was the Raj at its most racist and militaristic; indeed, even the British agreed, Winston Churchill famously denouncing the episode as 'Prussian' in its unwarranted violence.[15] Nehru imposed his Buddhist and modernist iconographic programme on the monument, commissioning American modernist architect Benjamin Polk and the Indian architect T. R. Mahendra to build the memorial.[16]

Yet, while the modernising Nehru could enthusiastically denounce the extreme violence of Dyer he was more ambivalent about commemorating the rebels of 1857. Many in Congress at that time saw the Mutiny in Marxist terms, as 'feudal and backward-looking' – not as a popular uprising, but as the last stand of the Old Regime, led by the hated princes who then became loyal clients of the Raj at its most pseudo-aristocratic. Moreover, in *The Discovery of India*, Nehru's most sustained reflection on the history of India, he had this to say about memorialising the rebels:

> The rebel Indians sometimes indulged in cruel and barbarous behaviour; they were unorganised, suppressed and often angered by reports of British excesses. But there is another side to the picture also that impressed itself on the mind of India, and in my own province (UP) especially the

11.1 The Jallianwala Bagh National Memorial, inaugurated in 1961

memory of it persists in town and village. One would like to forget all this, for it was a ghastly and horrible picture showing man at his worst, even according to the new standards of barbarity set by Nazism and modern war. But it can only be forgotten, or remembered in a detached impersonal way, when it becomes truly the past with nothing to connect it to the present.[17]

There were those who interpreted the 'Mutiny' as 'The First War of Indian Independence', but they were principally on the Hindu nationalist right, who in this period were closely aligned with India's former princes.[18] This helps to explain why Nehru refused vociferous lobbying from the Hindu nationalist opposition party, the Jan Sangh, to demolish the British Mutiny Memorial, and to build a monument to the rebels. It was only after Nehru's death that very minor changes were made to the signage. However, Nehru was in part driven by pragmatic considerations. He was keen not to alienate the British and their allies, the former princes, too much, at a tense time after the Partition crisis. As he explained in 1957, answering a parliamentary motion that statues of British colonists in and around Delhi be removed immediately:

There are various kinds of statues; some may be considered historical, some may be considered artistic and some may be considered, well, rather offensive in themselves . . . Our general attitude has been, first of all, to remove such as might be considered offensive, and that too, gradually without making too much fuss and without doing anything to raise ill will between countries . . . and raise up old questions which are dead and gone.[19]

This reluctance to interfere in the Raj's cityscape extended to much of the civic statuary of Delhi. The most striking example of Nehru's intransigence was his refusal to allow the removal of the colossus-like statue of George V situated beyond the War Memorial on the central vista of Raj Path. Only in 1968 did it finally go to Coronation Park, having been the victim of minor vandalism three years earlier.

This ambivalence towards the Raj was not confined to Congress elites. There is also evidence of a positive popular memory of the Raj – though this, at least in some cases, was founded on a support for the aristocratic and hierarchical aspects that Congress reviled. From the 1860s onwards, the British had deliberately associated themselves with Indian kingship (the 'Durbar' or 'courtly' Raj), and British rule, whether indirectly through kings or directly through District Officers, had adopted an aristocratic style of governance.[20] And while popular attitudes to aristocracies and kings varied, there is evidence for enthusiasm for this form of paternalism. This is suggested by the election of ex-princes and 'Rajmatas' (Queen Mothers) to the Lok Sabha in 1952.[21] Meanwhile the British monarchy itself seems to have benefited from the appeal of aristocratism. Queen Elizabeth II and Prince Philip received a rapturous welcome in Madras and Bangalore when they visited in 1961. *The Hindu* newspaper reported: 'Hundreds of thousands of people lined the nineteen-mile route from the Meenambakkam airport to the heart of Madras, to give an unprecedented welcome to the Queen'.[22]

Such attitudes to the British monarchy were not new. Popular songs sung at celebrations of Queen Victoria's Diamond Jubilee celebrations in 1897 revealed a strong approval of monarchic paternalism: 'Oh Jagadamba (Goddess)! Look up once. By granting mother a long life, save poor India'. Or: 'Take up the British flag and cry out in joy! Empress Victoria virtuous wife and mother of orphans, so long as she is present in our land the sun will never set'.[23]

Approval of the Raj also had more pragmatic roots, as popular groups appealed to Raj-era forms of government in protest at what they saw as the excessive centralisation of Independent India. For instance in 1966, the inhabitants of the 'tribal' kingdom of Bastar in central India chose their former British-backed king to lead a rebellion against their absorption into the new state of Madhya Pradesh, evoking the ideas of Verrier Elwin, a British anthropologist who studied and wrote about the region from the 1920s to the 1960s.[24]

The regionalisation of Indian memory (1967–85)

These popular groups, then, saw the British both as paternalistic protectors and co-creators of their sub-national states. It was this latter 'memory' of Raj that became important in the later 1960s, as Congress dominance waned, and regional parties waxed. In 1967, Congress lost power to regionalist parties in eight states, most dramatically in the south, and for these potentially sub-nationalist movements, the Raj was particularly important. Like Nehru and early Congress, they approved of the Raj's modernising features, but they 'regionalised' them, seeing the Raj as a co-creator of modern regional identities against the pretensions of Delhi and Congress.

Statues and commemoration have been, and still are, central features of campaigns for self-assertion by Indian sub-national and caste parties, and they played a much more important role in marking the symbolic arrival of the Tamil Nadu sub-nationalist party, the DMK (Dravida Munnetra Kazhagam). The DMK traced its roots to the southern factional politics of the early twentieth century, and presented itself as the victim of north Indian 'Brahminical colonialism', of which the Congress Party was seen as the latest manifestation. For these groups, and the party that emerged from them, the Raj was principally remembered as allies, for the British had created separate electorates and other forms of privileged 'reservations' in higher education and government jobs for non-Brahmins.[25] The British had also supported the Tamil cultural and linguistic revival of the late nineteenth century, and British philologists had established that Dravidian languages were entirely separate from, but as sophisticated as, northern Sanskritic languages.[26]

After the election of 1967 the new DMK government set about imposing its vision of the Tamil past by 'colonising' the Raj-era mile-long esplanade – the Marina – with statues of heroes of the Tamil past. These included Robert Caldwell, former Bishop of Tinnevelly, who had produced the first *Comparative Grammar of Dravidian or South-India Family of Languages* in 1856, and George Pope, another missionary who wrote several Tamil textbooks and dictionaries before becoming lecturer in Tamil and Telugu at Oxford in the 1880s, where he translated various Tamil great texts. Both were declared to be honorary Tamilians and 'noble sons' of the 'Tamiltay family'.[27]

It was not only Congress and Delhi that were the targets of this southern pro-Raj sentiment. Memories of the British could also play a role in intra-regional politics. A striking example of this was the battle over the British cenotaph in Bangalore (Karnataka), honouring the British soldiers who had died during the battle for that city in 1791–92. In 1949 the City Corporation proposed that the cenotaph be demolished and replaced with an Ashoka pillar in keeping with the Nehruvian Buddhist iconography of the new Indian state. It was, the corporation declared, necessary to do this to erase the memory of historic humiliation. However, there was some resistance to the demolition from influential Tamils, who had benefited from British rule in Karnataka at the expense of the indigenous Kannada-speaking population. The cenotaph therefore survived and it was only in 1964, when language conflicts between Kannada and Tamil-speaking groups boosted the influence of Kannada-speaking lobbies, that the cenotaph was finally destroyed and replaced by a statue of Kempe Gowda, the Kannada founder of Bangalore. This assertive Kannada pride eventually brought about a backlash in 1977, when Tamil-speaking groups successfully lobbied to prevent the removal of three Raj-era statues of British eminences from Bangalore's Cubbon Park. By the 1990s, British statues, and especially that of Queen Victoria, had become the official rallying point for middle class civic action groups protesting against what they regarded as a corrupt 'nativist' Kannada government, while their rowdier (according to the press) opponents rallied in the nearby M. K. Gandhi Circle.[28]

Congress and the Hindu right: two different visions of the Raj (1980s–2000s)

If contested memories of the Raj were crucial to the politics of the regions in the 1960s and 1970s, in the 1980s and 1990s they moved back to the national centre as conflicts between the increasingly powerful Hindu right and Congress were played out through debates over the nature of the British legacy. As has been seen, the Hindu right had objected to Nehru's admiration for the more modernising, technocratic features of the Raj, and his denigration of militaristic and aristocratic rebels. However, their message had little purchase at a time when the Indian middle classes broadly endorsed the Nehruvian vision. Yet by the 1980s, the political environment was very different. The perceived economic failures of Nehru's socialism, now disdainfully dismissed as the 'Permit Raj', strengthened a pro-market critique, which traced Congress's alleged 'bureaucratism' to the malign influence of British imperial government. This link was overtly made by the newly reformed Hindu nationalist right party the Bharatiya Janata Party.[29] Meanwhile, the successful political and social assertion of low-caste groups and Muslims, particularly in north India, triggered a high-caste Hindu backlash, which could take the form of enthusiasm for great Indian, anti-imperial (whether anti-British or anti-Moghul) militaristic kings and heroes – like the sixteenth-century Rana Pratap and the seventeenth-century Shivaji.[30]

Much of this debate took place at a popular level, as politics became increasingly democratised. The Hindu right's viewpoint was very effectively propagated in the cartoon story-book series *Amar Chitra Katha* (Immortal Picture Stories), which were designed for children and teenagers, and sold 90 million copies each year in India. The comics promote a Hindu nationalist, even xenophobic, reading of Indian history, which presents a range of Hindu heroes, both religious and secular, pitted against various foreign enemies – the British and the Mughals being most prominent.[31]

However a more sophisticated critique of the Raj was promoted by the governments of 1998–2004 dominated by the Hindu nationalist BJP, which launched the 'textbook wars', demanding the rewriting of Congress-era school textbooks on the grounds that they propagated a British imperial view of history. But this 'imperial' approach was not the whiggish triumphalism or militarism one might expect. Rather, the Raj was seen as the precursor of Nehruvianism and Nehru's effete liberalism. This outlook was alliteratively reduced to slogans denouncing the terrible trio – 'Macaulay, Marx, Madrasa'. Macaulay, the creator of the 1835 Education Act that ushered in English-medium education for the elites, was seen as the progenitor of the 'Brown Englishman' – a bureaucrat, a socialist and an appeaser of low-caste and Muslim malcontents.[32] This hostility to a supposedly left-liberal, bureaucratic Raj found its apogee in the views of Gujarat Chief Minister Narendra Modi, who actively encouraged the use of school textbooks in his state not only to denigrate the British, but to praise Hitler and other inter-war nationalist authoritarian regimes.[33]

Yet surprisingly, rather than rejecting this attempt to associate it with British-style state-building, Congress has been willing to embrace it even more explicitly than in the Nehru era. Nehru's efforts to indigenise modernity through the use of Buddhist and Ashokan symbolism has been abandoned, and since the 1980s Congress has been prepared to associate itself with a supposed legacy of British 'good government'. One of the first things the Congress government did on displacing the BJP in 2004 was to begin the process of recommissioning school textbooks. After some debate it was conceded that the old Nehru texts were out of date and should be rewritten, but the BJP replacements were deemed hopelessly amateur and amounted, in the words of more than one critic, to the 'Talibanisation of school history'.[34]

The new text-books marked a real departure from their Nehruvian and BJP predecessors. In the books designed for 16 and 17 year olds, there was barely any criticism of the British at all, and where there was, it was aimed at the commercial imperialism of the East India Company era. This sympathy for certain aspects of the British legacy can even be seen in discussions of the Gandhian nationalist period. Efforts were made to present a balanced picture, and particular individuals who helped the nationalists were given small sections within the text and singled out for praise, such as B. G. Horniman, the editor of *The Bombay Chronicle*, who smuggled embargoed photographs of the Amritsar Massacre to England, and Judge R. S. Broomfield, who had famously praised Gandhi as 'a great patriot and a great leader', even while convicting him of sedition in 1922. Meanwhile, the chapter on the Partition of India of 1947 refused to blame the British for deliberately fuelling communal tensions, as previous Congress-era textbooks had done, and the opening sentence insisted that 'The political landscape was complex – not only Indians against the British'. The treatment of the Mutiny/Rebellion meanwhile, was dealt with even more even-handedly, as might be expected given Congress's long-standing coolness towards this supposedly aristocratic-led uprising. Rather than weighing up the pros and cons of either side, the students were invited to reflect on issues of representation, and the desire of both sides to demonise the other.[35]

If there was one British hero in the textbook, it was Lord Wellesley, who was seen as the epitome of stern, incorruptible good government. Students were expected to sympathise with the British youth arriving in Bengal for the first time from chilly Scotland, and they were then invited to agree with Wellesley on the subject of good governance: 'It is the primary duty of government to provide for health, safety and convenience of the inhabitants, to improve streets, roads and drains'. Another lengthy chapter in the same textbook deals approvingly with British urban planning and development in the later nineteenth century.[36] The British of the late nineteenth century were censured for their obsession with racial segregation when organising urban space, but Wellesley, who lived at a time of less rigid racial hierarchies, escaped this criticism. Indeed, a book published to mark the complete renovation of Government House (Raj Bhavan) in Kolkata in 2003, praised Wellesley's sober and racially inclusive developmentalism:

[Wellesley] clearly conceived of the project along with that projected at Barrackpore as part of comprehensive reordering and redevelopment of Kolkata. . . . Moreover Indian wealth and enterprise (no matter how dubious) played more and more part in realising that total design. The city of palaces was not built exclusively by the raj[37]

The redevelopment of the neo-classical Government House has been part of a more general promotion of the 'modernising' architecture of the Raj – whether that of the early nineteenth century, or the inter-war period. In 1984 the Indian National Trust for Art and Cultural Heritage (INTACH), a 'National Trust'-style organisation, was founded under the sponsorship of India's then prime minister, Rajiv Gandhi. INTACH was dominated by the anglicised Indian upper-middle classes and often criticised for what some saw as its excessive concern to preserve Raj-era architecture.[38] Even more striking was the Indira Gandhi Centre for Arts, built in 1986 to honour the former prime minister after her assassination. It was based on a scheme by the architect Ralph Lerner, explicitly intended to 'reinforce Lutyens' plan' for New Delhi.[39]

Yet it was the Wellesley era that served as the ideal 'usable past' for the Congress of the 1980s, 1990s and 2000s. Finally turning away from Nehruvian socialism and planning, they were seeking a more market-oriented model, but one which still accorded higher status to the state bureaucracy than private business. Wellesley's British could be seen as the precursor of this 'managed', developmental neo-liberalism. Manmohan Singh, the Oxford-educated, technocratic Finance Minister (1992–97) and Prime Minister (2004–14) expressed this view of the British very clearly in his 2005 speech in Oxford, when he praised the legacy of 'good governance' and opined that, 'the relationship between individual Britons and Indians [was] relaxed and benign'.[40]

The centenary celebration of Government House showed even more clearly how Congress expected Wellesley to be viewed – as a liberal developmentalist, but also a tamer of the free-market capitalism at times defended by the BJP, and symbolised by the pre-Wellesley East India Company:

> Let us go back to Wellesley's advocacy of the 'ideals of the prince' above those of mere traders ... Wellesley and his successors set about implanting the grandeur of an imperial order upon these mundane operations of trade. The process culminated in 1857 when the Indian empire was placed under the British Crown ... The East India Company spawned a new decentred and despoiling growth that sucked forth the economic soul of the nation. Such unsustainable prosperity could not come without a fall.[41]

The conflict between the Congress and BJP visions of the Raj can be seen most vividly in the contrast between two hugely popular 'Bollywood' films of the early 2000s: Ashutosh Gowariker's *Lagaan*, or 'Land Tax', made in 2001, soon after the election of a BJP-dominated government, and Ketan Mehta's *Mangal Pandey: The Rising* made in 2005, shortly after the election of a Congress-led coalition. *Lagaan* presents a set of classic BJP themes. Set at the height of the Raj in

1893 it features a comically cruel British District Officer who seeks to humiliate the local Indian prince with a crippling land tax on his village, but then offers to waive it if the villagers can beat the British in a cricket match. The village then puts together a cricket team which is a BJP vision of an ideal Hindu community, hierarchical but cohesive. In a nod to the *mores* of the 2000s, there is a positive white character, a woman, who helps teach them the rules of cricket, a token Muslim, and even a Dalit, though his name – Kachra – means garbage. The film inevitably ends with the triumph of this integrated Indian team over the haughty, tax-obsessed Raj.[42]

In *Mangal Pandey*, in contrast, it is the trading aspect of the Raj that is condemned, and the film features a British hero who is willing to help create a radical, non-hierarchical India. The film centres on the *Bildung* of Mangal Pandey, who begins as a narrow-minded 'Brahmin', but develops into a socially conscious and liberal 'Indian'. He befriends not only a white British soldier, William Gordon, but also a Muslim. He is even shown in a relationship with a prostitute. Gordon, the Briton, is presented extremely positively, as a man alienated from the East India Company, appalled at its dealing in opium, and cynical about claims that such a corrupt organisation could really be bringing 'Free Trade'. The film ends on the eve of the Mutiny/ Rebellion of 1857, with a montage of Pandey being hanged by the evil Company. But as the noose is tightened his face dissolves into that of Queen Victoria, which then dissolves into Gandhi, then Nehru, and finally the National Flag – establishing a clear continuity between the post-Company British state and Indian nationalism. A voice-over solemnly intones that a British soldier called Gordon fought for India in the Great Rebellion.[43]

Mangal Pandey sparked an immediate outcry from the BJP right, who accused it of insulting a rebel hero by associating him with prostitutes and Muslims, and called for the film to be banned. Meanwhile, its lead actor, Aamir Khan, made the film's sub-textual critique of post-liberalisation India overt in his extensive blog. He explained that his main interest was the theme of freedom, drawing overt parallels between the East India Company's exploitation of India in the eighteenth century and American corporate power and Indian commercialisation in the present.[44]

It is clear, then, that far from forgetting empire, the Raj had been and remains close to the centre of Indian politics. The lack of interest in memorialising the various traumas of imperial rule can be understood in the context of Congress's increasing desire to appropriate aspects of the Raj's heritage. But this is understandably challenged on the right, and the conflict is likely to intensify, as shall be seen.

The place of Indian memory in post-colonial Asia

The place of the empire in contemporary Indian memory and politics differs markedly from that in many other post-colonial Asian states. In China and South-east Asia, post-colonial elites developed a more unified view of the imperial past – as a wholly negative phenomenon. In these states communists and nationalists could portray empire as militaristic, reactionary and uncomplicatedly racist. In Vietnam, the French could be seen as collaborators with the Japanese who were clearly defeated in war, and as a revolutionary state, communist Vietnam sought to destroy continuities with its European imperial predecessor. The Chinese state, too, has a more clear-cut nationalist story and historiography: the British aggressively challenged Chinese sovereignty, sought to flood the country with opium and even went so far as to equate the Chinese with animals (as shown in the outrageous 'No Dogs or Chinese' Shanghai Park poster). The leaderships of these states were also much more successful than was Nehru in obscuring the cultural links between colonial and post-colonial modernity, by invoking their own indigenous Confucian genealogies of bureaucratic modernity, or by appealing to a Marxism that was both international and indigenised. These were far more convincing than Nehru's Ashokan Buddhism.

But paradoxically this wholesale rejection and derogation of the colonial past has removed empire from the field of contemporary ideological conflict, and it has been easier for empire to become an object of nostalgic desire, which can then be commercialised. This commercial imperative is particularly evident in Vietnam, and the phenomenon of 'Indochic' has already attracted some historiographical attention. As Christina Schwenkel argues, the Vietnamese government has deliberately sought to promote tourism by repackaging the country as a site of old-school colonial glamour and languor.[45] This is a Vietnam of elephant rides, 1930s Citroëns and sundowners on the veranda. Helped by the films *Indochine* (1992) and *The Lover* (1992), this strategy has attracted Western tourists, but it has also created a domestic middle class market. Prosperous Vietnamese honeymooners frequently choose to stay at these imperial hotels such as the colonial-era Dalat Palace.[46]

A rather different type of tourism that appeals only to Westerners has been built around the American neo-colonial era and the Vietnam War. The War Crimes Museum in Ho Chi Minh City (Saigon) has been renamed the War Remnants Museum, and the underground guerrilla passageways have been widened to accommodate Western tourists, complete with rest rooms and souvenir bays, and tours are conducted by young Vietnamese women in Vietcong-like garb. Tourists can even enjoy the life of a US GI on R&R at the Rex Hotel – well known in many a war film as a haunt of bachelor officers during the war.[47]

We see similar, if less extreme, trends in parts of China, and especially in Shanghai. Zhu Rongji, the former mayor of Shanghai (1989–91) and China's one-time Premier (1998–2003), unabashedly used Shanghai's colonial experience with commerce and finance to attract potential investors, and 'Shanghai nostalgia' has 'became entangled with a fervour to embrace global capital and its ideology'.[48] Old buildings in the Municipal Concession and small villas in the West End have been renovated in order to attract Western filmmakers and tourists. The Sinified cafes and European restaurants that had managed to survive communism embraced their original Western identities. The famous Red Mansion Coffee House, for example, once again became Chez Louis.

Since the 1990s, India has been subject to similar commercial forces, and the Raj is also being increasingly commoditised – though more in its aristocratic than its modernising Company/trading form. And Indian elites, both Congress and Hindu right, have been increasingly eager to associate themselves with this high-status colonial lifestyle. The British associations have also been less sensitive for BJP elites since the 2000s. In the 1990s, the BJP was broadly pro-American and anti-British, but since 9/11, the United States' imperial turn, and the efforts of neo-conservatives to draw parallels between American and British imperialism, they have been more willing to embrace the British past. The gap between elite Indians over the British legacy has therefore narrowed, and both Hindu nationalists and Congress can see themselves as 'winners' in the global order, happy to draw on old imperial traditions (though there are still subtle differences of emphasis between them). However, the struggle over Raj memory continues, with less privileged sub-elites resisting this comfortable accommodation with the colonial past.

In some respects, Raj nostalgia echoes Indochic or Bund nostalgia. As the architectural historians Vikram Bhatt and Peter Scriver commented in 1990: 'Hoteliers, developers and architects sensitive to commercial trends have begun to exploit a burgeoning revival of appreciation for the pomp and splendour of the British Raj'.[49] Indian and other Asian colonial nostalgias are also focused on one particular aspect of colonialism: its pseudo-aristocratic hierarchies and luxurious lifestyles. Hotels make no secret of the fact that this is the Raj's main appeal, and have spent considerable sums restoring their buildings and emphasising the imperial past. According to Sanjeev Sharma, General Manager of the Nilgiris Taj Hotel in the old British hill station of

Ootacamund: 'The hotel created a historic ambience – attractive counters in the dining hall with images of the British Raj. Flags and colours bearing the "England" name. The persons in the displayed pictures were all British sahibs [sirs]. The waiters were dressed in the Indian waiters' uniform of the Raj era.'[50] Raj nostalgia was a definite selling-point, as Sharma explained: 'There is a definite direct link to the British life here. We get guests asking us about the past. Our hotel buildings themselves have Raj look. So, we decided to host a Nilgiris British Raj Nostalgia festival'.[51]

There has also been a revival in an equally aristocratic but rather less luxurious aspect of the Raj – its food. Pragya Vinod Kumar, a college student attending a 'Historic Food Festival' at the same hotel enthused over:

> Dishes based on the secrets of the chefs for the British sahibs: 'Cotton's Button' – a snack of mushroom with spinach and nutmeg, served on fried bread. 'Railway Lamb Curry' was a typical item on the menu of the Sahibs when they were travelling by train! And, the 'Dak Bungalow Murgi Roast' was what the Sahibs used to enjoy in their camp quarters after returning from work.[52]

One entrepreneur even established a chain of restaurants called 'The Solar Topee', after the pith helmet that was worn by scores of British and Indian bureaucrats and soldiers to keep out the sun – and indeed came to symbolise everything British. Its advertisements boasted of its 'sepia-tinted scrapbook styled menu', its Lady Curzon mulligatawny soup and Kipling's prawn cutlets, and its stewards in khaki safari uniform.[53]

However, there is a striking difference between Indian Raj nostalgia and other Asian counterparts: its principal consumers are the Indian middle classes, not foreigners, and the colonial aristocratic hierarchies it celebrates have penetrated Indian life much more profoundly than the kitsch hotels of Vietnam. So while the Vietnamese have renovated their hill resorts as fantasy retreats for foreign tourists and honeymooners, India's old Hill Stations seem to have become a genuine model for the future among some Indians dissatisfied with Nehruvian modernism. The architectural historian V. Bhatt contrasted an appealing colonial aesthetic with what he saw as the harsh modernism of the new city of Chandigarh, commissioned by Nehru in the 1950s: 'Just as certain positive elements of the British heritage, particularly parliamentary democracy, civil administration and language have become an integral part of modern India, likewise the hill resort has become part of Indian life and culture. Where the large public spaces of the capital complex in Chandigarh had left me cold, the scale of

Simla (a hill station) – the relations of its streets to the public spaces and buildings – felt comfortable and welcoming. It was ironic that Chandigarh, considered a model of free and democratic India, should feel alienating – forbidding almost – compared to Simla, a product of British colonial rule'.[54] The hill stations, established in part as educational centres for British children who were to be kept away from the 'Indianising' influences of the plains, have now become the places where Indian middle classes want to send their children, and resorts like Dehra Dun, Mussoorie, Ootacamund and Panchgani have become hosts to the Etons and Harrows of India, and their cheaper imitators.

The influence of the Raj stretches beyond public spaces, like schools and hotels, to the domestic sphere. Many of the Indian middle classes aspire to live in the 'the classic British bungalow, with its aristocratic sobriety, and its authoritarian connotations softened by time'.[55] Developers are therefore keen to create 'cantonment-style' housing, the types of buildings favoured by the Europeans after the Mutiny in racially segregated areas of colonial towns.[56]

Yet most striking is the appropriation of the archetypal symbol of British racial arrogance – the colonial club. In Ahmedabad in the late 1980s, the Rajpath (Kingsway) Club invited two architects, Kamal Mangaldas and Devendra Shah, to redesign their 1960s modernist clubhouse in a more imperial style. Club members felt that their bland concrete building was 'grievously lacking in the desired social atmosphere of a club'. The architects decided to take its name (Kingsway) as their inspiration and the new clubhouse paid extravagant homage to its Raj-era models echoing their 'extensive verandas, balconies, colonnades, large overhanging tile roofs, delicate wooden balustrades and polychromatic stone floors'.[57]

However, as the Raj is commoditised, and increasingly globalised elites and aspirational groups become more willing to consume its culture, so more discontented and excluded local sub-elites continue to challenge it. In 2009 efforts by the Indian Tourist Development Council to renovate the public garden surrounding the Jallianwala Bagh Martyrs Memorial were met with furious local opposition, and police baton-charged thousands of students whose leader claimed that commerce was undermining the sanctity of this monument to anti-imperial resistance: 'The so called development would deprive the coming generation of the rich heritage of Punjab. These stages would eventually be used for portraying vulgar shows for the visiting VVIP's cars from the newly constructed VIP gate at the entrance'.[58]

A similar protest against the commercialisation and alleged trivialisation of sites of anti-imperial memory erupted in September 2007, when a 'Mutiny Commemoration Tour', organised by a British tour operator for descendants of British men killed in 1857 to visit their graves, was seriously disrupted. British graves in the New Delhi satellite town of Ghaziabad were smashed by a gang of twenty-five youths following several days of inflammatory anti-British rhetoric by local politicians and Hindi-language newspapers. When they arrived at Meerut, the Bishop refused permission to lay flowers on the graves, and the two tour parties were forced to travel under armed guard. They were met with black-flag protests in Agra and rowdy demonstrations in Gwalior. In Lucknow, scene of a pivotal battle between rebels and British forces, they were pelted with plastic bottles, pebbles and cow dung and spent two days confined to their hotels for their own safety before leaving.[59]

Conclusion

Memory of the Raj will continue to be contested. At an elite level, it is the aristocratic and hierarchical elements that will probably continue to be influential in the culture, as a globalised Indian elite, both Congress and Hindu nationalist, see them as markers of social status. It is therefore only to be expected that sub-elites will challenge this culture, and denigrate the Raj more generally. It is also likely that Congress will continue to legitimise its technocratic, state-led marketisation project with judicious reference to aspects of the Raj, while more anti-state politicians will condemn the Raj for precisely those reasons – though the importance of this debate may well decline. It is, however, an open question which Raj will prevail – will it be the hierarchical Raj reborn as the neo-cantonment life of the nouveau-riche Hindu right, or the sober administrative propriety, good governance and civic action recently rediscovered by Congress?

Notes

1 H. C. Fanshawe, *Delhi Past and Present* (London: John Murray, 1902), p. 85.
2 M. V. Hasan, *Monuments of Delhi* (New Delhi: Aryan Books International, 1916 reprinted 1997) vol. II, p. 282.
3 N. Lahiri, 'Commemorating and Remembering 1857: The Revolt in Delhi and Its Afterlife', *World Archaeology* 35:1 (2003), p. 56.
4 N. Lahiri, 'Commemorating', p. 57; N. Gupta, *Delhi between Two Empires 1803–1931* (Delhi: Oxford University Press, 1981), p. ix.
5 P. Varma, *Being Indian: Inside the Real India* (Delhi: Penguin Viking, 2004), chapter I.
6 T. Guha-Thakurta, *Traversing Past and Present in the Victoria Memorial* (Calcutta: Centre for Studies in Social Science Occasional Paper no. 153, 1995), p. 2.
7 N. Lahiri, 'Commemorating', pp. 56–7.
8 A. L. Stoler and K. Strassler, 'Castings for the Colonial: Memory Work in "New Order" Java', *Comparative Studies in Society and History* 42:1 (2000), p. 38.

9 R. M. Brown, 'Inscribing Colonial Monumentality: A Case Study of the 1763 Patna Massacre Memorial', *Journal of Asian Studies* 65:1 (2006), pp. 92–3; P. Chatterjee, *The Black Hole of Empire: History of a Global Practice of Power* (New Jersey: Princeton University Press, 2012), pp. 4–5, 26.

10 T. R. Metcalf, *An Imperial Vision: Indian Architecture and Britain's Rule* (Delhi: Oxford University Press, 2002), pp. 10–16, 219–39.

11 T. R. Metcalf, *An Imperial Vision*, pp. 55–104, 105–41; G. H. R. Tillotson, *Jaipurnama: Tales from the Pink City* (Delhi: Penguin, 2006), pp. 141–4.

12 B. Prasad, *The State in Ancient India: A Study in the Structure and Practical Working of Political Institutions in North India in Ancient Times* (Allahabad: India Press, Ltd. 1928); D. R. Bhandarkar, *Ashoka* (Calcutta: University of Calcutta, 1925); V. R. Dikshitar, *Mauryan Polity* (Madras: Madras University Historical Series no. viii, 1932); R. K. Mookerjee, *Asoka* (London: n.p., 1928); N. N. Law, *Aspects of Ancient Indian Polity* (Oxford: Oxford University Press, 1921).

13 J. Nehru, *The Discovery of India* (Delhi: Oxford University Press, 1946 reprinted 1999), pp. 122–7; S. Jha, 'The Indian National Flag as a Site of Daily Plebiscite', *Economic and Political Weekly* 43:43 (2008), p. 107.

14 J. Nehru, *Discovery*, p. 281; J. Nehru, *Glimpses of World History* (Delhi: Oxford University Press, 1934–35 reprinted 1999), p. 434; B. Zachariah, *Developing India: An Intellectual and Social History, c. 1930–1950* (Delhi: Oxford University Press, 2005), pp. 23–8; B. R. Tomlinson, 'Historical Roots of Economic Policy', in S. Roy and W. E. James (eds), *Foundations of India's Political Economy: Towards an Agenda for the 1990s* (London: Sage, 1992), pp. 303–27.

15 D. Sayer, 'British Reaction to the Amritsar Massacre 1919–1920', *Past and Present* 131:2 (1991), pp. 130–64.

16 B. Polk, *Building for South Asia: An Architectural Autobiography* (Delhi: Abhinav, 1993), pp. 17–19.

17 J. Nehru, *Discovery*, p. 324.

18 V. Savarkar, *The Indian War of Independence, 1857* (London, n.p., 1909); H. L. Erdman, 'India's Swatantra Party', *Pacific Affairs* 36:4 (1963–64), pp. 403–4.

19 J. Nehru, *Lok Sabha Debates* vol. 1, (New Delhi: Government of India 1957), 13 May.

20 B. Cohn, 'Representing Authority in Victorian India', in E. Hobsbawm and T. Ranger (eds), *The Invention of Tradition* (Cambridge: Cambridge University Press, 1983), pp. 165–209.

21 W. Richter, 'Princes in Indian Politics', *Economic and Political Weekly* 6:9 (27 February 1971), p. 537.

22 *The Hindu* (20 February 1961).

23 I. Chowdhruy-Sengupta, 'Mother India and Mother Victoria: Motherhood and Nationalism in Nineteenth-Century Bengal', *South Asia Research* 12:20 (1992), p. 34.

24 N. Sundar, *Subalterns and Sovereigns: An Anthropological History of Bastar, 1854–1996* (New York: Oxford University Press, 1997), pp. 103, 227.

25 E. F. Irschick, *Politics and Social Conflict in South India* (Berkeley: University of California Press, 1960), pp. 55–89.

26 S. Ramaswamy, *Passions of the Tongue: Language Devotion in Tamil India, 1891–1970* (Berkeley: University of California Press, 1997), pp. 189–94.

27 S. Ramaswamy, *Passions*, p. 189.

28 J. Nair, *Battles for Bangalore: Re-Territorialising the City* (Bangalore: Centre for the Study of Culture and Society, n.d.), pp. 3–5.

29 Y. K. Malik and V. B. Singh, 'Bharatiya Janata Party: An Alternative to Congress(I)?', *Asian Survey* 32:4 (1992), pp. 328–9.

30 C. Jaffrelot (ed.), *Hindu Nationalism: A Reader* (New Jersey: Princeton University Press, 2007), pp. 19–27, 255–69.

31 K. McLaine, *India's Immortal Comic Books: Gods, Kings and Other Heroes* (Bloomington: Indiana University Press, 2009), pp. 137, 157–9, 183–4.

32 A. Beteille, *Ideology and Social Science* (Delhi: Penguin, 2006), pp. 24–9.

33 H. Mehta, 'In Modi's Gujarat, Hitler is a Textbook Hero', *Times of India* (30 September 2004).

PART III: REMEMBERING AND FORGETTING

34 V. Sanghvi, 'Talibanising Our Education', *Hindustan Times* (25 November 2001).
35 NCERT e-textbook, *Themes in Indian History*: www.ncert.nic.in/ncert.textbook/textbook.htm. Class VIII: From Trade to Territory; NCERT, *Themes*, Class XII: 'Rebels and the Raj' pp. 288–316, 'Understanding Partition', pp. 376–405.
36 NCERT, *Themes in Indian History*, 'Colonial Cities', pp. 316–46.
37 S. Chaudhuri, 'City, Palace and People', in I. Puri (ed.), *Raj Bhavan of Kolkata: 200 Years of Grandeur* (New Delhi: Penguin, 2003), p. 115.
38 M. E. Hancock, *The Politics of Heritage from Madras to Chennai* (Bloomington: Indiana University Press, 2008), pp. 92–5.
39 J. Lang and M. Desai, *Architecture and Independence: The Search for Identity 1880–1980* (New Delhi: Oxford University Press, 1997), p. 253.
40 Manmohan Singh quoted in S. Bannerjee, 'Pitfalls of Neo-Nationalism', *Economic and Political Weekly* 40:33 (2005), p. 3629.
41 S. Chaudhuri, 'City', p. 120.
42 G. Lichter and S. Bandhyopadhay, 'Indian Cinema and the Presentist Use of History', *Asian Survey* 48:3 (2008), pp. 443–9.
43 R. Majumdar and D. Chakrabarty, 'Film and History', *Economic and Political Weekly* 42:19 (2007), pp. 1771–8.
44 Aamir Khan in *The Times of India* (28 July 2005).
45 C. Schwenkel, 'Recombinant History: Transnational Practices of Memory and Knowledge Production in Contemporary Vietnam', *Cultural Anthropology* 21:1 (2006), p. 7.
46 E. Jennings, 'From Indochine to Indochic: The Lang Bian/Dalat Palace Hotel and French Colonial Leisure, Power and Culture', *Modern Asian Studies* 37:1 (2003), pp. 191–3.
47 C. Schwenkel, 'Recombinant History', pp. 9–16.
48 Pan Tianshu, 'Shanghai Nostalgia: Historical Memory, Community-Building, and Place-making in a late Socialist City', web paper, Department of Anthropology, Harvard University, n.d., pp. 6, 13–14.
49 V. Bhatt and P. Scriver, *Contemporary Indian Architecture: After the Masters* (Ahmedabad: Mapin, 1990), p. 142.
50 Quoted in P. S. Sundar, 'Nilgiris British Raj Nostalgia', in *Hospitality Business Weekly* (8 August 2005).
51 *Ibid.*
52 Pragya Vinod Kumar quoted in P. S. Sundar 'Nilgiris'.
53 Arun Khanna quoted in P. S. Sundar 'Nilgiris'.
54 V. Bhatt, *Resorts of the Raj: Hill Stations of India* (Ann Arbor: University of Michigan Press, 1998), p. 14.
55 V. Bhatt and P. Scriver, *Contemporary Indian Architecture*, p. 143.
56 *Ibid.*
57 *Ibid.*, p. 162.
58 Sandeep Kaur quoted in *Asian News International* (13 February 2009).
59 P. Foster, 'Arrests after Indian Mutiny Graves Smashed', *Daily Telegraph* (27 September 2007); R. Ramesh, 'Protests Force Indian War Grave Visitors to End Tour', *Guardian* (27 September 2007).

[206]

CHAPTER TWELVE

'Forgive and forget'?
The Mau Mau uprising in Kenyan collective memory

Winfried Speitkamp

'We must have no hatred towards one another. Mau Mau was a disease which had been eradicated, and must never be remembered again'.[1] When Jomo Kenyatta spoke these words in 1962, he was referring to the Mau Mau uprising against British colonial rule, which was among the bloodiest colonial wars in history. It began in the Kikuyu region in the late 1940s and reached its peak between 1952 and 1954 before being crushed by the British. More than 10,000 Kenyans lost their lives; some 100,000 suffered years of brutal imprisonment, while at least that many again were resettled. Kenyatta himself was arrested by the British in 1952 as an alleged rebel leader and was not released until 1961. In recent years new studies have pointed to the violence and atrocities of the Mau Mau wars. Britain's policy against the Mau Mau fighters has even been compared to National Socialism and Stalinism, especially with respect to the use of detention camps.[2]

In 1963 Kenyatta assumed the leadership of a newly independent Kenya. In terms of dealing with the memory of Mau Mau, the term 'forgive and forget' soon became the motto of his government. However, the official call to forget stood in contrast to the significance of remembering Mau Mau. No other African colonial war has generated such heated discussions and bitter conflicts with regard to public memory. This has included scholarly theses, memoirs, novels, songs, plays and films as well as monuments and street names. But the treatment of the Mau Mau legacy has remained controversial. Protest and opposition against the politics of remembrance as propagated by the Kenyatta regime started very early. Repeatedly, Mau Mau veterans demanded appropriate consideration in Kenya's public life and politics. They claimed that Mau Mau had not been limited to the Kikuyu but had constituted a truly national movement, a significant step on the way towards integrating and emancipating the Kenyan nation. The Mau Mau legacy was thus tied to the present.

As a result, the Mau Mau wars have remained central to internal Kenyan debates and a key factor within the determination of the Kenyan self-image. It is because the wars could not be reduced to a simple equation of British foreign rule on the one side and African rebellion on the other, but reflected a complex mix of interests and interactions, of collaboration and betrayal, that their classification and treatment came to be a burden for Kenya's post-colonial identity. The Mau Mau debate, as considered in this chapter, is not, in the first place, a post-colonial debate between Britain and Kenya. The focus here will be on a Kenyan national debate revolving around founding fathers, heroes, political achievements and Kenyan collective memory.

This chapter will discuss these developments in four steps: First, it will seek to reconstruct some main features of the Mau Mau uprising and the following war against the so-called freedom fighters. Second, it will survey the different phases of how issues connected to Mau Mau and its remembrance have been addressed. Third, it will focus on the politics of remembrance propagated in the Kenyatta and Moi eras. Finally, it will examine the changes during the Kibaki years in the context of transnational collective memories.

Background: the Mau Mau uprising

Mau Mau was a conglomeration of different movements, interests and actions. Even its name – 'Mau Mau' – was first used by the British and only later adopted by the rebels themselves. The movement had its roots in the inter-war years and underwent a process of radicalisation towards the end of the Second World War. The declaration of the state of emergency by the British in 1952 was the catalyst for the rebellion.[3]

One source of conflict was the colonial economic order. In 1950, the African population of the Kenyan colony numbered about 5.5 million, made up of various ethnic groups. The largest group, with over a million members, were the Kikuyu, who lived and worked the land mainly in southern and central parts of the colony. Apart from the Africans and about 120,000 Asians, there were some 30,000 Europeans in Kenya, 9,000 of whom were settlers in the fertile Highlands of the Kikuyu. The settlers needed land and workers, which led to the Kikuyu being forced into reservations and their land taken. These reservations did not offer the means for self-sufficient living and thus many Kikuyu had to work on the European plantations, either as labourers or as so-called squatters. The squatters were given a small piece of land for a vegetable garden and a few head of livestock on the European plantations, in return for which they and their families had to work a certain number of days for the settler, sometimes as many as 270 days a year.[4] After the Second World War, social pressure on the Kikuyu increased: the population grew rapidly, the squatters' work duty was raised and many were sent back into the reservations where the food situation deteriorated dramatically. The migration of tens of thousands into the city of Nairobi only served to shift the problem to a different location.

Another source of conflict was the interference with the Kikuyu political order. When the British were installing colonial rule, they were looking for stable political structures and native leaders who could be invested with administrative functions. The Kikuyu on the other hand did not have rigid and centralised political structures. They were linked by little more than language, culture and religion. Villages and neighbourhoods were their political administrative units. Leaders were chosen according to specific rules, and their functions were limited to that of speakers and representatives, while decisions were reached by the consensus of a council. The leaders' term of office was also limited. In a complicated system of 'generation rule', the leadership was transferred to a new generation every twenty-five to thirty years. Now the British interfered with that system. They stopped the generation transfer, established waged chiefs-for-life and gave them extended powers. However, these new chiefs had no legitimate standing with the Kikuyu.

A further source of conflict was the change colonial rule brought to the Kikuyu culture. The missionaries in particular posed a threat to traditional rites and customs. While the Kikuyu were willing and able to adopt some Christian ways, they rejected those demands that threatened the fundamental structure of Kikuyu society. Among the main issues were polygamy and circumcision. The circumcision of boys and girls was one of the most important initiation-rites of the Kikuyu. Family and society were built on it, and those not circumcised remained excluded. The missions on the other hand had a rather effective point of leverage: they refused circumcised girls access to their schools. This in turn led to the Kikuyu founding their own independent schools from 1930 onward. There, traditional customs were mixed with Christian elements and – as happened in other colonies – new, syncretistic forms of religion were developed.

The independent school associations reflected an increasing tendency towards self-organisation in associations and unions, which had been going on since 1920. At the end of the Second World War, the Kenya African Union was formed as an umbrella organisation according to the congress principle. Its demands were participation for Africans, abolition of racial barriers, constitutional rights and the improvement of working conditions, all to be realised legally. At the same time a rather more radical movement, the Kikuyu Central Association, became active partly from within, partly from without the Kenya African Union. In the 1940s, its members were increasingly calling for a more aggressive struggle. British policy only aggravated the conflict: contrary to some wartime promises, the colonial administration did little to increase participation. Only a few nominated African members were accepted into the legislative council, which remained dominated by Europeans. In the course of the so-called Second Colonisation, exploitation and rule were even intensified. Moreover, the settlers, too, were calling for self-determination, according to the Rhodesian model.

Disappointed expectations after the war, increasing exploitation and social hardship against the backdrop of a deep cultural crisis on the part of the colonised Kikuyu led to growing unrest towards the end of the 1940s, and in the Kikuyu homeland a full-blown revolt erupted. At its centre, the uprising was an expression of social protest. It was supported mainly by three groups: poor peasants from the reservations, driven-out squatters and the urban jobless. The first impulse might have come from the Kikuyu Central Association, but in the long run its leaders could not control the movement and there was neither a common name nor a firm organisation – only some councils and forms of cooperation.

The basis of the movement was apparently an oath. In the Kikuyu tradition, oaths were a common means of ensuring commitment and had already been used by Kikuyu organisations in the 1920s. People were sworn in secretly at night. The ceremony combined traditional elements with Christian elements and newly invented parts. The terms of the oath compelled the individual, on pain of death, to serve the community and to work towards the eviction of the Europeans. However, the wording was not standardised and became increasingly radical. In 1952 it was supplemented by a warrior oath, which called for the unconditional readiness to kill. These rituals and oath ceremonies in particular, only partially and distortedly known by the Europeans, conjured up an image of a superstitious, bloodthirsty and atavistically wild tribal movement.[5]

There was no unified programme. Intentions have to be deduced from the oaths, songs and, later, accounts of participants.[6] Land and liberty were the main goals. The return of land annexed by the British was a central demand which was to be taken literally, but also appeared as a general condition for liberty, because the land issue was the basis for the calls to evict the British. There is no consensus on whether the movement can be called nationalistic as such. Many of its elements were rooted in Kikuyu tradition, added to which were references to African values and Kenya as a political entity. The movement as a whole was exalted by a syncretistic religion. The return to tradition was part of the struggle for a new identity, which comprised elements of forming a nation-state based on ethnicity, without statehood ever being mentioned as a political goal.

The methods of warfare were marked by exceptional brutality on both sides.[7] On the British side some 100,000 natives were fighting as part of the Home Guard. These so-called Black Europeans, the assimilated Africans and collaborators, were pursued with particular hatred by the Mau Mau. After the British had declared the state of emergency in 1952, the rebellion, which had to fall back on guerrilla warfare, was quickly dissipated and dissolved. Punitive measures against the Kikuyu included arrest, internment, execution, torture, starvation and other forms of maltreatment. There were also rigorous re-education and resettlement programmes. Militarily, the British had unequivocally emerged as victors from the war, while the Kikuyu were beaten and humiliated.

Mau Mau in historiography and memory

The real struggle about what Mau Mau meant for Kenya and what would be worth remembering began only after the end of the conflict. During the rebellion and until 1960, the image of the uprising was almost exclusively shaped by the British. Press coverage by British journalists, descriptions and memoirs by the settlers, scholarly analyses as well as official accounts – they all combined to portray Mau Mau as an eruption of primitive, atavistic tribalism, as a throwback to barbaric times. The Mau Mau warriors came across as bloodthirsty savages or simply terrorists. Most interpretations carried racist undertones: while the settlers regarded Mau Mau as proof that Africans could not be civilised, anthropologists interpreted it as an expression of a psychosocial crisis, as a kind of collective sickness of the Kikuyu, who simply could not cope with the pace the Europeans set for their modernisation. However, all were united in their calls for the repression of the revolt.

Ever since Kenya gained her independence in 1963, Mau Mau has appeared in an entirely different light. The memories of the participants played a pivotal role in this re-evaluation and would from then on form the core of Mau Mau research. Two preliminary points need to be made: firstly, the memories of the participants were regarded as a very reliable source. The statements given in memoirs or interviews were usually deemed to be authentic and correct. This holds true for British and American as well as for Kenyan researchers. The wealth of detail generated was ascribed to the Kikuyu's impressive powers of memory, honed by their long oral tradition. It was rarely taken into account that in Kenya history is primarily remembered for communal and topical purposes, although many of the memoir-writers and interviewees had stressed that they were only willing to remember and answer because they wished the present to learn a lesson.

Secondly, most of the testimonies were prompted by people not involved in the events. Indeed, it was often British researchers who initiated, published, introduced or edited them. Some scholars would employ their writers for a few months as research assistants in order to give them time to write down their memories. The arguments within the testimonies and the scholarly works therefore appear to be closely interlinked. This accounts for the fact that the written eyewitness accounts addressed a fairly similar catalogue of aspects and topics. It appears that the authors were reacting to the expectations of their potential readers as well as to those of the researchers.

In view of this, four stages of dealing with Mau Mau can be identified.[8] The first stage covers approximately the 1960s. In contrast to the former British-dominated image, research turned to key motives and intentions for the rebellion on the basis of three volumes of memories by prominent Mau Mau members which were published between 1963 and 1967. These accounts shared two distinctive features: they were bent on portraying the struggle as a war of liberation, and focused on refuting the British view. Mau Mau warriors no longer appeared as terrorists, but as heroes fighting for a common cause, and the movement was considered as a whole rather than a set of local manifestations and differences. Secondly, the accounts represented the Mau Mau wars as an important, if not decisive, step towards national integration and statehood in Kenya. Accordingly, Mau Mau was a national project with a view to the future. Tradition – namely the Kikuyu tradition – was accorded only marginal importance. This point of view was also adopted by contemporary British researchers, as is reflected in the prefaces to the printed memories and in 'Nationalism in Kenya', which appeared in 1966.[9] The Mau Mau rebellion was now widely regarded as the breakthrough of a national movement in Kenya and many felt that Mau Mau was well on its way to being integrated into a Kenyan national identity. This interpretation was by no means shared by all Kenyans, though. Because of Mau Mau's exclusive claim on national tradition, it was met with sharp criticism by some Kenyan historians.

The second stage in the treatment of the Mau Mau legacy began at the end of the 1960s. Memories of participants were now being published in quick succession.[10] These new testimonies, no longer authored only by leading members of Mau Mau, conveyed a rather local perspective, were more detailed and differentiated in their descriptions and offered insights into the diversity within Mau Mau. Many of these memories shared a strong commitment to Kikuyu tradition. At the same time, social hardship as a mobilising factor moved to the centre of attention and the future-oriented elements of the old narrative lost their clear definition. The struggle now seemed primarily determined by local hardship and suppression, not necessarily by some utopian national fantasy. Even though the authors still thought of Mau Mau as a fight for liberty in the service of the nation and a future state, they did so rather in the sense that some higher logic had guided the course of historic events, and rarely credited Mau Mau with a thought-out plan or a defined goal.

The testimonies and interrogations of contemporary witnesses prompted a series of historical studies on the social origins and structural prerequisites of Mau Mau. The uprising was now regarded as the consequence of the Kikuyu suppression, provoked by the land issue, the situation in the overcrowded reservations and the squatter problem, but also as an answer to the destruction of the traditional Kikuyu social order. In all this, Mau Mau was not interpreted as backward tribalism, and only very rarely as a Marxist expression of class struggle, but rather as a social movement, reacting to the combined challenges of colonial rule, settler economy and Christian mission with the rediscovery of old traditions, new forms of community and modern political tools, thus demonstrating flexibility and the ability to act.[11]

The third stage in the public treatment of the Mau Mau memory broadened the perspective even more. While during the 1970s the focus had been on the socio-historical prerequisites for Mau Mau over the following years, research turned to the social realities of the uprising itself and to the collective and individual experiences of those involved. In terms of method this meant, besides the incorporation of written accounts, systematically including more and more general interviews with participants, even if they had not occupied leading positions. Mau Mau no longer appeared as a primarily national political or social movement, but as an ethno-cultural attempt at reconstruction, with concrete national and cultural results. The colonial situation was increasingly understood as a complex fabric of social interrelations, which undermined the old society, threatened the existence of the community and eroded old and trusted values. The

Kikuyu's 'moral economy' as well as that of the Mau Mau was now under scrutiny, and the experiences of those concerned moved into focus. In view of this, ethnicity once again appeared as a real driving force of history, albeit not as pre-modern tribal thinking, but as the sum of social traditions and cultural values, as expressions of specific virtues and codes of honour, which were said to have their roots in Kikuyu society. Ethnicity, according to John Lonsdale, was nothing exclusive and consequently not a tribal manifestation.[12]

During the fourth and latest stage of dealing with Mau Mau, which began in the late 1980s, the focus moved beyond the experiences to the memories of Mau Mau, not least because the generation directly involved was increasingly retiring from active public life. This phase was accompanied by renewed publications by Mau Mau veterans, who again presented their view of events and reaffirmed their claim on the interpretation monopoly. This meant that the historical event moved out of sight in favour of a reappraisal of Mau Mau's impact on contemporary Kenya. Since the beginning of the 1990s, several works have made the memory of Mau Mau the focus of their endeavours.[13]

The politics of remembrance in the Kenyatta and early Moi years

This development underscores, once again, that the memory of Mau Mau had become an element within the political discussion. Repeatedly, Kenyatta called for forgetting Mau Mau:

> Let us have independence in peace. I am requesting you strongly not to hold any secret meetings or support organisations. We are determined to have independence in peace, and we shall not allow hooligans to rule Kenya. We must have no hatred towards one another. Mau Mau was a disease which had been eradicated, and must never be remembered again.[14]

And in 1963 during the celebrations of independence in Nairobi Kenyatta set out:

> Our march to freedom has been long and difficult. There have been times of despair, when only the burning conviction of the rightness of our cause has sustained us. Today, the tragedies and misunderstandings of the past are behind us. Today, we start on the great adventure of building the Kenyan nation. As we start at this great task, it is right that we . . . should remember and pay tribute to those people of all races, tribes and colours who – over the years – have made their contribution to Kenya's rich heritage: administrators, farmers, missionaries, traders and others, and above all the people of Kenya themselves. All have laboured to make this fair land of Kenya the thriving country it is today.[15]

The Kenyatta administration argued in the same vein:

> Let us remember the struggle for our national independence; . . . Above
> all remember . . . Mzee Jomo Kenyatta, who designed our struggle and
> independence. Then let us not look backwards but forward with confi-
> dence. Let us not remember the past with bitterness. . . . Let us follow
> and support all that our beloved father of nations, with his Government,
> plan for us in order to build a strong nation and prosperity.[16]

In fact, the attempts to eliminate the Mau Mau memory were largely
fruitless, despite the fact that Kenyatta and his successor Daniel arap
Moi tried to enforce their intentions with rather drastic measures.
First, the policy of 'forgive and forget', as propagated by Kenyatta,
meant not only that the remaining British settlers were protected
after 1963, but also that loyalists and collaborators did not have to
fear persecution. A cleansing or final reckoning did not take place.
African members of the British colonial troops were incorporated
into the new government. This happened because of pragmatic considerations and was meant to ensure administrative continuity and
stability. Collaborators and loyalists were too numerous and also
too important to the state. Some Mau Mau veterans argued that
even in colonial times Kenyatta's stance had been overly moderate
and legalistic. Moreover, while the Kikuyu dominated in the new
state, the Mau Mau activists did not. The Kikuyu administrative
elite consistently tried to interpret Mau Mau not as a national opposition, but as a Kikuyu achievement, and thus to secure their own
dominance in the state over other ethnic groups. As a result, Mau
Mau became an ethnic issue or, to put it in another way, the Kikuyu
as an ethnic unit claimed legitimacy as the national governing elite.
The new elite thus presented itself as the fulfilment of the Mau Mau
legacy.

Secondly, the Kenyan state denied the Mau Mau warriors any
material privileges. Contrary to expectations and demands, they were
not granted any land, especially not in the disputed Highlands; the
property of the British settlers remained untouched. That alone
provoked the Mau Mau veterans' anger. In their view, British land-
ownership was illegal and the British should be expropriated without
compensation. The government approach was different: if the settlers
did not want to remain in Kenya, they could sell their land to the
state. That land was then offered to Africans but, since it was fertile
agricultural land, at a price which made it unaffordable for the majority of Mau Mau veterans. Strictly speaking, the decision not to redis-
tribute the land meant that Mau Mau had ultimately failed, since the
land question had been at the heart of Mau Mau.

Thirdly and finally, the state did not allow Mau Mau a prominent place in official acts of remembrance. Mau Mau was treated as *one* expression of dissent among many during colonial times. Kenyatta stressed over and over again that there had been many contributions to the successful struggle for national independence. He included more or less openly not just the passive stance of other ethnic groups but even collaboration with the colonial government. Mau Mau was not promoted as a state-building myth, even though this might have been consistent in view of the material and arguments generated by the first published memories and accounts from the years 1963–67. Instead, with regard to its relevance and impact Mau Mau was systematically historicised and contextualised. On this level, the memory of Mau Mau was rather cleverly accepted and interpreted as an episode in Kenyan history in Kikuyuland.

At the end of the Kenyatta and Moi years there was no central Mau Mau Monument in Kenya. The great Uhuru Momument in Nairobi showed Kenyans of all generations erecting the Kenyan flag. It was initiated in 1983 by Kenyatta's successor, Daniel arap Moi. Nairobi and Mombasa both feature an Uhuru [freedom, independence] Park – but there was no reference to Mau Mau. On the other hand, in small towns in the Mau Mau heartland some Mau Mau memorials were erected with official support – but clearly as regional and localised acts of remembrance. The place where the rebel leader Kimathi was arrested, for instance, was marked, and, additionally, a Kimathi Library was built in Nyeri. However, there was no central Mau Mau Museum. The Kenyan National Museum in Nairobi is divided into several sections: Nature, Culture, Religion and History are all represented equally, and within the historical divisions there was a section dedicated to Mau Mau, but it presented its topic in a rather low-key fashion alongside many other episodes in the history of Kenya and the East African peoples. Some leaders of the Mau Mau movement were honoured with street names. This, however, was usually limited to secondary roads. Nairobi's central axis and longest street remains Kenyatta Avenue; in Mombasa it is Moi Avenue. Other important streets commemorate African statesmen like Nyerere from Tanzania or Nkrumah from Ghana, and it is only way down the list that one finds the occasional Mau Mau street name.[17]

The Mau Mau legacy remained controversial. Protest and opposition against the politics of remembrance as propagated by the Kenyatta regime started very early. Repeatedly, Mau Mau veterans demanded appropriate recognition in Kenya's public life and politics. Their self-image was no longer that of beaten victims, but of freedom fighters, of martyrs for the great national cause, ultimately even of victors in the Mau Mau wars, whose sacrifice was eventually justified by the foundation of the state of Kenya. They claimed that Mau Mau had always been intended as a national movement and that it constituted one of the high points in Kenyan nationalism. Moreover, for them it represented a significant step not only on the path to the formal recognition of independence, but also towards integration and emancipation of the Kenyan Nation. To that extent, they said, Mau Mau was not just history but a legacy, which the survivors along with their successors would have to live up to. Naturally, the interpretation of this legacy would have to be left to the Mau Mau veterans.

The Mau Mau veterans, though, far from being united, moved even further into the background, not least because of their age. This is not to say, however, that the storm around the Mau Mau debate was abating. Although the vast majority of the now 25 million or so Kenyans had no first-hand memory of Mau Mau, the conflict about the correct interpretation of the war continued. It was driven by younger opposition politicians and authors for whom Mau Mau was not merely a Kenyan national myth, but provided a model of self-confidence, courage and the desire for freedom. Among these is the writer Ngugi wa Thiong'o, whose treatment of the subject was expressed in essays and plays. His interpretation of Mau Mau was that of a progressive inheritance and he emphasised the integrating national character of Mau Mau, which he said was based on supra-tribal unity and alliances that went beyond class boundaries. Thus the undiminished political relevance of Mau Mau was stressed as well as the political legacy it had bequeathed to the present; moreover, the idea of betrayal circulated again. All of this meant that Mau Mau remained such a dangerous topic that those in power felt the need to resort to restrictions, censure, prohibition and even arrests.

The Mau Mau wars have thus constantly been of central importance to internal Kenyan debates and a key to the Kenyans' self-image. It is precisely because the wars were not a simple equation of British foreign rule on one side and African rebellion on the other, but showed a complex mix of interests and interactions, that their classification and treatment came to be a burden on Kenya's post-colonial identity. Remembering and forgetting were therefore not a question of time. The explosive nature of the memories could still be utilised long after the event had become history. In fact, Kenyatta did not really want to eradicate the memory of Mau Mau, he just sought to give it regional and ethnic connotations in order to marginalise the Mau Mau warriors and ultimately defeat them. In fact the Mau Mau veterans were starved of public attention and although Kenyatta met Mau Mau veterans he never granted them a public role or rewarded them for their fight. Instead Kenyatta presented himself as father of all Kenyans and fore-father of national unity and liberty.

Mau Mau memories in the Kibaki years

A dramatic change in memory politics has taken place since the 1990s. In 1991 a multi-party-system was introduced. Semi-free elections fol-lowed in 1992. The problems of dealing with Mau Mau could now be discussed openly, veterans claimed compensation, and the questions of collaboration and resistance in the colonial period became a topic of election campaigns. Since then parliamentary and presidential can-didates have used Mau Mau to gain popularity. Now the Mau Mau warriors are celebrated as national heroes fighting the British in order to free the Kenyan nation. Even South African ANC leader Nelson Mandela, who visited Kenya in 1990, referred to one of the most famous Mau Mau leaders, Dedan Kimathi, who was executed by the British administration in 1957, in a public address. 'Kimathi died, but the spirit of independence, the spirit of liberation, remains alive and that is why the people in Kenya are free today'.[18] Now President Danial arap Moi insisted that the unification of the Kenyan nation was one of the key goals of the Mau Mau freedom fighters. Though Moi did not change the politics of remembrance pursued by Kenyatta he acknowledged the contribution of Mau Mau to emancipation and freedom. On Kenyatta Day in 1993 he declared:

> This day is set aside to remember the gallant sons and daughters from across the nation who paid with their lives so that we could be free. This day though named after the Founding Father of this nation, the Late Mzee Jomo Kenyatta, is dedicated to all the nationalists who waged a relentless struggle against the oppressive colonial rule.
>
> We fought with one resolve, irrespective of our ethnic backgrounds so that all communities could equally enjoy the fruits of independence.[19]

In 2002 Mwai Kibaki won the presidency. A former minister in Kenyatta's government, Kibaki emphasised the value of Mau Mau in Kenyan national history and thus distanced himself from Kenyatta's memory politics. In fact Kibaki did not support material compensation for the veterans either but he instigated plenty of symbolic action to elevate the profile of Mau Mau commemoration. In 2003 the ban on Mau Mau was finally lifted. On the occasion of Kenyatta Day in 2004 Kibaki emphasised the importance of the Mau Mau years. He especially remembered the famous 'Kapenguria Six', leading members of the Kenyan independence movement who were arrested after the outbreak

[218]

of Mau Mau and were tried at Kapenguria on the basis of dubious evidence for taking part in the uprising:

> We have gathered here to commemorate a special day in our national history. Fifty years ago, on 20th October, 1952, Mzee Jomo Kenyatta, Paul Ngei, Kungu Karumbah, Fred Kubai, Achieng' Oneko, Bildad Kaggia and other heroes were arrested and jailed because of their love for this country.
>
> These heroes were willing to sacrifice everything – including their own lives – to win our freedom. We remember these patriots and many others whose sacrifices played a prominent role in shaping the destiny of our nation.[20]

The Kibaki government integrated the Mau Mau veterans into the official memory. On 1 June 2007 the widows of both Kenyatta and Dedan Kimathi were invited to attend the public celebrations of Independence Day. Treating both widows as equal suggested that their husbands had made an equal contribution to national history. Now Mau Mau had moved to the core of national narrative. According to this reading of the past, the Kikuyu fighters had mobilised the whole country and unified Kenya against the British administration. In the same year Kibaki initiated a monument for Dedan Kimathi in Nairobi, fifty years after his execution by the British government. It was unveiled in February 2007 and showed Kimathi with a knife and a rifle on a pedestal about three metres high. The inscription praised him as 'gallant soldier, Mau Mau freedom fighter and nationalist', which, of course, he never was. And he was quoted with a heroic utterance: 'It is better to die on our feet than live on our knees for fear of colonial rule'. Another inscription emphasised the role of President Mwai Kibaki as the initiator of the monument. During the unveiling ceremony Kibaki praised Kimathi as a shining example for the nation:

> In Kenya, Uganda and Tanzania, and many other African countries, there are streets named after Kimathi. It is simply an admiration most people in these nations hold towards him, a poor fellow who mastered the courage to take up arms and fight injustices perpetrated by a seemingly undefeatable power. Field Marshall Dedan Kimathi was a gallant soldier, a Mau Mau freedom fighter and nationalist. He defined his generation, the history of Kenya and left lasting memories that are still engraved in our national psyche.[21]

And Vice President Moody Awori declared:

> By unveiling this statue dedicated to one of the gallant freedom fighters, the late Dedan Kimathi, the Government has indeed demonstrated that

it is committed to identify, recognise and honour Kenya's heroes/ heroines. I know more will be identified as time goes by and they will get the recognition they deserve.[22]

The Kimathi monument was the first central monument dedicated to Mau Mau in Kenya (Figure 12.1). The Mau Mau veterans were invited to the ceremony but they did not play an active role. Even now their demands for compensation and financial aid were neglected. Little wonder, then, that the new monument was subsequently mocked

12.1 The Kimathi monument in Nairobi, unveiled in 2007

in the daily press. A caricature showed Kimathi's widow in front of it and remarking with some bitterness: 'At last we've got our own begging spot'.[23]

Nevertheless, in the years of the Kibaki administration the Mau Mau veterans hoped to attract more attention to their goals and especially finally to receive compensation for their historical sacrifices. Numerous new veteran organisations were founded, such as the 'Mau Mau Original Trust', 'Mau Mau War Veterans Association', 'African Mau Mau Union' and 'Mau Mau War Council of Elders'. They all claimed to represent the interests of Mau Mau veterans. But as the *Daily Nation* noticed, 'among the war veterans, talk of hatred, rivalry and betrayal has been the singsong'.[24] Even new groups arose claiming to follow the footsteps of the nationalist forefathers of the Mau Mau movement and taking part in electing campaigns. In the end the veterans did not receive any compensation. The newspapers reported the disappointment and 'rising disillusionment by freedom heroes', and a Mau Mau veteran was quoted: 'Our main reason to fight the colonialists was to get back our land and forests, yet many of us have none'.[25] Two years later the comment ran: 'How many have they rewarded? Who will address us on Madaraka [independence] Day? How can those who did not fight tell us about the fight? Even the President should not address us on that day'.[26] In fact, all the veterans' hopes and demands were rejected. The Kibaki administration even refused to support the demands for compensation which the veteran organisations presented to the British government in 2006. So far, these claims have been rejected, but in 2012 the veterans won the right to sue the British government.[27] On the other hand, the Kibaki administration has used the Mau Mau memories to attract attention and gain legitimacy. Kibaki's repeated appeals for unity have often been underpinned with references to Mau Mau.

The importance and popularity of Mau Mau in the Kenyan public is highlighted by an incident which occurred in 2002.[28] At the end of the Mau Mau uprising one of the famous Mau Mau generals, Stanley Mathenge, had fled to Ethiopia and was never seen again. At the beginning of 2002 rumours circulated that Mathenge was living as a farmer in Ethiopia. Several Kenyan journalists went to Ethiopia and reported that they had found Stanley Mathenge who everyone had believed to be dead. No expense was spared when he was brought back to Kenya in May 2003: he was treated as a state guest; the administration paid for Mathenge and his entourage to fly to Nairobi and put them up in a four star hotel; he was given an enthusiastic welcome. At the airport a large crowd had gathered. The situation was almost out of control. Mathenge was brought back to his home town of Nyeri. A government spokesman proclaimed: 'This is the greatest day for this country since independence. It is the first stage of reclaiming our heroes and heroines lost glory'.[29] The newspaper coverage was intense and the Kibaki government did everything it could to profit from the popularity of Mau Mau.

But soon serious doubts were raised as to the man's identity. Mathenge would have been 84 years old, but the man from Ethiopia seemed to be younger. He was not as tall as Mathenge. He did not speak the Kikuyu language, his supposed mother tongue. And his family in Kenya was not sure about his identity either. Finally the government withdrew its invitation to the Independence Day celebrations and had the DNA of the supposed Mathenge analysed. The result was only published four years later: the man was not Mathenge. The whole affair had been a media phenomenon but it shows how important and explosive Mau Mau memories in Kenya still are – more than fifty years after the events.

Mau Mau has become a national site of memory in modern Kenya. But obviously it is, in the first place, not a colonial site of memory. It does not serve to commemorate the colonial past and to allow for the discussion of the burdens of history; it does not serve to address the problems of colonial domination, the activities of the chiefs, the question of collaboration or the politics of Kenyatta. Rather, it serves to shine a light on the present situation and the defaults of politics and public in Kenya. Interestingly enough, in the context of the Mathenge affair public debate did not focus on the history of Mau Mau, but on the state of politics and the nation at present. Mau Mau is a site of national identity. It stands for common achievements, heroes and founding fathers of the nation – and, disputed though it remains, Mau Mau still forms a core element of the Kenyan national narrative.

Notes

1 J. Kenyatta: *Suffering without Bitterness. The Founding of the Kenya Nation*, (Nairobi: East African Publishing House 1968), p. 189. Parts of this article draw on my earlier articles 'Spätkolonialer Krieg und Erinnerungspolitik: Mau Mau in Kenia', in H. Berding et al. (eds), *Krieg und Erinnerung. Fallstudien zum 19. und 20. Jahrhundert* (Göttingen: Vandenhoeck & Ruprecht, 2000), pp. 193–222, and 'Colonial Wars and the Politics of Remembrance: Mau Mau in Kenya', in C. Charbonneau, *Définitions de la Culture Visuelle IV: Mémoire et Archive* (Montréal: Musée d'art contemporain de Montréal, 2000), pp. 141–53.
2 C. Elkins, *Britain's Gulag. The Brutal End of Empire in Kenya*, (London: Jonathan Cape, 2005); D. Anderson, *Histories of the Hanged. The Dirty War in Kenya and the End of Empire* (London: Weidenfeld & Nicolson, 2005); D. Branch, *Defeating Mau Mau, Creating Kenya. Counterinsurgency, Civil War, and Decolonization* (Cambridge: Cambridge University Press, 2009); H. Charton, 'Acteurs, victimes et

témoins de la violence dans l'histoire. L'exemple mau mau (Kenya)', *Cahiers d'études Africaines* 201/1 (2011), pp. 169–92. For a comparison between Mau Mau and the Algerian war see R. Aldrich and S. Ward, 'Ends of Empire. Decolonizing the Nation in British and French Historiography', in S. Berger and C. Lorenz (eds), *Nationalizing the Past. Historians as Nation Builders in Modern Europe* (Basingstoke: Palgrave Macmillan, 2010), pp. 259–81.

3 For this survey on the Mau Mau years see J. Lonsdale and B. Berman, *Unhappy Valley. Conflict in Kenya and Africa*, 2 vols., (London: James Currey, 1992); W. Maloba, *Mau Mau and Kenya. An Analysis of a Peasant Revolt* (Bloomington: Indiana University Press, 1993); G. Kershaw, *Mau Mau from Below*, (Oxford: James Currey, 1997); D. Throup, *Economic and Social Origins of Mau Mau 1945–53* (London: James Currey, 1987); C. Presley, *Kikuyu Women, the Mau Mau Rebellion, and Social Change in Kenya* (Boulder: Westview Press, 1992).

4 See T. Kanago, *Squatters and the Roots of Mau Mau 1905–63* (London: James Currey, 1987).

5 F. D. Corfield, *The Origins and Growth of Mau Mau. A Historical Survey* (London: Her Majesty's Stationery Office, 1960).

6 See for example D. Barnett and K. Njama, *Mau Mau from Within. Autobiography and Analysis of Kenya's Peasant Revolt* (London: Macgibbon & Key, 1966); M. Kinyatti, *Thunder from the Mountains. Mau Mau Patriotic Songs* (London: Zed Press, 1980).

7 Cf. n. 2.

8 See M. S. Clough, *Mau Mau Memoirs: History, Memory, and Politics* (Boulder: Rienner, 1998).

9 C. G. Rosberg and J. Nottingham, *The Myth of 'Mau Mau': Nationalism in Kenya* (New York: Praeger, 1966).

10 See for example, B. Kaggia, *Roots of Freedom* (Nairobi: East African Publishing House, 1975).

11 See A. Clayton and D. Savage, *Government and Labour in Kenya 1895–1963* (London: Frank Cass, 1974).

12 See J. Lonsdale, 'Moral Ethnicity, Ethnic Nationalism and Political Tribalism: The Case of the Kikuyu', in P. Meyns (ed.), *Staat und Gesellschaft in Afrika. Erosions- und Reformprozesse* (Hamburg: Lit, 1996), pp. 93–106; J. Lonsdale, 'The Moral Economy of Mau Mau: Wealth, Poverty and Civic Virtue in Kikuyu Political Thought', in J. Lonsdale and B. Berman (eds), *Unhappy Valley* (London: Currey, 1992), vol. 1, pp. 315–504; C. Presley, *Kikuyu Women, the Mau Mau Rebellion, and Social Change in Kenya*; W. Maloba, *Mau Mau and Kenya*.

13 M. S. Clough, *Mau Mau Memoirs*; W. Maloba, *Mau Mau and Kenya. An Analysis of a Peasant Revolt*; F. Furedi, *The Mau Mau War in Perspective* (London: Currey, 1989); B. Berman, 'Nationalism, Ethnicity, and Modernity: The Paradox of Mau Mau', *Canadian Journal of African Studies* 25 (1991), pp. 181–206; S. Howe, 'Flakking the Mau Mau Catchers', *The Journal of Imperial and Commonwealth History* 39:5 (2011), pp. 695–7.

14 J. Kenyatta, *Suffering without Bitterness*, pp. 188–9.

15 J. Kenyatta, *Harambee! The Prime Minister of Kenya's Speeches 1963–1964* (Nairobi: Oxford University Press, 1964), p. 15.

16 Quoted in *East African Standard* (20 October 1964).

17 H. Charton, 'Jomo Kenyatta et les méandres de la mémoire de l'indépendance du Kenya', in H. Charton and M.-A- Fouéré (eds), *Héros nationaux et pères de la nation en Afrique*, in *Vingtième Siècle. Revue d'histoire* 118:2 (2013), pp. 45–59.

18 Quoted in M. Clough, 'Mau Mau and the Contest for Memory', in: E. Atieno-Odhiambo and J. Lonsdale (eds), *Mau Mau and Nationhood* (Oxford: James Currey, 2003), pp. 251–64, 251.

19 *Daily Nation*, Nairobi, 21 Oct. 1993, quoted in T. Heid, 'Kolonialgeschichte in der Kontroverse: Die kenianische Presse und Mau Mau' (Master's thesis, Justus-Liebig-Universität Gießen, 2009), p. 84.

20 *The Standard* (21 October 2004), quoted in T. Heid, 'Kolonialgeschichte in der Kontroverse', p. 96.

21 *Sunday Standard* (18 February 2007).
22 *Sunday Standard* (18 February 2007), quoted in T. Heid, 'Kolonialgeschichte in der Kontroverse', p. 100.
23 *Daily Nation* (20 February 2007).
24 *Daily Nation* (20 October 2004), quoted in T. Heid, 'Kolonialgeschichte in der Kontroverse', p. 102.
25 *The Standard* (20 October 2004), quoted in T. Heid, 'Kolonialgeschichte in der Kontroverse', pp. 103–4.
26 *Sunday Standard* (22 October 2006), quoted in T. Heid, 'Kolonialgeschichte in der Kontroverse', p. 104.
27 *The Guardian* (5 October 2012), www.guardian.co.uk/world/2012/oct/05/maumau-court-colonial-compensation-torture (accessed 29 April 2013).
28 See T. Heid, 'Kolonialgeschichte in der Kontroverse', pp. 98–9, 156–61.
29 *Saturday Nation* (31 May 2003), quoted in T. Heid, 'Kolonialgeschichte in der Kontroverse', pp. 98–9.

CHAPTER THIRTEEN

Exploration and exploitation: German colonial botany at the Botanic Garden and Botanical Museum Berlin

Katja Kaiser

Museums are not by definition sites of memory, in the sense of Nora's *lieux de mémoires*, but they provide influential interpretations of the past and the present. By displaying selected objects, embedded in constantly transformed narratives, they help to shape collective memory.[1] During the colonial era, museums located at the imperial centre played a crucial role in the production and popularisation of knowledge about the colonies. The stories told at the time revolved around the alleged modernity and supremacy of Europe, marking a sharp contrast to the supposed backwardness of the colonised territories. Moreover, the period witnessed a massive expansion of museums that enlarged their collections by adding ethnographic and natural-history objects from overseas. The Botanic Garden and Botanical Museum in Berlin is an apt example for this colonial entanglement of museums. To date this has been a greatly neglected dimension of its history. The particular fascination of the Berlin institution consisted in how museum, greenhouses and an outdoor area interacted to offer a unique sense of the colonies' vegetation and plant products. After the loss of Germany's overseas territories in 1920, the former colonies could be remembered here – at a site of imperial commemoration that remained largely unchanged until 1945. In the years that followed and until very recently the museum provided a place where the history of German colonialism could conveniently be forgotten.

After a brief overview of the history of the Botanic Garden and Botanical Museum during the colonial era, this chapter will go on to explore its function as a showcase of imperial Germany's colonial project. Then it will analyse its transformation of the institution into an imperial site of memory from 1920 until the 1940s. It will also consider the effects of German ventures in the field of colonial botany on landscapes and societies in the colonies, indigenous reactions to exploitation and the post-colonial memory of German botanists and planters.[2] Finally, the oscillation between the remembering and the forgetting of the institution's colonial legacy since 1945 to the present day will be explored in the context of public debates on Germany's colonial past and colonial collections in museums.

The history of the institution

Even before the German Reich became a colonial power, Berlin's Botanic Garden and Botanical Museum had already obtained botanical finds from overseas. Germans exploring foreign lands had gathered plants for Berlin, and renowned scholars like the naturalist and explorer Alexander von Humboldt had bequeathed their herbarium specimens to the Botanical Museum.[3] Following the acquisition of German protectorates in Africa, in the Pacific and in China after 1884, the institution's geographical and thematic focus shifted completely. Now it concentrated on the search for useful plants to be cultivated in the German colonies. This shift was initiated by the German government promoting colonial botany as a means towards an efficient agricultural exploitation of the newly acquired tropical regions. Plants had always been of great importance for the political and economic expansion of the European states and were seen as key to national wealth and power.[4] In the German Empire colonial agriculture was regarded as central to making the colonies profitable, because they lacked significant mineral resources and were unsuitable for large scale European settlement.[5] It is thus not surprising that the first scientific facilities established in the German colonies were experimental gardens.[6]

In order to supply these gardens with economically valuable plants or seeds, a research centre for colonial botany was needed, and so in 1891 the *Botanische Zentralstelle für die deutschen Kolonien* (Botanical Research Centre for the German Colonies) was founded at Berlin's Botanic Garden, the leading German institution of its kind. The *Zentralstelle* was supposed to be largely funded by the Foreign Office, but the bigger share of the running costs was actually met by the Prussian Ministry of Education, to which the Botanic Garden was affiliated.[7]

The *Zentralstelle* organised the circulation and examination of botanical material for commercial purposes on a global scale. It distributed living plants and seeds from its own stock to experimental gardens or private businesses in the colonies and arranged shipments of plants from other European or colonial botanic gardens to the German stations where their economic potential was analysed. Soil and plant samples were examined, and promising plants were propagated, improved by hybridisation and later sent back to the colonial gardens for trial and distribution to German farmers. The dissemination of knowledge and skilled labour was also part of the activities. The *Zentralstelle* gave advice to farmers in the colonies, public authorities and commercial companies. It trained the gardeners selected for colonial service that later worked at the German, British or Dutch research stations overseas, whilst botanists from Germany, Britain, France and the Netherlands visited the European and colonial gardens of the other colonial powers. By exhibiting and explaining tropical plants, the garden and the museum in Berlin also fostered public interest in the colonies. In addition, taxonomic work was conducted and standard works on German colonial botany were published. Thus during the years of Germany's colonial expansion the work of the institution was characterised by a mixture of political, scientific and economic interests.[8]

Like its role model, the Royal Botanic Gardens at Kew near London,[9] the Botanic Garden Berlin operated as a central point within an international network of botanic gardens, political institutions and companies that stretched across the whole world. Plants, knowledge and people circulated within this network. At the scientific level, a remarkably high degree of cooperation existed beyond the limits of nation and empire. Yet in view of nonetheless intense competition, it might seem too far-fetched to label the scientific networks a 'fraternity'.[10]

The manifold tasks of the *Zentralstelle* and the numerous acquisitions from the colonies pushed the Botanic Garden and Botanical Museum to its limits and made a transfer to a more spacious location inevitable. Not only did the large quantities of specimens, dried or preserved in alcohol, and of plant products from the colonies exceed the storage capacity of the museum, but the experimental beds and glasshouses were also bursting at the seams. Furthermore, the Botanic Garden was originally founded in 1679 as the palace's kitchen and pleasure garden in the village of Schöneberg, southwest of Berlin. By the late nineteenth century the former village had been incorporated into the capital. Streets and houses around the garden meant that plants and trees suffered from a lack of fresh air and light. A suitable new location was found in Dahlem, on the outskirts of Berlin. At 42 hectares it was four times larger than the old garden. In 1899 the enormously laborious venture of relocating trees, plants and the museum collections started. It took eleven years until the official opening of the new garden and museum could be celebrated in 1910.[11] Kew's size, functions, scientific reputation and popularity again served as a benchmark for the new venture, especially with regard to its expressly colonial tasks.

Adolf Engler, the director of the Botanic Garden and Botanical Museum Berlin between 1889 and 1921, fundamentally shaped both the concept and design of the Dahlem facilities as well as the work of the *Zentralstelle*. He was first and foremost a pragmatic scientist and not – like many of his fellow botanists – an enthusiastic advocate of the German colonial empire. Yet he quickly realised the opportunities colonial botany offered to increase the scientific prestige of the Botanic Garden and Botanical Museum, as well as his personal standing. Engler ambitiously formalised and defined the Foreign Office's vague instructions regarding the tasks of the *Zentralstelle*, going well beyond the official demands and using his privileged position as government consultant to secure the institution's dominant position as the most significant German research centre for colonial botany.[12]

It is worth exploring the new facilities in Dahlem – the outdoor area, greenhouses and museum – and the institution's objectives more closely because Engler's concept of the new garden and museum and its implementation highlight the importance of colonial botany at this time. Moreover, the facilities remained unchanged until the 1940s and provided an impressive backdrop for a vividly celebrated commemoration of the German colonies and their alleged natural wealth.

With respect to the aims of the Botanic Garden and Botanical Museum, Adolf Engler wrote in 1891: 'With a collection of tropical plants as complete as possible in the garden and a rich collection of plant products in the museum, the institution shall offer everyone who leaves for the colonies the opportunity to become familiar with these things'.[13] Thus the contemporary scientific goal of an encyclopaedic classification of the plant world intermingled with didactic intentions that were particularly directed at botanists, students, trainee gardeners, travellers, civil servants, farmers, missionaries and others heading for the tropics. In general, Engler considered the Botanic Garden and Botanical Museum as a scientific institution and regarded non-academic visitors as a nuisance, hindering staff and 'the better part of the visitors'[14] in their work and studies.

At the same time, however, he suggested from the beginning that the Botanic Garden and the Botanical Museum should be used to disseminate knowledge of tropical plants and their products to a broader public. In accordance with his overall concept for the new garden Engler planned to present all tropically useful plants together in one area, rather than scattered over different parts of the garden and the greenhouses as had been the case in Schöneberg.[15] This should also have the desired effect of convincingly demonstrating the great variety of useful plants in the colonies and hence the economic viability of the German overseas territories.

Showcasing Germany's colonial empire

The outdoor departments proved very attractive to the wider public. In the first season – the outdoor area opened as early as 1903 – some 5,000 people visited every Sunday to marvel at tropical plants like tobacco, peanuts, coffee, tea, rubber, spices and sugar cane.[16] A 1910 guide stated that 'these departments, which primarily serve practical purposes, find the interest of the public is obvious every visiting day and is only natural considering the great colonial interest that can generally be found in Germany now'.[17] In addition, there was a veritable plant craze at the time and a fascination with all things exotic.[18] The Botanic Garden offered everybody the chance to experience tropical plants with all their senses, not only to look at exciting non-native plants, but also to smell and perhaps even touch them.[19]

This sensual experience was further enhanced in the greenhouses, especially in the big tropical house: spectacular palm trees and unusual looking plants, arranged in a romanticised jungle, were there to enchant the visitors. Engler wrote in the foreword to a garden guide: 'Here the German people, who are beginning to feel as colonial masters, shall have the opportunity to see images of tropical vegetation'.[20] Clearly, rather than pursuing the merely didactic purpose of imparting knowledge of useful tropical plants, Engler intended to heighten the German people's interest in the colonial idea by engaging all senses, feelings and the imagination. The tropical landscapes presented were an imaginative construct, though, reflecting the worldviews of the botanists and the taste of the public.[21] In particular, the big tropical house proved to be a real crowd puller. Its dimensions – 28 meters high, 60 meters long and 30 meters wide – and its elaborate glass and steel architecture, unparalleled anywhere in the German Empire, added to a lasting impression.

The appearance of the new Botanical Museum was equally ambitious: a three storey building in the Wilhelmine style, mirroring in its representative and monumental architecture the prestige and importance of botany at that time. The museum was a matter of particular concern for Engler. The main functions, he decided, were first to house a rich collection of plant species for scientific studies; secondly to bring together an exhaustive collection of material for the aims of applied or economic botany; and thirdly to display the collection to the public.[22] The aims of colonial botany dominated all of these functions: acquisitions mainly from the German colonies and other tropical territories meant that the study collection of plant specimens grew so dramatically that it proved impossible for the staff to cope with the abundance of material. The desired-for completion of a systematic record of the plant world seemed to be a long way off, but a massive colonial archive was piling up, typical of the imperial power's 'fixation with the central collection of information . . . and a fantasy of knowledge made into power'.[23] With regard to the museum's second function, a collection of plant products for economic botany, Engler focused exclusively on plant products from the colonies and the display collection presented tropical crops in two sections: the first was dedicated to useful plants in general and the second, the colonial department, was assigned to the plants and their products native to the German colonies.[24]

Engler conceptualised the colonial department of the Botanical Museum as a teaching aid, but it also became the popular central showcase for the plant treasures of the colonies.[25] In eighty-six display cases plants and plant products from the colonies were presented alongside ethnographic artefacts such as necklaces and clothes that demonstrated the indigenous population's use of the plants. Photographs of the typical vegetation of each colony and coloured drawings of plants complemented the displays, which were intended to give a better overall impression of the flora overseas.[26] The interpretation of the objects was determined by labels and guides. It is possible to reconstruct the context in which the objects were presented and the meaning ascribed to them. Scientific information on the plants and their products naturally had priority, but the exhibition as a whole also asserted the colonial order of things. Collecting was a form of conquest and the transport of objects from the peripheries to the imperial centre established Berlin symbolically as the heart of empire. In the museum the objects were then ordered according to Western taxonomies, demonstrating knowledge of and authority over the territories overseas.[27] The multitude of plant products on display documented the natural riches of the colonies and suggested that the exploitation of the colonies could be profitable when German plantations had replaced peasant production, which was regarded as inefficient and inadequate (Figure 13.1).[28] Products of indigenous agriculture and artefacts were often used to visualise a social evolution from African or Asian cultures to the more advanced industrialised 'civilisations' of the West. They served as a 'springboard for Western imagination'[29] and the confirmation of European conceptions of non-Western cultures. In this regard the exhibition at the Botanical Museum did not differ from the display of objects in ethnographic museums during the colonial era.[30]

As a matter of course, colonial botany was not the sole task of the Botanic Garden and Botanical Museum at that time, but in his annual reports on the work of the *Zentralstelle* Engler constantly complained

13.1 The economic plants department in the Dahlem Botanical Museum between 1910 and 1943 (Archiv Botanischer Garten, Berlin-Dahlem)

that it occupied all the time of his staff members.[31] Its public image was also that of a colonial institute: the Botanic Garden and Botanical Museum co-organised scientific colonial conferences and in this context the curator of the *Zentralstelle*, Georg Volkens, presented the experimental stations that were maintained in the colonies.[32] At the Berlin Trade Exhibition of 1896 the Botanic Garden and Botanical Museum participated and displayed tropical plants.[33] It was the aim of the trade fair, which included a 'colonial exhibition', to promote the colonial project through the use of popular colonial products such as coffee, cocoa or cigars. Seven million visitors came to gaze at innovations in technology and industry, tropical plant products and indigenous people from the German colonies.

Morphing into a site of memory

The German Reich officially lost its colonial empire in 1918 after its defeat in the First World War, but this did not mean the end for German colonial botany. As scientific, political and economic interests in the colonies remained, the Botanic Garden and Botanical Museum Berlin still functioned as a research centre for colonial botany, albeit to a lesser extent. At the same time, the grandeur of the museum and the greenhouses with their extensive collections and rich variety of living tropical plants were used to keep alive the memory of the colonies and their alleged economic importance to the German Reich. This development must be seen in the context of political claims for the restitution of the German colonial empire – a near-unanimous

13.2 The Botanic Garden and Botanical Museum's stall for the 700th anniversary of the city of Berlin in 1937 (Archiv Botanischer Garten, Berlin-Dahlem)

demand in Germany well into the early 1940s – which was accompanied by nostalgia for the colonial era (Figure 13.2).[34]

Scientific research now concentrated on the flora of the former German territories in Africa. A large number of acquisitions from previous years were still waiting to be properly analysed and in addition, new plant specimens were sent to Berlin by German farmers who had returned to Cameroon or the former German East Africa during the second half of the 1920s. At the same time, German botanists resumed their research in Togo, Cameroon, South-West Africa and the former German East Africa. They would continue their work there even during the Second World War.[35] The results were published in multi-volume publication projects supported by the *Kolonialwissenschaftliche Abteilung* (Department of Colonial Sciences) of the *Reichsforschungsrat* (State Research Council),[36] in periodicals like the *Notizblatt* (Infosheet), published by the Botanic Garden and Botanical Museum Berlin, or the more popular *Tropenpflanzer* (Planter in the Tropics), published by a private colonial interest group, the *Kolonialwirtschaftliche Komitee* (Colonial Economic Committee). Along with facts on tropical plants and colonial agriculture, these publications occasionally offered revisionist optimism about the time 'when Germany gets her nice colony Cameroon back'.[37] Articles also defended German efforts in colonial agriculture and medicine against allied claims of Germany's unworthiness as a colonial master: 'The principle (to take good care of the native population of the colonies) has contrary to all falsehoods always been . . . the determining factor of Germany's colonial politics'.[38] Remarks

[232]

like this, or the protestation that 'we still feel close to our black fos-terlings',[39] were meant to refute the doctrine of the German Reich's guilt as a uniquely cruel colonial master. Furthermore, books were recommended which stated the 'uneconomical use (of the former German colonies) by the mandatory powers'[40] and argued that the economic prosperity of these territories could only be possible under German rule. The alleged importance of colonies for the German economy was highlighted, even though the figures were sobering: although the trade in rubber and cocoa from Cameroon as well as in cotton from German East Africa and Togo had increased until 1914, the total share of the import from the colonies never reached more than 0.5% of the German Reich's total imports.[41]

The *Zentralstelle* was dissolved in 1920, yet private colonial inter-est groups such as the *Colonial Economic Committee* and the *Deutsche Kolonialgesellschaft* (German Colonial Society) continued to pursue their projects and initiated the reactivation of the *Zentralstelle* in 1939. Now called *Botanische Zentralstelle für die Kolonien*, it was initially financed by these two organisations, which merged to form the *Gruppe Kolonialwirtschaftlicher Unternehmungen* (Group of Colonial Economic Enterprises). After its official reopening in 1941 it was subsidised by the National Socialist government. As before, the *Zentralstelle* examined economically valuable plants, advised public authorities and commercial companies and prepared publications. It organised lectures and guided tours through the unchanged colonial departments in the garden and the museum. The participants were mainly members of the *Reichskolonialbund* (Reich Colonial League), a collective body of all German colonial organisations during the Third Reich, students and teachers at the *Institut für Überseegeschichte und Kolonialpolitik* (Institute for the History of the Overseas Possessions and Colonial Policy) as well as police and army officers destined for missions in Africa.[42] A new greenhouse for tropical plants was built, plants and plant products were loaned to support colonial exhibitions and on the occasion of the 700th anniversary of the city of Berlin the Botanic Garden and Botanical Museum contributed a presentation on its colonial department.[43]

The most striking feature of the institution's function as a site of memory is thus how little its duties in the field of colonial botany were affected by the loss of Germany's colonies. These activities now took on a new meaning. By presenting an unaltered picture of the tropical nature of the colonies with an emphasis on their economic importance and by pursuing further botanical research in these areas, Berlin's botanic institutes helped to perpetuate German demands for colonial revisionism. They commemorated a colonial empire that was intact and flourishing. In this respect Dahlem resembled many other scientific organisations and colonial associations which also attempted to preserve the pre-war status and voiced eager public claims for a return of Germany's erstwhile colonies. Besides, the exhibitions at the Botanic Garden and the Botanic Museum served a continuing public desire for colonial exoticism.[44] All in all, as a site of imperial memory from 1920 until the 1940s the botanic institutes were much more a centre of colonial activity than a place of quiet contemplation.

German colonial botany at the periphery

German ventures in the field of colonial botany affected indigenous societies and landscapes in the former African colonies. They accelerated a process of social and environmental transformation that continued to unfold long after the end of German rule.[45] The founding of the experimental stations Amani (1902) and Kwai (1896) in German East Africa (today mainland Tanzania) removed land from the local inhabitants and evicted them, partly by destroying their homes. As a result, the local population migrated to other areas. Yet at Amani, African families were soon resettled on station land to meet the institute's need for 200–300 workers to cultivate the extensive experimental fields.[46] On the private German coffee, cocoa, sisal and cotton plantations African workers were scarce as well. In Togo, German East Africa and Cameroon plantation companies and the local colonial government collaborated in expropriating land and using taxation to force African men to work on the plantations. Colonial labour demand destabilised rural subsistence economy, as well as household divisions of labour and social hierarchies by taking young men out of their families and communities. Many forced workers died owing to the harsh working conditions and poor hygiene on the plantations. These coercive measures and the enforced growth of crops for export repeatedly led to uprisings against German colonial authorities, and to acts of sabotage and resentment towards German farmers.[47]

The *Zentralstelle* was involved in these events through their support of the experimental stations, governmental gardens, German settlers and plantation owners with the dissemination of practical agricultural knowledge and plants.[48] It also received regular reports from the stations. Yet, even though these topics were controversially discussed by a wider public, Engler and his colleagues at the Botanic Garden and Botanical Museum Berlin did not take a public stand on the issues of colonial labour or the suitability of indigenous peasant production compared to small-scale farming by settlers and large-scale plantations.[49] The scientific articles and monographs that have been examined so far give no indication that there was an awareness of the social and political consequences of the German efforts in the field of colonial botany.

Botanical gardens, agricultural research stations and changed landscapes in today's Togo, Cameroon and Tanzania all have German origins. Indeed, the German governmental gardens and research stations are far more than just sites of memory of colonial rule and agricultural aspirations. The mandatory powers which took over the former German territories after 1919 continued the botanical research at these facilities. Some of them are still part of a global botanical network, such as Amani and the 'Limbe Botanical Garden', established as governmental garden Victoria. Today, the latter comprises less than half of its former area and the old library and laboratory have become the 'Atlantic Beach Hotel'.[50] Dar es Salaam's Botanical Garden, founded as a governmental research garden and now a small fraction of its original size, is a well-known tourist attraction thanks to its neat park and lavish flower beds. Its tree nursery used to provide avenue trees, which can still be found in many parts of Tanzania.[51] German botanical experiments carried out at the stations initiated and shaped ecological changes that continue to the present day. The stations introduced exotic crops and trees, and some of these became quite aggressive invaders, dominating and devastating naturally grown ecosystems. Far more severe was the ruthless destruction of huge parts of nature by German planters and commercial companies. Near Amani, coffee planters cleared thousands of hectares of rainforest for their plantations and in Cameroon large areas were affected by the overexploitation of rubber. The extensive alienation of land from indigenous use for plantation agriculture certainly had the most lasting effects on the landscape and indigenous societies.[52]

Altogether, and viewed from an African perspective, the memory of German colonial botany is ambivalent. In these countries, the creation of botanical gardens and experimental stations is honoured as the beginning of agricultural research, and many plants introduced by German botanists are now important commodities for export. In his study of Amani and Kwai Christopher Conte calls it an ironic situation that today's local farmers at Kwai preserve a memory of the German efforts by growing wheat and other exotic crops introduced in the time of German colonialism which their predecessors had opposed.[53] The memory of injustice and exploitation under German rule seems to be, if not forgotten, overwritten by the experience of the mandatory power's colonial rule.

[235]

Remembering and forgetting

In Berlin, after the Second World War, all signs pointed to a new beginning. In 1943, bombs had hit the herbarium and the library of the Botanic Garden and Botanical Museum Berlin and the majority of the preserved collections and books were burnt. In the same year, the glasshouses were destroyed by air raids and in 1944 the exhibition wing of the museum building was also damaged. Before the war, the collections in Berlin were considered to be the second largest in the world and their loss became known as the 'Dahlem catastrophe'. After 1945, the reconstruction of the buildings, now situated in the American sector, was slow, as was the rebuilding of the collections.[54] Little had survived of the colonial departments in the garden and the museum. In the new concept for the garden and the museum's permanent exhibition, the former colonies played no further role.

This corresponded to the general way that colonial memory was dealt with in West Germany and West Berlin immediately after the Second World War.[55] The memory of National Socialism dominated collective memory, and Germany's colonial past was omitted. It was only in the 1960s during the student movements and their anti-imperialist orientation that street names and monuments recalling German colonial rule provoked fierce yet locally limited conflicts. Ever since then there has been a discernible anti-colonial attitude in public discussions and historical research. At the same time a positive memory of the colonial era was cultivated in societies like *Verein für das Deutschtum im Ausland* (Association for Germanness Abroad) and by veterans' clubs continuing colonial traditions such us wreath-laying ceremonies at colonial monuments until very recently.[56]

Yet, the Botanic Garden and Botanical Museum did not cut all ties with its colonial past. Togo became the new focal point of scientific study of the African flora. A vegetation map of Africa, prepared between 1939 and 1942 was published for the first time in 1963 as 'testimony of Dahlem's Africa tradition'.[57] The institution's colonial era was not explicitly addressed in any other way, though. On the occasion of the garden's 300th anniversary in 1978 a comprehensive history of the institution was published, presenting the colonial era simply as one of the many chapters of its past. A first systematic study of German colonial botany, the work of the *Zentralstelle* and botanical research in post-colonial times appeared as late as 1987 in the form of a short article in English in a journal with only a limited readership.[58]

Today, the Botanic Garden and Botanical Museum focus on the future, not the past. Its homepage claims that 'plants are our future', and the central aims are 'to explore, document, present, explain and preserve plant diversity'.[59] The institution profiles itself as a modern research facility and part of Freie Universität Berlin; general information on its history is available but it takes several clicks to get there. For visitors to the garden and the museum traces of the colonial past are difficult to discern as well, even though they are omnipresent: the location Dahlem, the museum building and the greenhouses, parts of the collections, a small plant named for the Amani Station in German East Africa in a glasshouse and a bust of Adolf Engler in the museum's hallway – all these are reminders of colonial days. Yet, labels that would allow visitors to appreciate the historical dimension of the place and the collections are missing. In 2010 a temporary exhibition on the 100th anniversary of the Botanic Garden and Botanical Museum at its present location in Dahlem highlighted only a few aspects of the institution's colonial entanglement, concentrating on botanical issues but neglecting political and economic connections.[60] Whereas its historical role model Kew unabashedly acknowledges the importance of its colonial tradition, the Botanic Garden and Botanical Museum's handling of the issue seem to be less confident. A possible reason for this might be that the institution's colonial history and its remaining collections from colonial times still await a systematic analysis.

Recent developments in different areas have put pressure on museums to explore their colonial legacy, however, and to address their history of collection formation and exhibition concepts. On the one hand there is increasing research on the link between science and imperial expansion as well as on the importance of museums in popularising the natural sciences. The museums' approaches to collecting and displaying are now analysed within the context of the ideological views they sought to convey.[61] On the other hand a couple of museums have already started their own research projects. The Charité, Berlin's university teaching hospital, is investigating its anthropological collections from colonial times in view of restitution claims. The research of its Human Remains Project at the Centre for Anatomy and the Museum of Medical History began by analysing its collection of skulls and its first objective was to establish the provenance of the specimens. A second aim was the comprehensive exploration of the history of the collections and their collectors. In 2011, twenty skulls of Namibian origin were returned to Namibia. The Human Remains Project and the German Museums Association are currently working on guidelines regulating the treatment of human remains in museums.[62] In the meantime the discussion among museum experts has expanded from human remains to plaster casts from human skulls, voice recordings and ethnographic objects. There are now demands that further research be conducted into the circumstances under which objects were gathered.[63]

[237]

Berlin's botanical institutions have already received such appeals. In 2009, an article discussing the Botanic Garden and the Botanical Museum as a site of colonial environmental history laid out a broad agenda for investigation, ranging from exploring whether plant material for the herbarium and other collections was brought together by force, to wondering whether in the colonies new plants were introduced against the wishes of the local population. It also encompassed the topics of biopiracy and thoughts on establishing a policy of sharing research results on specific plants with the countries of their origin.[64]

Recent years have not just witnessed increased academic research on the connections between museums and empire or museums self-critically examining their own colonial legacy. There has also been a broader public debate on Germany's colonial past triggered by the occasion of the 100th anniversary of the war against an indigenous population, the Herero, in the colony of German South-West Africa (today's Namibia). Fearful of claims for financial compensation, both the German Federal Chancellor and the Foreign Minister carefully avoided an official apology during their visits to the country. But the question of an appropriate recollection of the colonial era remains. This has become even more pressing in view of current debates on the highly contested memory of the colonial past in some of the former colonies, which will not leave the discussion in Germany unaffected.[65]

Local initiatives in Germany are already finding alternative ways of imparting knowledge of German colonial history to a wider public, and guided tours through former imperial centres such as Berlin and Hamburg are offered. Unofficial guided tours by freelance historians through the permanent exhibition of the German Historical Museum in Berlin, which provide critical additional information on Germany's colonial past, are also well attended.[66] Furthermore, an extensive list of imperial sites of memory in Germany has been published with a broader audience in mind.[67] Criticism has been justifiably directed at the fact that the list referred mainly to 'places of forgetting', for in the majority of cases the colonial importance of the institutions, monuments and personalities mentioned is not widely remembered.[68] Still, the publication can be seen as an attempt to recover these histories from oblivion and to contribute to establishing a broader public awareness of Germany's colonial past, which despite the developments described above still holds a marginal position in the collective memory.

Current debates and developments make it inevitable that museums, including the Botanic Garden and Botanical Museum, examine their institutional and collection history as it relates to colonialism. Until lately, museums have constituted themselves as 'recorders of history' rather than as committed participants.[69] Yet the Botanic Garden and Botanical Museum with the *Zentralstelle* was actively involved in the colonial project in various ways, as were ethnological museums and others. Further research into the roles of the Botanic Garden and Botanical Museum as actors in German colonial history as well as into the circumstances under which objects were gathered will throw a different light on the objects, the museum building and the garden. Visitors will have a more historically aware museum experience and with its self-reflection the institution could, in addition to its tasks as a modern research centre, have a share in anchoring the colonial past in the collective memory.

Notes

1 P. Nora, 'Comment écrire l'histoire de France?' in P. Nora (ed.), *Les lieux de Mémoire*, vol. 3: Les Frances (Paris: Gallimard, 1992), pp. 9–32, p. 20.

2 This chapter is related to the author's doctoral thesis *German Colonial Botany – The Botanic Garden and Botanical Museum Berlin 1884–1918* (Freie Universität Berlin; supported by Villigst Foundation). Since the activities of the Botanic Garden and Botanical Museum were mainly directed at the African colonies of Cameroon, German East Africa and Togo, the discussion will be limited to these areas.

3 F. K. Timler and B. Zepernick, *Der Berliner Botanische Garten. Seine 300-Jährige Geschichte vom Hof- und Küchengarten des Großen Kurfürsten zur wissenschaftlichen Forschungsstätte* (Berlin: Presse und Informationsamt des Landes Berlin, 1978), pp. 25–32.

4 L. Schiebinger, *Plants and Empire. Colonial Bioprospecting in the Atlantic World* (Cambridge: Harvard University Press, 2004), p. 5. See also L. Schiebinger and C. Swan (eds), *Colonial Botany. Science, Commerce and Politics in the Early Modern World* (Philadelphia, PA: University of Pennsylvania Press, 2005).

5 H. Schnee (ed.), 'Da das wirtschaftliche Gedeihen der Schutzgebiete in erster Linie auf der landwirtschaftlichen Produktion beruht . . .' ('Because the economic prosperity of the protectorates is primarily based on the agricultural production'), *Deutsches Koloniallexikon* (Leipzig: Quelle und Meyer, 1920), vol. 2, p. 428. (All translations by the author.)

6 J. Ruppenthal, *Kolonialismus als 'Wissenschaft und Technik': Das Hamburgische Kolonialinstitut 1908 bis 1919* (Stuttgart: Steiner, 2007), p. 27.

7 Geheimes Staatsarchiv Preußischer Kulturbesitz, Berlin (hereafter GStA PK), I. HA Rep. 76, Va, sect. 2, tit. X, nr. 89 B, vol. I, duplication of contract between Foreign Office and Ministry of Education, 1 July 1890, p. 154 and GStA PK I. HA Rep. 76, Va, Sekt. 2, Tit. X, Nr. 89 B, vol. II, letter Foreign Office to Ministry of education, 8 June 1898, pp. 179–81; GStA PK I. HA Rep. 76, Va, Sekt. 2, Tit. X, Nr. 89 B, vol. II, letter Ministry of Education, internal note, 14. April 1898, p. 173.

8 Cf. B. Zepernick, 'Die botanische Zentralstelle für die deutschen Kolonien' , in U. van der Heyden and J. Zeller (eds), *Kolonialmetropole Berlin: Eine Spurensuche* (Berlin: Berlin Edition, 2002), pp. 107–12; F. K. Timler and B. Zepernick, 'German Colonial Botany,' *Berichte der Deutschen Botanischen Gesellschaft* 100 (1987), pp. 143–68, esp. pp. 147–9; K. Kaiser and H. Hartmann, 'Berlin: Botanischer Garten und Botanisches Museum,' in U. van der Heyden and J. Zeller (eds), *Kolonialismus hierzulande: Eine Spurensuche in Deutschland* (Erfurt: Sutton, 2007), pp. 145–9, p. 145.

9 On Kew: L. H. Brockway, *Science and Colonial Expansion. The Role of the British Royal Botanic Gardens* (London: Academic Press, 1979); R. Drayton, *Nature's*

PART III: REMEMBERING AND FORGETTING

Government. Science, Imperial Britain and the 'Improvement' of the World (Yale: University Press, 2000); R. Desmond, *The History of the Royal Botanic Gardens Kew* (Kew: Kew Publishing, 2007 [2nd edn]). On Kew's imperial network: D. P. McCracken, *Gardens of Empire: Botanical Institutions of the Victorian British Empire* (London: Leicester University Press, 1997). On Kew as a role model for Berlin: H. W. Lack, 'Kew – ein Vorbild für Berlin-Dahlem?', in Stiftung Preußische Schlösser und Gärten (ed.), *Preußische Gärten in Europa: 300 Jahre Gartengeschichte* (Leipzig: Edition Leipzig, 2007), pp. 182–5.

10 D. P. McCracken, 'Fraternity in the Age of Jingoism. The British Imperial Botanic and Forestry Network', in B. Stuchtey (ed.), *Sciences across the European Empires, 1800–1950* (Oxford: Oxford University Press, 2005), pp. 49–62.

11 Cf. H. W. Lack (ed.), *Humboldts grüne Erben: Der Botanische Garten und das Botanische Museum in Dahlem 1910 bis 2010* (Berlin: BGBM Press, 2010), pp. 42–5; F. K. Timler and B. Zepernick, *Der Berliner Botanische Garten*, pp. 42–54.

12 GStA PK, I. HA Rep. 76, Va, sect. 2, tit. X, nr. 89 B, vol. I, letter from Adolf Engler to Ministry of Education, 7 January 1890, pp. 112–18.

13 *Notizblatt des Königlichen botanischen Gartens und Museums zu Berlin* 10 (1897), p. 301.

14 *Ibid.*, p. 304.

15 GStA PK, I. HA Rep. 76, Va, sect. 2, tit. X, nr. 89 B, vol. I, letter Adolf Engler to Ministry of Education, 7 January 1890, p. 117.

16 *Notizblatt* 33 (1904), p. 107.

17 K. Peters, *Führer zu einem Rundgang durch die Freiland-Anlagen des Königlichen Botanischen Gartens zu Dahlem bei Berlin* (Berlin: Selbstverlag des Königlichen Botanischen Gartens Dahlem, 1910), p. 51.

18 D. P. McCracken, *Gardens of Empire*, p. X.

19 On the links between museum display and imperialism, the sensorial dimension of collections and the dominance of sight in the modern museum: C. Classen and D. Howes, 'The Museum as Sensescape: Western Sensibilities and Indigenous Artifacts', in E. Edwards, C. Gosden and R. B. Phillips (eds), *Sensible Objects: Colonialism, Museums and Material Culture* (Oxford: Berg, 2006), pp. 199–222.

20 A. Engler, *Führer zu einem Rundgang durch die Gewächshäuser des Königlichen Botanischen Gartens zu Dahlem bei Berlin* (Berlin: Selbstverlag des Königlichen Botanischen Gartens Dahlem, 1916), p. 28.

21 N. Stepan, *Picturing Tropical Nature* (London: Reaktion Books, 2001), pp. 149–79.

22 K. Krause, *Führer durch das Schaumuseum des Königlichen Botanischen Museums in Berlin-Dahlem, vol. 2: Führer durch die pflanzengeographische und die koloniale Abteilung* (Berlin: Selbstverlag des Königlichen Botanischen Gartens Dahlem, 1916), pp. VI–VII.

23 T. Barringer, 'The South Kensington Museum and the Colonial Project', in T. Barringer and T. Flynn (eds), *Colonialism and the Object: Empire, Material Culture and the Museum* (London: Routledge, 1998), pp. 11–27, p. 11.

24 K. Krause, *Führer*, pp. IX–X.

25 Cf. E. Cittadino, *Nature as the Laboratory: Darwinian Plant Ecology in the German Empire* (Cambridge: Cambridge University Press, 1990), p. 137.

26 K. Krause, *Führer*, pp. 53–87.

27 Cf. T. Barringer, 'South Kensington Museum', p. 11; C. Classen and D. Howes, 'Museum as Sensescape', p. 209.

28 Ministerium der geistlichen, Unterrichts- und Medizinalangelegenheiten (ed.), *Der Königliche Botanische Garten und das Königliche Botanische Museum zu Dahlem* (Berlin: Horn & Raasch, 1909), p. 135.

29 C. Classen and D. Howes, 'Museum as Sensescape', p. 203.

30 Cf. C. Classen and D. Howes, 'Museum as Sensescape', pp. 199–211; Barringer, 'South Kensington Museum'.

31 GStA PK, I. HA Rep. 76, Va, sect. 2, tit. X, nr. 89 B, vol. 2, annual report Adolf Engler to Ministry of Education, 4 March 1895, p. 6.

[240]

32 Cf. Deutscher Kolonialkongress, *Verhandlungen des Deutschen Kolonialkongresses* (Berlin: Kolonialkriegerdank, 1903), pp. 4, 18, 182–93.

33 GStA PK, I. HA Rep. 76, Va, sect. 2, tit. X, nr. 89 B, vol. 2, pp. 42, 44, 53.

34 Cf. S. Conrad, *Deutsche Kolonialgeschichte* (München: C.H. Beck, 2008), pp. 117–19; W. Speitkamp, *Deutsche Kolonialgeschichte* (Stuttgart: Reclam, 2005), pp. 160–72.

35 *Notizblatt* 14 (1938–39), p. 60; F. K. Timler and B. Zepernick, 'German Colonial Botany', pp. 159–61.

36 Cf. F. K. Timler and B. Zepernick, 'German Colonial Botany', p. 158.

37 *Der Tropenpflanze* 40:1 (1937), p. 2.

38 *Ibid.*

39 *Ibid.*

40 *Der Tropenpflanzer* 45:1 (1942), p. 287.

41 H. Gründer, *Geschichte der deutschen Kolonien* (Paderborn et al.: Schöningh, 2000 [4th edn]), pp. 136, 144, 180, 238.

42 *Notizblatt* 15 (1940–44), pp. 599, 653; *Führer durch den Staatlichen Botanischen Garten zu Berlin-Dahlem* (Berlin: Preußische Druckerei- und Verlags-AG, 1935), pp. 41, 71.

43 *Notizblatt* 14 (1938–39), p. 208.

44 S. Conrad, *Deutsche Kolonialgeschichte*, p. 117.

45 Cf. C. A. Conte, 'Imperial Science, Tropical Ecology and Indigenous History: Tropical Research Stations in Northeastern German East Africa 1896 to the Present', in G. Blue, M. Bunton and R. Croizer (eds), *Colonialism and the Modern World* (Armonk, NY: Sharpe, 2002), pp. 246–61, p. 247.

46 Cf. C. A. Conte, 'Imperial Science', p. 256; D. Bald and G. Bald, *Das Forschungsinstitut Amani: Wirtschaft und Wissenschaft in der deutschen Kolonialpolitik Ostafrika 1900–1918* (München: Weltforum, 1972), p. 67.

47 Cf. T. Sunseri, 'Famine and Wild Pigs: Gender Struggles and the Outbreak of the Majimaji War in Uzaramo (Tanzania)', *Journal of African History* 38 (1997), pp. 235–59; H. Gründer, *Geschichte der deutschen Kolonien*, pp. 127–65; A. Eckert, *Grundbesitz, Landkonflikte und kolonialer Wandel: Douala 1880–1960* (Stuttgart: Steiner, 1999), p. 75.

48 Institutes: Victoria/Cameroon, Amani/German East Africa; experimental gardens and government's gardens: Windhuk, Okahandja/German South-West Africa, Bismarckburg, Misahöhe, Lome/Togo, Dar es Salaam, Kwai/German East Africa, Buea, Bamum,/Cameroon, Rabaul/New Guinea.

49 Cf. H. Schnee, *Deutsches Koloniallexikon*, vol. 1, pp. 71–2; Conrad, *Kolonialgeschichte*, pp. S. 57–8; H. Gründer, *Geschichte der deutschen Kolonien*, pp. 134–5, 137, 143, 150–2; Conte, 'Imperial Science', p. 249.

50 http://bgbm3.bgbm.fu-berlin.de/BGBM/museum/ABT/ABT/TEXT/afrika.htm (accessed 6 November 2012).

51 D. Bald and G. Bald, *Amani*, p. 39.

52 Cf. C. A. Conte, 'Imperial Science', pp. 256, 258.

53 *Ibid.*, p. 259.

54 Cf. F. K. Timler and B. Zepernick, *Der Berliner Botanische Garten*, pp. 67–93; H. W. Lack (ed.), *Humboldts grüne Erben*, pp. 92–5.

55 Cf. W. Speitkamp, *Deutsche Kolonialgeschichte*, pp. 172–87; S. Conrad, *Deutsche Kolonialgeschichte*, pp. 8–11, 119–21. In the GDR imperialism was condemned as the highest stage of capitalism. Colonial monuments were removed and street names changed. Speitkamp, *Kolonialgeschichte*, p. 173.

56 Cf. S. Conrad, *Deutsche Kolonialgeschichte*, p. 120; W. Speitkamp, *Deutsche Kolonialgeschichte*, p. 175. At least until 2005, veterans' clubs and other traditional societies met annually at a monument for German colonial troops for commemoration and wreath laying ceremonies. More information and pictures on http://offene-kartierung.de/wiki/go?DerSogenannteTansaniaPark#10_Traditionskr_nze_und_Gegendemonstration_2005 (accessed 6 November 2012).

57 *Willdenowia*, suppl. 1 (1963), p. 2.

58 F. K. Timler and B. Zepernick, 'German Colonial Botany'.

59 www.bgbm.org/default_e.htm (accessed 6 November 2012).
60 H. W. Lack (ed.), *Humboldts grüne Erben*, pp. 42–5, 88–9.
61 Cf. for further reading, B. Stuchtey (ed.), *Sciences across the European Empires*, pp. 4–6.
62 http://anatomie.charite.de/geschichte/human_remains_projekt/ (accessed 6 November 2012).
63 Cf. B. Lange, 'Sensible Sammlungen', in M. Berner, A. Hoffmann and B. Lange (eds), *Sensible Sammlungen: Aus dem anthropologischen Depot* (Hamburg: Philo Fine Arts, 2011), pp. 15–40; for another approach: S. Legène and J. van Dijk (eds), *The Netherlands East Indies at the Tropenmuseum. A Colonial History* (Amsterdam: KIT, 2011), pp. 6–14.
64 L. Kreye, 'Der Botanische Garten und das Botanische Museum in Berlin-Dahlem – ein Schauplatz der kolonialen Umweltgeschichte?', in B. Herrmann and U. Stobbe (eds), *Schauplätze und Themen der Umweltgeschichte: Umwelthistorische Miszellen aus dem Graduiertenkolleg. Werkstattbericht* (Göttingen: Universitätsverlag, 2009), pp. 127–43, esp. pp. 133–7.
65 Cf. S. Conrad, *Deutsche Kolonialgeschichte*, pp. 121–3; W. Speitkamp, *Deutsche Kolonialgeschichte*, pp. 176–87.
66 www.freedom-roads.de/pdf/FRRDPresseND_KKB.pdf (accessed 6 November 2012).
67 U. van der Heyden and J. Zeller (eds), *Kolonialismus hierzulande*.
68 Cf. review by Michael Pesek, http://hsozkult.geschichte.hu-berlin.de/rezensionen/id=13087 (accessed 6 November 2012).
69 T. Barringer, 'Introduction', in T. Barringer and T. Flynn (eds), *Colonialism and the Object*, p. 4.

CHAPTER FOURTEEN

Recollections of rubber

Frank Uekötter

There are many ways to lose a war. One of the more embarrassing ones is to run out of rubber. That prospect was haunting Americans in 1942 when the country was gearing up its war economy. In the months after Pearl Harbor, Japan had occupied the rubber plantations of South-east Asia, forcing the US to find other suppliers. The search turned into a frenzy. In March 1942, the federal government launched a huge Emergency Rubber Project to enlist a vast array of experts in its quest for the precious material. At the same time, the government stepped up recycling efforts to lay its hands on every piece of rubber already in the country. When New York Governor Herbert Lehman donated his tennis shoes to the collection drive, it made front-page news in the *New York Times*.[1]

Almost half a century later, 120 rubber tappers were gathering at the University of Brasília to draw attention to their miserable fate. Brazilian rubber was under pressure on international markets and a bitter conflict with their powerful bosses threatened not only the economic existence of the tappers but even their lives. It was quite an achievement to rally together workers who lived deep in the jungle, and the long trip to Brasília made for a challenge of its own, all the more so because many tappers had never before travelled more than a day on foot or by boat. However, when they assembled in the auditorium of one of the country's leading universities in October 1985, they were in an upbeat mode. One of their chief weapons was the story of how rubber from the Amazon rainforest had helped the United States to overcome its chronic rubber shortage during the Second World War. To their consternation, the rubber tappers found that no one cared.[2]

The two stories demonstrate the importance of commodities to lives and economies in the modern era, but they are also testimony to the precarious place of commodities in collective thought. They typically occupy a twilight zone in the realm of memory: resources are surely important, and they obviously have a history, but that does not necessarily stimulate awareness. As long as commodities are cheap and readily available, the modern consumer tends to focus on other things. This makes for a curious blend of alertness and amnesia: commodity histories typically bear the hallmark of dramatic oscillations between burning needs and carelessness. Commodities are thus tricky subjects for explorations of imperial memories: how can recollections of rubber be examined when popular awareness is notoriously sporadic?

The selectiveness of memory

Among the numerous commodities of the modern era, rubber seems particularly well placed to produce a broad trail of imperial memories. It is a crucial resource that is inseparably intertwined with modern life. Natural conditions allowed rubber to be produced in vastly different parts of the world, making for a network that truly spans the globe. There is also plenty of fodder for the historical imagination, as the story features a number of archetypes of imperial history: the intrepid daredevil, the plantation, the scientific network. However, commodities such as rubber suffer from a number of complications when it comes to imperial memories.

Most commodity histories are geographically diverse. Places of extraction, refinement, trade and consumption are often scattered over different continents. The challenges that people are wrestling with at these individual stages are vastly different, and it is often difficult to understand them without a reference to other stages along the commodity chain. The concept of *sites* of memory goes in the opposite direction: it encourages a focused approach, the concentration on one event and one locale in the hope that an in-depth discussion that concentrates on this one entity leads to a distinct world of imaginations. In other words, while sites of memories are akin to trees, with different branches that go back to a common trunk, commodity chains operate as intricate, polycentric webs.

We can discern the ensuing problems in existing memory projects. Some three decades after Pierre Nora's pioneering work, there has been a wide array of entities figuring as sites of memory: battles, buildings, books, pieces of art and so on. Networks rarely make it onto the coveted list, and if they do (as in the case of the *Stasi*, East Germany's infamous secret police, or the mafia in Italy's memory project), there are usually other reasons for their inclusions. Going through the three volumes on Germany's sites of memory, the closest approximation to the topic at hand is probably the Hanseatic League.[3]

For some reason, networks are having a hard time entering collective memory: most people seem to feel more comfortable when thinking about the past in terms of places, faces and events. Whether the twenty-first century's obsession with networks and networking will change that is a matter of speculation.

However, perhaps the most important reason for the selectiveness of commodity memories is that people – or, to be specifically, *some* people – can *afford* to be forgetful. People can consume resources without having to engage with any memories. In fact, consumption is often easier in the absence of intellectual baggage. Talk about 'banana republics' tends to spoil one's appetite for fruit, just as few people like to think about abattoirs when consuming meat. However, the situation is different on the other end of commodity chains: consumers may forget where their material supplies came from, but producers rarely do, and rarely can. The rift between these two perspectives is a recurring theme in this chapter.

Given all these complications, should memory scholars continue to shun commodities and head for other, easier topics? This chapter suggests that the opposite may be more rewarding. We can turn the selectiveness of memory into an advantage by looking at the mode of selection: how do societies come to devote their attention to specific places and events along complex commodity chains? Why do specific events enter collective memories, and for whom? In this chapter, we will search for answers along the trail of rubber in world history, making stops in the Amazon rainforest, South-east Asia, Great Britain, Germany, the Congo and Liberia. Along the way, we will encounter a number of sites that could have entered collective awareness but failed to do so, such as the Putumayo, guayule, or kok-saghyz.

We will consider how recollections of rubber became enshrined in specific sites of memory. In fact, we will conclude with some reflections on how a new, more materialist understanding of memory is emerging from this discussion. We will also see that there may be yet another reason for the contested place of commodities in memory studies: the obscene toll that the modern system of resource allocation exacts. The story at hand is a tragic one, and memories of rubber are often painful. Commodity history is not for the faint-hearted.

The Brazilian connection

Among the group of commodities with an imperial past rubber is a latecomer. It emerged in the nineteenth century when the need for a buffer material became more and more pressing. Wherever engineers had to construct a flexible connection between two components, or where adverse conditions required insulation, rubber was an option, and often the preferred one. Inflatable tyres boosted the global demand for rubber when bicycles became mass products in the late nineteenth century, soon to be followed by automobiles. Rubber is behind products as different as erasers, dummies and condoms. The rubber scare during the Second World War shows that rubber was also a crucial resource for war, as tanks and battleships needed it to function. Without rubber, life in the modern age would look very different.

Rubber is a natural product, though one that requires significant processing. It derives from latex, the milky substance naturally produced by plants. Until Charles Goodyear and others introduced vulcanisation in the 1840s there was little industrial use for what was, from a chemical standpoint, an emulsion of polymers. By adding heat, sulfur, and catalysts, engineers could turn the liquid into the durable substance that we know as rubber. Twentieth-century chemistry found ways to produce synthetic rubber, but to this day natural rubber has remained the preferred option for a number of uses. For instance, aircraft designers usually shun synthetics for tyres because natural rubber copes better with the extreme conditions during take-off and landing.

Many plants produce latex, but only a few have achieved commercial significance. By far the most important one is *hevea brasiliensis*, a tree that gives off the precious liquid from incisions in its bark, a labour-intensive process commonly known as 'tapping'. The Latin name points to the plant's origin: *hevea brasiliensis* is native to the Amazon River basin, and Brazil, Peru and Bolivia are the only countries where the plant grows naturally. A commodity that owes its existence to the combined forces of modern science and industry thus had its roots in the depth of the Amazon rainforest.

The Amazon basin had been part of a Portuguese colony since the sixteenth century and became the hinterland of Brazil when the country gained its independence in 1822, but before the age of rubber this hardly impacted on the indigenous population. For a long time, the Portuguese presence remained confined to coastal regions, and when the colonisers moved inland, they preferred more southerly regions. The Amazon rainforest combined an inhospitable climate with an even more inhospitable array of plants and animals, and that reduced the white man's presence to the forays of a handful of daredevils like Alexander von Humboldt. Until the middle of the nineteenth century, few residents of the Amazon knew that they were colonial subjects.

Hevea brasiliensis brought the remote area into the global economy. For a number of decades, the Amazon rainforest held a monopoly on rubber production. As early as the 1850s, some 25,000 people were engaged in the business of tapping, mostly around Belém.[4] When industrial demand picked up after 1880, the city of Manaus, almost 1,000 miles upstream from the mouth of the Amazon River, became the scene for developments reminiscent of Gold Rushes in other parts of the world. The best-known illustration of this was the opera house, built completely from imported materials between 1891 and 1896 and funded from rubber profits. But the opera was by no means the only indicator of a bustling boomtown in the middle of the rainforest. Manaus was also the first South American city boasting an electric streetcar line.[5]

Wealth accumulated particularly among a small band of 'rubber barons'. The situation was less favourable for the tappers who were collecting rubber in the jungle. While slavery was not abolished in Brazil until 1888, tapping was the province of independent workers. Tappers decided by themselves on the manner and intensity of rubber collection, but their freedom was only relative. They were selling their rubber to intermediaries who in turn provided them with supplies. The system was prone to exploitation because intermediaries could manipulate the price of supplies. In response, tappers could turn to independent suppliers or switch dealers, but the location of their trade severely limited their range of options. In fact, quite a number of tappers eventually realised that they were operating at a loss.[6]

Labour conditions in the Amazon became subject to international scrutiny when the muckraking British weekly *Truth* began to publish a series of sensationalist articles in September 1909. The charges focused on the Putumayo, a frontier region in which four South American countries – Colombia, Ecuador, Peru and Brazil – had a stake. The Putumayo was unusual in that one company, the Peruvian Amazon Rubber Company, controlled most of the region, depriving tappers of the option to play one dealer off against another. Furthermore, rubber collection was in the hands of Indians, whereas tappers were usually *mestizos* or *caboclos*. Finally, the Peruvian Amazon Rubber Company was registered in London, and when *Truth* published allegations about torture, abuse and rape, it touched a nerve in the motherland of abolitionism. Under pressure from the Anti-Slavery and Aborigines Protection Society, the British Foreign Office ordered the British consul general in Rio de Janeiro, Roger Casement, to investigate. After collecting evidence in the region in late 1910, Casement confirmed that there was reason for concern, estimating that more than 90% of the natives had suffered whippings. The scandal simmered on for a few years.[7]

From a local perspective, the scandal was merely a reflection of a sad normality. The Peruvian Amazon Rubber Company simply drew on the Amazon tradition of forced labour and slavery. According to Michael Stanfield, 'Northwest Amazonians had traded human beings for goods prior to the rubber boom and continued to do so thereafter'.[8] International attention clearly reflected European standards and did not stimulate deeper interest in the region and its customs. Interestingly, the Putumayo scandal is one of the few situations in colonial history where the plight of non-white natives ranked higher than that of people with a Caucasian background. Coverage in *Truth*, and abolitionist activism highlighted abuse of the indigenous population while ignoring the fate of the more than 100,000 rubber collectors who had migrated into the Amazon. Late-twentieth-century authors have criticised rubber collection in the Amazon as 'one of the strangest, most brutal forms of labour exploitation in modern history', but the contemporary perspective was different.[9] In the late nineteenth century, tappers were simply self-employed entrepreneurs, at least if seen from distant Europe. If they were out of luck, that was their own problem.

The Putumayo scandal followed on the heels of outrage over King Leopold's Congo, which will be discussed below. However, while the Congo affair has gained some publicity in recent years, the Peruvian story has received only scant attention. As of May 2014, neither the Putumayo scandal nor key figures like Benjamín Saldaña Rocca or Walt Hardenburg had Wikipedia entries. Perhaps it plays a role that the Putumayo scandal occurred in a notoriously unequal society, where abuse of labour is expected rather than feared? After all, forgetfulness of this story meshes nicely with Eric Hobsbawm's famous diagnosis that Brazil was 'a monument to social neglect'.[10] Be that as it may, it is striking that Amazon rubber has received far less publicity for how it produced rubber than for the way in which it lost its biological monopoly.

Theft

One might argue that it was only a matter of time until *hevea brasiliensis* would grow outside the Amazon. After all, plants from the New World had been coming to Europe and other parts of the world since soon after 1492, a transfer that has come to be known as the 'Columbian Exchange'.[11] Yet the transfer of rubber seeds became a modern legend, nourished not least by its protagonist, Henry Wickham, who retold the story in so many versions that the precise sequence of events remains shrouded in mystery. 'There was always an air of the fantastic to Wickham's exploits, an extravagant blend of Edgar Rice Burroughs and Lord Dunsany, and even today, historians seem uncertain what to make of him', Joe Jackson wrote in his biography of Wickham.[12]

We can see the story's enigma at work in the reception of Jackson's book: it won acclaim as a finalist for the 2009 Mark Lynton History Prize of the Columbia University Journalism School and rose to the number-two spot in *Time* magazine's Top Ten list of non-fiction books in 2008.

In May 1876, Wickham secretly brought 70,000 rubber seeds aboard a ship bound for Liverpool and assured its transfer to the Royal Botanic Gardens at Kew. It was quite an achievement to collect that number of seeds in the rainforest – an earlier transfer with fewer specimens had failed. Handling the load, which weighed three quarters of a ton plus packaging, was no small feat either. But that surely did not suffice to earn Wickham enduring fame. The story gained its thrust from the unresolved question lurking behind the theft: who owns the genetic potential of plants? In spite of international and bilateral agreements, no consensus has emerged on the issue to this day, and the secrecy of Wickham's mission obviously betrayed a guilty conscience. In Jackson's view, Wickham 'pulled off one of the most successful and far-reaching acts of biological piracy in world history'.[13]

The theft still resonates in Brazil's collective memory and continues to frame political decisions. 'Biopiracy haunts Brazilian history, beginning with Henry Wickham, an Englishman who smuggled rubber seeds out of the country in the 19th century and broke Brazil's global rubber monopoly', an Associate Press article declared in 2005. Nowadays, it noted, these fears were hampering research in the Brazilian Amazon.[14] Environmental historian Warren Dean took a similar view in 1987: 'In the Brazilian popular imagination the removal of *hevea* seeds to Southeast Asia continues to be resented, and to be regarded as a tremendous economic loss'.[15] After all, the years of the rubber monopoly were just too good to be true. During its peak between 1898 and 1910, rubber amounted to 26% of Brazil's export revenues, second only to coffee (leather made for a distant third, with 4%).[16]

However, the lament draws on a rather simplistic view of rubber production. The collective imagination takes it as a given that Amazon rubber production would have been sustainable and that rubber consumption would have continued to rely on *hevea brasiliensis*. Both of these assertions can be doubted. Resource monopolies usually perished during the modern era, and industrial buyers would have had a powerful incentive to search for substitutes. Furthermore, conditions in the Amazon implied severe limits to growth, and it is unsure at best whether it could have supplied the automobile age. Finally, the rain forest was on the periphery of Brazil's economy, implying a significant risk of clashes with the powerful provinces of Minas Gerais and São Paulo farther south: the rubber monopoly was surely no model for Brazil's economy in general, and as revenues went mostly to a small band of rubber barons, its political leverage was limited. All in all, there are good reasons to agree with Dean in that 'Brazil might well be worse off' if it had retained its biological monopoly.[17]

The Brazilian state of Amazonas imposed a heavy export tax on rubber seeds in 1884, and Brazil banned their export entirely in 1918.[18] However, the fact that these measures came into force eight and forty-two years after Wickham's feat clearly suggests that the shock was long in coming. The golden years of Brazilian rubber came *after* the theft: the ground-breaking ceremony for the opera house in Manaus was still a decade and a half away when Wickham's ship weighed anchor in Santarém harbour. It was not until 1906 that the South-east Asian rubber plantations were mentioned in the Brazilian Chamber of Deputies.[19] As late as 1908–10, the rubber barons of the Amazon still schemed to boost the price of rubber on world markets.[20] But then things fell apart.

Imperial Kew

The transfer of rubber seeds does not end with Wickham's departure from Santarém. It was one thing to export *hevea brasiliensis* seeds from Brazil, but quite another to turn the seeds into plants at Kew, and another still to make them grow into actual trees in Africa and Asia. Dean observed that Wickham's enterprise 'was not so much an adventure as it was a complex bureaucratic project, some fifty years in the execution'.[21] For anthropologist Michael Dove even this is too much praise: for him the endeavour 'was far too uncoordinated and happenstance to merit the term *project'*.[22]

The institutions that took part in the transfer naturally took a different view. The quasi-official history of the Royal Botanic Gardens at Kew, written by its Chief Librarian and Archivist Ray Desmond, boasts that rubber 'completely redeemed Kew's reputation'.[23] In order to share the sense of excitement in June 1876, Desmond quotes the recollection of Kew's Assistant Director, William Thiselton-Dyer: 'We knew it was touch and go, because it was likely the seeds would not germinate. I remember well on the third day going into the propagating houses where they were planted and seeing that by good luck the seed was germinating'.[24] In the end, only 4% of the seeds germinated, but that made for 1,900 healthy plants ready for shipment to Kew's satellites in Asia in August 1876. Botanical Gardens were traditionally working as networks, constantly exchanging seeds and other biological material, and Kew's nineteenth-century network of biological stations all over the empire was second to none.

In a nod to post-colonial sentiments, Desmond touches briefly on 'whether it was an honourable thing to take the natural resources of a country and in so doing deprive it of some commercial advantage', though the legitimacy of the endeavour is ultimately beyond doubt for him. Kew's nineteenth-century leaders probably had even fewer qualms, since they did not treat seeds as a national property. *Hevea* plants did not only go to Ceylon and Singapore but also to the Dutch East Indies, the German East Africa Company, and Portugal's Mozambique.[25]

The cumulative result of all these efforts was that *hevea brasiliensis* became a plantation crop. The first plantation-grown rubber reached world markets in the late 1890s, and by 1910, production was large enough to destroy the monopoly of Amazon rubber within a few years. Plantations had been a defining feature of colonialism since the Caribbean sugarcane plantations of the early modern era, but even huge stands of rubber trees generated little excitement. They were perceived as just another plantation system at work. We can see this divergent interest in the vastly different space that John Loadman devotes to the different themes in his *Story of Rubber*. Loadman devotes forty-one pages to the Congo but only twelve to Malaysia and none to Liberia.[26]

A properly functioning plantation is apparently a dull thing, at least for people from the West. (We will get to the perspective of the locals in a moment.) The Asian rubber plantations gained only a brief moment of transnational fame when Japan occupied them in 1942. The plantations emerged unscathed from the war, and while the industrialised world was grateful that Japan abstained from a torched earth strategy, this decision also meant that rubber failed to achieve a high profile in collective memory. In the popular imagination it was oil, not rubber, that was the resource that defined the Pacific War.

The scientists and boosters in Asia whose work was more demanding than that of the gardeners at Kew did not get much attention either.[27] In a baffling omission, the British botanists had failed to bring knowledge of the relevant techniques along with the seeds from Brazil, which forced the colonists in South-east Asia into a lengthy process of reinventing the wheel. Even a colourful figure like the director of Singapore Botanic Gardens Henry Nicholas Ridley, whose penchant for *hevea brasiliensis* earned him the sobriquet of 'Mad Ridley' (he invented the V-shaped or 'herringbone'-style of bark cutting, among other things), never won much acclaim beyond expert circles.[28] While Joe Jackson wrote a popular book about Henry Wickham's life, Henry Ridley only achieved biographical fame when Singapore's Research Institute of Economic Plants in the Tropics started a book series on 'developers of the rubber industry of Singapore and Malaysia' in 1969. As far as can be ascertained, the project collapsed after the first volume.[29]

In the end, the botanists' wisdom pales in comparison with an element of luck. In their Amazon homeland, *hevea brasiliensis* plants are threatened by South American leaf blight, a lethal fungus that (unbeknownst to the heroes at Kew) had not joined the seeds on their journey to Asia. How great a threat the South American leaf blight actually was became evident when it sealed the fate of Henry Ford's rubber plantation project in Brazil in the 1930s, a story recently resurrected from oblivion by Greg Grandin's best-selling book.[30] Mindful of these experiences, the rubber-producing countries in Asia and Africa have always been wary of the fungus and its potentially devastating effect. With that, these countries, weak as they were when it came to the production of imperial memories, at least became recipients of Amazon experiences.[31]

Rice-eating rubber: a smallholder's nightmare

As we have noted earlier, lukewarm interest in commodity chains is a characteristic phenomenon of consumer societies. Producing regions could barely forget plantations and their consequences. What looked stable from a distance was, upon closer inspection, a story full of tensions. On the Malaysian Peninsula, rubber trees had claimed 250,000 hectares by 1910 and 891,000 hectares eleven years later, mostly driven by the prospect of reaping pioneer profits. However, prices on world markets were fluctuating wildly after the first two decades of cultivation, and Malaysia, whose economy essentially revolved around rubber and tin until the 1960s, learned the painful consequences of export dependency.[32] In Liberia, the Firestone Tyre and Rubber Company not only maintained a huge plantation, but the size of the investment and the need to cope with a labour shortage also meant that it enjoyed a controlling position in national politics. A system of contract labour that put recruitment in the hands of native chiefs drew allegations of forced labour, and the system became subject to a League of Nations inquiry in 1930.[33] Firestone's role in Liberia has remained controversial, and a 'Stop Firestone' campaign exists to the present day.[34]

Dependency was a theme that ran through these cultures and even shaped the collective imagination. This is powerfully illustrated in an indigenous myth that emerged among smallholders in Borneo in the 1930s: the dream of the rice-eating rubber tree. Smallholders could integrate rubber production into their swidden cycle of rice cultivation, and did so with great commercial success. However, the dream cautioned them not to neglect subsistence food production: it tells of rice that mysteriously disappears and is then found in a hollow rubber tree. As Dove has argued, the 'dream of the rice-eating rubber illuminates Bornean tribespeople's consciousness of the threat posed by overcommitment to global commodity markets'.[35]

The dream spread against the background of the International Rubber Regulation Agreement, which was also designed to protect rubber production on estates against the competition from smallholders. However, that merely slowed their demise: while Asian rubber plantations were productive enough to marginalise Amazon rubber, they were not strong enough to rule in their own region. Over the course of the twentieth century, the share of estates in Indonesia's rubber production sank from over 90% to about 20%, and smallholders now dominate the market – a remarkable achievement in the absence of support for smallholders from the Indonesian government. A flexible labour regime, which allows smallholders to shift between subsistence- and market-oriented activities at short notice, has given them a lasting edge over large, capital-intensive plantations.[36]

King Leopold's heart of darkness

Few colonial rulers are more notorious than King Leopold II of the Belgians. His reign over the Congo Free State became an international scandal in the early 1900s and entered world literature through Joseph Conrad's *Heart of Darkness*. Conrad had spent six months in the Congo in 1890, when ivory was still the main commodity, and the book 'was, among other things, an early expression of what was to become a worldwide revulsion from the horrors of Leopold's exploitation of the Congo'.[37] In the years after Conrad's visit, rubber became the mainstay of the colonial economy, and that brought with it a regiment of terror: hostage taking of women and children, chopping off of hands, and random killings were all means to force the natives into collecting their allotted quota of rubber (Figure 14.1). When the true character of his reign became known, a transnational wave of outrage, particularly in the Anglo-Saxon world, forced King Leopold to accept civilian control over his colony. According to a recent study, the Congo was 'perhaps the grimmest episode of the rubber boom', and considering that the story of rubber in general was not exactly an uplifting one, that surely means something.[38]

The atrocities were shocking, but they were also hidden in the jungle, and that made gaining reliable information a challenge of its own. King Leopold had heralded his personal reign over the Congo as a crusade for civilisation and against slavery and won international

PUNCH, OR THE LONDON CHARIVARI.—November 28, 1906.

IN THE RUBBER COILS.

Scene—*The Congo "Free" State.*

14.1 'In the Rubber Coils', *Punch*, London (28 Nov. 1906)

acclaim for his endeavour. However, when an office clerk, Edmund Dene Morel, turned whistle-blower and made his insider knowledge public, the image began to collapse. Morel positioned himself in the grand British tradition of humanitarianism, and when the House of Commons passed a resolution expressing concern in 1903, the Foreign Office wasted no time in requesting a report from His Majesty's consul in the Congo.[39]

The consular report confirmed the accusations, and the campaign gained momentum. Authors like Arthur Conan Doyle and Mark Twain rallied to the cause. As colonial culprits go, Belgium was an easy target. It was not an imperial power of long standing, and its precarious European setting hemmed in by mighty neighbours made it vulnerable to international criticism. For colonial powers with baggage, criticising the Congo was a good opportunity to highlight their own civilising missions, and Great Britain, which had just fought the hugely controversial Boer War, seized the chance with particular gusto.[40]

An awareness of the connection between rubber and terror remained alive in the Congo, which was hardly surprising in a society with an uncounted number of limbless people. When a Belgian agricultural expert tried to induce villages in the Congo to increase production during the Second World War, he recognised that the memory of 'red rubber' was still haunting the people.[41] Furthermore, rubber was merely the first of several instances where commodities proved a curse for the Congo, and the victimisation by international resource interests became a running theme in the country's history. The Congo was unfortunate in that it provided a key commodity for every era. When rubber declined as a consequence of both scandal and Asian competition, a copper mining boom set in. During the Cold War, the country supplied uranium to the West, and in the twenty-first century, the Congo became known (or perhaps notorious) for its coltan.[42] As the editor of the *New African* declared in a recent issue: 'It may be currently unfashionable to assign Africa's troubles to colonialism and external powers, but in the case of the continent's second largest country, DRCongo, it would be difficult to come to any other conclusion'.[43]

One factor that kept these memories subdued was the Cold War. After a chaotic release into independence, which included the Western-backed assassination of its first Prime Minister Patrice Lumumba in 1961, the Democratic Republic of Congo became a faithful ally of the NATO powers, particularly after General Joseph D. Mobutu's putsch in 1965. In such a setting, any commemoration of colonial atrocities was obviously inopportune, especially since access to resources was subject to perennial negotiations with the Congo government. It was only after the end of the Cold War that pressure on Mobutu began to mount, eventually leading to his resignation in 1997.

In 1998, Adam Hochschild published *King Leopold's Ghost*, a study that more than any other raised awareness of the country's troubled past. However, the book is just as remarkable as the fact that the author admitted to knowing next to nothing about the Congo just a few years before he published it. He had stumbled across the topic in a footnote in a book he read during a night-time flight, and Hochschild realised the importance of the story as he read more: in his judgment, it was 'the first major international atrocity scandal in the age of the telegraph and the camera'.[44] A documentary based on the book came out in 2006, and there were translations into several European languages. French and Dutch versions followed swiftly (and then translations into German, Swedish, Italian, Danish, Spanish, Portuguese, Finnish, Norwegian and Polish), but it is revealing that they were published outside Belgium, in Paris and Amsterdam. In the country of the perpetrators, the Congo affair provoked not so much soul-searching but rather an embarrassed silence, which is characteristic of the way the country is dealing with its colonial history. As a German public radio broadcast declared in 2010, 'the question of postcolonial guilt is generally ignored in Belgium'.[45]

The wonders of chemistry and the ghosts of autarky

Church bells were ringing when the submarine *Deutschland* returned to the German seaport of Bremen in August 1916. People came in droves to the dikes along the Weser River to watch a marvel of German engineering. In the midst of the First World War, one might expect that the cause of the spectacle was the glorious return of a warship, but the *Deutschland* had not fired a single shot during its mission. In a way, it was the most peaceful submarine in military history, as the vessel did not carry any weapons at all. What the submarine did have was plenty of storage room, which was filled with nickel, tin and rubber. The submarine had bought these goods in Baltimore (after US officials had verified that there were indeed no torpedoes on board), and had smuggled them through the Allied sea blockade. Cut off from its traditional supply routes, Germany was in desperate need of natural rubber.[46]

The event mirrored a new chapter in the history of rubber. Since the invention of vulcanisation, rubber had by and large lived in the Ricardoan world of free trade, where the cheapest supplier won the day. But since 1914, new rules applied, and they would remain in force for some three decades. War economies favoured secure lines of supply: it spelled trouble if a country no longer had access to the open sea (like Germany in both world wars) or if a country conquered key plantations (like Japan in the Second World War). Furthermore, restrictions and tariff walls increasingly hindered global trade, particularly after the onset of the Great Depression. Finally, the shifting geography of rubber production created a new type of market power. After the demise of Amazon rubber, Great Britain produced about three-quarters of the world's rubber supply, and the United States consumed about three-quarters of global production. Since Britain was heavily in debt to the United States after the First World War, it was an obvious idea to use the latter's dependency for profit. The Stevenson Plan, which sought to increase prices by limiting exports, directly led to Firestone's investment in Liberia.[47] In 1934, Great Britain, India, the Netherlands, France and Siam signed a more significant production control accord, the International Rubber Regulation Agreement, which lasted into the world war.[48]

One solution was the development of synthetic alternatives. German industrial chemistry was particularly active in this regard: the giant IG Farben Company developed a process to turn lignite coal into synthetic rubber and sold the product under the trade name 'buna'. In fact, a German 'commodity novel' of 1938 celebrated buna rubber as a 'triumph of reason', describing German chemistry as a victory 'over hardness and brutality that allowed "free" trade to have a go at nature and man alike'.[49] But in the end, the German chemical industry was not so much interested in civilisatory advancement as in profits, and the vagaries of global supply routes and German rearmament made a compelling case for synthetics. In 1926, a US author declared that 'German synthetic rubber is dead. It is too expensive'.[50] But this was only true in a world of free trade, and that world was crumbling.

The obsession with autarky was no German peculiarity. It was also the prime motivation that brought Henry Ford into the Amazon jungle: the settlement, named Fordlândia after its driving spirit, never produced a drop of rubber.[51] Ford also paid Thomas Edison to experiment with domestic rubber plants. During the Second World War, the quest for domestic American rubber led to the Emergency Rubber Project, which aimed at the cultivation of alternatives like goldenrod and guayule. None of these projects made a significant contribution to US wartime production, but they show that synthetic rubber, which eventually provided the lion's share of supplies, was not the only option on the table.[52]

Notwithstanding its pride in buna rubber, Nazi Germany pursued its own natural rubber programme. One of its foci was kok-saghyz, a species of dandelion native to Central Asian highlands that Soviet scientists had studied in the 1930s. The German project drew heavily on knowledge from these scientists while maintaining the familiar racial hierarchy between Aryans and Eastern 'sub-humans': a classified report on rubber production in Russia issued by the *Institut für Ostforschung* pointed to 'the Soviet system's inability to produce achievements'.[53] The project became truly ghastly when the Germans moved towards field trials, which hinged on the exploitation of forced labour in the occupied East. That, and the failure to produce significant quantities of rubber, obscured the memory of the kok-saghyz project after the end of the war. Researchers learned about it only a decade ago when the Max Planck Society funded a large research project about its own Nazi past.[54]

Post-war amnesia and a sense of remorse

In 1946, 230,000 pounds of guayule seeds were sold to a farm supply company in Bakersfield, California. With victory in the war, access to rubber plantations restored and industrial chemistry at hand, government officials saw no better use for the formerly precious seeds than cattle feed.[55] It was a fitting move by a post-war society that quickly forgot about resource exigencies. Faced with a cornucopia of products, cheap and available in every desired quantity, it seemed pointless for US citizens to ponder questions as to where commodities came from. The corporate giants that ruled the tyre market were not interested in these issues any longer. Their PR efforts stressed the marvels of science and engineering, along with their favourite marketing ploy such as classical music programmes (The Voice of Firestone) or gourmet guides (Michelin).

In the case of rubber, forgetfulness proved particularly easy because rubber production was remarkably trouble-free during these years. Indigenous pathogens continued to spare rubber trees in Africa and Asia, and South American leaf blight stayed where it was, in the Amazon jungle, making for a remarkable exception from the general trend towards what Emmanuel Le Roy Ladurie has called the microbial unification of the world.[56] According to the Singapore International Chamber of Commerce, 'natural rubber's most critical years' came when strikes and riots plagued political life in Singapore as the British government was conceding the first steps towards self-government in the 1950s.[57] Only non-whites saw things in a different light: when Morel's anti-Leopold book *Red Rubber* eventually received a reprint in 1969, the publisher was Negro University Press.[58]

It would take a major change of the political scene to stimulate interest in commodities and their origins again. That change took place in the late sixties and seventies. The oil price shock of 1973/74 rocked the industrialised world and brought a realisation that resources were not cheap by nature. A young generation, born in an age of affluence, took a more critical look at the consumption habits of their elders. A resurgence of Marxism brought the plight of workers back into focus and raised fundamental questions about capitalism. Latin America became an area of concern for people who did not like military dictatorships, particularly US-backed ones. Environmentalists were opening yet another line of criticism.

The man who brought all these strands together was Francisco Alves Mendes Filho, better known as Chico Mendes, a union leader who emerged as an internationally recognised figure in the fight for the Amazon. Even by Brazilian standards Mendes came from a remote region: his home province of Acre was originally a part of Bolivia that became incorporated into Brazil with the Treaty of Petrópolis in 1903.[59] While working as a rubber tapper, he recognised the need for organisation and formed a powerful union. Working as he did under a military regime and in the wake of endemic violence against union officials, this was no small achievement. He achieved fame beyond the nation's borders when he merged his union interests with the international environmental movement: while some tappers had never heard of Asian plantations and synthetic rubber, Mendes presented Amazon tapping as an effort in environmental conservation. Rubber tapping made judicious use of the jungle as it was, and thus offered an economically viable alternative to cattle ranching. By designating special 'extractive reserves', the government could save the rainforest from destruction and the tappers' jobs at the same time. The manifesto that emerged from the 1985 conference at the University of Brasília declared, 'We demand to be recognized as [the] genuine defenders of the forest'.[60]

When Mendes emerged on the international environmental scene, he was immediately greeted with enthusiasm. Deforestation of the Amazon rainforest was a problem that worried environmentalists in many parts of the world, and they were grateful for a domestic spokesperson. Mendes was invited to meetings and conferences abroad to deliver speeches and receive awards. Meanwhile, there were encouraging signs in Brazilian environmental policy as the country was inching out of the shadow of the military dictatorship. However, Mendes would not live to see the fruits of his work: after numerous threats from ranching interests, the prime agents of deforestation in Acre, he was killed in December 1988, three days before Christmas.

The murder made headlines around the world and put the man and his cause into the spotlight of global attention. Whereas murder cases in the Amazon usually fall into the jurisdiction of local policemen, who frequently investigate in a lacklustre manner, the chief of the Federal Police oversaw the Mendes case; the killers were arrested and sentenced to prison. Chico Mendes remains an internationally recognised icon with 1.5 million hits on Google, and when environmentalists around the world recalled his achievements on the twentieth anniversary of his death, some 20 million hectares were under protection in extractive reserves.[61] The Amazon remains a region of environmental concern.

[259]

However, a few years before Chico Mendes became world famous, another event had offered a different perspective on rubber in the Amazon. In 1981 the German director Werner Herzog released a film with a spectacular plot set in the years of the Amazon rubber boom. The main character, Fitzcarraldo – unforgettably portrayed by Klaus Kinski – is obsessed with the idea of building an opera house in the Peruvian rubber town of Iquitos. In order to fund the project, he plans to collect rubber in a part of the rainforest inaccessible by ship. The extraction project thus required hoisting a steamship over a mountain ridge from a parallel river. Fitzcarraldo eventually achieves his goal with the help of native tribes, but they thwart his plan by cutting the ship adrift and sending it down the rapids to appease their river gods.

The film was based on a real story, although the original Fitzcarraldo had the wisdom to dismantle his ship before its transport overland. However, to the consternation of Hollywood producers, Herzog insisted on having a real steamer pulled uphill in full.[62] In the end, the ship made it over the hill, and the film reached cinemas in 1982. It evoked several familiar themes: the rich rubber barons, the challenges of tapping, the harshness of the rainforest, and the opera house in Manaus. It offered spectacular footage of the landscape, but the jungle setting was ultimately the background for a story about an obsession and the realisation of dreams: the film ends with a smiling Fitzcarraldo watching a piece of opera being performed on his steamer. There was no moral in the film, and certainly none about tappers, natives or rubber. The world is as it is, and Fitzcarraldo tries to make the best of it.

Fitzcarraldo's jungle was fundamentally different from that of Chico Mendes's. This was not the fragile biological system that environmentalists and tappers sought to defend. Fitzcarraldo's jungle was vast, mysterious and lawless except for the laws of nature: when Herzog returned to the production site twenty years later, he found that the rainforest had swallowed everything.[63] This was the jungle of Theodore Roosevelt, who went on an expedition along one of the least explored tributaries of the Amazon, the River of Doubt (henceforth Rio Roosevelt or Rio Teodoro) after his time in the White House. For Roosevelt, the rainforest was a challenge for real men, rather than mother earth, making thoughts about extractive rubber reserve pointless at best and unmanly at worst. This nature, Roosevelt wrote in his book-length account, 'is entirely ruthless, no less so as regards types than as regards individuals, and entirely indifferent to good or evil, and works out her ends or no ends with utter disregard of pain and woe'.[64] Citizens of a globalised age recognised that nature well: it is the perfect parable for the neoliberal world of perennial, no-holds-barred competition.

Both ideas of wilderness are still with us, and the prevailing state of awareness in Western societies can be located somewhere between the poles of Chico Mendes and Fitzcarraldo. The modern citizen knows better than ever that resource extraction comes at a price, economic and otherwise. The films *Blood Diamonds* and *Killer Coltan* have now joined *Red Rubber*; the environmental destruction that goes along with rare earth mining is nowadays a matter of public record; and people have heard Saudi Arabia's oil minister Ahmed Zaki Yamani declare, 'All in all, I wish we had discovered water'.[65] And yet awareness of this toll rarely leads to action, and the resource hunger of modern societies continues almost unabated. Modern consumers, surrounded by a plethora of rubber products, may be forgetful most of the time, but there are moments where memories of rubber are haunting them – all the more because of an uncomfortable feeling that the blood-stained history of rubber is probably not all that special.

The commodity of memory and the memory of the commodity

These remarks are obviously sketchy, but this much should be clear: if commodities are underrated in memory studies, this is surely not for lack of stories. A century and a half of rubber extraction has produced a trail of events that left a deep impression in societies around the world. Furthermore, it is a story that separates into two general strands, a tragic and a heroic one. While Brazil is angered by the memory of Wickham's theft, Britain fondly recalls the combination of adventurism and science in action. Malaysia is reading the disastrous failures of Brazilian plantations as a warning of the constant threats to which monocultures are exposed, and specifically as an illustration of the need to keep South American leaf blight off its soil at all costs.

Stories in the West and the Global South diverge not only in their moral overtones. Interestingly, only in the Global South have memories led to action: namely Brazil's wariness of bio-piracy and Malaysia's fear of epidemics. In contrast, the British memory is of a nostalgic kind – an exciting tale, but also one from a bygone era. A few American enthusiasts continue to experiment with guayule, but as it stands, their only claim to fame is that they have made guayule 'perhaps the nation's best-understood plant in technical and scientific terms that still is not in widespread commercial production'.[66] Exigencies from the times of autarky and the Second World War have faded from awareness in the wake of post-war consumerism, and figures like Chico Mendes have changed that only to a limited extent.

A new generation of scholars has explored paths beyond this binary of memory, uncovering forgotten events in the history of rubber and Western involvement in atrocities in and beyond the Global South. It is a matter of speculation whether their work will lead to a new stage in collective awareness, but the success of Hochschild and others in the book market, fuelled by a growing unease about globalisation, is surely encouraging. What is still lacking, though, is the connection between these events. Modern societies are still struggling fully to acknowledge the mutual entanglement and the moral complicity that go along with global commodity chains.

The selectivity of memory is plain when we see the previous places and events against the full extent of the commodity chain that brought rubber from the tropics to Western consumers. If the metaphor were not so inappropriate for a tropical plant, one might speak of an iceberg phenomenon, where much of the actual story is hidden below the surface. The full rubber network obviously defies collective memory, and tracing the paths of collective memory leads to a skewed picture of the history of rubber that is reminiscent of the famous fable about the blind men and the elephant: each party picks the part that it can best make sense of and ignores the rest.

So maybe it is time to move beyond the sphere of culture and embrace a broader concept of memory. Ever since Pierre Nora's pioneering project, investigations of sites of memory have focused on acts of communication. In fact, Maurice Halbwachs went so far as to doubt the existence of individual memories, arguing that collective memory was purely a result of social (usually group-specific) discourses.[67] It goes without saying that this tradition has proved immensely stimulating for both researchers and the general public, but it is reaching its limits when it comes to the non-human world. Here we need a broader concept of memory that looks beyond discourses. South American leaf blight lacks the power to speak, but it can surely make a statement.

We can see this material dimension of memory at work in the story of rubber. Brazilians remember Wickham not just because of his prolific storytelling but also – and perhaps mainly – because they recognise the experience. The opera house in Manaus is one of many ghost town relicts that remain of boomtowns after the bust. The horrors of King Leopold's Congo evoke the familiar trepidations that enlightened consumers share about colonial and post-colonial resource extraction. The dream of rice-eating rubber is one of many myths that help indigenous people to cope with outside interference. And the fungus scares Malaysia, Indonesia, Liberia and all the other places where rubber is grown because they have learned about the destructive power of pathogens in a monoculture – and not just from Fordlândia. In all these cases, memories grow not just from communication but also from people's encounters with their surroundings.

Commodities have their own ways of producing memories. They operate not only through discourses but also through shared experiences. Commodities offer revelations to humans through their material essence: every *hevea* plant is susceptible to South American leaf blight, no matter where it grows. To be sure, there is no tension between discourses and material experiences here. Quite the contrary, memories are arguably most powerful when transnational communication and personal experiences converge: it is one thing to receive rumours about problems with a certain commodity, but quite another to witness them first-hand. In any case, as we strive to identify memories in a global context, we should take note that memories travel also in the commodities' material cores: in the DNA of plants and animals and in the atoms and molecules that define a resource. Commodities link people in different parts of the worlds, and they are frequently the *only* things that link them, and that makes for a nonverbal type of communication that we should bring into the study of memories. By virtue of their involvement in commodity chains, people share experiences, hopes and fears even when they do not speak to each other. It is only through a study of these shared experiences, transmitted in words as well as in matter, that we can truly understand the global recollections of rubber.

Notes

I would like to thank Sebastian Eigen, Claas Kirchhelle, Annka Liepold, Corey Ross, Veronika Schäfer, Sarah Waltenberger, and Amir Zelinger for their helpful comments on this chapter.

1 M. R. Finlay, *Growing American Rubber: Strategic Plants and the Politics of National Security* (New Brunswick: Rutgers University Press, 2009), p. 1.
2 A. Revkin, *The Burning Season: The Murder of Chico Mendes and the Fight for the Amazon Rain Forest* (Boston: Houghton Mifflin, 1990), pp. 195–201.
3 D. Schümer, 'Die Hanse', in E. François and H. Schulze (eds), *Deutsche Erinnerungsorte*, vol. 2 (Munich: C. H. Beck, 2001), pp. 369–86.
4 W. Dean, *Brazil and the Struggle for Rubber: A Study in Environmental History* (Cambridge: Cambridge University Press, 1987), p. 11.
5 J. Jackson, *The Thief at the End of the World: Rubber, Power, and the Seeds of Empire* (London: Duckworth Overlook, 2008), p. 253n.
6 W. Dean, *Brazil*, pp. 37–40; Z. Frank and A. Musacchio, 'Brazil in the International Rubber Trade, 1870–1930,' in S. Topik, C. Marichal and Z. Frank (eds), *From Silver to Cocaine: Latin American Commodity Chains and the Building of the World Economy, 1500–2000* (Duke and London: Duke University Press, 2006), p. 278
7 Cf. M. E. Stanfield, *Red Rubber, Bleeding Trees: Violence, Slavery, and Empire in Northwest Amazonia, 1850–1933* (Albuquerque: University of New Mexico Press, 1998), pp. 132, 138, 206.

8 *Ibid.*, p. 207.
9 A. Revkin, *Burning Season*, p. 44.
10 E. Hobsbawm, *The Age of Extremes: A History of the World, 1914–1991* (New York: Vintage Books, 1996), p. 577.
11 A. W. Crosby, *The Columbian Exchange: Biological and Cultural Consequences of 1492* (Westport: Greenwood, 1972).
12 J. Jackson, *Thief*, p. 10.
13 *Ibid.*, p. 9.
14 http://news.mongabay.com/2005/1030-ap.html (accessed: 2 February 2013).
15 W. Dean, *Brazil*, p. 166.
16 B. Fausto, *A Concise History of Brazil* (Cambridge: Cambridge University Press, 2006), p. 176.
17 W. Dean, *Brazil*, p. 166. Similar Z. Frank and A. Musacchio, 'Brazil', p. 277.
18 J. Jackson, *Thief*, p. 191.
19 W. Dean, *Brazil*, p. 44.
20 B. Weinstein, *The Amazon Rubber Boom 1850–1920* (Stanford: Stanford University Press, 1983), p. 215.
21 W. Dean, *Brazil*, p. 7.
22 M. R. Dove, *The Banana Tree at the Gate: A History of Marginal People and Global Markets in Borneo* (New Haven: Yale University Press, 2011), p. 116.
23 R. Desmond, *The History of the Royal Botanic Gardens, Kew* (2nd edn, Kew: Kew Publishers, 2007), p. 231.
24 *Ibid.*, p. 233.
25 *Ibid.*, p. 233n. Quotation p. 233.
26 J. Loadman, *Tears of the Tree: The Story of Rubber – A Modern Marvel* (Oxford: Oxford University Press, 2005).
27 E. J. Salisbury, 'Henry Nicholas Ridley, 1855–1956', *Biographical Memoirs of Fellows of the Royal Society* 3 (1957), pp. 141–59, 145.
28 M. R. Dove, *Banana Tree*, pp. 103n, 113. His achievements were recognised within insider circles, though, as Ridley received the Rubber Planters Association's Gold Medal in 1914, the Frank Meyer medal for foreign plant introduction in 1928, and the Colwyn medal of the Institute of the Rubber Industry in 1955. (R. E. Holttum, 'Henry Nicholas Ridley, C. M.G., F.R.S. 1855–1956', *Taxon* 6 [1957], p. 4.)
29 Research Institute of Economic Plants in the Tropics, *Developers of the Rubber Industry of Singapore and Malaysia, vol. 1: H. N. Ridley, 1855–1956* (Singapore: The Institute, 1969).
30 G. Grandin, *Fordlandia: The Rise and Fall of Henry Ford's Forgotten Jungle City* (New York: Metropolitan Books, 2009).
31 W. Dean, *Brazil*, p. 166.
32 J. H. Drabble, *An Economic History of Malaysia, c. 1800–1990: The Transition to Modern Economic Growth* (New York: Macmillan, 2000), pp. 53n, 108.
33 G. E. Boley, *Liberia: The Rise and Fall of the First Republic* (New York: St. Martin's Press, 1984), pp. 41, 43; J. H. Mower, 'The Republic of Liberia', *Journal of Negro History* 32 (1947), pp. 265–306; G. Mitman and P. Erickson, 'Latex and Blood: Science, Markets, and American Empire', *Radical History Review* 107 (2010), pp. 45–73.
34 D. E. Lee, *Human Rights and the Ethics of Globalization* (Cambridge: Cambridge University Press, 2010), p. 137.
35 M. R. Dove, 'Rice-Eating Rubber and People-Eating Governments: Peasant versus State Critiques of Rubber Development in Colonial Borneo', *Ethnohistory* 43:1 (1996), pp. 33–63. Quotation p. 35.
36 M. R. Dove, *Banana Tree*, p. 6n.
37 I. Watt, *Conrad in the Nineteenth Century* (Berkeley: University of California Press, 1979), p. 139.
38 S. C. Topik and A. Wells, 'Commodity Chains in a Global Economy', in E. S. Rosenberg (ed.), *A World Connecting 1870–1945* (Cambridge and London: Belknap Press of Harvard University Press, 2012), p. 683.

39 As it happened, that consul was the same Roger Casement who was sent to the Putumayo seven years later. Casement was later executed for supporting Irish independence during the First World War. He was also gay. Little wonder that Casement remains alive in collective memory! (M. E. Daly [ed.], *Roger Casement in Irish and World History* [Dublin: Royal Irish Academy, 2005]).
40 A. Hochschild, *King Leopold's Ghost: A Story of Greed, Terror, and Heroism in Colonial Africa* (Boston: Houghton Mifflin, 1999).
41 D. Van Reybrouck, *Kongo: Eine Geschichte* (Berlin: Suhrkamp, 2012), p. 235.
42 *Ibid.*, p. 148.
43 B. Ankomah, 'They Are At It Again! The Sponsors of African Wars', *New African* 47:524 (2013), p. 10.
44 A. Hochschild, *King Leopold's Ghost*, p. 4.
45 www.dradio.de/dkultur/sendungen/weltzeit/1213597/ (accessed 2 February 2013).
46 W. Fleischer, 'Hundert Meter tief im Nordatlantik und einen Bauch voll Kautschuk: Die Fahrten des Handels-U-Bootes Deutschland,' in U. Giersch and U. Kubisch (eds), *Gummi – Die elastische Faszination* (Berlin: Nicolai, 1995), pp. 152–4.
47 J. H. Drabble, *Economic History*, pp. 127–32.
48 P. T. Bauer, *The Rubber Industry: A Study in Competition and Monopoly* (Cambridge, Mass.: Harvard University Press, 1948), p. 84.
49 K. Fischer, *Blutgummi: Roman eines Rohstoffes* (Berlin: Kommodore Verlag, 1938), p. 243.
50 D. Culross Peattie, *Cargoes and Harvests* (New York: D. Appleton & Co., 1926), p. 73.
51 G. Grandin, *Fordlândia*.
52 M. R. Finlay, *Growing American Rubber*.
53 E. Kahn, *Der russische Raum als Kautschukerzeuger* (Königsberg: Institut für Ostforschung, ca. 1941), p. 2.
54 S. Heim, *Kalorien, Kautschuk, Karrieren: Pflanzenzüchtung und landwirtschaftliche Forschung in Kaiser-Wilhelm-Instituten 1933–1945* (Göttingen: Wallstein, 2003), pp. 125–98.
55 M. R. Finlay, *Growing American Rubber*, p. 219.
56 E. Le Roy Ladurie, 'Un Concept: L'Unification Microbienne du Monde (XIVe-XVIIe Siècles)', *Schweizerische Zeitschrift für Geschichte* 23 (1973), pp. 627–96.
57 A. Coates, *The Commerce in Rubber: The First 250 Years: Commissioned by the Singapore International Chamber of Commerce, Rubber Association* (Singapore: Oxford University Press, 1987), p. 339.
58 E. D. Morel, *Red Rubber: The Story of the Rubber Slave Trade Flourishing on the Congo in the Year of Grace 1906* (New York: Negro Universities Press, 1969 [first published in November 1906]).
59 B. Fausto, *Concise History*, p. 152.
60 A. Revkin, *Burning Season*, p. 203.
61 http://blogs.edf.org/climatetalks/2008/12/24/edfs-schwartzman-remembers-chico-mendes/ (accessed 2 February 2013).
62 C. David, *Kinski: Die Biographie* (Berlin: Aufbau-Verlag, 2006), p. 301.
63 W. Herzog, *Eroberung des Nutzlosen* (Munich: Hanser, 2004), p. 329.
64 T. Roosevelt, *Through the Brazilian Wilderness* (New York: Charles Scribner's Sons, 1914), p. 147.
65 T. L. Karl, *The Paradox of Plenty: Oil Booms and Petro-States* (Berkeley: University of California Press, 1997), p. 187.
66 M. R. Finlay, *Growing American Rubber*, p. 17.
67 Cf. M. Halbwachs, *On Collective Memory: Edited, Translated, and with an Introduction by L. A. Coser* (Chicago: University of Chicago Press, 1992).

SELECT BIBLIOGRAPHY

Anderson, D., *Histories of the Hanged. The Dirty War in Kenya and the End of Empire* (London: Weidenfeld & Nicolson, 2005).

Arjun, D. (ed.), *Poisoned Bread* (Mumbai: Sangam Books, 1992).

Assmann, J., 'Collective Memory and Cultural Identity', *New German Critique* 65 (1995), 125–33.

August, T. G., *The Selling of the Empire: British and French Imperialist Propaganda, 1890–1940* (Westport CT: Greenwood Press, 1985).

Baddeley, J. F., *The Russian Conquest of the Caucasus* (London: 1908, Reprint: RoutledgeCurzon, 2003). Bandyopadhyay, S., *From Plassey to Partition: A History of Modern India* (Hyderabad: Orient Longman, 2004).

Barnett, D. and K. Njama, *Mau Mau from Within. Autobiography and Analysis of Kenya's Peasant Revolt* (London: Macgibbon & Key, 1966).

Barringer, T., 'The South Kensington Museum and the Colonial Project', in T. Barringer and T. Flynn (eds), *Colonialism and the Object: Empire, Material Culture and the Museum* (London: Routledge, 1998), pp. 11–27.

Barringer, T. and T. Flynn (eds), *Colonialism and the Object: Empire, Material Culture and the Museum* (London: Routledge, 1998).

Barton, C. E. (ed.), *Sites of Memory: Perspectives on Architecture and Race* (New York: Princeton Architectural Press, 2001).

Bayly, C. A., *Origins of Nationality in South Asia: Patriotism and Ethical Government in the Making of Modern India* (Delhi: Oxford University Press, 1998).

Beltz, J., *Mahar, Buddhist and Dalit: Religious Conversion and Socio-Political Emancipation* (New Delhi: Manohar Publishers, 2005).

Benjamin, R., *Orientalist Aesthetics: Art, Colonialism, and French North Africa (1880–1930)* (Berkeley: University of California Press, 2003).

Berenson, E., *Heroes of Empire: Five Charismatic Men and the Conquest of Africa* (Berkeley: University of California Press, 2010).

Betts, R. F., *Assimilation and Association in French Colonial Theory, 1890–1914* (New York: AMS Press, 1970, 1960).

Bhatt, V., *Resorts of the Raj: Hill Stations of India* (Ann Arbor: University of Michigan Press, 1998).

Bose S. and A. Jalal, *Modern South Asia: History, Culture, Political Economy* (London: Routledge, 1998).

Bowen, H. V., *The Business of Empire: The East India Company and Imperial Britain, 1756–1833* (Cambridge: Cambridge University Press, 2007).

Branch, D., *Defeating Mau Mau, Creating Kenya. Counterinsurgency, Civil War, and Decolonization* (Cambridge: Cambridge University Press, 2009).

Breen, J. (ed.), *Yasukuni – the War Dead and the Struggle for Japan's Past* (London: Hurst and Co., 2007).

SELECT BIBLIOGRAPHY

Breitenbach, E., *Empire and Scottish Society: The Impact of Foreign Missions at Home, c. 1790 to c. 1914* (Edinburgh: Edinburgh University Press, 2009).

Brubaker, R., M. Feishmidt, J. Fox and L. Grancea (eds), *Nationalist Politics and Everyday Ethnicity in a Transylvanian Town* (Princeton: Princeton University Press, 2006).

Bucur, M. and N. Wingfield (eds), *Staging the Past: The Politics of Commemoration in Habsburg Central Europe* (West Lafayette: Purdue University Press, 2001).

Cain, P. J. and A. G. Hopkins, *British Imperialism: 1688–2000* (London: Pearson Education, 2002).

Cannadine, D., *Ornamentalism, How the British saw their Empire* (London: Penguin Books, 2002).

Çelik, Z., *Empire, Architecture, and the City: French-Ottoman Encounters, 1830–1914* (Seattle: University of Washington Press, 2008).

Çelik, Z., J. Clancy-Smith and F. Terpak (eds), *Walls of Algiers: Narratives of the City Through Text and Image* (Washington: University of Washington Press, 2009).

Chafer, T. and A. Sackur, *Promoting the Colonial Idea: Propaganda and Visions of Empire in France* (New York: Palgrave, 2001).

Chakravarty, G., *The Indian Mutiny and the British Imagination* (Cambridge and New York: Cambridge University Press, 2005).

Chandral, S. and T. J. Vogelsang, 'Change and Involution in Sugar Production in Cultivation-System Java, 1840–1870', *The Journal of Economic History* 59:4 (1999), 885–911.

Chatterjee, P., *The Black Hole of Empire: History of a Global Practise of Power* (Princeton: Princeton University Press, 2012).

Chaudhary, Z., 'Phantasmagoric Aesthetics: Colonial Violence and the Management of Perception', *Cultural Critique* 59 (2005), 63–119.

Cittadino, E., *Nature as the Laboratory: Darwinian Plant Ecology in the German Empire* (Cambridge: Cambridge University Press, 1990).

Clayton, A. and D. Savage, *Government and Labour in Kenya 1895–1963* (London: Frank Cass, 1974).

Clough, M., *Mau Mau Memoirs. History, Memory, and Politics* (Boulder: Rienner, 1998).

Coates, A., *The Commerce in Rubber: The First 250 Years: Commissioned by the Singapore International Chamber of Commerce, Rubber Association* (Singapore: Oxford University Press, 1987).

Collins, S., *The 1940 Tokyo Games: The Missing Olympics: Japan, the Asian Olympics and the Olympic Movement* (London: Routledge, 2007).

Connerton, P., *How Societies Remember* (Cambridge: Cambridge University Press, 1989).

Coombes, A. E., *Reinventing Africa: Museums, Material Culture and Popular Imagination* (New Haven, CT: Yale University Press, 1994).

Coser, L. A. (ed.), *Maurice Halbwachs: On Collective Memory* (Chicago: The University of Chicago Press, 1992).

Cox, J., *The British Missionary Enterprise since 1700* (New York and London: Routledge, 2008).

Crosby, A. W., *The Columbian Exchange: Biological and Cultural Consequences of 1492* (Westport: Greenwood, 1972).

Daly, M. E. (ed.), *Roger Casement in Irish and World History* (Dublin: Royal Irish Academy, 2005).

Darwin, J., *After Tamerlane: The Rise & Fall of Global Empires, 1400–2000* (London: Penguin Books, 2008).

Dean, W., *Brazil and the Struggle for Rubber: A Study in Environmental History* (Cambridge: Cambridge University Press, 1987).

Desmond, R., *The History of the Royal Botanic Gardens Kew*, 2nd edn (Kew: Kew Publishing, 2007).

Drabble, J. H., *An Economic History of Malaysia, c. 1800–1990: The Transition to Modern Economic Growth* (New York: Macmillan, 2000).

Edwards, E., *Raw Histories: Photographs, Anthropology and Museums* (London: Bloomsbury Publishing PLC, 2001).

Elkins, C., *Britain's Gulag. The Brutal End of Empire in Kenya* (London: Jonathan Cape, 2005).

Escott, H., *A History of Scottish Congregationalism* (Glasgow: Congregational Union of Scotland, 1960).

Evans, M. (ed.), *Empire and Culture: The French Experience, 1830–1940* (New York: Palgrave Macmillan, 2004).

Farr, M. and X. Guégan (eds), *The British Abroad since the Eighteenth Century: Travellers and Tourists*, vol. 1 (Basingstoke: Palgrave Macmillan, 2013).

Farr, M. and X. Guégan (eds), *The British Abroad since the Eighteenth Century: Experiencing Imperialism*, vol. 2 (Basingstoke: Palgrave Macmillan, 2013).

Finlay, M. R., *Growing American Rubber: Strategic Plants and the Politics of National Security* (New Brunswick: Rutgers University Press, 2009).

Fisher, J. L., *Pioneers, Settlers, Aliens, Exiles: The Decolonisation of White Identity in Zimbabwe* (Canberra: ANU E Press, 2010).

Foucault, M., *Power (Essential Works of Foucault 1954–1984)*, J. D. Faubion (ed.), vol. 3 (London: Penguin Books, 2002).

Furedi, F., *The Mau Mau War in Perspective* (London: Currey, 1989).

Gammer, M., *Muslim Resistance to the Tsar: Shamil and the Conquest of Chechnia and Daghestan* (London: Cass, 1994).

Gosnell, J., *The Politics of Frenchness in Colonial Algeria, 1930–1954* (Woodbridge: Boydell & Brewer Ltd, 2002).

Grandin, G., *Fordlandia: The Rise and Fall of Henry Ford's Forgotten Jungle City* (New York: Metropolitan Books, 2009).

Greenlee, J. G. and C. M. Johnston, *Good Citizens: British Missionaries and Imperial States, 1870–1918* (Montreal: McGill-Queen's University Press, 1999).

Guha-Thakurta, T., *Traversing Past and Present in the Victoria Memorial* (Calcutta: Centre for Studies in Social Science Occasional Paper no. 153, 1995).

Gupta, N., *Delhi between Two Empires 1803–1931* (Delhi: Oxford University Press, 1981).

Halbwachs, M., *On Collective Memory*. Edited, translated, and with an Introduction by L. A. Coser (Chicago: University of Chicago Press, 1992).

Hall, C., and S. O. Rose (eds), *At Home with the Empire: Metropolitan Culture and the Imperial World* (Cambridge: Cambridge University Press, 2006).

Hervieu-Léger, D., *Religion as a Chain of Memory* (Cambridge: Polity Press, 2000).

Hobsbawm, E. and T. Ranger (eds), *The Invention of Tradition* (Cambridge: Cambridge University Press, 1983, 16th edn 2008).

Hochschild, A., *King Leopold's Ghost: A Story of Greed, Terror, and Heroism in Colonial Africa* (Boston: Houghton Mifflin, 1999).

Holmes, R., *Sahib: The British Soldier in India 1750–1914* (London: HarperCollins, 2005).

Jackson, J., *The Thief at the End of the World: Rubber, Power, and the Seeds of Empire* (London: Duckworth Overlook, 2008).

Jaffrelot, C. (ed.), *Hindu Nationalism: A Reader* (New Jersey: Princeton University Press, 2007).

Jeal, T., *Livingstone* (New Haven, CT: Yale University Press, 2001).

Judson, P. and M. Rozenblit (eds), *Constructing Nationalities in East Central Europe* (Cambridge, Mass.: Harvard University Press, 2005).

Kenyatta, J., *Suffering without Bitterness. The Founding of the Kenya Nation* (Nairobi: East African Publishing House, 1968).

King, A. D., *Colonial Urban Development: Culture, Social Power and Environment* (London: Henley, and Boston: Routledge and Kegan Paul, 1976).

Kshirsagar, R. K., *Dalit Movement in India and its Leaders, 1857–1956* (New Delhi: M.D. Publications, 1994).

Kuhn, A. and K. McAllister (eds), *Locating Memory: Photographic Acts* (Oxford: Berghahn Books, 2006).

Kushner, B., *The Thought War – Imperial Japanese Propaganda* (Honolulu: University of Hawaii Press, 2006).

Kushner, B., *Dreams of Empire: Japanese Propaganda Textiles* (Brussels: MHJ Collection, 2011).

Lahiri, N., 'Commemorating and Remembering 1857: The Revolt in Delhi and Its Afterlife', *World Archaeology* 35:1, The Social Commemoration of Warfare, (June, 2003), 35–60.

Lang, J. and M. Desai, *Architecture and Independence: The Search for Identity 1880–1980* (New Delhi: Oxford University Press, 1997).

Lawrence, J., *Raj: The Making and Unmaking of British India* (London: Little, Brown, 1997).

Lawson, P. H., *The East India Company: A History* (London: Longman, 1993).

Layton, S., *Russian Literature and Empire: Conquest of the Caucasus from Pushkin to Tolstoy* (Cambridge: Cambridge University Press, 1994).

Legène, S. and J. van Dijk (eds), *The Netherlands East Indies at the Tropenmuseum. A Colonial History* (Amsterdam: KIT, 2011).

Leonhard, J. and U. von Hirschhausen, *Empires und Nationalstaaten im 19. Jahrhundert* (Göttingen: Vandenhoeck & Ruprecht, 2009).

Loadman, J., *Tears of the Tree: The Story of Rubber – A Modern Marvel* (Oxford: Oxford University Press, 2005).

Lonsdale, J. and B. Berman, *Unhappy Valley. Conflict in Kenya and Africa*, 2 vols. (London: James Currey, 1992).

SELECT BIBLIOGRAPHY

Lorcin, P. M. E. (ed.), *Algeria and France, 1800–2000: Identity, Memory, Nostalgia* (New York: Syracuse University Press, 2006).

MacKenzie, J. M., *Propaganda and Empire: The Manipulation of British Public Opinion, 1880–1960* (Manchester: Manchester University Press, 1984).

MacKenzie, J. M. (ed.), *Imperialism and Popular Culture* (Manchester: Manchester University Press, 1986).

MacKenzie, J. M., *Orientalism: History, Theory and the Arts* (Manchester: Manchester University Press, 1995).

MacKenzie, J. M. (ed.), *European Empires and the People: Popular responses to Imperialism in France, Britain, the Netherlands, Belgium, Germany and Italy* (Manchester: Manchester University Press, 2011).

Maloba, W., *Mau Mau and Kenya. An Analysis of a Peasant Revolt* (Bloomington: Indiana University Press, 1993).

Maxwell, A., *Colonial Photography and Exhibitions: Representations of the "Native" and the Making of European Identities* (London: Leicester University Press, 2000).

Maylam, P., *The Cult of Rhodes: Remembering an Imperialist in Africa* (Cape Town: David Philip, 2005).

McCracken, D. P., *Gardens of Empire: Botanical Institutions of the Victorian British Empire* (London: Leicester University Press, 1997).

McLaine, K., *India's Immortal Comic Books: Gods, Kings and Other Heroes* (Bloomington: Indiana University Press, 2009).

Mendelsohn, O. and M. Vicziany, *The Untouchables: Subordination, Poverty, and the State in Modern India* (Cambridge: Cambridge University Press, 1998).

Metcalf, T. R., *An Imperial Vision: Indian Architecture and Britain's Rule* (Delhi: Oxford University Press, 2002).

Metcalf, T. R., *Forging the Raj: Essays on British India in the Heyday of Empire* (New Delhi: Oxford University Press, 2005).

Nehru, J., *The Discovery of India* (Delhi: Oxford University Press, 1946 reprinted 1999).

Nish, I., 'Regaining Confidence – Japan after the Loss of Empire', *Journal of Contemporary History* 15:1, special issue on Imperial Hangovers (1980), 181–95.

Nora, P., 'Between Memory and History: Les Lieux de Mémoire', *Representations* 26 (1989), 7–24.

Nora, P., *Realms of Memory: Rethinking the French Past*, vol. I (New York: Columbia University Press, 1996).

Nora, P. (ed.), *Les Lieux de mémoire.* 3 vols. (Paris: Gallimard 1997).

Nwoye, R. E., *The Public Image of Pierre Savorgnan de Brazza and the Establishment of French Imperialism in the Congo* (Aberdeen: Aberdeen University, 1981).

O'Hanlon, R., *Caste, Conflict and Ideology* (Cambridge: Cambridge University Press, 2002).

Omvedt, G., *Dalits and the Democratic Revolution: Dr. Ambedkar and the Dalit Movement in Colonial India* (New Delhi: Sage, 1994).

Orr, J., *The Victim as Hero: Ideologies of Peace and National Identity in Postwar Japan* (Honolulu: University of Hawai'i Press, 2001).

Osborne, P. D., *Travelling Light: Photography, Travel and Visual Culture* (Manchester: Manchester University Press, 2000).

Pelizzari, M. A. (ed.), *Traces of India: Photography, Architecture, and the Politics of Representation, 1850–1900* (Montréal, New Haven: Canadian Centre for Architecture, Yale Center for British Art, 2003).

Pettitt, C., *'Dr. Livingstone, I Presume?' Missionaries, Journalists, Empire* (London: Profile Books, 2007).

Phillips, R., *Mapping Men and Empire: A Geography of Adventure* (London: Routledge, 1997).

Pitts, J., *A Turn to Empire: The Rise of Imperial Liberalism in Britain and France* (Princeton: Princeton University Press, 2008).

Porter, A., *Religion versus Empire? British Protestant Missionaries and Overseas Expansion, 1700–1914* (Manchester: Manchester University Press, 2004).

Presley, C., *Kikuyu Women, the Mau Mau Rebellion, and Social Change in Kenya* (Boulder: Westview Press, 1992).

Prochaska, D., *Making Algeria French: Colonialism in Bône, 1870–1920* (Cambridge: Cambridge University Press, 2004).

Ramaswamy, S., *Passions of the Tongue: Language Devotion in Tamil India, 1891–1970* (Berkeley: University of California Press, 1997).

Ramteke, D. L., *Revival of Buddhism in Modern India* (New Delhi: Deep & Deep publications, 1983).

Rao, A., *The Caste Question: Dalits and the Politics of Modern India* (Berkeley: University of California Press, 2009).

Revkin, A., *The Burning Season: The Murder of Chico Mendes and the Fight for the Amazon Rain Forest* (Boston: Houghton Mifflin, 1990).

Reybrouck, D. Van, *Kongo: Eine Geschichte* (Berlin: Suhrkamp, 2012).

Robert, D. L., *Christian Mission: How Christianity became a World Religion* (Malden, MA, and Oxford: Wiley-Blackwell, 2009).

Rosberg, C. G. and J. Nottingham, *The Myth of 'Mau Mau': Nationalism in Kenya* (New York: Praeger 1966).

Ross, A. C., *David Livingstone: Mission and Empire* (London and New York: Hambledon Continuum, 2006).

Ruoff, K., *Imperial Japan at Its Zenith: The Wartime Celebration of the Empire's 2,600th Anniversary* (Ithaca: Cornell University Press, 2010).

Ruppenthal, J., *Kolonialismus als 'Wissenschaft und Technik': Das Hamburgische Kolonialinstitut 1908 bis 1919* (Stuttgart: Steiner, 2007).

Ryan, J. R., *Picturing Empire, Photography and the Visualization of the British Empire* (London: Reaktion, 1997).

Sampson, G. D., and E. M. Hight (eds), *Colonialist Photography, Imag(in)ing Race and Place* (London: Routledge, 2002).

Sayer, D., 'British Reaction to the Amritsar Massacre 1919–1920', *Past and Present* 131:2 (1991), 130–64.

Schiebinger, L., *Plants and Empire. Colonial Bioprospecting in the Atlantic World* (Cambridge: Harvard University Press, 2004).

Schiebinger, L. and C. Swan (eds), *Colonial Botany. Science, Commerce and Politics in the Early Modern World* (Philadelphia, PA.: University of Pennsylvania Press, 2005).

Schwartz, J. M. and J. R. Ryan (eds), *Picturing Place, Photography and the Geographical Imagination* (London and New York: I. B. Tauris, 2006, 2003).

Schwarz, B., *Memories of Empire, Volume I: The White Man's World* (Oxford: Oxford University Press, 2011).

Schwenkel, C., 'Recombinant History: Transnational Practices of Memory and Knowledge Production in Contemporary Vietnam', *Cultural Anthropology* 21:1 (2006), 3–29.

Sèbe, B., *Heroic Imperialists in Africa* (Manchester: Manchester University Press, 2013).

Sheftall, M. G., 'Tokkô Zaidan: A Case Study of Institutional Japanese War Memorialisation', in S. Saaler and W. Schwentker (eds), *The Power of Memory in Modern Japan* (London: Global Oriental, 2008), pp. 54–77.

Shimazu, N., 'Popular Representations of the Past: The Case of Postwar Japan', *Journal of Contemporary History* 38:1 (2003), 101–16.

Sindima, H. J., *The Legacy of Scottish Missionaries in Malawi* (Lampeter: Edwin Mellen Press, 1992).

Singer, B. and Langdon, J., *Cultured Force* (London and Madison: University of Wisconsin Press, 2004).

Sinha, A. J., 'Visual Culture and the Politics of Locality in Modern India: A Review Essay', *Modern Asian Studies* 41:1 (2007), 187–220.

Smith, K., 'The Shôwa Hall: Memorializing Japan's War at Home', *The Public Historian* 24:4 (2002), 35–64.

Smith, T., '"A Grand Work of Noble Conception": The Victoria Memorial and Imperial London', in F. Driver and D. Gilbert (eds), *Imperial Cities: Landscape, Display and Identity* (Manchester: Manchester University Press, 2003).

Stanfield, M. E., *Red Rubber, Bleeding Trees: Violence, Slavery, and Empire in Northwest Amazonia, 1850–1933* (Albuquerque: University of New Mexico Press, 1998).

Stanley, B., *The Bible and the Flag: Protestant Missions and British Imperialism in the Nineteenth and Twentieth Centuries* (Leicester: Apollos, 1990).

Stoler, A. L. and K. Strassler, 'Castings for the Colonial: Memory Work in "New Order" Java', *Comparative Studies in Society and History* 42:1 (2000), 4–48.

Sundar, N., *Subalterns and Sovereigns: An Anthropological History of Bastar, 1854–1996* (New York: Oxford University Press, 1997).

Sunseri, T., 'Famine and Wild Pigs: Gender Struggles and the Outbreak of the Majimaji War in Uzaramo (Tanzania)', *Journal of African History* 38 (1997), 235–59.

Tanaka, Y., T. McCormack, and G. Simpson (eds), *Beyond Victor's Justice? The Tokyo War Crimes Trial Revisited* (Leiden: Brill, 2011).

Tengatenga, J., *The UMCA in Malawi: A History of the Anglican Church, 1861–2010* (Zomba: Kachere Books, 2010).

Thomas, M. (ed.), *The French Colonial Mind*, vol. 2: *Violence, Military Encounters, and Colonialism* (Lincoln: University of Nebraska Press, 2011).

Thorne, S., *Congregational Missions and the Making of an Imperial Culture in Nineteenth Century England* (Stanford, CA: Stanford University Press, 1999).

Throup, D., *Economic and Social Origins of Mau Mau 1945–53* (London: James Currey, 1987).

Tillotson, G. H. R., *Jaipurnama: Tales from the Pink City* (Delhi, Penguin, 2006).

Totani, Y., *The Tokyo War Crimes Trial: The Pursuit of Justice in the Wake of World War II* (Cambridge, Mass.: Harvard University Asia Center, 2008).

Urry, J., *The Tourist Gaze*. 2nd edn (London: SAGE Publications, 2002).

Varma, P., *Being Indian: Inside the Real India* (Delhi: Penguin Viking, 2004).

Weinstein, B., *The Amazon Rubber Boom 1850–1920* (Stanford: Stanford University Press, 1983).

Williams, C. P., *The Ideal of the Self-Governing Church: A Study in Victorian Missionary Strategy* (Leiden: Brill, 1990).

Wilson, K., 'Empire, Gender, and Modernity in the Eighteenth Century', in P. Levine (ed.), *Gender and Empire* (Oxford: Oxford University Press, 2007).

Wingfield, N. (ed.), *Creating the Other: Ethnic Conflict and Nationalism in Habsburg Central Europe* (New York: Berghahn, 2003).

Winter, J., *Sites of Memory, Sites of Mourning: The Great War in European Cultural History* (Cambridge: Cambridge University Press, 1995).

Zachariah, B., *Developing India: An Intellectual and Social History, c. 1930–1950* (Delhi: Oxford University Press, 2005).

Zelliot, E., *From Untouchable to Dalit: Essays on the Ambedkar Movement* (New Delhi: Manohar, 1992).

INDEX

Smith, Anthony 73
Smith, Kerry 74
Smuts, Jan 160
Société de Géographie 101, 104
South Africa 97, 109, 160, 163
South America 247, 258, 261–3
South Korea 72, 83
Soviet Academy of Sciences 177–8
Spain, Imperial Spain 13, 256
St Petersburg 170, 174, 180
Stanard, Matthew G. 11
Stanfield, Michael 248
Stanhope, Philip Henry Earl of 141
Stanley, Henry Morton 97–8, 104, 155
Stead, Henry Wickham 248–51, 261–2
Steevens, George Warrington 100
Stewart, James 155
Stoler, Ann Laura 188
Strassler, Karen 188
Student Volunteer Missionary Union 159
Sudan 106
Sudan, Anglo-Egyptian 95, 105
Sudi, Tom Peter 165
Susi, Abdullah 164
Suvorov, Alexander 180
Sweden, Kingdom of Sweden, Swedish 256
Switzerland 101, 158
Szabó, Zoltán 56
Szapáry, Gyula 58–9

Tajima, Ryûjun 77, 80, 88
Tak van Poortvliet, Johannes 126
Tamil Nadu (India) 194
Tanaka, Nobumasa 83
Tanzania 216, 219, 234, 235
Texier, Charles 26
Theodorescu, Răzvan 65
Thiong'o, Ngugi wa 217
Thiselton-Dyer, William 250
Thollens, Hendrik 123
Thorbecke, Johan Rudolph 126
Thornycroft, Sir Hamo 107–8
Tiger Kloof 161
Tisza, Kálmán 58
Togo 232–6
Tôjô, Hideki 85
Tokyo 70, 72–3, 82, 84, 86
Tokyo, monuments in 72, 75–7, 79–80, 82–5, 88
Toyoda, Kumao 81–2
Turkey, Ottoman Empire 13, 32, 59, 177, 180
Twain, Mark 254
Tweed, John 143

Udal, Nicholas R. 105
Uganda 219

United States of America xiv, 3, 71–2, 76, 78, 111, 157, 191, 199–201, 212, 236, 243, 247, 252, 256–8, 261
Unowsky, Daniel 55

Varma, Pavan 188
Vasile, Radu 65
Verderevskii, Evgenii A. 173
Vereenigde Oostindische Compagnie (Dutch East India Company) (VOC) 1, 115–18
Verdun 96
Verhoeff, Pieter 117
Versailles 96
Victoria (Queen of Great Britain and Ireland) 29–31, 107, 193, 195, 199
Victoria Falls 153–4, 160, 163
Vienna 53, 55–6, 58, 61
Vietnam 200–2
Vittal Rao, Beldona 147
Vlaicu, Aurel 63
Volkens, Georg 231
Voortrekker Monument 163

Walder, Dennis 6
Warburg, Aby 6
Washington, Booker T. 158
Washington DC 260
Wehry, Geo 119
Wellesley, Arthur 144
Wellesley, Richard 197–8
Wertheim, Abraham Carel 125
Wilberforce, William 156
Wilhelmina (Queen of the Netherlands) 126–7
Williams, John 156
Wilson, Frank 163
Wilson, Hubert 163, 166
Wilson, Woodrow 158
Wingate, Reginald 111
Woking 107
Wood, John 148
Wurssbain, Johann Sigmund 122

Yamamura, Tsuru xiii
Yamani, Ahmed Zaki 261
York 104
Yoshida, Shigeru 79

Zala, György 57–8, 61
Zambia 109
Zanu-PF 153
Zanzibar 156, 164–5, 167
Zhukov, Georgy 180
Zimbabwe 109, 153–4, 167
Zimmermann, August Eduard 126
Zuiderzee 111